BRING WARM
CLOTHES

*Letters and Photos
from Minnesota's Past*

PEG MEIER

MINNESOTA
HISTORICAL
SOCIETY PRESS

The publication of this book was supported though a generous grant from the Elmer L. and Eleanor Andersen Publications Fund.

mnhspress.org

The Minnesota Historical Society Press is a member of the Association of University Presses.

Manufactured in the United States of America

10 9 8 7 6 5 4 3 2 1

∞ The paper used in this publication meets the minimum requirements of the American National Standard for Information Sciences—Permanence for Printed Library Materials, ANSI Z39.48-1984.

The title *Bring Warm Clothes* comes from the advice Polly Bullard's friend gave her in 1908 about moving to northern Minnesota: "Bring your warm clothes; for 35 below zero means it is cold."

The cover photo shows the sledding family of Louis Benepe, a St. Paul dentist, in about 1885. *MNHS collections*

Back cover: top, load of logs, 1899, *Carlton County Park Commission*; middle, child in sled, 1898, *MNHS collections*; bottom, World War I nurse, *MNHS collections*.

International Standard Book Number
ISBN: 978-1-68134-274-0 (paperback)

Library of Congress Cataloging-in-Publication Data
    Bring warm clothes : letters and photos from Minnesota's past / collected by Peg Meier.
        p. cm.
Originally published: Minneapolis: Minneapolis Tribune, [1981].
ISBN-13: 978-0-87351-639-6 (pk. : alk. paper)
ISBN-10: 0-87351-639-7 (pbk. : alk. paper)
    1. Minnesota—History—Sources.
    2. Minnesota—Social life and customs—Sources.
    3. Minnesota—History—Pictorial works.
    4. Minnesota—Biography.
    5. American letters—Minnesota.
    I. Meier, Peg, 1946–
F606.B837 2009
977.6'04—dc22   2008024956

*This book is dedicated to people who record their lives
with good letters, diaries and photographs.
And to those who keep and treasure the documents.*

CONTENTS

INTRODUCTION TO THE 2023 EDITION

More than forty years have passed since *Bring Warm Clothes* first was published. We didn't know if Minnesotans would like it. You did!

It was an odd history book. I wanted to give you stories about regular people, in their own words. You could get the "important" stuff of Minnesota history elsewhere, in many formats. I wanted this book to be informal and a pleasure to peruse.

Decades ago, I loved having excuses to explore the collections of the Minnesota Historical Society and other history archives. I was then a reporter for the *Minneapolis Tribune* and wondered if I could take a leave of absence and do just that. Maybe I could get a grant from the Saint Paul Foundation to put together a book.

Bingo. That worked. For seven glorious months in 1980, I paged through old letters and diaries. I examined photos. I read decades-old newspapers on microfilm. I bugged librarians and historians around the state to tell me which collections stirred their hearts. Every once in a while, I got so excited about a find that I'd whoop with joy. Not every scholarly researcher working in those quiet places appreciated that.

I especially liked the writing left behind by ordinary people, not necessarily by politicians or the rich guys for whom our streets were named. Rather, I searched for words of housewives, farmers, immigrants, students. Maybe their correspondence is like letters from your own family, generations ago, or in texts you exchanged last week.

I'll never forget finding Samuel Bloomer's tiny diary, which he stitched together between two scraps of cardboard. A Civil War soldier from Stillwater, he was injured in the Battle of Antietam. In teeny penmanship to conserve paper, he wrote on September 17, 1862, "I was left on the field all day as the shot & shells of both armies playing in or about there . . . made it a very dangerous place"

A few days later, Sam penciled into his diary, "This day will long be remembered by me for about 8 oclock A.M. the Doctors put me on the table & amputated my right leg above my knee and from thence suffering commenced in earnest." I bet. No anesthesia in those days, you know.

I told a newspaper colleague about Sam Bloomer. She was unimpressed. That was so long ago, she reminded me, about someone we didn't know. Who cares about him? My enthusiasm momentarily was crushed.

But I protested to her that Sam returned

to Stillwater, was elected mayor, married, lost his wife, remarried, outlived three of his four children, and lived to age eighty-two. His is a great narrative! She just didn't see it. I had to realize not everyone loved local history as I did. Oh, well. Somebody would.

These stories and great old photos did fill a niche. Book sales were terrific—way more than 200,000 since 1981, in twenty-some printings. Twin Cities Public Television liked the book and made a film that's still available.

Over the decades, I've received amazing feedback: From a man who wanted to buy a second copy so he could use both sides of each page to wallpaper his guest bathroom. From a woman who gave the book to her mother as a birthday gift on Christmas Day, and inside the family found a wanted poster for grandpa, charged with bastardy. From women who sympathized with Margaret Kerr, who in 1874 was visited for ten days by a friend with four children under seven, to add to her own flock of five kids under nine. Both families took ill with chicken pox.

Despite the enthusiasm for the book, after forty years some buyers were put off by the size. The original was horizontal, 9x11 inches, which some thought was cumbersome to read in bed, boat, or bathtub and on the toilet. (Minnesotans are fervent readers.)

And now the Minnesota Historical Society Press has reprinted *Bring Warm Clothes* in a more compact and vertical format, 8.5x11 inches. While the press was at it, we removed some language that was acceptable in the 1980s but no longer.

So here we are. The book is easier to hold, still fun, still crammed with fascinating REAL people.

One suggestion: May you leave behind some of your own stories. Write them down. Or tell and preserve your stories on recordings or video. Today. No better day. Nothing fancy. Someone will cherish your words someday. I promise.

Peg Meier
June 2023

OPPOSITE
Rock carving of an atlatl, a notched stick used by Natives to throw a spear (see page 5). *MNHS*

A hand, carved many centuries ago. *Jeffers Petroglyphs Historic Site, photo by John Cross, MNHS*

GENERATIONS AND GENERATIONS

One of the oldest messages in Minnesota

For generations upon generations, people have lived in the place we now call Minnesota.

Carved in a rock by a hunter about five thousand years ago is a picture of an "atlatl," a spear-throwing device similar to the harpoon the Inuit used later. When a hunter used an atlatl, he could throw his spear hard and far. Starting in about 3000 BCE, people used pointed rocks to peck symbols in a twenty-three-mile-long outcrop of rock. This was near what is now the town of Jeffers, on the prairie of southwestern Minnesota. Many people from different tribes carved the pictures over a long span of time—up to 1750 CE.

A large number of the carvings were destroyed before their importance was recognized. However, about five thousand of the Jeffers petroglyphs (rock pictures) still exist.

There are carvings of bison, turtles, wolves, bear, elk, bows and arrows, harpoons, medicine men, dragonflies, and stick men. Some of the stick men wear bison-horn headdresses. Many carvings defy description, and some anthropologists believe they are ancient doodles. Some carvings are more than three feet across; others are only a few inches.

The oldest symbols depict the atlatls. From about 3000 BCE to 500 CE, big-game animals provided most of the food for people living in this area. The huge bison (a now-extinct ancestor of today's bison, often called buffalo) was the most important animal that was hunted. Small bands of hunters followed the migrating bison herds and drove them over cliffs or into narrow ravines. Hunters then could easily kill them with their spears and atlatls.

A French view of the new world, just before 1700. *MNHS*

1700s

European contacts with the Native Americans living in this area, begun in the second half of the 1600s, increased in this century. French and British governments sent expeditions to explore territories that were unknown to them but fully occupied by Indigenous nations. French and British corporations sent traders to bring back valuable furs. Beaver pelts and the search for the Northwest Passage were the prime attractions. The Dakota (also called Sioux, meaning "snake," by enemy tribes and whites), originally a woodland people, were forced westward onto the plains by Ojibwe (Chippewa) people. And the Ojibwe had been forced from their homelands in the east by Europeans. Because the Europeans left written records, the stories we have from this time reflect their perspectives. →

JONATHAN CARVER

"This country is coverd with grass which affords excellent pasturage for the buffeloe which here are very plenty."

European explorers and fur traders, under various flags, came to Minnesota over the decades. After the French and Indian War in the 1760s, control of the Minnesota land went from France to England. The British were interested primarily in the fur trade, then in exploration. One of the earliest English explorers was Jonathan Carver. Carver wrote a book that was very popular in Europe. Some of his observations were less than accurate, but his descriptions were vivid.

JUNE 4, 1767. Came to the great medows or plains. Here I found excellent good land and very pleasant country. [This is the area near Lake Pepin on the Wisconsin-Minnesota border.] One might travel all day and only see now and then a small pleasant groves of oak and walnut. This country is coverd with grass which affords excellent pasturage for the buffeloe which here are very plenty. Could see them at a distance under the shady oaks like cattle in a pasture and sometimes a drove of an hundred or more shading themselves in these groves at noon day which afforded a very pleasant prospect for an uninhabited country. We killd several of these buffeloes, one of which we all judgd would weigh fifteen hundred weight and if the same could be fed as is common to fatten our tame cattle undoubt-edly would weigh three thousand, they being by far the largest creatures in bulk that I ever saw. . . . Here is a great plenty of elk, the largest that ever I had seen. As it was after they had shed of their horns, they apeard at a distance on the plain like droves of horses. A hunter might get very near to these as they was very tame and would hardly move out of our way till fired upon.

Their [the Dakota] marriage customs are very peculiar. When two young people are about to joyn in wedlock they walk out both together on the parade which is generally in the middle of the camp where a number assembles to assist in the ceremony. Among

Jonathan Carver. *MNHS*

these is one of their underchiefs who in a short speach informs the spectators that them two, calling over their names, are come there that the whole may witness that they love each other that he takes her for his wife . . . to get wood, dress his victuals, take care of the tent both while he is at home and out a hunting and at war, after which they take hold of each others' hands, and the whole of the spectators discharge their arrows over the heads of the bride and bridegroom, after which the man turns his back to the bride. She gets on him and he carrys her to his tent. The spectators give a loud cohoop and wish them happy all their days. Thus ends the ceremony.

John Parker, ed., *The Journals of Jonathan Carver and Related Documents 1776–1770*, MNHS Press, 1976

PETER POND

"no Snakes But Small ones which is not Pisenes"

European interest in Minnesota was due in large part to a small and frivolous item valued across the ocean: the beaver hat. From the early 1600s to the middle of the 1800s, no proper European gentleman appeared in public without one. The fashion spread to America. Many early explorers and most traders in what is now northern Minnesota and Canada were after the beaver pelt.

For Europeans, politics on the northern frontier consisted largely of claims over trapping areas, and their concern about the Ojibwe and the Dakota often boiled down to concern about pelts they had. For several hundred years, the lifestyle remained the same for the fur traders and the French-Canadian men who paddled the big canoes loaded with furs and supplies.

Peter Pond was a skilled explorer and trader in the Upper Mississippi country in the 1770s and 1780s. It is said Pond furnished Benjamin Franklin with information about the Great Lakes area that enabled Franklin

Dakota people, painted by Karl Bodmer

to bargain well with the British during boundary negotiations. But Pond was not a skilled writer or speller, as this piece of his autobiography shows:

On acount of the fase of the Cuntrey & Soile the Entervales of the River St Peter is Exsaland & Sum Good timber the Banks

A Dakota village,
painted by Seth Eastman

Bend the Intervals are High and the Soile thin & lite the River is Destatute of fish But the Woods & Meaddoues afords abundans of annamels Sum turkeas Buffeloes are Verey Plentey the Common Dear are Plentey and Larg the Read & Moose Dear are Plentey hear Esesly [especially] the former I have sean fortey Kild in One Our By Surounding a Drove on a Low Spot By the River side in the Winter season, Raccoons are Verey Large, no Snakes But Small ones which is not Pisenes Woolves are Plentey thay follow the Buffeloes and often Destroy thare yoang & Olde Ones in winter the Natives near the Mouth of the River Rase Plentey of Corn for thare one Con-cumtion—The Manners and Custams of ye Yantonose [Yanktons, a band of the Dakota] The Band I Saw up the River are Notawases by Nation But By Sum Intornal Disputes thay ware Seaperated into Six Different Bands Each Band Lead By Cheafes of thare One Chois. . . . Thay Leade a wandring Life in that Exstensive Plane Betwen the Miseeurea & Misisippey thay dwell in Leather tents Cut Sumthing in form of a Spanis Cloke and Spread out by thirteen [poles] in the Shape of a Beel the Poles Meet at the top But the Base is fortten In Dimert [diameter] thay Go into it By a Hole Cut in the Side and a Skin Hung Befour it By way of a Dore thay Bild thare fire in the Middel and [d]ue all thare Cookerey over it at Night thay Lie down all round the Lodg with thare feat to the fire thay Have a Grate Number of Horseses and Dogs which Carres thare Bageag when thay Moove from Plase to Plase thay Make yous of Buffeloes Dung [for fuel] as thar is But leattle or no wood apon the Planes they are [contin]uely on the Watch for feare of Beaing Surprised By thare Enemise [who are] all Rund them

Charles M. Gates, ed., *Five Fur Traders of the Northwest*, MNHS Press, 1965

JOHN MACDONELL

John Macdonell was born in Scotland and migrated to New York and Canada. He was twenty-five years old and on his first trading trip when he kept this diary:

WEDNESDAY 11TH [SEPTEMBER 1793]. Supped upon a Bear killed by the hunters and while at supper a Snake came into the Tent and was not perceived till it got half its length across Mr Neil Mackay's plate.

THURSDAY 3RD OCT. After walking till 3 PM. I mounted a high round hill from the summit of which I spyed three Buffaloes on a hill at some distance. Having got two men to accompany me we killed one of the three, a thigh of which I carried to our campment to make Steaks.

Five Fur Traders of the Northwest

Map of the Great Lakes, 1762. *MNHS*

Shooting the rapids, painted by Mrs. F. A. Hopkins. Look closely: Mrs. Hopkins may be aboard.
Public Archives of Canada C-2774

1800s

The area came under the jurisdiction of the United States in 1803 under the Louisiana Purchase. Voyageurs (the canoeists of the fur trade) and fur traders carried on the region's commerce. →

GEORGE NELSON

"Whenever this country becomes settled how delightfully will the inhabitants pass their time."

George Nelson was only sixteen years old when he became an apprentice clerk in a fur-trade company called the XY Company. He left his parents' home near Montreal, Canada, in 1802 to work in the St. Croix Valley of what is now Minnesota. At first Nelson, the oldest son of a schoolmaster, was homesick and shocked by the rough ways of the traders and the Ojibwe people around him. As these segments (written later in his life) show, he learned to adjust and to like the people.

By this time [just thirty miles away from his parents in Montreal] I began to accustom myself to the ways. That heaviness of heart peculiar to youth when they leave home for the first time began to wear away, and finding myself a free, an irresponsible agent, entirely master of my own will & actions, I soon began to "run riot." I ran into all the excesses of foolish language; freed from the shackels of a Strict parent; & no one out of compassion or justice to say "Hold." I gave into all the foolish & vulgar language of the lowest of our crew, most fortunately my propensities never led me further.

On the 15th [of September 1802] Smith [William Smith, another XY employee] shot a duck. I was very glad, because I was already tired of corn; for they had "made no allow-ances" for me. But when I saw the manner he

was dressing it! He plucked, Singed, scraped off the ashes that had adhered to the bird in singing it on the coals, pulled out a few of the longest of the stumps, split it open, & threw it into kettle, wherein the indian corn, for our supper, was boiling.

He did not even rince it in the lake. This procedure shocked me terribly. He then broiled the entrails of the duck on the coals & eat them himself! "O, what a barbarian! what a hog! Am I to become like that!—is it for this I have left my father's house, the affection-ate care of the best of mothers, deprived of the society of my brothers & sisters!"—My heart swelled almost to bursting point with disgust, indignation, horror & grief. "But I shall not remain long here. I will save my earnings, return to the "civilized" (!) world, buy a farm & pass my life quietly & com-fortably." How easily is the mind consoled & the heart relieved, with reflections that are not, can never be realized, very often from the influence of the very cause that give rise to them! Alas! poor human nature! The duck was soon cooked. . . . Smith offered me a very reasonable share,—I refused, thanking him; he rightly guessed the cause, "What? said he, because forsooth I did not wash it! oh, lah!— that squeamishness of yours will soon vanish. Why did you remain hooked to your mothers apron?" This, accompanied with many oaths

"North" Canoe on Lake Superior —

Canoe on Lake Superior, painted by George Seton. *Public Archives of Canada, C-1052*

The Laughing Waters,
painted by Seth Eastman

Lake Superior, engraved by Charles Mottram. *Public Archives of Canada, C-13584*

& ribaldry, called with there, only served to increase my pain & cause me more to feel my wretchedness.

[Nelson's first impression of the Ojibwe people was not favorable:]

We soon entered the Ste Croix & glided gently down its placid bosom, but little obstructed with rapids. . . . The indians, the moment they saw us gave the whoop. They were all drunk, the N. W Co. [the North West Company, a competing firm] had a little before given liquor. They came rushing upon us like devils, dragged our Canoe to land, threw the lading ashore, ripped up the bale cloths, cut the cords & Sprinkled the goods about at a fine rate. Such a noise, yelling & chattering! "Rum, Rum, what are you come to do here without rum?"—after a while, when they saw we had no rum, they gradually dispersed. A few of the more quite [quiet] remained; they entered into friendly intercourse with Smith whom they knew for many years; & it is but bare justice to say that he acquitted himself like a man, both as regards prudence & courage on this critical and trying occasion. It was enough to test the nerve of any man. I soon became the object of their attention. They gathered round me, spoke kindly, laughed with me & tapped me friendly on the Shoulders & head. But I understood nothing of what they said. Smith done all the needful in this business for me. . . . They were the first I had seen in numbers & at their homes. Men of the common Stature, most of them besmeared black, with bruised charcoal & grease, being most of them in mourning for some of their relations, killed the year before in a drunken quarrel on this very spot. There were five killed out-right & six very severly & dangerously wounded, with knives, only with a Capot & brich cloth on, their Tommy haw-pipes & knives in their hands. They look fierce, & were so. Strait as arrows, their motions & their eyes showed plainly, how frequently these faculties must have been bro't to the test.

[His attitude was to change. Over the years, he came to know Ojibwe customs. He wrote that he found their mourning ceremonies no more strange than an Irish wake. He discovered the people of the St. Croix to be courageous and full of character, and he eventually married an Ojibwe woman.]

The indians took great pity upon me. One of them adopted me as his Son, & told his own Son, a lad of about my age, to consider me as his Brother & to treat me so, and he did indeed the very few times we happened to meet after this.

We had two [Native] widows, one very old, to pass the winter by us in a wretched hut. They had two daughters & two boys, between 12 & 14 years of age. I surprised to remark the boys frequently with black faces, upon enquiring, I found they were fasting. They sometimes dreamed of their departed friends,—"on those occasions, when they awake in the morning, they bruise soft charcoal in their hands, with which they rub their faces so as not to leave one spot of the natural color, take their guns or bow & arrows & go into the woods a hunting, and to mourn & weep where they may not be seen nor heard." They return at even & eat after Sun Set! The old woman would frequently go out to the foot of the hill some distance off, & weep & mourn & moan, addressing her departed husband & friends in accents & a tone of voice not to be misunderstood even by me, young, thoughtless & boistrous as I was.

What is this? is it Barbarism? if so, what signify the "Irish wakes"? our own wailings on the departure of those dear to us? after a few months, & not unfrequently only some days,

& we return to the busy occupations of life, & finally become quite reconciled & oblivious:—here, children after several years, go into the woods & bewail their departed friends in quiet & solitude, fasting the whole day. An old woman, many years after the melancholy events, goes & hides herself at the foot of a tree & holds a "talk" with them; complaining of her bereavement & asking forgiveness if she had ever injured, offended, or hurt their feelings! On their return, they would generally be cheerful, as if it had not been them who but a moment before were making such wailing, or, as if they had just been pouring off all their grief! I have very often witnessed such scenes: I was very young & reckless, but being a Christian, & civilized, these superstitious barbarities were beneath the attention of my superior knowledge; but they have left an indelible impression.

[Nelson dropped his fear of the Ojibwe, yet some of their practices disturbed him. This one, for example:]

The men were out a hunting & returned towards evening. They were all highly pleased to see us. They had some furs & plenty of meat. They cooked a large Kettle full for us & helped us generously but Smith eat very

Scene on Lake Superior, painted by W. Armstrong. *Public Archives of Canada, C-11748*

little being disgusted with the woman. One of her children had a "looseness," [diarrhea] & the little black devil was running about the lodge squattering out yellow stuff like mustard; she scolded & laying the bratt on her lap opened the cheeks & with the back of her knife Scraped off the Stuff, scolded him again for a dirty little dog, wiped her knife upon the brush, scooped water with her right hand out of the Kettle in which our meat was, to wash both, & finished cutting up, with the same knife, a piece of beautiful fat meat, as a relish to what she had put on before. I was sadly disappointed, for I was hungry & always had a strong appetite. I kept my eyes upon her during the whole performance, which certainly was dirty enough. But the knife was cleaned. There was nothing on her hands.

[Early in January 1803, they feared the Dakota were after them.]

We retreated a few hundred yards off, & finding a thick cluster of wild rose bushes we beat them down, & passed the night upon them; each one taking his turn in the middle, to keep from freezing; for we had no blankets, & had only taken a glass of rum in the morning, so as to have a better appetite!. . . . It was very cold & windy—nothing to cover us, no fire & empty Stomacs, with only a few rose bushes to keep us from the Snow.

[All in all, Nelson thought the area beautiful:]

There are a great number of Lakes in the whole extent of the Country: some of them beautiful, nay magnificent bodies of water, & well furnished with fish. Many a time in walking over them have I thought: Whenever this country becomes settled how delightfully will the inhabitants pass their time. There is no place perhaps on this globe where nature has displayed & diversified land & water as here. I always felt as if invited to settle down & admire the beautiful views with a sort of joyful thankfulness for having been led to them. There is nothing romantic about them, frightful rock, & wild & dashing water falls. Nature is here calm, placid & serene, as if telling man, in language mute, indeed,—not addressed to the Ears, but to heart & Soul: It is here man is to be happy: a genial & healthy climate—the rigour of winter scarcely three months, & in that time no very severe cold: I have diversified the land with hundreds of beautiful lakes all communicating with each other by equally beautiful streams, full of excellent fish, & ducks of twenty Species, Swans & geese with abundance of rice for you & them. The borders well furnished with grapes, plums, thorn apples & butternut &c. &c. The Woods Swarming with Dears & bears & beavers: not one noxious or venimous animal insect or reptile: come my children, come & settle in this beautiful country I have prepared for you, & be happy.

George Nelson papers, Metropolitan Toronto Library Board

Fort Snelling, several decades after construction, painted by Edward K. Thomas.
Minneapolis Institute of Arts

1820s

Fort Snelling was completed and served as the military and social hub of the frontier. The area was dotted with more than forty fur-trading posts, tiny operations scattered along riverways through a broad territory. A few white settlers arrived. The first steamship reached the fort in May 1823, expanding trade and bringing the beginning of tourist trade. People who survived childhood diseases could expect to live to about age forty-five. →

LAWRENCE TALIAFERRO

"My advice to you is that the bloody war club be buried deep in the Earth."

Construction of Fort Snelling was begun by the US government in 1819 at the confluence of the Mississippi and Minnesota Rivers near what is now the Twin Cities. This area was known to the Dakota as Bdote, and it was considered sacred as the site of one of the Dakota creation stories. For decades, the fort was literally on the edge of the frontier: white farmers were forbidden to settle on lands that had not yet been taken by treaties. To the west were only a scattering of cabins and an occasional fur post, hundreds of miles apart and each with only a dozen or so people. Fort Snelling—with about three hundred soldiers, officers, and dependents—was the center of white occupancy and civilization. It had a school, library, church, theater, and dances. Never the scene of battles, it was mostly involved in encouraging and regulating trade with Native American tribes. It was established primarily because the US government wanted to prevent Indigenous trappers from trading their furs to the British.

Major Lawrence Taliaferro (pronounced Tol-i-ver) of Virginia arrived at Fort Snelling in 1820 to serve as US Indian agent to the Dakota, Ojibwe, Ho-Chunk, and other Native tribes in the larger region. Unlike many corrupt and incompetent Indian agents on the frontier, Taliaferro was generally respected by the Native people he dealt with. He was honest, considerate, and dignified. His duties included trying to keep peace among the tribes, protecting them from fur traders' exploitation, and encouraging them to switch from hunting to farming. By the 1830s, the beaver had become scarce, and American fur traders were after muskrat. Settlement obviously was coming, and the Native people were being squeezed out.

In his diary in July of 1821, Taliaferro recorded a speech he made to "chiefs and head men of the Chippeways on a visit to this post, to meet the Sioux and to settle their

Lawrence Taliaferro. *MNHS*

View of the Minnesota River

long differences in my presense." The language is elaborate and, by modern standards, patronizing. He spoke in English. Taliaferro never learned the Native languages; he relied on interpreters.

Chippeways, my friends and children—
The Great Spirit has brought you and the Sioux together this day—lend me your ears that you may listen.

Many of you that are assembled here to day have never been under the sound of my Voice. Hear me Chippeways, when you call on your American Father you will find him allways ready to adjust all difficulties that may be happening in your nation. You have long listened to a Father across the great water. His Chiefs have told you more than they have ever fulfilled or have ever taken place. They have made you promises. They made you presents and strewed their Medals & Flags through your nation, for what. That your blood might flow the more freely for them.

My Children.

None of you this day, under the sound of my voice but knows this talk to be the truth. I am glad to see you here to day Chippeways and Sioux, that I may tell you these things. Your American Father never wished either your assistance or your Blood in any of his wars he was & is still able to fight his own Battles against the red coats, red skins or any other Nation.

It is true your American Father was once like a Small Tree, but that day has long since passed and he has grown up like a tall Oak, and the branches extend to all parts of the world. Nothing does he owe to any Nation and what passes through my hands & into yours is an evidence of his good will to those who listen to my council and conduct themselves like Chiefs & good men.

Chippeways

The language I make use of this day to you is the same which I spoke to the Sioux on my first arrival in their Nation It is now time that all Red Skins should have but one Ear—for the American Nation is too strong to acknowledge any Master. This Flag (a large Am. Flag in my left hand) floats and is waved on the Waters of every Nation and the Eagle looks proudly upon the many stars in her nation that surround her.

Chippeways

One word more, listen to me. I have a heart for all Red Skins, and if the great Spirit had have gifted me with the knowledge of your tongue and that of the Sioux, Blood should cease to flow, and not a tear again shed in either Nation. When you have however listened to my words half as long as you have to your English Father, my councils will be found more conducive to your happiness & that of your wives & children.

My children

Much blood has been shed in the long war between your Nation and the Sioux and it will benefit both Nations if you this day pass around the calumet of peace & friendship. I do not say you must be at peace but my advice to you is that the bloody war club be buried deep in the Earth that both Nations may enjoy the same fire side.

My children

The Roads are smooth about my house always keep them so, and the Great Spirit will Smile upon you.

Lawr Taliaferro
Ind agent
for the Upper Mississippi

[Even Taliaferro could not use words to sweep away the problems of the Native nations. Cultural traditions of glory earned in warfare, frictions between Ojibwe and Dakota people brought about by pressures from whites, the white man's greed, the liquor given to the Native customers by the traders (and even by Taliaferro)—they all contributed to the continued battles, raids, and scalpings. But while the truce he tried to enforce between the Dakota and Ojibwe was frequently broken, the peace between the whites and the Native nations lasted all the time he was agent. He left in 1839.]

Lawrence Taliaferro papers, MNHS

MNHS

JAMES E. COLHOUN

Fort Snelling

James E. Colhoun was a member of a US expedition to Minnesota in 1823. His journal differs from those of other explorers because it reflects his education and travels, mostly in South America and the Orient. He read widely and had some familiarity with at least four foreign languages.

FRIDAY, JULY 18, 1823. Fortunately the nights are sufficiently cool to permit our sleeping with our boots on & our heads covered with the blanket. It is hardly an exaggeration of the traders that in the summer season on the St. Peter's [now known as the Minnesota River] the one whose office it is to strike fire will find it impossible to perform his duties, unless protected from the mus-quitoes by some of his company. Although I have a veil for the purpose, I find it necessary to keep a soldier constantly employed to brush away these troublesome insects while I am making Observations, & even with that aid I am seldom able to make them in a satisfactory manner. So soon as supper is ended we hurry to our coverts. The horses crowd into the smoke of our fire, & several times have been so much distracted by stings of musquitoes as to rush over our baggage & into the midst of the party. They have no respite in the day time, for then they have to bear the torment of horseflies.

MONDAY, JULY 28, 1823 . . . We made our supper of the spoils of the hunt, which we had brought fastened to our saddles. We found the elk-meat, though inferior to that of the buffalo, a lighter colored & better kind of venison; the chief objection to it was the too great taste of tallow. The udder was delicious, perhaps the more because our meal had been postponed & the appetite consequently increased. It was cooked in our usual way by inclining to the fire the sharpened stick thrust through it & stuck into the ground. Meals that I have ate with most zest have been those prepared in this rude manner, no doubt borrowing much from attendant circumstances.

Lucile M. Kane, June D. Holmquist, and Carolyn Gilman, eds., *The Northern Expeditions of Stephen H. Long: The Journals of 1817 and 1823 and Related Documents*, MNHS Press, 1978

Hunting buffalo, painted by Karl Bodmer

1830s

Native guides showed Schoolcraft the way to Lake Itasca, allowing him to claim that he discovered the source of the Mississippi River. The US government used fur trade debts and incursions by white settlers to force Ojibwe and Dakota people to sell large tracts of land. Lumbermen and farmers began to move in. The fur trade was on the decline. Missionaries focused their work on the Native people. The panic of 1837 slowed development. A sawmill was built at Marine-on-St.-Croix in 1839. Stillwater, a lumber town, was soon to follow. →

NATHAN JARVIS

"If they do not dance with grace they at least make it up in strength & duration, generally continuing it from 8 oclock in the evening until 8 in the morning."

Dr. Nathan S. Jarvis was an army surgeon at Fort Snelling from 1833 to 1836. He was from New York and took steamboats on the Ohio and Mississippi Rivers to get to Minnesota. He wrote to his family.

Nathan Jarvis. *MNHS*

Fort Snelling, Upper Mississippi
OCTOBER 10, 1833
Dear Sir:

I was much gratify'd in receiving your letter which by the by is only the second one I have rec'd since my departure from home, a period of nearly 7 months, and as our express starts tomorrow I embrace the opportunity of answering it and the enquiries you make.

As to news, little can occur in this distant region, secluded from the world. We pass our time something in the way of exiles, banish'd from the pleasures and I may add follies of civiliz'd life. Still there are charms even in savage life and the wilderness, as proof of which there are many men in this country acting as Indian traders and possessing talent who after accumulating fortunes by the profits of the trade, marry indian wives and settle themselves down for life, abandoning any idea of ever returning to the places of their birth or their friends. If we have but little news here we occasionally, altho' extremely rare see a straggler in this distant region nor travellers nor traders, but those idle wandering fellows who have no home and going they know not where nor do they care and without any earthly motive. 2 such arrived here this summer and both from the state of New York. One of them in a log canoe paddling alone all the way against the strong current

Harvesting wild rice, painted by Seth Eastman

of the Mississippi and part of the time without anything to eat. His object he stated in coming here was to see the country and fight the Indians. To gratify his last ambition they persuaded him to enlist. The other's motive was likewise to see the country and he said he came from New Windsor, N.Y. he had neither shoes, clothing or provisions and was anxious he said to go further on to the Red River settlement a distance only of 800 miles thro' numerous bands of hostile indians, who would have scalp'd him before he had got half the way if he ever got so far without starving. He concluded, however, to remain here at present and chop wood at 50 cts. a day, a business to which he says he was brot up. Here is ambition & enterprise for you. A missionary or more properly a teacher by the name of Ayres, sent out by Amer. Board of Missions [headquartered in Boston and representing the Congregational, Presbyterian, and Dutch Reformed churches], arriv'd here a day or two ago from 300 miles east in the Chippeway country, where he is stationed with a wife and young woman as teacher in the midst of savages, this being the nearest post to him where there is a white man. He came for provisions and letters. . . .

My expenses at this post including mess, servant, washing, horse keeping, etc., amount to about $25 a month. My pay is $82 a month and I likewise receive about $100 a year from the Ind. agent for attending sick Indians and about $100 more from private practice, making in all nearly $ 1,200 a year. . . .

I have one of the best rooms in the garrison, the hospital range being built of stone. But what is of more importance in this climate and such winters as we have here, is that we received this summer between 30 & 40 large stoves for the use of the garrison. Speaking of winter, everything betokens its near approach. Immense flocks of wild geese and myriads of ducks flying south. More are kill'd than are count'd. The ducks are the finest I have ever eaten. The winter generally sets in the beginning of November, when everything remains in thick ribb'd ice until nearly the middle of April. What think you of the thermometer being as low as 30 degrees below zero? Such is the case every winter in this climate. We keep a regular diary of the weather at the posts, consequently I know the state of the weather, by referring to the book, ever since the post was established. Last winter the thermometer for every day during the month was nearly ten degrees below zero. 2000 cords of wood are generally consumed during the winter at the post.

As to your inquiry respecting my rank, medical officers do not, as it were, belong to the line of the army, but the general staff and rank accordingly. The only occasion in which their rank is bro't in with that of the line is in choice of quarters and then it depends on length of service whether a surgeon rank with a Major or Captain or assistant with Capt. or Lieut.

As to how the sabbath is observ'd here, the only way it is known is by a relaxation of the men from their daily fatigue duty (not garrison duty) and Sunday inspection. Otherwise it is unknown here—

The sound of the church going bell
These rocks and these valleys ne'er heard,
and by a late general order it will be some years before any of us heard the signal of civiliz'd life, for no officer can have a furlough for 7 months until 6 years' service. The officers are very agreeable men, altho' too much addicted to cards, which is the prevailing vice in all these outposts where men are shut out from amusements during the long and severe winters. We have almost all trades among the men here, as shoemaker, silversmith, bookbinder, tailor, etc., who are accordingly employed in their leisure time for whatever we want made.

You make inquiries respecting the width & current of the Mississippi here—opposite the fort it is about 300 yards and the current runs about 4 miles an hour. The water is now at its lowest stage and in the channel is not more than 6 or 8 ft. and elsewhere is easily forded. It is now about 8 ft. below high-water mark . . . I will in some future letter give you a description of the surrounding country, its timber and productions. We receive at the post newspapers from New York, Philadelphia, Washington, Boston, etc. Our last news from the East is August 9th, over 2 months since.

[Here Jarvis wrote to his sister, Mary:]

Fort Snelling Upper Mississippi
FEBY. 2ND 1834
For Mary
. . . Little has taken place as we have all been most of the month shut up in the fort and confin'd to our Rooms owing to the excessive cold . . .

Our latest New York Papers were up to the 14th of December. . . . Major Bliss appointed me the other day Librarian & Inspector of the Post school, offices I more trouble than honor. Our library contains about 400 vols of excellent books to which is attach'd a

Reading Room which is abundantly suppl'd with Newspapers & Periodicals. The school has about 20 children belonging in and out of the Fort. Between these and one's professional duties and occasionaly sleigh riding I contrive to pass my time agreeably enough.

My horse took it into his head to die the other day and there goes $50 out of my pocket and what is worse has left me horseless. I had him drawn under the walls of the Fort for a purpose that you will consider a very ungrateful return for all his services to me vis as wolf bait which soon attracted their notices—

And nightly on my poor chevel
They made a glorious carnival.

We however had some sport in chasing them with dogs . . .

The soldiers amuse themselves by having Balls in the Fort twice a week and it is amusing sometimes to visit them. Their partners are mostly those ladies of the garrison yclept Camp women together with the ladies without. If they do not dance with grace they at least make it up in strength & duration, generally

continuing it from 8 oclock in the evening until 8 in the morning. I have lately been practising on snow shoes and have gone several miles on them thro' a deep snow. . . . I have got some pretty Indian curiosities I will send you next spring if an opportunity affords. My Room looks something like a Museum hung around with pipes, tomahawks war clubs, &c. Mary all I want now is a wife can you pick out one. As for me I never shall have a chance of [illegible] thro' a regular courtship for I have to stay here a long time and must therefore like royal personages court by proxy! Therefore select one for me and describe to me her qualities & accomplishments & C., &c. The mail is closing and I must therefore close my letter by asking you to give my love to all the family & friends.

Yours affectionately
N.S. Jarvis

Malloch Rare Book Room, New York
Academy of Medicine Library

WILLIAM T. BOUTWELL

". . . to a person unaccustomed to a voyageurs life, what a beast of burden man may become from habit, and the burdens he will carry through mud and water, where it would be impossible for a dumb beast to pass!"

A missionary who traveled with the canoeists called voyageurs (French for "travelers") was amazed at their strength. The writer was the Rev. William T. Boutwell, a Protestant who in 1833 became a missionary among the Ojibwe at Leech Lake. He wrote that September in his diary:

It is absolutely passing belief, to a person unaccustomed to a voyageurs life, what a beast of burden man may become from habit, and the burdens he will carry through mud and water, where it would be impossible for a dumb beast to pass! I had merely a musket, 1 paddle, and 2 umbrellas upon my shoulder,

Horse races, painted by Karl Bodmer

and yet I could not keep in sight of the greater part of our men, unless I ran faster than I chose. We reached the head of the portage at half past six. Here we overtook the Red Cedar and Leech Lake baggage, which left Fond du Lac some four or five days before us. I was hungry, wet, and tired, to say nothing of mud, when I reached here. Hardly had I pulled off my muddy socks and moccasins, before I was requested to relieve a poor fellow who was suffering from a defective tooth. Supped upon a piece of wild goose and pork.

William T. Boutwell papers, MNHS

EDMUND ELY

"This has been a day of deep interest & anxiety in the Family. About 11 o'clock Catharine was delivered of a Daughter."

Edmund F. Ely was a Protestant missionary among the Ojibwe in northern Minnesota in the 1830s. He was with the American Board of Commissioners for Foreign Missions. When he wrote the first of these entries, he was twenty-four years old. Ely wrote in great detail of the Ojibwe, his struggle over his soul, his travels and his aggravation that the Ojibwe made the sign of the cross (Catholic priests had reached them before the Protestants did). He rarely mentioned his family. In fact, the references to his wife and child quoted here are among the few he penned. Many men of his times tended to write more about business and weather than about family.

SABBATH EVENING SEPT. 21 [1833]. This has been a business Sabbath with us. Our room has been so much visited by Indians & children, that we have not found time to pray 10 minutes, without a Rapp at our door. Whenever an Indian is visited in his lodge, he lays aside all business & attends to his visitor—& they expect the same from us. consequently we spend our time when they are here & at all hours, in reading & Singing to them. Spent an hour or more this morning in Mr. S.'s lodge according to appointment—& also this Evening—20 to 30 individuals were present. Nearly all joined—especially the women & children.

FRIDAY EVE. 27TH SEPT. The autumnal wind howls without. The Moon is obscured by dark clouds. How naturally does the mind that heeds such an Evening, sympathize in the general gloom! The domestic fireside & the dear circle which were wont to surround

Edmund Ely. *Northeast Minnesota Historical Center*

Sugar camp, painted by Seth Eastman

Dakota funeral scaffold, painted by Karl Bodmer

it—the recollection of beloved friends & associates, with whom stout counsel & prayer have been often enjoyed—all force themselves before the mind. How sad the review. The domestic circle broken—Parents moulding in the grave. Their offsprings scattered far & wide—their prospects various associates—separated by a long distance. No one to mingle his voice with prayer & praise to the God of our Mercies. Sad retrospect—& a lonely life to one, who for the first time breaks away from friends & privileges—to stand alone in the wilderness. Yet, although my sympathies dwell on this subject I will not wish myself back. No, God has sent me here to "cast up an Highway for them." but—how unworthy—how unfit. What meanness in one so honoured! Thou Lord knowest my wants.

SATURDAY EVE. SEPT. 28, 1833. Another week has rolled away. The first week of my labours as Teacher [to the Ojibwe children]. It has been delightfully spent. I love to see improvement—& feel encouraged when I see but little. It distresses [me] to be "dumb"—my lips can utter very few words intelligible to my scholars—but am gaining slowly . . .

WEDNESDAY EVE [OCT. 16]. This morning was called to see a little Boy's face, which had swollen very much during the night. I made him a Poultice—as the most simple Remedy. This evening he was in great pain with it—& the system much excited. He could not bear a warm poultice—came home & prepared a linament—& returned—but in the meantime the Mother & Boy had gone to the neighboring Lodge of an Indian, who was singing over him.

Left word that I would attempt nothing—unless they would let their drumming alone—in half an hour the Mother sent for me to come & apply my remedy. I conjecture the cause to be—a hull of Wild Rice sticking in the Cheek or Goom—shall Call

in the morning to see the effect. The Chief called—& wanted I should see his Mother & daughter, who were unwell did not call. A little Knowledge of medicine [would be] very desirable in this region—great suffering might be relieved.

FRIDAY EVENING, OCT. 18. After Supper this afternoon 5 oclk went with Mr. Davenport to procure some dry wood—as our Man whose duty it is was absent hunting Cattle. Loaded an old leaky log Canoe & I navigated it while crossing the river to the house—it was so dark that I could not well see to balance the Canoe—as the Canoe was,—with its load,—having leaked ½ full of water—within an inch of the water's Edge. As the current struck my unwieldy vessel, it caused it to roll & take water—& balancing back it filled. I pulled with all my might—for the other shore—was about the middle of the river & it—very deep. The load being wood, & being bouyed partially by the water—it did not immediately go down. But I twice succeeded in preventing it from Capsising—although it was six inches under water—by balancing myself against the Current. Had it upset [I] should have lost two axes—& perhaps my life—as I was somewhat encumbered by a heavy coat—& the current strong. But in that situation—keeping the Canoe right side up with one end just out of water—succeeded in bringing my Canoe & load to shore with the loss of not one stick. I was wet to my hips in the Canoe.

SABBATH EVENING—OCT. 20. This has been a pleasant Sabbath—a lovely autumnal day. . . . Explained to Mr. D. the nature of Chr. Baptism. He had formerly requested Baptism for a dying Child, [from] Rev. Mr. Ferry of the Mackinaw mission, which was refused, on the ground of neither parents being believers. He appeared Satisfied with Mr. F[erry]'s course now—although had felt very hard toward him . . .

MONDAY EVENING, OCT. 21ST. Today Mr Aitkins Men arrived from St Peters, with corn—have Made the voyage in twenty five days. Have this evening had another scholar in English—a Frenchman [probably a fur trader] who is to winter here. . . . Mr. A Received Papers [newspapers] from St. Peters, which is the first I have seen, of dates since my leaving the states. Often have I longed to know what was the state of things in the states—whether Our eastern Cities have been visited by Cholera this season. I see that Cincinnati & St Louis have been visited—we are safe in God's hand O—how little confidence do I find in myself.

The thought of this terrible disease—for a moment, makes me recoil. Yet God holds the pestilence in his hand . . .

WEDNESDAY MORNING, 6 OCLK, NOV. 13TH 1833. A little before 5 oClk was waked by one of our Men to get up—said that the stars were falling in every direction, like hail. There was no one at the post who knew any thing of Meteorology except Myself. Whether they thought that "the end of all things was at hand," I did not enquire—but evidently they imagined them ominous of something very Serious. I told them that I thought it ominous of Cold weather. This Phenomenon was discovered about 4 oClk—& when I first saw it—had diminished greatly in frequency—at ½ past 5—Counted upwards of forty in about a minute. . . . What Indians here—are somewhat frightened. They are very Superstitious on Such points. Some years since a remarkably red appearance of the Aurora Borealis—was observed, in the Summer. The next Summer—the Measles swept through this region making awful ravages among the Poor Indians. This remarkable Aurora Borealis—they then Said, was omenous of the Sickness. The Indians here—have never observed a similar Phenomenon to that of this morning, & it would be almost useless to attempt to persuade

them that this does not forebode some Evil thing. One of the best Men in this band (about 40 yrs old) came up into my room as I was writing the first part of this Article. He had seen the whole & Said that he had never seen or heard anything of the Kind in this country. I afterwards explained to him that they were not "Stars" that fell—but Electric or Gaseous Phenomena in the atmosphere.

SATURDAY EVE. NOVR. 16TH. To-day, with the exception of my School hours in the morning, I have spent in religious Exercises—to wit—reading Scriptures—meditation—Prayer—reading life of David Brainard. I find myself very far from God—& the humble Spirit which a Missionary should possess. An amasing insensibility—& hardness of heart . . .

THURSDAY EVE. FEBY. 27, 1834. I today, for the first time, heard an Indian use profanity. He was endeavoring to repair a trap . . . but was not succeeding, he gave vent to his vexation in an imprecation of the most horrid kind—in English—that some ungodly man has doubtless learned him. There is nothing in the Indian language capable of Expressing oaths as used in Eng. & French. They sometimes Call each other "Mojianim"—or a bad Dog—that is the extent of their profanity.

FRIDAY, MAY 30 1834. [while traveling to conduct business] Mr. D. & myself supped with Messrs Belangie & Fairbanks—our meal consisted of dried Sturgeon—boiled. I found the Gills of the Sturgeon, a delicacy—to my good appetite. We then had some Griddle Cakes, made of Sturgeon Eggs, with a little flour which, we ate with Maple Syrup. This is the first thing I have seen in shape of Bread for many weeks. I partook heartily—every part of a Sturgeon is eated—even the Skin of the back (crisped) of which I ate little yesterday, is deemed good, & in fact I should not Starve on Sturgeon.

WEDNESDAY, OCT. 15 [1834]. This evening Mons. Cotte requested me to desist praying in their meetings & after reading. For himself—he said my prayers were very good—but I did not make the cross—did not love it—& the Catholic Indians would not stay in the room when I prayed, (this I have observed—once or twice but did not know the Cause). They did not wish to learn any other prayers. . . . He reminded me that all the Children were Catholic Children, & did not wish I should teach them otherwise—as also the Praying Indians did not wish me to mention the subject to them.

I Enquired—Do you mean all Ind's?

Ans. No. You may speak to others, but they will not hear you.

Ques. Do you object to my praying or talking with any Indian, if so requested by him?

Ans. No.

Ques. Do you mean that I should not pray in my School?

Ans. No.

I then briefly stated, that I attended their meetings—read sung & prayed by invitation that I had not forced myself upon them—that I did not feel at liberty in their meetings to do what was unedifying to them. It was a rule with me to pray in my school—which I could not relinquish—that I did not deter the Scholars from making the Cross—that while they performed that Ceremony at Commencement & close of my prayer. I waited—giving them opportunity. That I came to teach & do good—& not to make war on the worship & opinions of others.

[Ely's broadmindedness wasn't constant. Later he remarked about the Catholics converting the Indians, "It is distressing that so many poor & ignorant should be led in so deceptive a Road."]

SABBATH AUGT. 30 [1835]. This P.M. I was married to Miss Catharine Bissell, of the Mackinaw [Mich.] Mission. Ceremonies in Church—[conducted] by Br. Boutwell.

SABBATH MAY 29 [1836]. This has been a day of deep interest & anxiety in the Family. About 11 o'clock Catharine was delivered of a Daughter both mother & daughter are doing well.

NOV. 29, 1838. Last Friday, I wounded myself, apparently very slightly Just above & close to the Knee pan of my left leg, with Knife. I took little notice of it, Was a little lame. On Tuesday finding my knee becoming rather stiff, I examined it, found it somewhat inflamed—discovered that I had cut a small Tendon—& probably taken cold in it. Saw the necessity of immediately using means for relieving it. Mr. Landre recommended an application of the Bark of the Red Tamarack. The young tree is only used—say 2 inches in diamter. Cut into Short pieces & boil about one hour. Peel the outside bark, then take off the inner bark & pound it—until it is soft. Save the presence of the fine fibres—the preparation would not be distinguished from a Salve. Apply a plaster, covering the affected parts. Wash the wound in the Liquor in which it was boiled—also, wet the Plaster freely with the same. It should be removed twice or thrice a day. The Soreness & Swelling is decreasing—the wound is cleansed & in a healing state. Has now been applied 24 hours. Am dependent on Mr. L. for the care of My Cattle—stovewood &c &c.

Edmund F. Ely and Family papers, St. Louis County Historical Society Collection, Northeast Minnesota Historical Center, University of Minnesota, Duluth

CATHARINE ELY

"Mary is very fond of sucking rabbit bones & bread. She is likewise fond of hasty pudding. Night before last her father corrected her for crying at night, wanting to be taken up."

The journal of Ely's wife, Catharine, is much different from his. She wrote almost exclusively about her children. Most of the sections here are about the early childhood of their firstborn, Mary.

Catharine Ely. *Northeast Minnesota Historical Center*

NOV. 25 [1835]. This day I suppose I am 18 years of age.

NOV. 26. Visited an Indian Lodge in which were two women, read to them the word of God. They seemed very much interested, & seemed anxious to be instructed.

JAN. 25 [1836]. Monday. My dear husband arrived this afternoon from Lapointe after an absense of three weeks. I received letters from several individuals. The church at Lapointe are in a very interesting state. God is in the midst of his children there. One soul, they trust, has been brought out of natures darkness into God's marvellous light.

JULY 16. Mary Wright Ely, born Sabbath May 29th. We think her on the whole a pretty good baby. She does not seem to complain without some reason. She begins to notice those around her & appears pleased when noticed. She is now seven weeks old.

JULY 18, MONDAY. Usually wairysome at Evening for a little while—last evening particularly so. This morning oppressed by heat, her father spoke to her & she instantly began to cry & struggle, in order to see if it came from peevishness, he spoke to her again—with the same result—but she soon belched

An Ojibwe woman, painted by Seth Eastman

Falls of St. Anthony, painted by Seth Eastman

wind—unable to decide the cause of her apparently repulsive conduct.

THURSDAY [JULY] 28. Baby's fond of listening to music, sometimes she shows pleasure at the sound of the flute, rather fretful this afternoon.

AUG. 2. Not very troublesome to day, inclined to talk. She loves company. When she is awake she is always looking for some one to pay a little attention to her & chat with her.

AUG. 3. M. has been quite disposed to sleep. It may be on account of the state of her bowels, nothing has passed her since yesterday—& it is now near night.

SEPT. 20. This afternoon M was determined not to lie in the cradle. She cried & strugled to have me take her. I thought it was not duty to have her indulged. She continued crying I spatted her legs & let her see by my countenance & talk that she must lie still. She accordingly droped to sleep. She has several times showed an unwillingness to lie in her cradle. Her will is beginning to show itself.

NOV. 29. She is now six months old & has two teeth. For some days past we have held out our hands to have her come. We thought, she was learning a bad habit of going to those, only she wanted to. We thought it best, that when ever we wanted to have her come to us to take her right up. This afternoon I had been washing her sore ears I held out my hands to take her. She would not come. Her will is gaining ascendancy.

DEC. 5. Mary is very fond of sucking rabbit bones & bread. She is likewise fond of hasty pudding. Night before last her father corrected her for crying at night, wanting to be taken up.

JAN. 1837. She can sit alone on the floor. Very playful. She love[s] her father very much. She will sometimes cry for him. . . . She has had her hand spatted more than once for taking hold of books when they were in her way. She understands that she must not meddle with them.

APRIL 22. M. has for some time tried to blow her whistle. Today she succeeded to her great gratification, & amusement. She repeated it several times. She has been quite uneasy to day. This morning I tied her on the rocking chair. She let her peace of bread fall & in bending to take it the chair turned over. She bruised her head sadly. She has sat out on the green grass this morn, for sometime amusing herself.

MAY 27. Mary can stand up alone. She began to stand alone a month ago. She also tries to sing when told to.

SEPT. 22, 1837. Mary commenced walking in June the latter part. She now gabbers but cannot talk yet. She can say papa. Mamma, Man. We are learning her to fold her hands when the blessing is asked at table & returning thanks.

OCT. 17. Mary can say, dirty hand, & several other words such as potato. My dear Mamma. She will repeat words after me.

FEBRUARY 21, 1839. Mary can read in words of three or four letters. . . . She can also write, a, b, c, o. She is now learning the 3 chapter of Prov. [Proverbs] has learned 14 verses. She has also learned to repeat several hymns, such as, Lord in the morning those shalst hear. May God who makes the sun to Show. And now another day is gone. Though I am young a little one.

Edmund F. Ely and Family papers, St. Louis County Historical Society Collection, Northeast Minnesota Historical Center, University of Minnesota, Duluth

Lake Pepin, painted by Seth Eastman

MATHIAS LORAS

"Our arrival was a cause of great joy to the Catholics, who had never before seen a Priest or Bishop in those remote regions."

In 1839 Mathias Loras, the Roman Catholic bishop of Dubuque, visited St. Peter (now called Mendota) and found a "considerable number" of Catholics. Bishop Loras wrote this to his sister:

DUBUQUE, 26TH JULY, 1839
My Dear Sister,
I have just returned from St. Peter's, where I made my second mission or episcopal visitation. Though it lasted only a month, it has been crowned with success. I left Dubuque on the 23d of June, on board a large and magnificent steam vessel, and was accompanied by the Abbe Pelamourgues and a young man, who served us as interpreter with the Sioux. After a successful voyage of some days along the superb Mississippi and the beautiful lake Pepin, we reached St. Peter's. This fort, built at the confluence of a river of the same name [the St. Peter River is now called the Minnesota River], and the Mississippi, is advantageously situated; the soil is very fertile, and the mountains around of no considerable elevation. Our arrival was a cause of great joy to the Catholics, who had never before seen a Priest or Bishop in those remote regions; they manifested a great desire to assist at divine worship, and to approach the Sacraments of the Church. The wife of our host, who had already received some religious instruction, was baptised and confirmed: she subsequently received the sacrament of matrimony and made her first communion. The Catholics of St. Peter's amount to one hundred and eighty-five . . .

[From another Loras letter, written in July 1839:]

On Thursday, the sixty-third anniversary of the independence of the United States, I was at the altar, offering my prayers to heaven, in favour of my adopted country, when a confused noise suddenly burst upon my ears. A moment after, I perceived through the windows a band of savages, all covered with blood, executing a barbarous dance, and singing one of their death-songs. At the top of long poles brandished fifty bloody scalps, to which a part of the skulls was still attached, the horrible trophies of the previous hard fight of the preceeding days. You may well imagine what an impression such a sight made upon my mind. I finished the service as well as I could, and recommended to the prayers of the audience, those unfortunate beings.

Acta et Dicta, a publication of the St. Paul Catholic Historical Society, July 1907

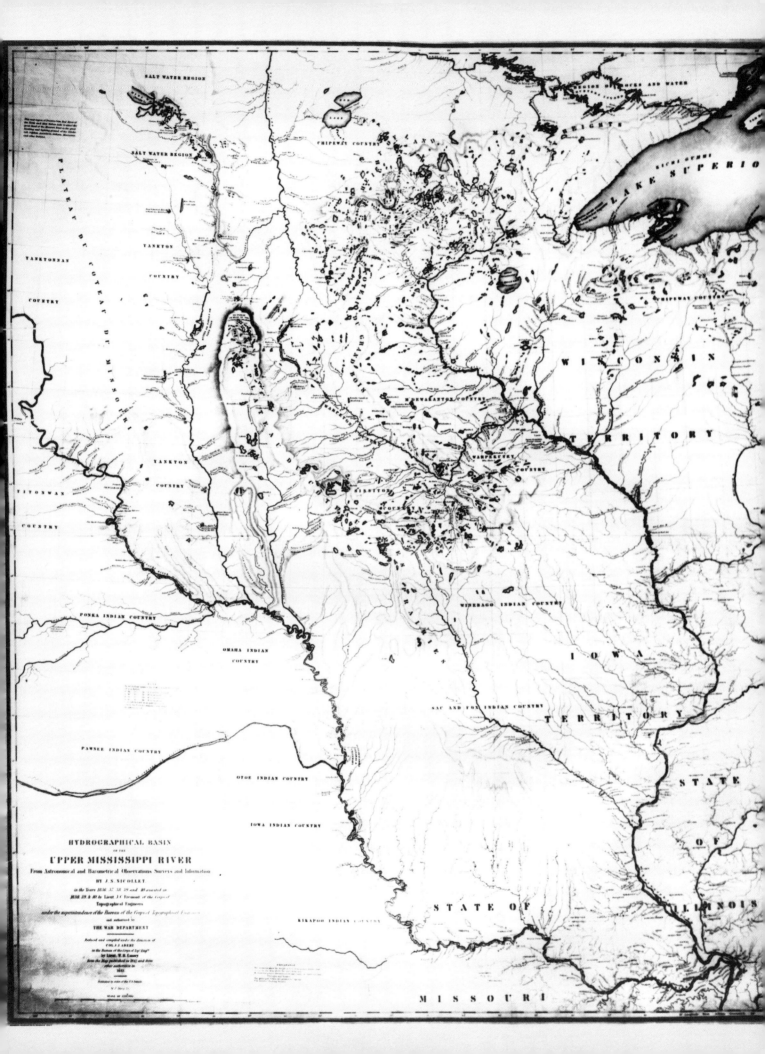

SALT WATER REGION

SALT WATER REGION

PLATEAU DU COTEAU DU MISSOURI

YANKTONNAN COUNTRY

YANKTON COUNTRY

YANKTON COUNTRY

SITONWAN COUNTRY

CHIPEWAY COUNTRY

LAKE SUPERIOR

CHIPEWAY COUNTRY

WISCONSIN TERRITORY

M'DEWAKANTON COUNTRY

WARPEKUTE COUNTRY

SISSITON COUNTRY

WINEBAGO INDIAN COUNTRY

IOWA TERRITORY

PONKA INDIAN COUNTRY

OMAHA INDIAN COUNTRY

SAC AND FOX INDIAN COUNTRY

PAWNEE INDIAN COUNTRY

OTOE INDIAN COUNTRY

STATE OF ILLINOIS

IOWA INDIAN COUNTRY

STATE OF

KIKAPOO INDIAN COUNTRY

MISSOURI

HYDROGRAPHICAL BASIN
OF THE
UPPER MISSISSIPPI RIVER
From Astronomical and Barometrical Observations Surveys and Information
BY J. N. NICOLLET
in the Years 1836 37 38 39 and 40 assisted in
1838 39 & 40 by Lieut. J C Fremont of the Corps of
Topographical Engineers
under the superintendence of the Bureau of the Corps of Topographical Engineers
and authorised by
THE WAR DEPARTMENT

Reduced and compiled under the direction of
COL. J J ABERT
in the Bureau of the Corps of Top¹ Eng⁵
by Lieut. W.H. Emory
from the Map published in 1842 and from
other authorities in
1843

OPPOSITE: A map of the Upper Mississippi, by Joseph Nicollet. *MNHS*

JOSEPH NICOLLET

Joseph Nicollet was a gifted astronomer who is remembered for producing the first accurate, detailed map of Minnesota. The US government sponsored his expedition to determine and record the resources of the land between the Missouri and the Mississippi.

TUESDAY, JUNE 19, 1838 . . . Now some families of Indians occupy these islands [in what is now Nicollet County], to live on the tipsinna [prairie turnip] and a little hunting. These are the families of the warriors that we met at the Traverse des Sioux as they were going down to St. Peter's with Sleepy Eyes [chief of the Swan Lake band of Sisseton]. I promised these warriors that I would help their wives and children. This I did with pleasure. The old mother of Sleepy Eyes has come herself on canes to offer me as a present a duck already cooked and skinned, which they were without doubt about to eat when they learned of our arrival. Here are the barbarians who take food from their mouths to help the traveler!

SUNDAY, JUNE 24, 1838. Today everyone is in camp, quiet and peaceful, as a day of rest which follows great fatigue, as a day of grace and as an act of acknowledgment for him who, like myself, should thank Providence for the success that accompanies my enterprise thus far. The day is fine, neither too hot nor too cold; it invites prayer, contemplation, and thought, saying to the traveler: Leave your heart and memories behind you.

WEDNESDAY, JULY 4, 1838. . . . Our Indians have left us this morning, pleased with us and we with them. Nothing equals the reserve and discretion of these good people, and, as is generally true, once they know who you are, what you are doing, and that you treat them well, it takes so little to make them your friends that I cannot conceive why so many whites blunder in their dealings with them. All this comes without doubt from failure to understand or realize the ways of the respective parties. Kindness and language are the two avenues for reaching the heart of the Indian. A little tobacco and a few words will do what an army cannot do.

Edmund C. Bray and Martha Coleman Bray, trans. and eds., *Joseph N. Nicollet on the Plains & Prairies: The Expeditions of 1838–39*, MNHS Press, 1976

Joseph Nicollet. *MNHS*

1840s

Fur traders and other businessmen sought opportunities to the west, toward the Red River and the plains country. A village of a few houses and cabins developed around the steamship landing in St. Paul. A sawmill opened in 1848 in St. Anthony (now part of Minneapolis). Congress established the Minnesota Territory in 1849. Fewer than four thousand whites lived in the territory, which included large parts of what are now North Dakota and South Dakota. →

JOHN AND ANN NORTH

"You must take for granted that we are both happier than ever before, and that I am infinitely obliged to you for giving me so good a wife."

John Wesley North and his wife, Ann, left New York state in 1849 for the pioneer territory of St. Anthony (now part of Minneapolis). He was a lawyer suffering from intestinal distress, fatigue, and other problems that seem to have been caused by nervous strain. He thought his health would improve in the West. It did.

In the thriving little village of St. Anthony, the Norths could not find a house. They had one built on Nicollet Island. Ann North fell in love with Minnesota; she wrote to her parents that it might be "too new for you, but just the place for us." Here are excerpts from a letter to her parents in Syracuse, New York, just as the Nicollet Island house, a two-room log cabin, was being finished.

ST. ANTHONY, NOV. 25, 1849
My dear Parents,
Once more I seat myself to hold communion with my dearly loved home friends—but under somewhat different circumstances from those under which my last was written. We were then boarding—and I was obliged to write while a gossiping old lady talked to me. Now we are alone, in our new home. Mr. North [is] writing too. Everything as quiet as we choose to have it, for the river separates us from all other inhabitants. The carpenter did not leave here till last night. We came here, on

Thursday, put down the carpet in one room, and unpacked some things. As the windows were not all in, we could not sleep here. Friday morning we had our trunks brought and have remained, since, ourselves.

Yesterday, a man painted the woodwork. We cannot get settled till he has put on another coat. Everything stands in the middle of the floor, and every time we stir we get daubed [smeared with paint] and more than we should if we had handles on the doors. None of them are thus blessed except the outside one, which has a nail driven in, to open and shut it by and a button to hold it together. But I don't think of fretting—they'll all come in due time. We have now no place to set our crockery. A cupboard is to be made for us this week. Our table answers for cupboard, pantry, dressing table, dining table secretaire, and various other purposes. But even with all the inconveniences, it is more pleasant than boarding anywhere. You wished me to give you a description of our house and the arrangement of things in it, which I shall be most happy to do, when we get them arranged . . .

But oh! my cooking! I find I can fry pork, and cook potatoes—even warm them over—but I want milk and butter in greater abundance. But the cranberry pie. I made a slight blunder. I did not, in the first place, put in sweetening enough. Then I put it in so hot an

Ann and John North. *MNHS*

oven that the crust was, as Uncle Garret used to say, "a dark, handsome snuff' color, and the juice all ran out into the oven. You may imagine what a cranberry pie without any sugar and burnt crust would be. Mr. North [her husband] eats it by pouring molasses over it and mixing it all together. He won't complain, for fear of discouraging me, I suppose. How I do wish we had some of your good apples.

Of the small glass dishes you gave me, only three are whole. I suppose the other were broken at the upsetting. [Their stagecoach overturned near Galena, Illinois.] All our furniture, except the piano, was somewhat injured, though the most of it, very little. Three of the legs of the dressing bureau were broken off. The articles in it came nicely. One of the back legs of the sofa was broken off Mr. North fastened it on again. The bookcase was considerably injured . . .

He purchased of a half barrel of pork (shoulders) for $7, a barrel of cranberries for $4, a barrel of flour for $6, 40 bushels of potatoes at 75 [cents] per bushel. . . . Our common bedstead cost $4. Our stove and a good deal of furniture at Galena $23. Our common table of black walnut $3 ¾, kitchen chairs, wooden, one set, $4 ½. I thought all this might interest you and Grandma . . .

You can scarcely imagine how much I think of you all. But I am happy here. Why should I not be? We have so much more for our comfort and happiness than many of our neighbors. Give my best love to all the dear DeWitt friends—tell Mrs. Otis that spoon is quite a treasure—and I scarcely take it in my hands (which I do so many times a day) without thinking of her. But there is something to remind me of home every half hour. My dear, dear Father, do write to me. I love to know you think of me so often, but be not anxious. I am in good hands. With much, and my warmest, love to every one of you, I remain, your ever aff[ectionate] daughter,

Ann L. North

The Norths' house. *MNHS*

[John North took up his pen and added to her letter:]

. . . We have got settled in Minnesota with less trouble and inconvenience than we expected, and all things considered about as cheaply. It cost us between $29 and $30 to get our goods to Chicago, $43 to get them to Galena, $15 to get them to St. Paul and between $9 & $10 to get them to our house. Then there were house charges and our board at hotels while waiting for them . . .

My health is good and I am becoming more strong and hearty every day. I have been out looking [at] land and walked fifteen miles in one day. At another time I got up at 11 o'clock at night and went with another man to get the preemption [homestead rights] of a lot of land about 2½ miles from the village. We lost our way and walked some 7 or 8 miles before we got to the land. . . . The reason of my being called up in the night to go and take possession of the land was that others were calculating to take possession of the land that night and the man that went with me overheard their conversation. We had been calculating to go the next morning. . . . It is a choice lot and lies so near town as to make it valuable . . .

What land I get I want to secure soon for it is being taken up quite fast. The village here at the falls has increased at least one half since I was here in September, and the land in the country is being taken in proportion to the increase in the village. There will be a great filling up here in the spring. Tell Mr. Wicks to send on his warrant if he wants a lot of land and I will secure it in the same way I do for others . . .

I like this country more and more. I would not go back to Syracuse on any account. It would be pleasant to be with our friends but health and business are better here, and we hope to see some of you here in the spring. Just come out and see how nicely we live, out here in the middle of the river with a snug little home and one of the best housekeepers in the Territory. Ann meets the emergencies of western life like a Philosopher, and acts her part nobly. She is just commencing the duties of housekeeping, and feels some anxiety about her success, but for my part I have no fears. We are both very happy in our new house and the future seems bright, and the prospect cheering. I have never enjoyed better spirits than since I have been here. But I can not write half the good things I want to. You

must take for granted that we are both happier than ever before, and that I am infinitely obliged to you for giving me so good a wife. Write to us often.

Affectionately yours,
J. W. North

[The Norths prospered. In 1852, John North wrote to his father-in-law that he had real estate holdings of $81,000 and indebtedness of $2,000. He owned farm and town property. Three years later he decided St. Anthony Falls was at its financial peak; he moved the family south to the Cannon River valley, ripe for development. He founded the city of Northfield. The Norths left Minnesota in 1861, moving first to Nevada and then to California, where he died in 1890.]

Henry E. Huntington Library, San Marino, California

GUSTAVUS OTTO

"Be sure to have them educated orderly, that they may not become so unhappy as their forsaken, unhappy father."

Gustavus Otto, an army private, led a miserable existence at Fort Snelling and was eager to get out of the military. In those days, the army was a haven for fugitives. Otto hinted he was forced to become a soldier. This is a translation from the German of a letter to his wife.

FORT SNELLING 7TH APRIL 1849
Iowa Territory
Dear Louise,
Although I intended several times to write you, circumstances, labors and feelings did not allow me to do this. As I come to day from my watch duty and it is a rainy day, I have so much time to do this. . . . We were ordered for this spring to our old post Fort Marcy now Fort Gaines, but through the deeds of our General

received the order to remain here, which we like very much, although we are plagued by the hardest tasks and watch guards. The country is very pleasant here, only very mountainous on the banks of the Mississippi river. On the height all is prairie with pleasant hills, our fortress lies very high on the mountain, and is built of stones. All the goods, which come with the Steamboat we must take up to the mountain and here arrive weekly. One mile from here is a little village with several stores which carry on trade with the Indians. The place is called St. Peters. 6 miles from here is a little town, which increases every day in size and is very good for provision dealers, is called St. Pauls. This place and the surroundings are settled with Indians, Frenchmen & Yankees; in general there are a great many Indians here & these bring in enough fishes, prairie fowl, wild ducks & geese. This winter we had also 3 prisoners here, accused of the murder of whites but all escaped again and we could not find any trace of them until now. Several of the soldiers took also flight and many of the soldiers will desert this summer yet. The winters are very cold here, particularly this one; we are in thick stone buildings and had, each 2 men 3 woolen blankets and haystacks, and yet we had to make a fire in the midst of the night in order not to freeze; we had to release some times one another at guard every ¼ or ½ hour; many had a watch duty (in the morning 8½ o'clock) frozen their ears, noses & feet. I myself had my face & ears frozen but I am cured again. Then we had to procure for 2 miles, wood, hay & water, where one's life was not safe one minute not to slip and to fall down with the wood, which we had to throw down from the mountain. I have not been sick until this winter, when I caught a severe cold & had to pass several days at the hospital. I am better of it and would feel entirely well again, but the daily thoughts, the dreams & restlessness, which I have almost every night, for my poor children, begins to make me every day more languid, also the thought to stand thus yet 4 years, frightens me more for I forget entirely my business. One has also no prospects to save anything for one has to get here more extra clothes & shoes not to freeze than one gets here and these are very dear here. One has also to provide himself with other provisions if one does not want to get the scurvy, for we get only Saturday and Sunday fresh beef with potatoes, the other days (that is, every day) boiled pork and bean soup in the morning, cold pork, bread and coffee, in the evening one slice of bread with coffee; now you can think what soldier life is. The only thing which keeps one up is the cleanliness, for lice. I have not met with any more. Then we have many Irish in our Company with which we have to bear much; when they are intoxicated they knock everything down & want nothing but fight. The Courthouse is always full of them. Thank God, I have not come into it as much as I know that our Captain loves me much. I have also painted the window curtains of my Captain's orderly Sgt; he was much pleased with it and I said that it was a pity that I was soldier, while I could earn my bread so well. He would make me free if he could, but he thinks that you can do it. Since two months, 3 soldiers have already been released by their sgt, also today one had got free again, he is from Baltimore. You could also do it if you wanted to do it. And my only request to you is to do it. I will not return to you, if you do not want it, for you live perhaps happier without me, which I wish from all my heart, but I am no drunkard any more and have learned to work and if I was free, I could any how do some thing for my poor children, and save, in order to enjoy my old age, if I should reach this. I would get every day, in the little town of St. Paul $2 from a master, who has often come to see if I was free. I could also get $10 in Galena, St. Louis, Louisville, but my hands are tied, and 5 years of my life are gone, without helping my children at all, also to get a place in the army, the prospects are rather bad, as always such are taken who have been in Mexico; no land is given anymore. I beg you once more from all my heart do for me what you can, God will reward you. If you wish I shall come home I will do it until fall when I have earned money, for I shall then take care as husband & father. I am still innocent of adultery as I was before, although the temptations for it are strong enough here. Do you not wish to have me free again, write as soon as possible, as I want to go to California then, to establish a new home there and let me learn to forget my dear poor children. Be sure to have them educated orderly, that they may not become so unhappy as their forsaken, unhappy father. Tell them a heartful farewell, greet & kiss them from me. While I must close now, I beg you for a speedy answer, for it might be that we are transferred again to another place. I can have an answer here in 3 days, while it is only 600 miles from Detroit. God grant you altogether health all happiness and well wishes

from your
lonely Gustavus Otto
Comp. E 6th Infant. Reg.
Capt. Woods
Fort Snelling Iowa Territory

[Otto was unable to solve his problems and deserted from the army the next summer.]
Gustavus Otto papers, MNHS

WILLIAM BROWN

William R. Brown was a pioneer farmer in the St. Croix Valley. He wrote in his diary about his vegetables rotting. In those days, a common means of food preservation was to dig a hole, put the food in it and fill in the hole with dirt and straw.

SUNDAY THE 14TH [OF DECEMBER, 1845] . . . This morning I discovered that 2 of my turnip holes have commenced rotting & caved in. they had on them 3 inches of straw & 2 of dirt and small chimney fixed in top with a flow [of air] inches square, these have been stoped up when the weather set in very cold, but still the rutabagas were too warm.

Last year I put in my rutabagas about 8 or 10 inches of dirt & lost most of these in consequence of their being too warm. This year I put on 4 inches & still they are rotting, this is astonishing to me for we have had very cold weather since winter set in.

[Brown made a note January 8, 1846, on prices of the day:]

While at Stillwater I bot. 1 pair coarse boots $3.00, 1 table cloth 60 cents, 1 pr pants $3, 1 small chisel 25 cents.
William Reynolds Brown papers, MNHS

NEWSPAPER CLIPPINGS

JOY TO THE WORLD GEORGE ZANE
Having completed his new Saloon, on Third street opposite the St. Paul House, takes pleasure in announcing to the citizens of St. Paul, that he is now fully prepared to administer to their wants. He will at all times keep on hand the choicest Liquors, Cigars, Oysters, Sardines, etc.

Minnesota Chronicle, May 31, 1849

Never enter a sick room in a state of perspiration, as the moment, you become cool your pores absorb. Do not approach contagious diseases with an empty stomach nor sit between the sick and the fire, because the heat attracts the vapor.

Minnesota Pioneer, April 28, 1849

The art of butter-making:
Milk is set in six quart pans, for twelve hours. It is then set over a small kettle of hot water for a short time to heat and is then set away for twelve hours or twenty-four hours; but is not allowed to stand until it becomes rancid. The cream is churned as soon as there is enough obtained—time of churning from three to five minutes only. The churn used is the common dash churn. By heating or scalding the milk, I think it adds to the quantity and quality of the cream. I know that better butter can be made in this way than by the old method. Some may think it is too much trouble to heat the milk, but if they have only two or three cows, it will more than pay them in time of churning.

Minnesota Pioneer, June 28, 1849

Religious services are held in St. Paul as follows:
By Rev. Mr. Ravoux at the Catholic Chapel on every alternate Sunday, commencing Sunday after next.

By Rev. Mr. Gear, of the Episcopal Church on every Sunday in the Capitol at four P.M.

By Rev. Mr. Hobart, of the Methodist Episcopal Church, every Sunday morning at the School House.

By Rev. Mr. Parsons, of the Baptist denomination, every other Sunday at the Capitol, commencing next Sunday.

By Rev. Mr. Neill, at the Presbyterian Lecture Room, every Sunday morning at half-past ten o'clock.

Minnesota Pioneer, August 16, 1849

STEAMBOATS—It would be a great convenience to the public, and probably a benefit to the owners of boats, if they would arrange it so as to scatter their arrivals at St. Paul through the week, instead of all coming at about the same time. As boats scarcely need a convoy in our waters, we do not see why they need to go in flocks.

Minnesota Pioneer, September 13, 1849

House and Lots for Sale. [St. Paul]
The subscriber offers for sale his house and two lots 132 feet front on Stillwater street, running back on a corner. The house is 16 by 25 feet, 1½ stories high, 5 rooms and a buttery, 3 below and 2 above, lathed and plastered with flues for stoves, a good stable and root house, good water adjoining the lot, the house entirely new.

It will be sold for $600, one half cash and the balance on time. A great bargain, being less than the cost of the buildings. A large cooking stove goes in with the property. Call and see.

James Hoffman

Chronicle & Register, November 10, 1849

Blessed be steam! It is the very pulse of the world. The rivers and the lakes are the veins and arteries through which it throbs, carrying vitality, enterprise and civilization into the remotest interior. See that superb vessel with her tall black flues; but yesterday, as it were, she leapt from her moorings at New Orleans, from the levee crowded with bales, boxes, barrels, shining negroes, and hurrying drays, dashed along between the luxuriant plantations of the South, threading her rapid but devious way between the bluffs into colder regions, where nature does less and man does more, and now she has reached her journey of thousands of miles, and lies panting and listening to the roar of the Falls of St. Anthony, where all is bleak and leafless, ready to return again to the blooming South; for as yet the highest bred steamboats—the very Fashions and Peytonas of our river craft—have not the bottom and stride to leap the Falls. Here she lies, resting as it were; for a steamboat always seems to be in a state of natural repose, sweetly slumbering, when her paddle wheels are unlocked, and the well-oiled engine throbs like the heart of a slumbering giant. Up! Arouse this manufactured leviathon. Cast off her lines. And now, like a pair of dislocated shoulders slipped into joint, her wheels are locked, she swings into the stream—her hot breath is poured upon the air, and with a power which makes her very frame tremble, she smites the waters with her paddles, and now bluffs and trees—the very shores seem to be flying by.

On the Mississippi, the liquid highway of our continent, how many old acquaintances are formed! Let those who cannot find good company at home, travel on this river, and they will always find intelligent men and refined women. The steamboat is our floating saloon—our place for reunions and conversations. There is more discomfort and annoyance in one mile of staging than in one hundred miles of steamboating. On a good boat, with good company, we take no note of time. For instance on Thursday night we take a berth on the steamboat Senator, at St. Paul—pass Friday in pleasant conversation, and on Saturday morning awake in Galena.

St. Paul Pioneer, May 19, 1849

"Soap—How it is made best" made the front page of the *Minnesota Pioneer* on June 28, 1849. Here's the lesson:

The time for preparing this essential of household economy is near. Every family in city and country ought to make its own soap. The cost of this article is incredible when it is all to be purchased, while the manufacture costs so little as not be worth naming.

Every housewife knows how to make it; but all do not know the best way, nor how to overcome all the difficulties of it; nor the causes of these difficulties. Some are accustomed to mix the lye and grease; the latter consisting of old bones, bacon rinds, scraps of pork, and all refuse matter, just as it is, and boiling them til the soap 'comes' as it is called, or till the lye and grease unite. A better way is to 'cleanse' the grease—that is, extract it from the refuse matter, by boiling in weak lye, till it is all separated, when it is set by to cool; and the grease will rise to the top, when it may be skimmed off for use.

Now have the lye good and strong—such as will bear up an egg—heat it to boiling, and pour it into the soap barrel, mix in a proper quantity of grease. If both are good, they will unite and form soap. Add lye until the grease is all taken up.

Sometimes the soap will not 'come' for want of 'luck,' though the lye will bear up an egg, especially if the ashes are made of beach, oak or some other sort of wood. Hickory ashes give little trouble. The reason is, that the lye is not caustic enough.—It contains a considerable quantity of carbonic, or sulphuric acid; and unless this can be rid of, no soap can be made because the lye and grease will not mix. What is to be now done? Put in fresh lime. The acids immediately leave the lye to unite with the lime, and the lye becomes caustic. . . . Soap boilers who use ashes indiscriminately, put in a peck of quick lime to a bushel of ashes; and they never fail to get soap . . .

Oxcarts on the main street of St. Anthony in about 1855, delivering furs from the north and loading up with supplies for Red River Valley settlements. *Minneapolis Public Library*

1850s

The Dakota, forced to sign treaties surrendering most of their lands, retained only slivers of territory. Similarly, the Ojibwe were coerced to sign away much of the north country, land rich with pine and minerals. White farmers concentrated on oats, potatoes, corn, peas, beans, turnips, etc., and grew barely enough to supply local needs. Industrial growth included flour milling and lumber milling. A land rush lasted from 1854 to 1857. Most of the immigrants were from New England and New York; some were foreign-born. Many areas of land were surveyed. Steamboats ran the Rum River. Stagecoaches traveled the roads around St. Paul and a network of roads in southern Minnesota. Congress made land grants to railroad companies, but tracklaying did not begin. The nationwide Panic of 1857 slowed development here. Bankruptcy was common. Minnesota became a state in 1858. By the end of the decade, logging and milling were important, but the state was becoming fundamentally agricultural. →

THE FULLER FAMILY

"I have wanted fruit so much. I had two, three peaches the other day, the first I have ever seen in St. Paul."

Alpheus G. Fuller, the oldest of seven children of a Connecticut family, came to Minnesota in 1848 with hopes of improving his health. He became a fur trader, hardly a glamorous occupation. In a letter to his brother August 15, 1849, he wrote, "Have the most sport nights lying on the floor and hearing the Rattle snakes sing sometimes they get into bed with the traders or under their pillows."

He soon was followed to Minnesota by other family members. His brothers joined him in the fur trade, and his sisters established a home in St. Paul. They were active in the social life of the frontier capital. The letters they wrote to relatives in the East were full of gossip and discussions of a developing territory. Here Sarah Fuller wrote to a sister in Connecticut:

ST. PAUL, DEC. 12, 1852
Dear Sister,
. . . We were all invited to attend a small party at Gov. Ramsey's last week but I did not attend, for various reasons. There was a dance at the Mazourka hall last Wednesday, David wanted to know in the morning if I was going. I told him I thought not. We all went down to church in the evening and when I got home I found Mr. Randall and David here with a sleigh waiting for me, and nothing to do but I must jump in and go down, did not wait to dress it was so late, it was ten when I got there, and the party broke up at eleven, it was a very small select party, and a very pleasant one, only stayed an hour . . .
From your affectionate sister, Sarah

[Sarah wrote to sister Lizzie on January 2, 1853:]

My dear Lizzie,
Your letter of Dec. 9 was thankfully received Thursday, should have immediately answered

Abby Fuller Abbe. *MNHS*

A popular hairstyle of the 1820s

Fashions for July.

it had I not been engaged preparing for New Years, which was yesterday, but was it not too bad I had the sick headache so did not enjoy the day as well as I expected to. We had forty calls [visitors], not as many I believed as we had last year not as many went out making Calls as they did last year, and I was glad myself. And Emily not being well it rather fell upon Lilliore to entertain them. Emily got thrown a week ago by some drunken soldiers on horseback coming home from Church Sunday morn and really had quite a severe fall, but is setting up now in her double gown by the Stove. We were all very much frightened, thought she was dead at first—they carried her into Miss Stokes shop a few moments until she was able to ride home, then Mr. Lelly

took her into his sleigh and brought her home. Dr. Brisbine got thrown a few days since and broke two of his ribs Called for the first time since [then on] yesterday says he is in a good deal of pain yet, cant laugh it hurts his ribs so.

Miss Neilland and Mr Murray & Mr Keth-kog were home last evening and Emily being sick [I] had the peculiar pleasure of entertaining them myself, in the parlor, had a game of whist and really passed a very pleasant evening both of the gentlemen were strangers to me. I saw Miss Neilland Thursday and she told me she was going to get some beaux and was coming up in the evening, the parlour looks sweetly the prettiest room in St. Paul . . .

Good night, pleasant dreams.

Sarah.

EMIGRATION

UP THE MISSISSIPPI RIVER.

The attention of Emigrants and the Public generally, is called to the now rapidly improving

TERRITORY OF MINNESOTA,

Containing a population of 150,000, and goes into the Union as a State during the present year. According to an act of Congress passed last February, the State is munificently endowed with Lands for Public Schools and State Universities, also granting five per cent. on all sales of U. S. Lands for Internal Improvements. On the 3d March, 1857, grants of Land from Congress was made to the leading Trunk Railroads in Minnesota, so that in a short time the trip from New Orleans to any part of the State will be made in from two and a half to three days. The

CITY OF NININGER,

Situated on the Mississippi River, 35 miles below St. Paul, is now a prominent point for a large Commercial Town, being backed by an extensive Agricultural, Grazing and Farming Country; has fine streams in the interior, well adapted for Milling in all its branches: and Manufacturing

WATER POWER to any extent.

Mr. JOHN NININGER, (a Gentleman of large means, ideas and liberality, speaking the various languages,) is the principal Proprietor of **Nininger**. He laid it out on such principles as to encourage all **MECHANICS**, Merchants, or Professions of all kinds, on the same equality and footing; the consequence is, the place has gone ahead with such rapidity that it is now an established City, and will annually double in population for years to come.

Persons arriving by Ship or otherwise, can be transferred without expense to Steamers going to Saint Louis; or stop at Cairo, and take Railroad to Dunleith (on the Mississippi). Steamboats leave Saint Louis and Dunleith daily for **NININGER**, and make the trip from Dunleith in 36 to 48 hours.

NOTICES.

1. All Railroads and Steamboats giving this card a conspicuous place, or gratuitous insertion in their cards, **AIDS THE EMIGRANT** and forwards their own interest.

2. For authentic documents, reliable information and all particulars in regard to Occupations, Wages, Preëmpting Lands (in neighborhood, Lumber, Price of Lots, Expenses, &c., apply to

THOMAS B. WINSTON, 27 Camp street, New Orleans.
ROBERT CAMPBELL, St. Louis.
JOSEPH B. FORBES, Dunleith.

[Sarah wrote to Lizzie:]

ST. PAUL JAN 16—1853
Dear Lizzie,
. . . David [their brother] thinks of starting East in about 2 weeks I should go with him but it is so unpleasant travailing in cold weather, would like to see you all, and will I hope in the Spring, though think I will feel sadly when I leave for I have really become very much attatched to St. Paul, more particularly to the place than the people. David sits here eating mince pie and tells me to tell Lizzie that he cannot write before he leaves but will tell you all the news when he gets home . . .

I must tell you what a great dance we attended Wednesday eve at Mazourka [dance hall], greatest one there ever was in the teritory. If it was not the greatest I enjoyed it the most. Must tell you how I was dressed, wore my double skirted muslin and pink satin waist and short sleeves, three rows of lace round the neck and two round the sleeves and pink flowers in my hair good many [Army men] down from the fort [Fort Snelling]. I support it will be the only one I shall attend this winter, probably. I really dissapated a good deal last week. Monday spent the evening at Dr. Borups. Tuesday at Mrs. Basses, Wednesday Mazourka Hall, Thursday at a tableau party at Mr. Oakes

[Lilliore to Lizzie February 11, 1853:]

I have a bit of fresh news to communicate that you may possibly be interested to know. And what do you think it is? Well it is no more than that your old admirer Randall is reported to

Minneapolis in 1857, looking west on Second Avenue South from Washington. *MNHS*

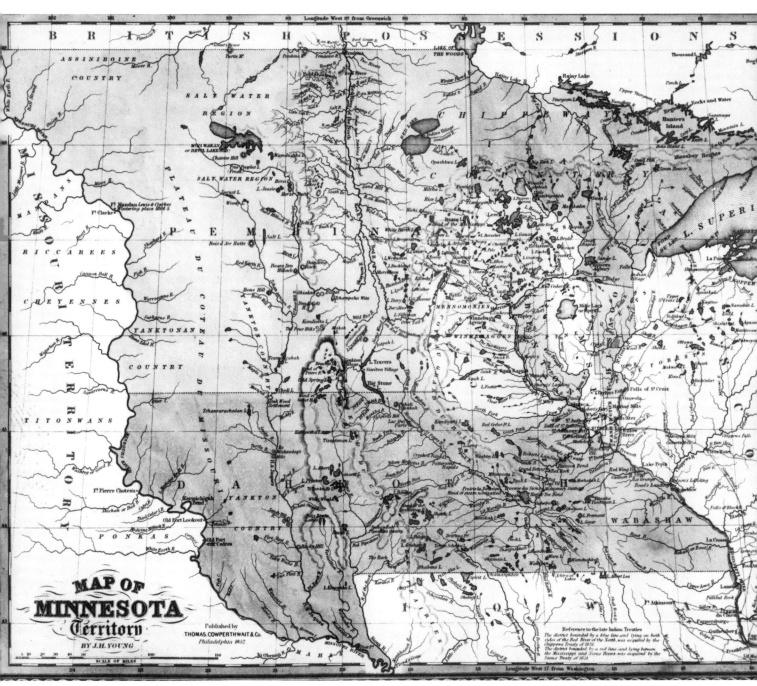

Map of the Minnesota Territory, which included much of what is now North and South Dakota, 1852. *MNHS*

be very much enamored with a Miss Langor who is visiting Mrs Monroe at the Fort and as report says actually engaged. Mrs. Simpson is our informer. She says he spends all of his evenings there, walks to and from church with her &c., and to cap the climax she presumes she will be married in the spring. She says Miss Langor is very pretty amiable and accomplished, plays the guitar and sings very pretty. She came to the fort late last fall, she is from Connecticut and has been teaching in Norwich. Sarah saw her at one of the dances but was not introduced. She has been invited to several of the parties here, but has recently had news of the death of a sister and does not go out. That is the reason I suppose it was been kept so quiet, he has shown her all the attention at home.

[Abby to an aunt on February 11, 1854:]

ST. PAUL FEB. 11, 1854

Dear Aunt Trootwood [Elizabeth Fuller]
Jane has been writing a letter to Father and Mother and trust it will appease their unquiet spirits & my duty is to you. It is perfectly ridiculous for any of you to worry about anything . . . but I am sorry that Father and Mother should be foolish enough to make themselves unhappy about eight grown children, the youngest more than twenty-one. Its time the tables were turned and the children worry for the parents . . .

I'm going to frighten you a bit by telling you that Sally and I came near meeting a serious accident the other night. Were in a close sleigh, six of us, going on the ice to Mendota to a little party, lost our way, broke through the ice, horses went in up to their necks, & the sleigh began to sink, but we just got out & fortunately we were over a sand bar and they extricated the team, but we were a wee bit frightened.

Good Bye, & God bless you all from
Abb

[The Fullers were doing their share of entertaining. Three days later Alpheus's wife wrote:]

Yesterday we prepared for a company of thirty. I have now discharged nearly all my obligations to my St. Paul friends, they were all married people. I am going to invite the unmarried ones for the girls Friday eve.

[Here Abby Fuller, one of the sisters, wrote to her sister Lizzie on July 26, 1854, about an outbreak of cholera in Minnesota. Cholera epidemics were not uncommon in the 1800s.

The disease, often transmitted by food, involved a sudden onset of acute diarrhea and sometimes vomiting. Most victims recovered in one to five days, but many died. Cholera outbreaks still occur, but there are modern vaccines.]

Am sorry Sarah is not well but I think it would be the height of inprudence to come here till the weather is cold when we hope these diseases will abate the cholera panic is not all over & there are many distressing cases of dysentary. Mr. Fillmore died yesterday morning with the disease & there are a great many cases in town they make as little stir as possible about it & probably there is no place on the Mississippi more free [of cholera] than this but that is not much & I advise our people to stay among those at England hills for the present. My health is improving a little by a very careful diet & all the preventatives have thus far escaped any touch of the disorder. We cook no vegetables eat no fresh meat but beef & are as careful all of us as though sick & we've all been well. Geo & David both got down from the upper country tonight looking as strong & well as bears. Alpheus had a serious attack of cholera, the first case in town and as hard a one as any, but his system was in a good state & his medicines worked well which was probably all that saved him. The River sickness has been frightful they said the last trip of the Admiral, from St. Louis, she averaged four deaths a day, all the way through, and the Galena arrived yesterday reported a great deal of sickness, though people have no way of finding the amount. Still we think the business is abating & that dysentary is taking its place, but a few weeks cool weather will remove it, perhaps so it will be safe to come.

. . . A party of my friends went to Lake Minnetonka & camped out a day or two fishing last week & they were all very anxious for me to go but I did not dare to though I did want to so much & we have had a theatre & series of concerts in town for a fortnight.

[Sarah to Lizzie, October 29, 1854:]

St. Paul has improved very much since I left—there has been some very handsome buildings built—but the greatest improvement are the sidewalks . . .

[Sarah to Lizzie, April 23, 1855:]

It seems so lively since the boats commenced coming and we can get mails again. Oh, Lizzie, I called upon Mrs. Randall last Thursday, at the Winslow [Winslow House, a St. Paul hotel] She is going to be in St. Paul a couple of weeks. Mr. Randall has gone down the river to be gone two weeks and she stays at the Winslow while he is absent. She is rather pretty, her hair curls naturally, a light brown, she had on a black silk and pink scarf and long black mits and came into the room with a bottle of salts in her hand smelling of it . . .

There is another [monetary] failure in town, Mr. Charles Parker the banker, people think there will be a great many more failures in St. Paul this year. Maj. Murphy [an Indian agent] and his wife from up country spent three days here last week, George [brother George Fuller] invited them here, but I for one was glad when they left, they were very plain people . . .

It has been very gay in St. Paul this winter, and it seems pleasant to be quiet although it will not be long before we shall have to take up our duds and walk, the lease to this house was out, the twelf of April, but we can stay here still. Mr. Parker, the man that owns the house told us to stay until the house was sold or rented. . . . George has bought a house off upon the bluff, a mile and a half out of town but it is not quite finished, it is to be plastered and painted before we can go into it. It was a house Mr. Brewster built for himself, I don't like the idea of being so far out of town but the girls think it will be pleasanter. ["So far out of town" was near where the capitol stands in St. Paul today.] This Spring there are a great many strangers here that have come up on the Boats, a great many emigrants.

Goodbye,
Sarah

[Sarah to Lizzie, July 10, 1855:]

So you see how we are living & I believe in any other climate on earth, so much running, care and dissipation would kill me, but my health is splendid—not uncomfortably fleshy as I used to be at home, but strong and vigorous & feel as though I could do anything under heaven I set out to do. [Another sister] Jane's health is perfect & she is happy as a clam.

[Sarah to the family back in Connecticut:]

JULY 21, 1855:
Blow ye the trumpet, for the Fuller family is increasing Alpheus has a son born this morning, tell Father there is one to bear up the name. Jenny says its head is shaped just like Father's.

[Sarah to Lizzie, September 2, 1855:]

O Lizzie I fancy you are eating peaches and what I would not give to help you. I have wanted fruit so much. I had two, three peaches the other day, the first I have ever seen in St. Paul these were brought up from below [from the south by steamboat], tasted very swell here, but could not have tasted as well in Connet. We have had some very good watermellons, and a few muskmellons.

Sam Abbe,
Abby's husband. *MNHS*

[Lizzie to Abby, July 12, 1857, after Lizzie took a vacation at a health spa in Madison, Wisconsin, called the Lake Side Water Cure Establishment:]

I took just one bath while there and attribute the splendid health I am now enjoying entirely to it. It was so cold that while there the very thought of the bath room made me shiver and we were obliged to warm our rooms to keep from freezing.

[Lizzie to Abby, October 20, 1857, during a recession:]

The times are awful. Men cannot get money to supply the private necessities of their families Workmen of all kinds are turned out of employ. Bass has stopped building his new house. Stewart who is building the finest house in town on Rice's bluff has stopped his . . . there are no failures of note yet but they must come if these times keep on.

[Abby to Lizzie, October 29, 1859:]

Things are hard but there is everything here in abundance to eat—but not a dollar of money. It has become almost obsolete. I told Sam. he chuckled over the fifty dollars I brought back [from the East] more than he would a town-site.

[The Sam of whom Abby Fuller wrote was Sam Abbe, the man she married. Her name became Abby Fuller Abbe. Her brother, George Fuller, married Sam Abbe's sister, Josephine Abbe. George and Josephine Fuller had a daughter and named her Abby Abbe Fuller. What a fun family.

Abby Abbe wrote to her "Aunt Trootwood," Elizabeth Fuller, shortly after Abby and Sam Abbe moved to Crow Wing, Minnesota.]

Crow Wing
DEC. 30, 1860
Sam wonders if you are as fat as ever. Pronounces you just the woman for this country in summer. Says a musquitoe would split his bill trying to bite you.

Abby Abbe Fuller and Family papers, MNHS

DANIEL FISHER

"I am teaching the Catholic School—my mission is among the dirty little ragged Canadian and Irish boys."

Daniel J. Fisher, a young seminarian from New York transferred to Minnesota, wrote a letter in 1852 to another seminarian. He was obviously fed up with pioneer life and with teaching "wild little fellows." He would prefer to be a martyr, he wrote here.

One soon gets sick of so much monotony and although the first few miles were pleasant enough, yet I should have rejoiced afterwards to see anything as high above the ground as a dunghill. But such rich soil as it is—and so deep—New Yorkers never dream of so much fertility . . .

St. Paul is a large town—when the boat arrived, there were a thousand persons collected on the shore although it was nearly 10 o'clock at night. The Catholics are very poor here—and what is worse very irreligious and indifferent—they are Half breeds, Canadians, and Irish—The Yankees have all the influence, the wealth and the power, although they are not near as numerous as the others. There are three papers published weekly here—there are six churches and any number of doctors, lawyers and parsons—but there is no money—as all the wealth is controlled by a Fur Company who own nearly all the shops and employ a great number of workmen and never circulate any money—they loan it at 60 per cent!! they pay their men in provisions, etc.—But I cannot say much about the place as I have been in it only a month.

What am I doing do you think? I am teaching the Catholic School—my mission is among the dirty little ragged Canadian and Irish boys. Every day, morning and afternoon, I practice patience with these wild little fellows—try to teach them who God is, and then to instruct them in the mysteries of A.B.C. I left N.Y. to go among the Indians and I was hoping for strength to undergo the hardships of a savage life, or to meet a martyr's death. I felt the difficulty of the sacrifice more than anybody thought—but the greatest trial was one that I never dreamed of—and to take the charge of these impudent and insulting children of unthankful parents was the greatest mortification I ever underwent. But it was a momentary feeling of pride which prompted these thoughts—I told the Bishop that I would undertake the school and having reflected that if this were so great a mortification it would be more acceptable to God, I went into the little low unplastered school room with so much love for my office as if I were Vicar Gen. of New York. Whenever I get time and my head ceases to ache, I study Theology—the Bishop told me the other day that he would ordain me in September; but whether he will ordain me priest or only Subdeacon I do not know. . . . It is well for those who thought of coming here that they did not come—I think they would have been disappointed in everything—the only thing that can sustain a New Yorker in this wild country is the hope of a speedy release from this life and a good place in the next.

Acta et Dicta, a publication of the St. Paul Catholic Historical Society, July 1907

***

According to a wise saw, it costs as much to keep a dog as it does to feed an individual. In these weak and piping times of little work and less pay, it behooves us all to economize—to cut off every source of waste and extravagant consumption. Scores of families who have to pinch and be pinched in order to provide food for themselves, are, nevertheless, addicted to dogs. These dogs prowl about town in search of food and et ceteras. They snap at passers by. They fight. Make night hideous. Frighten children. Break into gardens and trample down the tender shoots. Dogs in town are of no earthly use. They do nothing but yelp o'nights and multiply their species. They bring no revenue into the town treasury. We do not wish to be dictatorial or dogmatic, but if our will in respect to "dogs" was the law, every dam's son of them—mongrel, puppy, whelp, and hound—and especially curs of low degree, should be "retired" from general circulation. Their tails should be cut off close behind their ears; save and except in the case of those "animals" whose owners think them worthy of paying a tax therefor into the town treasury, and of wearing a collar.

St. Paul Pioneer & Democrat, July 2, 1859

MNHS

ANDREW PETERSON

"In the morning I did a bit of everything, also did an errand at Lundsten. In the afternoon I cut more hay."

Andrew Peterson was born in Sweden in 1818 and came to the United States in about 1850. Four years later he and other members of a Swedish Baptist church followed their minister from Iowa to Carver County in the Minnesota Territory. He staked his claim in the Waconia Township one summer day, planted potatoes the next day, and helped his neighbor build a cabin the day after that. The work went on and on. Peterson recorded it in his diaries, which he kept until he died in 1898.

Swedish author Vilhelm Moberg based a series of novels, starting with *The Emigrants*, on Peterson's diaries. The series was later made into movies. Here is a piece of Peterson's 1858 diary, translated from the Swedish. Notice how often he helps his neighbors and they help him.

August

1. Sunday

2. This forenoon I split the large maple into boards. In the afternoon we had a meeting for missions.

3. First in the morning I did some pick up jobs, then I hewed planks for the log ceiling.

4. Went to Mitchels and shocked wheat.

5. First I mended a scythe for Johannes and went over with it, then I hewed planks.

6. and 7. Hewed boards, etc.

8. Sunday.

9. Forenoon. Did nothing as Gronlund from the other settlement was here and hindered me and the same with Cornelius. In the afternoon I cut a maple and split into boards.

10. A.M. Was with Hammerberg and made a plan for his house. P.M. Hewed boards on the other side of the maple.

11. In the morning I dug around the grafts [this was the beginning of Peterson's apple orchard] and picked them clean of worms. In the afternoon I went to a meeting.

12. Broberg was here and helped me haul rye, etc. John and Cornelius cut wheat.

13. Cornelius and I cut wheat.

14. Cornelius and I cut wheat. John came later and helped us finish it.

15. Sunday.

16. Harvested at Mr. Nilsson, church day-work.

17, 18, 19, 20 and 21. Cut and tended to the hay for myself.

22. Sunday.

23. Went to Scandia and made a casket for Peter Swenson and we buried him in the evening.

24. Cut and tended hay.

25 and 26. Went with Elsa [his fiancée] down to the Swedish settlement at Carver.

27. Tended to my hay.

28. Broberg came and helped me haul hay all day.

29. Sunday.

30. Cut hay all day.

31. In the morning I did odd jobs and in the

afternoon Broberg helped me haul hay. Today my heifer took the bull.

September

1. Turned my hay.

2. In the morning I was over at Johannes and in the afternoon I stacked hay.

3. In the morning I went to Broberg and Mattson to hire a carriage for a trip to Chaska, then stacked hay and went to Johannes.

4. Elsa and I, together with Maja Stina [sister Maria] went to Chaska in Mattson's wagon.

5. Sunday.

6. A.M. Had a meeting at Mrs. Nilsson in regards to the school. In the afternoon I went and ground corn for Erickson.

7. Cut hay all day, also went over to Johannes.

8. In the morning I did a bit of everything, also did an errand at Lundsten. In the afternoon I cut more hay.

9. First I put up my heater, then I started to put in panels in my house.

10. In the morning I was over at Johannes. In the afternoon I stacked the hay on the

ABOVE. Peterson's diary. *MNHS*

BELOW. Andrew Peterson in about 1898, in front of the log cabin he built in the 1850s. *MNHS*

Elsa Peterson, later in life. *MNHS*

wheat. In the evening at 5 o'clock Elsa and my expectations became a reality, a marriage.

16. John was here and plowed and I cut corn also went to Bengtson after seed wheat.

17. Sowed and harrowed the wheat.

18. Forenoon—Cut down the corn. Elsa and Anna helped me. In the afternoon we went to a prayer meeting in preparation for the Conference.

19. Sunday.

20. The Conference started. Was there all day.

21. Went to the Conference which ended that day.

22. In the morning I stacked hay on the north bog. Erickson and Hammerberg helped. In the afternoon I started to put up bows on Nilsson's wagon. Elsa and Anna have chopped up corn today and this evening they have gone over to Cornelius's house.

23. Practically the whole day I was at Nilsson's house fixing the bows on the wagon, etc.

24. Were at a meeting all day. We had a baptismal service when August Johnson and his wife, Magnus Johnson's wife and Cornelius's wife were baptized.

25. Finished cutting corn.

26. Sunday.

27. Made pig-pens and went after my pigs at Johannes.

28. In the morning I cut rails and stakes to the fences.

29. Had Johannes's oxen and hauled the rails and stakes to the fences.

30. Fenced in a cow yard, etc.

Andrew Peterson papers, MNHS

meadow of the south claim. John and Erickson helped.

11. Turned the hay on the bog that is on mine and Nilsson's claims.

12. Sunday.

13. Stacked hay and then edged boards for the panel.

14. Put up panels in the house.

15. In the morning I was over at Johannes and chopped cornstalks. At noon John went with me home and started plowing for the

70

HARRIET GRISWOLD

"Allen's grave is in a pleasant spot, on the bank of the lake but a short distance from our cabin."

Near Cambridge, Minnesota, Allen Griswold was involved in real estate speculation. Both he and his wife, Harriet, were ecstatic about their new lives and the economic opportunities. She wrote October 17, 1856, to her brother:

Allen says he is quite pleased with the investment in lots at Cambridge, says they are selling rapidly.

[And Allen wrote:]

Saint Paul M T [Minnesota Territory]
APRIL 18TH 1857
Brother Henry
Sir
I will write you a few lines relative to our Lots in Cambridge, that you may learn that what was stated by me as to the price six months from that time, has been more than realized. My Brother RB has recently sold at the City of Holyoke, Mass., four lots in Cambridge for $500. GG has sold in Boston some twenty lots [for] something less, said he was offered $100 a Lot for one Block of twelve, a part of which had been previously sold. I hold now at $100 per Lot, about fifty five acres of my claim. . . . I think there never has been a time, in our day when a brighter prospect for successful speculation in Real Estate lay before us than the present, here in the present Territory and future State of Minnesota. . . . There are

extensive preparations making for building here this season, also in almost all parts of the territory. The grant of Land from Congress to the Territory for Rail Road purposes creates quite an excitement in all parts . . .
From your Brother,
H. Griswold

[But then misfortune hit. Allen died and the children were ill. Harriet's letter telling of the death is missing now, but this letter is the next one. In it, Harriet tried not to panic.]

CAMBRIDGE OCT. 24 [1857]
Dear Brother and Mother:
I received your letter dated Sept 28 soon after I wrote you of Allen's death. Albert [their son] was then quite sick but he continued to grow worse for nearly a week. I think his disease is worm fever, he is now better although he is not able to walk about yet. for a few days I feared he must soon lie by the side of his father. Allen's grave is in a pleasant spot, on the bank of the lake but a short distance from our cabin. Brother Gilbert stopped with us a week and kindly assisted in putting up our cabin, which Allen had not commenced when he was taken sick, the neighbors also were very kind both during our sickness and assisting about the cabin which we are sadly in need of for our old one is quite open and cold weather is upon us. besides you know it is only 12 feet square. During the week Gilbert was here I

MINNESOTIAN.

(Third Street, below Cedar.)   EDITORS AND PUBLISHERS.

A, FRIDAY MORNING, MAY 18, 1855.   NUMBER 8.

Early St. Paul newspaper

had 4 and 5 men to cook for beside our own family and taking care of Albert which I found wore upon me some. I am getting quite nervous, but I hope I shall not be sick as I was last fall. I think if we are prospered we may move into our new cabin the last of this week. We have a good crop of beans, but little corn, as the gophers and birds took a good share of it, and I should think we had about a hundred bushels of potatoes. I think I have been remarkably sustained during my affliction but I trust I have the presence of the Saviour and the guidance of his holy spirit but I tremble when I think of the care now resting on me and I fear it will be a burden which I shall not long be able to bear. Allen had taken a great interest in Cambridge and laboured hard for its welfare but he was not permitted to live to see the result, but I trust he is in a far better world than this. I very much dread the long dreary winter before us but I hope we shall suffer for none of the necessaries of life so long as Arnold is well he will be able to keep us in wood though we must depend on others to haul it as we have no team.

I regret very much that the children must be out of school so long. We expect some to move in this fall but I expect we shall have no school under a year. I hope we have your sympathy and an interest in your prayers.

With much love
from Harriet

[By the next spring Harriet Griswold was struggling to put her life back in shape. On April 29, 1858, she wrote to her brother:]

About 2 weeks ago I came to the conclusion that we could not get along without a team and as I had an opportunity to get a horse here, I thought best to do so, for the Land warrant and $25 I bought the horse, harness, and Sleigh, or the Sleigh was thrown in. I have the ground all plowed and Arnold has harrowed in a piece of oats with the horse. The plowing cost me $13 besides keeping the man and his team here a week . . .

Everyone is complaining of hard times here money scarse produce is very cheap. Corn 30 cts, oats 30, potatoes 15 cts, butter 15, eggs 6 and 8 flour costs me 5 dollars at Anoka and one dollar for freight here. If we had a wagon we could save paying out for

Four Dakota and six whites, part of an 1858 delegation to New York City and Washington, DC, to make a treaty with the federal government for Indian lands. *Minneapolis Public Library*

freight but I have not the means to get one at present.

The prospect for a school or meetings is less than it was one year ago and what am I to do with the children. Could I sell the improvements on the place for any amount I should be tempted to do so and go where we could have the advantages of a school &c but we can sell nothing now for no one has any money. . . . I am quite discouraged trying to farm it Arnold does not seem to have the ambition that most boys of his age do. I have tried to encourage him in every way I could, buying a horse &c. but he seems to lack energy. I can get none of the Children interested in their studies; and the thought again comes up—must we always stay here? There is over 20 dollars due me for board from those who were here one year ago but they are gone and I cannot collect any of it. While I had the care of the PO [post office] I furnished my own stamps consequently when I come to make out my account I found the department were indebted to me nearly 10 dollars. I am told now that I cannot collect this, because I should have sent for stamps at the time. The first of the winter I sent Allens watch down to Mr Frost at Anoka the man that Florence [her daughter] boarded with and requested him to change it for young [farm] stock. He gave me credit for the amount of her board and let the watch go to pay a debt of his own, he has now gone to Pikes Peak whether I will ever get the balance due me I do not know.

May 1st. This morning I found ice in a tub at the door over 2 inches thick wonder if you have as cold weather with you . . .

Yours Harriet

SEPT. 24:

It is a question in my mind whether it is my duty to stay here a great while longer. Sometimes it seems rather hard that we must live so entirely shut out from the world as we do but we have no reason to doubt our heavenly Father for we have thus far been provided for. Have been advised to go back east but whether it would be best even if it were possible I do not know, hope our duty will be made plain to us that we shall perform it faithfully.

With much love from Harriet

OCT. 17TH:
What would you say were I to tell you I have some thoughts of changing my name [getting married]. I am sure I do not know what is for the best and fear were I to do so it might be for the worse. Hope I shall be guided in the path of duty, have another letter to answer before the mail goes down so I must close, with much love to all

Yours, Harriet

[Apparently she did not marry. This is the last we hear of Harriet, written from Cambridge, October 16 of 1861 or perhaps 1862:]

Arnold is gone a good deal which brings all the care on me. He wants now to get a job of husking to get corn for our own use this winter, but they only propose to give every 9th bushel which hardly pays. He talks some of enlisting for the [Civil] war, is quite disappointed in not being able to go to school this winter. Tis not much crops he has to secure before cold weather perhaps 10 bushels of sound corn and 50 of potatoes which will go but a little way toward keeping us all for a year.

We are all of us well for which we have great reason to be thankful. We are having our indian summer. Weather mild and pleasant had no frost untill the last week in Sept. There is a very small yield of wheat generally in this country, corn pretty good, potatoes also. The man who took my place has not threshed the wheat out yet and will not till cold weather I have my flour all to buy. Excuse this short letter, have time to write no more now.

With much love from
Harriet

Harriet Griswold papers, MNHS

H. P. VAN CLEVE

"The Dutch beat the Yankees in swearing,
work hard, play hard & laugh loud."

H. P. Van Cleve.
MNHS

By the 1850s Minnesota's land was being surveyed. Whites were eager to buy property, and Natives were pushed farther westward. Horatio Phillips Van Cleve was a surveyor in Stearns County in 1857. His wife stayed in Long Prairie with their seven children. Those mentioned in this letter are Malcolm, age nineteen; Anna (nicknamed Nannie), age seventeen, and Lizzie, age ten.

SABBATH AFTERNOON AUGT. 30TH, 1857
Camp about ½ mile west of the City
of St. Joe, Stearns Co. Minnesota
My dear wife
Last Tuesday morning I started a letter to the Post office, for you, by a slow coach that I had discharged, & am somewhat fearful it may be a long time before it reaches you if it ever does. In it, I told you to direct my letters to St. Cloud, and also that my work was progressing but slowly; that I was suffering from sore feet, so that every step was taken with great pain; that I was almost destitute of friends & provisions diminishing with awful rapidity, and if I do not get relief soon my work must cease. This is a gloomy account of my affairs, which I regret today it is but too true. . . . My dear wife you little know what I suffer, mentally and bodily. . . . I regret to have to give so doleful an account of my affairs, but it is mournfully true. I have many times regretted that I entered in this service . . .

I have not told you all my blessings. The Sabbath comes once a week & I have a grand rest from my toil & hardships. I lie down & read and meditate and rest my weary limbs, and comfort my lame feet with easy slippers. And then I think of the dear ones at home that they are well & happy, making my own heart glad with the thought.

I mourn over my sins, my neglect of duty, looking to our Heavenly Father through Christ for mercy & forgiveness. Pray for me my precious one & thank God for all his goodness . . .

How do the children prosper? I suppose Malcolm has cut 18 or 20 tons of hay and will cut as much more before haying time is over.

I suppose Nannie and Lizzie relieve you of all the work about the house, so that you have all the leisure you wish. When you sit down at the dinner table with the children around you, you may think of me sitting on the ground, wherever noon may find us, satisfying our hunger with the bread and pork that we carry with us for lunch. If water is at hand in some marsh, we quench our thirst; if not, we wait till we come to some. Several times I have quenched my thirst dipped from a depression in a marsh made by my feet. In walking over such bogs, they shake for many yards around you, and you feel somewhat fearful of finding the underside. And again you go in over boot top and have the comfort of walking with boots full of water, and all the time it is "stick," "stuck," "stick," "stuck" "stick," "stuck," through the brush and over the marsh with thousands of mosquitoes singing in concert, "stick," "stuck," "stick," "stuck." I can give you but a faint idea of a surveyor's life. But you have sufficient to satisfy you that it is not an easy one.

I write this on the ground, supporting my head on my hand, and elbow on the ground—my paper on the old portfolio that could relate quite a history, if it could repeat all that had been written on it, by myself and others. It is now near sunset; the air is cool and pleasant after the heat of the day; the boys have left camp, all is quiet, save for the chirping of the crickets and occasionally a few notes from a bird, with the wind rustling gently through the tree tops. All that is wanting is the company of wife and children to make it to me a delightful Sabbath evening.

The town of St. Joe (or St. Joseph) contains two small groceries, which are also dwellings & stopping places for travelers, two or three dwellings, a Roman Catholic church & a high cross. The Red River trail passes through it. Lots have been laid out, & doubtless there are some in market if any of your friends wish to purchase. It is on the west side of the prairie. . . . A Dutchman is putting in a dam & intends to build a mill on it. All the settlers are Dutch.

Good bye. May God bless you all. Love to the children and all.

Love, your dear husband,
H. P. Van Cleve

[In a letter of August 15 Van Cleve mentioned the ethnic backgrounds of the people around him:]

Have just had my supper. Good biscuits, & good butter. Real Long Prairie butter. What better could a man want. But there are about 40 of the natives around all talking about their claims, which are getting somewhat twisted sometimes by my survey. Lines do not always run so as to please every body. Dutch are thick here, but there are also quite a good supply of Yankees. The Dutch beat the Yankees in swearing, work hard, play hard & laugh loud.

We are encamped by a brewery, where Dutch & English congregate to drink good beer. Was just invited to go & take some, but declined on two grounds. 1st It is the Sabbath. 2nd Do not like to drink with a crowd. Either objection is sufficient.

Horatio P. Van Cleve and Family papers, MNHS

Fresh Goods for the Market

DESIRE MICHAUD,

Grocery, Provision, Wine and Liquor Dealer.

Wholesale and Retail.

(Robert street, near the corner of Third street.)

DESIRE MICHAUD, begs to inform his friends and customers both in the city and surrounding country, that having succeeded ALEX. REY, Esq., in business at the old stand on Robert street, he is prepared to supply from extensive, complete and fresh stock, all orders with which he may be favored. No pains or expense have been spared, and he is certain he will be able to gratify every taste. In his stock will be found N. O. Sugar— every grade, Belcher, Clarified, P and B crushed and pow'd bbls and ½ bbls do. molasses N. O. re-boiled sugar, H syrup, golden syrup in quantity or 10 gallon kegs, N O molasses Rio coffee, Laguyra coffee, Java do Mocha coffee Tea of all descriptions, ground pepper, whole pepper, allspice, ground allspice, cassia, ground cassia, nutcloves,ground cloves, nutmegs, Swinborne's gelatine, nuts of every kind, dried currants, G A salt, Kanawha salt, rice, olive oil, sardines, Baltimore cove oysters mock turtle soup, clams, lobsters, and salmon, dried apples, dried peaches, cod-fish, No. 1, mackerel, fresh herrings, white fish, Mackinaw trout Lake herrings, mustard Lewis' vinegar preserves, caper sauce, pepper sauce, ketchups preserved fruits, pie fruits, extracts of lemon, vanilla, rose, &c. &c. yeast powders, green peas, beans, corn, asparagus, &c. Boston nails--every size, Manilla rope, pressed candles, star candles, palm soap, family soap, fancy soap, castile soap, chewing tobacco--all qualities, yellow bank, tin foil smoking tobacco--Goodwin & Murray, oakum, pitch tar, cotton batting, wrapping paper--four sizes, shot, percussion caps G D, rifle powder, M R raisins, pipes T D whiskey--Monongahela, Courbon, New York Brandy, Baltimore Gin, pure imported Brandy, Durand, Burgundy Wine, white do. claret wine, Heidsick, Sauterne, Brandy, Brooms.

And a large assortment of wooden ware, willow ware and an infinity of articles belonging to his line too large to enumerate. He has constantly on hand Flour, Pork, Lard, Bacon. Butter, and all kinds of Grain.

Nov 27, 1854--dtf

HARRIETT AND NANCY NICHOLS

"There was romance enough acted here to write as good a story as you will find in any novel."

Harriett Nichols was a young, unmarried missionary in what is now Morrison County, in a small three-year-old community called "Belle Prairie," French for Beautiful Prairie. She spelled it "Bell Prairie." She loved the adventure: "I tell you it is pleasant to be one of the first settlers in a new country." Here she told about a male missionary from another settlement who was out to find a wife in a hurry.

BELL PRAIRIE, JUNE 9, 1852
My dear Brother Henry,
. . . I suppose you are interested in courtship and marriage, and any thing of that nature so closely connected with your far off sister may not be uninteresting to you. . . . When the canoe came down for us a fortnight ago, Mr. Laferty, a young man who went up there as a missionary last summer, accompanied the boatmen, for the purpose of obtaining a wife in Bell Prairie. The missionaries there had advised him to get Miss Smith, as she had been in the territory so long, and they were acquainted with her. She had also heard of him before, and to confess the truth, was desirous of obtaining his hand. When he came, he was a little disappointed in her, or rather was better pleased with the rest of us than he expected. We have all four of us been here for some weeks, and he remarked to Mrs. Ayer [wife of the chief missionary] that she had got a fine lot of girls, and if he obtained any of them he should think he had a prize.

Now don't you think we were placed in rather delicate circumstances? I don't like this way of doing up the business. He was so anxious to please the missionaries that he had not independence enough to act for himself. I should judge from his appearance that he was a worthy gentleman, and would probably have made any of us a good husband. I really pittied him, not enough however to love him for I should want a longer time than a week to make up my mind. He said to the last moment that he did not love Miss Smith as he wanted to. You would have thought had you been here that we had a curious time, and I assure you we did. I would'nt like to pass through another such week, till I had had plenty of time to rest from the excitement. There was romance enough acted here to write as good a story as you will find in any novel. But I would not speak worse of my sister than the circumstances demand. She will probably make him a good wife, for she seemed to love him. The truth is she had been almost spoiled by being in this part of the territory so long with no other "sisters" to share the attention of the gents. In one week from the time Mr. L. first arrived here they were engaged, on the next morning married and in an hour afterwards he left in the canoe with the goods, and she proceeded with the company eight days after.

[On August 4, Harriett assured her brother that she was glad Miss Smith got the missionary.]

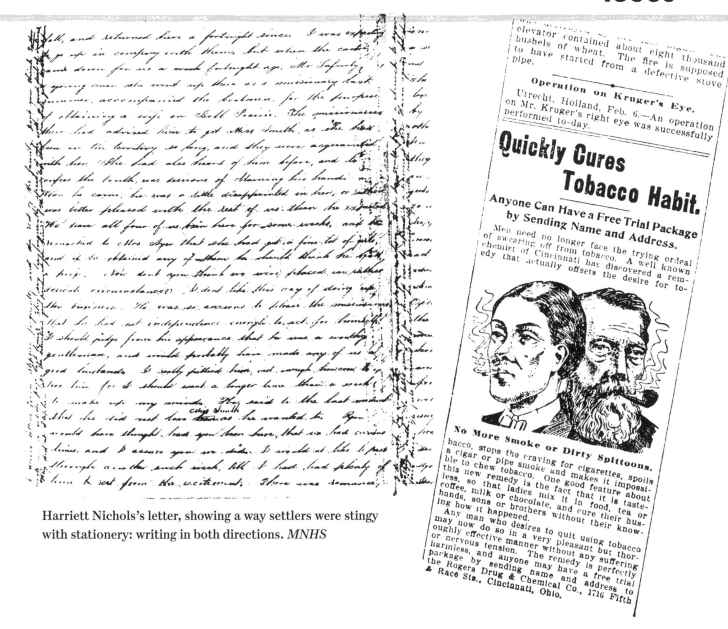

Harriett Nichols's letter, showing a way settlers were stingy with stationery: writing in both directions. *MNHS*

Then you thought I should be Mrs. Laferty if Miss Smith had not! Brother Henry, I shall be very particular in selecting a companion for life. A young lady in this country need not fear but she will have chances enough to get married, and I don't think it is best to take jump at the very first chance. By the way Mr. Lafery did not ask me. I should want one with a little more independence than he manifested.

[She found one. On November 4, 1853, her brother Henry's wife noted, "Have never seen him, should think from her description that

he was about perfect." She married William Harrison Fletcher, a farmer. She wrote to Henry on December 28, 1853:]

I am glad you are so well pleased with your new home, as I am with mine. We all form one family and get along nicely. I have quite a little family to take care of, two pigs and eighteen chickens. I feed them every day, and the chickens have got so they fly on to my shoulders almost every time I go out and then I am kept quite busy mending husbands stockings and mittens, and I go with him sometimes to draw water from the creek. He says I must tell

St. Anthony Falls, about 1855. *MNHS*

you to come up and see us, he dont feel like writing to strangers.

[Harriett was enchanted even with her married name. In a letter of May 16, 1854, she wrote, "Don't you think my name is prettier than it used to be?" By the time she wrote to her brother on January 17, 1855, the family had grown:]

We have recently taken two Indian boys (one ten and the other four years of age; their names are George Jay, James Bailey) to bring up until they are twenty one. It is a week today since we took them and they have done well so far. The oldest boy seems to like work and is very kind to the little one. He takes most of the care of him. Their father wants them to be brought up like white children. The youngest is partly white, has light hair and is an interesting child. Love to Nancy and the children.
　　Yours with much affection,
　　Harriett S. Fletcher

P.S. Harris is getting our rails this winters for a pasture. He has to haul them two miles. This keeps him quite busy.

WEDNESDAY, JAN. 31. As we did not succeed in getting this letter to the [post] office before, I will add a few words more. A little stranger arrived here last Thursday about four P.M. They all that have seen you, say he resembles you. I was taken sick about five in the morning, and on the whole had a comfortable time. I was obliged however to lie ten hours afterward, before all was over. We sent for Dr. Lewis, and he succeeded well in removing the difficulty. I have been gaining rapidly ever since. We call the baby "Charles Benjamin." Our sister-in-law, Mrs. Jane Fletcher, is with me. Let us hear from you soon. The little things you sent look sweetly on the baby.
　　Yours
　　H.S.F.

[Meanwhile, Harriett encouraged her brother and his family to come to Minnesota to be missionaries. They did. On August 5, 1853, Henry wrote to his parents:]

Well, I am in the Missionary work, most decidedly, with work enough to do for any one man. I have more farming business on hand than I like, it takes up too much of my time, another year I hope to give myself more entirely to the great work of preaching the Gospel. I do not yet know where we shall permanently locate. There is a settlement going up at the mouth of Rum River called Anoka, seventeen miles above St. Anthony. The people there are desirous I should come and reside at that place and form a church and preach to them. They offer me some land in a favorable position lying on the Mississippi river. It will be a fine point, and one of interest in its future growth. It will be a fine missionary field, which almost induces me to go. While on the other hand, at Minnetonka I do not see much for me to do as a minister.

[The family was at St. Anthony Falls in October 1853 when Henry's wife, Nancy, wrote to a niece:]

We are all well excepting Louise. She is now sick with a Fever. I think it is the Typhoid. The same that Uncle M had a few weeks ago. I think I never saw fever run so high as hers does, her face is scarlet, and her flesh burning hot, I gave her five [ice] packs yesterday, and washed her about fifteen times in cold water before I could inhibit the fever heat in the least. To day she is better—her fever does not rage as it did yesterday. I bathe her once in half an hour and succeed in subduing the heat to a great extend. I think by tomorrow I will conquer it entirely, and in a few days she will be as well as ever—This was the mode of my doctoring Mr. N. [her husband] with the dysentary and fever. We employ no physicians. After Mr. N. began to get better I was taken down quite hard sick with the dysentary brought upon me by being over him night and day; the day that I was taken [sick] one of the Physicians of the place hearing that my husband was sick called upon a friend to see him, and invited him to speak at the Temperence Convention, he saw me, said I was very sick, and should probably have a long sickness; he gave me of his own free will, and free of charge, some powders. I laid his powders on the shelf, and doctored myself by the blessing of the Lord I was able to attend the Convention in three days with my Husband, & children. We had a delightful time.

[Nancy Nichols continued the story on November 4, 1853:]

Well we are settled in Stillwater for the year—comfortably, pleasantly and happily thank the Good Lord. After I wrote [that] Louise was very sick with the Typhoid fever—we would not trust her with any physicians for they do not have good success at all, their patients run along seven or eight weeks and then die—we followed up our treatment of water and saw that it did better than those on other treatment—she was able to be moved over here in about three weeks lying down all the way and stopping once to rest three hours—distance twenty five miles—we have been here just a week tonight—she is recovering slowing can sit up only a part of the time, is the most emaciated little thing that I ever saw, she begins to look like herself a little now—You must think I had a little to do a sick child, not able to sit up but a few moments and packing [to move] and cleaning and not being rested from taking care of Mr. Nichols—I was in just the right state to be taken down with the same fever—for when I slept with L [Louise] I could feel my blood boil with fever as I took the heat from her. We moved into our house Friday and I worked all day to get righted and took cold and then I was sick and sick enough I was too with the same fever from Friday night till Tuesday night. Henry working over me most faithfully all of the time, my fever was subdued and I began to feel like myself again! thanks to the kindnesses of the Lord.

[Her husband apparently thought she had unduly upset their relatives with her letters about the illnesses. Henry wrote to Harriett November 5, 1853:]

We really felt like sympathizing with you in your sympathy for us, for really we did not intend to create so much feeling and if it had not been for Nancy's chattering pen, you never would have found out so much by me, about our circumstances. To use a western expression, it seemed for a while "a mighty poor show" for us. But the blessed promise "the Lord will provide" was most fully realized in its fulfillment to us.

Henry M. Nichols and Family papers, MNHS

JANE GREY SWISSHELM

"There is no good reason why any man should be buried until after he is dead."

J ane Grey Swisshelm was one of the state's foremost opponents of slavery and proponents of women's rights in the 1850s and 1860s. She came to Minnesota from Pennsylvania in 1857, already a well-known journalist. The following year she became owner and editor of a St. Cloud newspaper with the curiously spelled named of *Visiter*. Her writing, never tame, and her politics antagonized some prominent citizens. One night someone broke into her print shop, damaged the press, and threw type into the river. Swisshelm had something to write about all that, and the prominent citizens cried libel. A compromise was reached, and Swisshelm promised to print no more attacks in the *Visiter*. She kept her word; the next week her attacks appeared in a new newspaper she called the *St. Cloud Democrat*. Here are some of her thoughts:

Definitive: The experience of the past few weeks teaches us that we must "define our position" or be constantly liable to being misunderstood, and so to giving personal offence.

Well, our normal state is mutual antagonism to the superior sex; and contempt for their affectation of superiority.—No doubt this is very wicked; and we simply state it as a fact, so that our readers may not mistake every want of reverence on our part, toward any particular dignitary, as a sign of personal hostility, when, in many cases, it might arise from our natural lack of appreciation of

Jane Grey Swisshelm. *MNHS*

dignitaries in general. . . . We never do feel that antagonism towards any woman, seldom meet one for whom we do not feel some sympathy, respect or affection . . .

January 11, 1858

[That women in business, such as herself, had to pay taxes but could not vote infuriated

Swisshelm. She included this statement in her newspaper's creed and ran it in almost every issue:]

Paying taxes is as unwomanly as voting; and is a privilege which should be exclusively confined to "white male citizens, of this and other countries," until women share with them the responsibility of saying what shall be done with the money they are required to contribute to the public treasury.

The idea of social etiquette, whose rules require a woman to kiss or be kissed by all the tobacco chewers in a room full of company, is, certainly, in a very high degree revolting. How a delicate minded woman can argue herself into submission to such a rule is a little beyond ordinary comprehension, and, certainly no man of proper self respect wishes to

kiss any woman he does not love. To suppose that one loves all the women whom he meets in social gatherings is marking very large count on the size of his heart.

January 14, 1858

Why is it? Folks at a distance keep wondering that the men who destroyed the Printing Office at St. Cloud are not indicted and sent to States Prison; well, it is just because they are not fit subjects for that kind of punishment. They are not ruffians by nature, nor by any long course of practice.

The proper end of punishment is that amendment of the criminal. Men of this class could not be made better by that kind of proceeding. If the law had taken their case in hand we should have to drop it; and we greatly prefer attending to them in our own way. We have

Government lumber mill at St. Anthony, 1857. *MNHS*

got them on as far as "repentance" now, and hope yet, to see them as far as "newness of life;" and that will be much better than placing the brand of a common criminal outcast upon men, who with proper treatment, may be useful members of society.

August 19, 1858

The Effects of Tobacco on Intellectual Vigor— The Medical Press asserts that the Polytechnic Schools in Paris, have recently furnished some curious statistics bearing on tobacco consumers.

Dividing the young gentlemen of that college into two groups—the smokers and the non smokers—it shows that the smokers have proved themselves in the various competitive examinations, far inferior to the others. Not only in the examinations on entering the schools are the smokers in a lower rank, but in the various ordeals that they have to pass through in a year, the average rank of smokers had constantly fallen, and not inconsiderably.

October 7, 1858

Dancing: We regret to learn that some of our religious friends are having serious trouble on this question. It is painful to differ with good, earnest people; and did we regard this matter as unimportant or look upon dancing as many do, viz. a less evil than something it displaces, we should condemn it at once. But the amusements of a people are just as important as their religion. All animated beings require amusement, relaxation and will have it. It is a nessary of life as much as bread and water. . . . Dancing is one of the most universal of all the heaven-appointed means of happiness. All nature dances, the waves in the sunlight, the leaves on the trees. . . . The goats dance upon the mountains, the lambs upon the hillsides. . . . There is no good reason why any man should be buried until after he is dead.

February 9, 1860

GLORIOUS NEWS!!

MINNESOTA A STATE!!!

100 GUNS FIRED AT WINONA:

Winona Times, May 15, 1858. *MNHS*

Pro-Slavery Outrage: As it is a fashion with a portion of the press to deny or ridicule statements that peaceable citizens of the Free States are mobbed and lynched at the South when they have given no provocation for such outrages, we quote the following from the last issue which has reached us of the Atlanta Confederacy. It is not even pretended that the person outraged had done or said anything to provoke Pro-Slavery vengeance:

"Ride Side Up with Care—An old Abolition reprobate, calling himself Dr. Holacher, from Pennsylvania, was taken up in our city on Saturday, for having in his possession incendiary documents. The bird was stripped of his borrowed plumage, and treated to a coat of black [tar], a color more in accordance with his political principles, and marked to

'Horace Greely, Tribune office, New York City. Right side up with care.' Thus parcelled, he left for New York via Chattanooga and Norfolk. Horace, the Black Knight of the Tribune, will please inform us of the safe arrival of his 'Brother' in iniquity. This climate is too hot for Abolitionists."

May 3, 1860

Don't Do It, Girls

There is a practice, quite prevalent among young ladies of the present day, which we are old-fashioned enough to consider very improper. We allude to their giving daguerreotypes [pictures produced by an early photographic process] of themselves to young men who are merely acquaintances. We consider it indelicate in the highest degree. We are astonished that any young girl should hold herself so cheap as this. With an accepted lover it is of course all right. Even in this case the likeness should be returned if the engagement should by any misunderstanding cease. If this little paragraph should meet the eye of any young girl about to give her daguerreotype to a gentleman acquaintance, let her know that the remarks made by young men when together, concerning what is perhaps on her part but a piece of impudence or imprudence, would, if she heard them, cause her cheeks to crimson with shame and anger.

May 30, 1861

***

[By the 1850s, Minnesota's reputation as a paradise was widely promoted by people in Minnesota (especially those wanting to sell land) and even by some non-Minnesotans. Here a writer to the *Williamantic Medium*, a Connecticut newspaper, urged friends in the East to come to "the New England of the West." The St. Paul *Daily Minnesotian* reprinted the letter June 13, 1854, and added, "Good judges will not consider the description overwrought."]

If the farmers of New England could but see this country once, they would soon bid adieu to the rocks and hills of their old homesteads, and with their wives and children would locate upon some of the broad prairies of the New England of the West. One general objection that is raised against coming to a new country, is the scarcity and bad quality of the water; but this cannot be said of this Territory; for a better watered country I never saw. Springs, brooks and small lakes are scattered all over its surface. You can scarcely find a single 160 acres but what is well watered. Fish of the finest quality abound in the lakes and rivers. Another objection to Minnesota in particular, is that it is too far north. There you are mistaken again; for everything that can be raised in the New England of the East can be raised in the New England of the West. Wheat does well, producing from 30 to 40 bushels per acre; oats from 40 to 50, potatoes 200. In fact, vegetables grow almost spontaneously. Fruit of all kinds will undoubtedly do well. We are hardly apt to consider that for every two degrees we go west, it grows one degree warmer. Minnesota must become—it cannot be otherwise, possessing all the advantages she does, of climate, soil, and location— an important member of the Union. These advantages are being appreciated, and immigrants by thousands are constantly coming in, to people her vast domain. One year from now she will without doubt be a State. The neighing of the iron horse will soon be heard calling into use energies that have lain dormant since the creation. The telegraph will soon be extended here, and then distance will be annihilated, and we shall be within speaking distance of each other. The thunders of Niagara will then send their echoes here, and we can send back the pleasant ha ha of our own beautiful water-falls.

***

Who are Wanted in Minnesota

We want farmers—strong, robust, active men, who know the way, and have the will and means to tame our wild uncultivated soil, and develop its surprising fertility and unsurpassed resources. Let them if possible possess some means—enough at least to break and fence a few acres, and put up a cabin for a temporary home. More if possible, but this much is almost absolutely necessary. The best of land can be obtained, whether pre-empted or purchased of individuals on a credit of at least a year. But there are no farms in Minnesota, ready fenced and ploughed, to be given away or disposed of for a song. Farming is too profitable here to favor the idea of such generosity. Lands broken and fenced are worth from 10 to 30 and 50 dollars per acre according to situation. It is true that there is no western state where improvements will pay so certain and large a profit as in Minnesota. Large sums are annually sent out of the Territory for grain and provisions—not because we have not a soil which produces luxuriantly, nor a climate which does not ripen to perfection every vegetable and species of grass, grain, and fruit of the temperate zone, nor a cash market of the highest price at our own doors, but solely because there are not farmers enough to supply the market. Let it be distinctly understood then that farming is by far the most profitable business at present in Minnesota and is likely long to continue so.

Next, mechanics are wanted—men of industry, enterprise and who thoroughly understand their business. Such cannot fail to do well. There are not enough such to supply the demand; there is not sufficient competition to reduce the price of mechanical labor to its proper standard, as compared with other employments. Unless we are greatly mistaken, mechanics receive much higher wages in proportion, than professional men or farmers. The same is true of laboring men. Two and three dollars per day is a high price to pay an ordinary mechanic, and a dollar and a half is too much for a common hand, at hoeing corn and potatoes. The farmer cannot afford to hire at that high price. Let the laborer be well, even generously paid, for faithful toil. He deserves to be paid a good price for a good days work. And after all, any slight disproportion which may exist in the compensation of different employments can be only temporary. Time will make it all right. But it is a truth which all feel, that good mechanics are much wanted in Minnesota. With temperance, prudence and industry, none can fail to thrive—some will make fortunes.

Lawyers are wanted in Minnesota—men of education, character and refinement, who thoroughly understand both the science and practice of their profession—men who adorn that profession by irreproachable lives, and high moral virtues, men whose severe study, unswerving integrity and enlarged views evince their love for the noble science of the law, and afford security of their usefulness in society. A lawyer in Minnesota should be able to plead a cause in law, to advise a client of his rights, to wield an axe or handle the hoe. He will not have business in his profession to occupy all his time, and he must think no honest labor beneath him or whatever kind it may be. Our Territory is large, but there is no room for miserable pettifoggers, who gain a wretched subsistence by stirring up quarrels in the community—vampyres, who drain the blood of society, too lazy to work, too ignorant to harbor an idea, too stupid to have a sense of shame, hated of the gods and despised of man.

We want ministers—learned, pious, self-denying men, who have not entered the ministry as a darnier [last] resort, to get a living which they are too lazy or inefficient to earn by any other means. We want men of independent thought, untrammeled by creeds or dogmas,

> *"Let it be distinctly understood then that farming is by far the most profitable business at present in Minnesota and is likely long to continue so."*

who will preach the bible in its purity, whether or not it accord with the teachings of men or sects. Men especially, who shall not be afraid of work, who can plane a board, drive a nail, dig a well, stone a cellar or handle a spade none the less skillfully, than they preach with all the fervor and eloquence of a Paul or Apollos. Thank God, we have some such, hundreds more will be welcomed. Let them come.

Physicians who expect to live by the practice of their profession will find Minnesota a poor field for a location. If there is any one peculiar characteristic of this Territory, it is its exceedingly healthy climate. Life Insurance Companies are at a discount. There are already a goodly number of the disciples of Galen [doctors] among us, who will find "their occupation gone," as soon as they gave cured or killed, such desperate cases as come here infected with the thousand dangerous and complicated diseases of other parts of the Union, and have been given over by the "regulars" of eastern and more southern states.

Last, but not least, young ladies are wanted. By this term, it is not meant that class to which it is usually misapplied—so called genteel young misses, brought up to read yellow-covered literature, to idleness and tight lacing, to sing a sentimental song or play a tune on the piano, dance the polka and talk fashionable nonsense. There is no room for such in Minnesota. We use the term "young lady" in its legitimate sense, as meaning one who is ready to engage in any labor that may be useful and necessary, whether it be to wash or bake, mop the floor, clean house, or patch a worn garment. These are your true ladies, more worthy of honor than those to whom armed knights of old paid homage—who give dignity to labor by a noble example, render homes happy, and become ornaments to society. Such can command from two to three dollars per week for their work, break the hearts of industrious and enterprising young men by their charms, heal them by consenting to become happy wives and mothers, and become the founders of great and prosperous commonwealth. Let such young ladies come to Minnesota.

St. Anthony Express, June 21, 1851

NEWSPAPER CLIPPINGS

Down at Dayton's Bluff, almost within the corporation limits of St. Paul, is an extensive bed of bluish-white clay, ten feet in depth. There is also white clay, but not so convenient to the town. There is also plenty of pipe clay. I do not know about the common plaster. In the Cave two miles above St. Paul, and on the island opposite the town, is oceans of fine white sand, that would make the heart of any good housewife leap for joy. Lead is worth from $7 to $7.50 per 100 lbs. Any kind of pottery would pay well. There is also fine stone for the manufacture of stone ware.

Minnesota Pioneer, December 29, 1853

The cranberry crop this season has proved unusually abundant. The Indians have been in town almost every day for a week past, offering them for seventy-five cents per bushel. The marshes which yield this delicious fruit abound in this vicinity, and many of our citizens supply themselves with it without much labor or inconvenience. The usual method of gathering it is with a small rake constructed for the purpose, by means of which many barrels may be gathered in a day.

St. Anthony Express Weekly, September 3, 1853

Mr. Gottleib Seigal, a respectable German who has resided for some time in this city, was attacked with cholera yesterday and died during the night. We hear of no new cases in the city today. The German who was sick yesterday in the 3rd Ward, and for whose use a coffin had been prepared, is now convalescent, and has returned the coffin with many thanks to the board of health.
Minnesota Weekly Democrat, June 28, 1854

Some journeyman preacher would make a profitable trip up the Mississippi River, with a supply of blank marriage licenses; there being no person north of Saint Paul who is authorized by law to tie the nuptial knot. Many couples are represented to be in an awful state of suspense, more properly imagined than described.
Minnesota Pioneer, January 30, 1850

AN EXCELLENT LAW—Wives of inebriates are by law in Wisconsin allowed to transact business in their own names and dispose of their earnings as they may deem best.
Weekly Minnesotian, March 10, 1856

As navigation on the Mississippi is probably suspended for the next five months, we have been to some trouble to look over the number of steamboat arrivals at the port of St. Paul during the past season, and comparing them with the previous years. The following is the result of our labors:
Arrivals in 1850 . . . 104
1851 . . . 119
1852 . . . 171
1853 . . . 229
Minnesota Weekly, November 12, 1853

Six or seven of the sporting citizens of Saint Paul, started off about eight days since on a hunting and trouting excursion to Rush river. Having only 15 gallons of brandy along with them, they returned on the 8th day, being out of necessaries, with a supply of such luxuries as venison and trout.
Minnesota Pioneer, January 2, 1850

Yellow-feet ducks are coming in plenty, at twenty cents a pair. There is just now no other fresh meat in market.
Minnesota Pioneer, April 25, 1850

We would advise each immigrant to St. Paul this season, as we did last season, to come here prepared to build a cheap house immediately, without depending upon hiring a house. A rough and ready residence can be erected in a week, at a trilling cost.
Minnesota Pioneer, February 27, 1850

[About a July 4 celebration held at Belle Prairie, Benton County:]
The whole ceremonies of the day were conducted without the use of stimulating drinks, to the delight of all who were present.
Minnesota Pioneer, July 15, 1852

SHAKOPEE—This town is progressing rapidly. Some twenty-five buildings have been put up during the spring and summer. Several frames are being raised for dwellings, and the cellars and foundations for several more are ready for the frames. The large hotel built by Mr. Wasson is nearly completed. It is fifty-six by thirty-six feet, two stories of frame upon a stone basement. T. A. Holmes, Esq., has a new three story house completed.
Minnesota Pioneer, September 1, 1853

SCARCITY OF MECHANICS—During no time since our residence in Minnesota have we heard such a universal cry of the scarcity of mechanics as at present. Many of our master builders say that they could have done three times as much work this season as they have been able to do, but for the scarcity of mechanics. The lowest wages paid to carpenters at this time are two dollars per day, while plasterers and bricklayers receive $2.50 to $3.00.
Minnesotian Weekly, October 22, 1853

The Episcopalians have replaced the awkward and flimsy benches in their church with neat and comfortable pews.
St. Anthony Express Weekly, July 16, 1853

E. Howe, late of St. Paul, has removed to Mankato City and opened a Hotel, where he will at all times be pleased to see his friends.

Minnesota Pioneer, June 2, 1853

SNOW SKATES—Some of the Norwegians who reside here used the Lapland snow skates. . . . These skates are strips of smooth wood, about six feet long and three inches wide and turning up like sleigh runners before. The wearer partly shuffles along by moving alternately his feet, and shoves himself behind at the same time, with a long staff. One of these snow skates arrived in town last week from Lake Superior, having traveled at the rate of eighty miles or less a day.

Minnesota Pioneer, February 3, 1853

Fresh pork continues to come in, in quantities sufficient to supply the demand. It is ten dollars per hundred on an average. It is generally rather light. Pork is retailing at fifteen cents per pound from the barrel—28 to 30 dollars by the barrel. Chickens 12½ cents per pound; turkeys 20 cents; venison 8 to 10 cents; eggs 50 cents per dozen; butter 30 to 35 cents per pound; flour $6.50 to $7 per barrel; potatoes 50 to 75 cents per bushel; apples $2.50 to $3 per bushel; corn $1.25, wheat $1.25, oats 65 cents, per bushel.

St. Anthony Express Weekly, December 31, 1852

A Nuisance: We have heretofore called attention to an intolerable nuisance in the heart of the city, viz: a large drove of cattle that is kept in the street, this side of the University grounds. Some fifty or a hundred head of cattle have been obstructing the free passage of the street, creating a most disagreeable stench, trespassing on the grounds of the citizens in that vicinity, and offering a most unseemly spectacle to all passersby . . .

St. Anthony Express, September 1, 1855

Sweet has erected a new Soda Fountain in his store, and is dealing out a most delicious beverage to the crowds which daily throng his room.

St. Anthony Express Weekly, May 27, 1854

BEDS ON STEAMBOATS: One of the first reforms needed on steamboats in the west, is good comfortable beds, with so much clothing that you do not have to spread a newspaper over you at night, to prevent freezing. Why should a boat spread an extra table and fine carpets, and then send a poor fellow to a hard straw mattress, to shiver all night and take a severe cold, under a dirty sheet and a narrow comforter?

Minnesota Pioneer, May 6, 1852

FRAGMENT OF A LOVE LETTER—DOUBTFUL COMPLIMENT
How I wish, my dear Adelina, my engagements would permit me to leave town and go to see you! It would be like visiting some old ruin, hallowed by time, and fraught with a thousand pleasing recollections!

Weekly Minnesotian, November 3, 1855

Warning! There is a reaper whose name is Death; and since no one can tell when he will thrust in his sickle and cut us off from life, now is the time to have your Picture taken at Whitney's Gallery,—where as good a Dagurreotype can be procured [as at] any other establishment in the World.

Weekly Minnesotian, January 3, 1856

[St. Paul had a section of Blacks as early as the 1850s. A newspaper said of them:]

In the first place our Blacks are attentive to their business, and are no idlers, as they are represented to be in the slave States. Secondly, they are a useful class, and here on the confines of Barbarism do as much to put a civilized aspect upon the face of society as any other class. Their barber shops are favorite places of resort for many bachelor Whites who meet there, as on a social exchange. Thirdly, the Blacks are our musicians. A negro's music always has a charm for every ear—whether it is the music of the rosin and the bow, or the guitar, or the soft lubly voice; each separately or all combined, as of a stilly night, in a serenade.

Minnesota Pioneer, September 30, 1852

BROKEN UP—One of the lowest and most infamous dens of debauchery and prostitution in our city, which for eighteen months, or more, past has given much trouble to the police by frequent brawls, riots, fights, &c., has at last been broken up, not by the strong arm of the law, but by feuds among the inmates. It was the haunt known as "Frank Wilson's." The inmates yesterday moved for other quarters.

St. Paul Daily Minnesotian, February 16, 1859

It is estimated that two thousand people have arrived in the Territory the present week by water and land carriage. The immigration has now fairly commenced, and may be expected to continue undiminished for the next three months.

Daily Minnesotian, May 25, 1854

Capt. Tapper has woodmen employed in building a large and commodious ferry boat to ply between Nicollet Island and the west side of the river. This will probably be the last season that we shall require a ferry, as it is contemplated to have the bridge completed early in the fall.

St. Anthony Express Weekly, March 4, 1854

The first railroad in Minnesota is about to be erected on Nicollet island. It will be eight hundred feet in length, and will be equipped with a car to run constantly between its two termini. St. Anthony enterprise is certainly beginning to wake up.

Daily Minnesotian, May 25, 1854

Mr. LeDuc, on 3d street, St. Paul, has opened a book store—the first and only book store, we think, in Minnesota.

Minnesota Pioneer, September 26, 1850

Never was a city laid out so badly as St. Paul. The plat of the town with its numerous additions looks as if some accident had knocked all the streets into pi. Measures should be taken immediately to straighten and reform them as far as practicable, before it is too late.

Minnesota Democrat Weekly, September 30, 1851

[A St. Louis man wrote humorously of his trip to Minnesota in 1855. It reads in part:]

The house had a flat hay roof. The gentleman of the house, in reply to our inquiries as to how it shed rain, was kind enough to inform us that in Minnesota it never rains, except at night, and that the showers are never of longer duration than one hour; that his roof would hold water until the shower is over, and then, when it commences raining inside of the house, his wife and children, get under the umbrella, and he goes out of doors. In that way they keep dry and comfortable.

When we got to the brook, we fixed up our rods, and tried the trout with our flies. It's too new a country for flies. The trout are not educated up to that point yet. Moreover, the weeds are higher than your head, and between hanging your hook in throwing it, and the care necessary to avoid stepping on rattle-snakes, it is not easy to use your fly.

After dark we changed our bait, and caught some fish, some whoppers. I landed a two-pounder, who broke my hook and commenced a series of ground and lofty tumbles towards the brook. Determined to save him, I jumped into the stream, the water appearing to be about a foot deep, and went up to my neck. I felt somewhat astonished, and allowed the fish to give me the slip. As the temperature of the water was forty degrees, Fahrenheit, I soon recovered coolness enough to scramble out. Here I made a memorandum of the fact, that swearing is a very good institution to warm one up, when accidentally chilled.

Daily Minnesotian, September 1, 1855

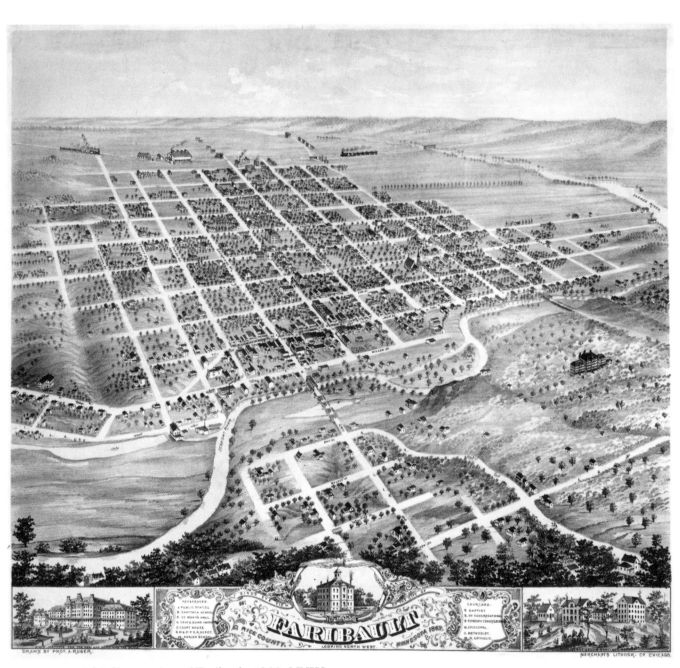

A bird's-eye view of Faribault, 1869. *MNHS*

1860s

This was a decade of great turmoil—the Civil War and the Dakota War—as well as rapid population growth and the emergence of farming as the chief industry. The Homestead Act, signed by President Abraham Lincoln in 1862, encouraged settlement. Settlers took 1.25 million acres under its provisions in Minnesota from 1863 to 1865. Immigrants consisted primarily of German and Irish people. A state Board of Immigration, established in 1867, sent agents to New York and Europe. The first railroad tracks were laid in 1862, between St. Paul and St. Anthony. Railroads encouraged immigrants to buy land and farm, thereby using rail services. Wheat farming became the main crop in the 1860s and 1870s. New demands surfaced for labor-saving farm machinery. The Grange Movement brought to light farmers' grievances, such as high freight and elevator rates, unfair grading of grain, and high interest rates. A school for the "indigent deaf and dumb" opened at Faribault in 1863, a hospital for the insane in St. Peter in 1866, and the Pence Opera House in Minneapolis in 1867. →

J. MADISON BOWLER

"Kiss Baby for me. Learn her to speak and revere the name of Abraham Lincoln, the people's friend."

"Dear Lizzie" began the writer boldly. Then he lost his nerve and explained for a page and a half of his four-page letter why he had the audacity to address her so familiarly.

ST. ANTHONY, APRIL 12, 1860
Dear Lizzie:
Perhaps you may think the above address [the salutation] rather too familiar in tone for me to use on so short acquaintance, but I believe it is one which custom allows to those who stand in our relation. Although I use it with its full force and meaning, yet I can but feel a little delicacy, since, with the exception of near relatives, you are the first and only lady whom I ever addressed in so familiar a manner. But, Lizzie, I believe we ought to write just as we feel toward each other, and I shall always try to do so as far as I am able, for I have not taken the step which I have, thoughtlessly or for the mere purpose of a flirtation, but in obedience to true affection and with none but honorable intentions. I assure you that it affords me much pleasure and is a great relief to have one whom I am at liberty to love above all others, and in whom I can confide, and at the same time feel the assurance that my love and confidence is reciprocated, especially one so worthy and kind-hearted as yourself. Now let me ask that our correspondence and intercourse with each other be characterized by plainness and freedom, and that neither of us shall be backward in giving or asking such explanations as will often be necessary at many times, as misunderstandings will often occur to make true the old saying, viz, "The course of true love never did run smooth."

I wish you were here today, everything is so nice and pleasant as I stroll about and meet old acquaintances and review the old scenes, such as the Falls, Nicollet Island &c. I partake in none of

Bowler's letter. *MNHS*

these pleasures without thinking how lonely you must be, and wishing Lizzie by my side to share them with me . . .

Remember me to your Father, Mother, Sisters, and your Aunts Henrietta and Sarah, and Amon, i.e., unless you are unwilling that they should know that we correspond.

Yours very truly,
J. Madison Bowler

[His letters must have had the desired effect on Lizzie Caleff's heart. They were married in 1862. Serving later in the Civil War, Bowler wrote this letter to his wife in April 1865:]

We have the sad intelligence of the death of President Lincoln; but have received no particulars. The first intimation we had of this painful event was from the firing of half-hour guns, commencing at sunrise. Shortly, however, an order from Dept. HdQrs., announcing it, was received. Everybody is to abstain from all business, except from necessity, Officers and soldiers to remain in camp, and half-hour guns to be fired from Fort Steele until sunset. I can think of no event which could create greater gloom in the hearts of patriots than the violent death of Abraham Lincoln. To think of good, honest Abraham Lincoln being struck down by an assassin, is enough to make the nation weep. All are sad indeed to-day. This fills the cup of vengeance to overflowing. I think now, that I never shall forgive the traitors who have brought about this terrible event. I can fight them with good will till I die, if necessary . . .

St. Anthony Falls, from the east side looking west, 1861. *Minneapolis Public Library*

THE PHILOPAIDIA!

THE GREAT

DIPHTHERIA CURE

Has been at last discovered by

REV. FATHER CLEMENS

COLLEGEVILLE, MINN.

And can now be Procured of MESSRS.

NOYES BROS. & CUTLER

ST. PAUL, MINN.

PRICE, $1.00 PER BOTTLE

The Medicine needs no puffs or recommendations, it has already stood the trial and has proved all it claims and more too. It is not gotten up to make money, but to exterminate diphtheria, which it will do. Wherever this disease prevails, this medicine ought to be on hand. We consider it superfluous to say more.

REV. FATHER CLEMENS, O. S. B.

Give love to all. Kiss Baby for me. Learn her to speak and revere the name of Abraham Lincoln, the people's friend.

Ever your loving,
Madison

James Madison Bowler and Family papers, MNHS

***

[Oakland Cemetery was organized in 1853 by citizens of St. Paul. The cemetery association bought "forty acres of rolling timber about two miles from the river landing; so far from the town as to be difficult of access, and with little probability that settlements would ever disturb its rural quiet." Now the cemetery is near the heart of St. Paul, about a mile north of the state capitol.

The following is part of a page from the 1865 records. On the page are thirty-eight names of the dead; half (nineteen) were children under age ten. The oldest of the thirty-eight was Elizabeth Summers, born in Scotland and dead at age sixty-five. The next oldest was Mary Ann Russell, born in Ireland and dead at forty-seven. The early deaths were not unusual for the times.]

NAME	AGE	NATIONALITY	DISEASE
Reinhardt Seidel	46 yrs.	Prussia	Lung fever
Orsen Colson Murray	21 years	Hancock Co, Ill.	Dysentary
Raphael Luther Weide	19 yrs	Madison, Ind.	Apoplexy
Anna Eastman	27 yrs., 10m, 28 days	Washington, D.C.	Remittent fever
Infant daughter of John H. Palmer	12 hours	St. Paul	——
Two infant sons of Henry Russell, Oscar and Otto	2 mos., 23 days	——	——
Mary Carver, daughter of Thomas Carver	6 mos.	McLean Township	Cholera infantum
Willis Will (Coloured)	21 yrs.	Munroe, La	Fever
John F. Morton	31 yrs.	Portsmouth, O	Consumption
Samuel Smart Colby	35 yrs., 1 mo, 10 days	N.H.	Chronic diarrhea
Ernest DeMontreville	4½ years	St. Louis, Mo.	Congestion of bowels
Emma Mealas Falk	1 yr, 29 da.	St. Paul	Teething
Henry Merrick Brooks	15 yrs, 5 mo	Willsboro, Ohio	Accidental shooting
Charles Keller	30 days	St. Paul	Cholera infantum
Carrie Jane Murray	9 yr, 7 mo, 11 da.	Centreville, Ind.	Dysentary

AMONG THE WHEAT-FIELDS OF MINNE-
SOTA. Minnesota is pre-eminently the wheat-
growing State of the Union. Almost the
youngest of the political sisterhood. With a
settlement and town history of hardly more
than a decade, she now boasts of a quarter of a
million of inhabitants, and contributes largely
to the wheat-markets of the East. Owing to
the peculiarity of her climate and soil, she is
the best adapted of any of the States to the
raising of this staple. Wheat is in fact almost
her exclusive object of production. None farm
here except for this. Her dry, clear, and for
the most part, cool atmosphere makes Minnesota the very paradise of wheat-growers.
As one stands on the boundless rolling prairies of this country, and looks around him on
every side, and sees the interminable reach of
slightly undulating soil, clad with golden-rod,
fire-weed and a vast variety of other flower-
ing plants intermixed with prairie-grass, and
notices the almost utter absence of forest,
and catches the onward rush of the fresh, cool
southern breeze that sweeps by with a voluminous force, he involuntarily thinks of the wide
expanse of the ocean, and snuffs the wind as
he would the sea-breeze itself.

Harper's Magazine, January 1868

Two Horse Plow. *MNHS*

Minneapolis's first hook and ladder
company, in front of a mortuary,
1869. *Minneapolis Public Library*

NEWSPAPER CLIPPINGS

We have been requested by an interested party to state that the ball the other night was conducted with great decorum, and that the rumor of strife, &c., is all a mistake. The pool of blood about the entrance and the alarming noise which disturbed the people in its vicinity, are all due to accident or some other cause.

Goodhue County Republican, February 21, 1862

In a new country like Minnesota, there is no use for idle, frivolous, lazy dandies, or dressy, fancy ladies, who think it is a disgrace to wash dishes, make their beds, do chamber work or knead bread. People come to a new country to better their condition. They leave all superfluities at home. They do not want drones. They fail to appreciate ladies who think more of senseless fashions than in assisting to lay up a few dimes to purchase frocks for the babies. Drawling words, affectation, fondness of dress, living beyond their means, won't do here. The country is too new.

Minneapolis Chronicle, January 27, 1867

Ladies Writing Class—O. F. Carver's class for the instruction of ladies in penmanship, commences this afternoon at 2 o'clock, at the College room, in Hayward's Block, those who are deficient in writing will do well to attend.

St. Paul Pioneer & Democrat, January 8, 1862

Notice!!
Whereas Mary Ann Levitt has left my bed and board without any just provocation, I hereby forbid all persons from boarding, harboring or trusting her on my account as I will not be accountable for any such acts from this date.

REDIC LEVITT

Stillwater Messenger, February 9, 1864

We learn that the second year of the Minnesota Institute for Deaf and Dumb at Faribault will commence on the 17th of September. A note from one of the officers of the Institute says: "All mutes who propose to attend during the current year, should be on hand at the first of the term. The State furnishes them with a home and tuition free,

3000 LABORERS WANTED

On the LAKE SUPERIOR AND MISSISSIPPI RAILROAD from Duluth at the Western Extremity of Lake Superior, to ST PAUL

Constant Employment will be given. Wages range from $2.00 to $4.00 per Day.

MECHANICS Are Needed at Duluth!

Wages to Masons and Plasterers, $4.00 per day; Carpenters, $3.00 per day.

10,000 EMIGRANTS

WANTED TO SETTLE ON THE LANDS OF THE COMPANY, NOW OFFERED ON LIBERAL CREDITS AND AT LOW PRICES.

Large bodies of Government Lands, subject to *Homestead* Settlement, or open to Pre-Emption. These Lands offer Facilities to Settlers not surpassed, if equalled by any lands in the West. They lie *right along the line* of the Railroad connecting Lake Superior with the Mississippi River, one of the most important Roads in the West. Forty miles of the Road are now in running order, and the whole Road (150 miles) will be completed by June, 1870. WHITE and YELLOW PINE, and VALUABLE HARDWOOD, convenient to Market, abound.

The SOIL is admirably adapted to the raising of WINTER WHEAT and TAME GRASSES. *Stock have Good Pasture until the Depth of Winter.* The waters of Lake Superior, in connection with the Timber, make this much the warmest part of Minnesota. The navigation season at Duluth is several weeks longer than on the Mississippi. The LUMBER interest will furnish abundant and profitable WINTER WORK.

FREE TRANSPORTATION over the completed portion of the Railroad will be given to Laborers and all Settling on the Lands of the Company.

At Duluth *Emigrants* and their families will find *free* quarters in a new and commodious *Emigrant House*, until they locate themselves, by applying at Duluth to LUKE MARVIN, Agent. *Laborers* will report to WM. BRANCH, Contractor of the Road. For information as to Steamers to Duluth, inquire at Transportation Office in any of the Lake Cities.

DULUTH, MINN., JUNE 14, 1869.

"DULUTH MINNESOTIAN" PRINT.

MNHS

98

without money and without price, but they must bring comfortable clothes and bedding, &c., whatever else they may want."

St. Paul Daily Press, August 30, 1864

A party of German emigrants arrived on the Albany yesterday morning, bound for the Sauk Valley. Our foreign immigration is very heavy this year. In some sections of the State it has more than made good, in point of labor, all that has been absorbed into the army.

St. Paul Daily Press, August 30, 1864

The price of logs is going up, up, up. The ruling figure to-day is $15.00 delivered at this point, and every log is eagerly snatched as soon as it arrives at the boom.

Stillwater Messenger, May 31, 1864

Madam Rose Lovejoy and Madam E. M. Robinson were arraigned yesterday on charge of keeping bawdy houses. Each of them was accompanied by four boarders. The proprietors were fined $20 each, and the other $5 each. We understand it is the intention of the authorities to repeat this dose once a month.

St. Paul Daily Press, February 21, 1864

A Curiosity—A farmer brought to town one day last week a perfectly formed lamb; or rather two lambs, joined together like the Siamese twins. The animal had eight legs, four eyes and two heads. It was bought by Mr. Bixby, who is having it stuffed, after which it will be on exhibition at his store.

Goodhue County Republican, February 5, 1894

Dental notice. Price reduced. I will hereafter extract teeth for twenty-five cents each. E. J. Sibley.

Mankato Semi-Weekly Record, March 12, 1862

Cook Wanted Immediately. Wanted at the Mankato House. A woman to do the cooking, wages $8 per month, and work not hard.

Mankato Semi-Weekly Record, March 5, 1862

The St. Paul city council has passed resolutions offering to pay $20 each to 75 men, citizens of Ramsey County, who will be the first to enlist in the Sixth regiment, and also $5 per month to the wife and children of every person so enlisting.

Mankato Semi-Weekly Record, July 30, 1862

Wanted—An Insane Asylum. The Iowa Hospital for the Insane, at which our Insane patients from this State have hitherto been placed, is now full, and no more can be admitted there. There are, it is estimated, at least fifty insane persons in the State who ought to be within the walls of an asylum, but unfortunately, there is no accommodation for them.

The last Legislature appropriated $15,000 for the erection of an Asylum, but it will take at least a year to get it ready. The Winslow House in St. Anthony has been suggested, and the University Building has also been surveyed. But the Regents object to that idea. The building is vacant at present, and will not be ready for its original purpose for over a year.

St. Paul Daily Pioneer, March 28, 1866

[A newspaper notice from an unhappy man voted out of office:]

A Card.

To the citizens of this township [Rushford Township, Fillmore County]; particularly the Norwegian voters. . . . I return my thanks to the old personal friends who have for years partaken of the crumbs from my table, and particularly those who have had fat slices, I wish joy in their hearts for the quiet stab given.

GEORGE G. STEVENS

Rushford, Mn., April 3, 1867

Charge of the First Minnesota regiment at Gettysburg, painted by Heisser. *MNHS*

CIVIL WAR

Minnesota had been a state only three years when the Civil War broke out in the spring of 1861. Governor Alexander Ramsey happened to be in Washington April 13 when the news came that Fort Sumter had surrendered. The next morning he volunteered a thousand Minnesota men. This was the first offer of Union soldiers. Patriotism ran high in Minnesota. But the Minnesota men were involved in some of the worst battles: Bull Run, a Union disaster; Antietam, called the bloodiest single day of the war; Gettysburg, where a Minnesota regiment was sacrificed to buy time for the Union forces. That regiment, the First Minnesota, ranked twenty-third of 2,047 Union regiments in percentage of men killed during the war. In all, about 25,000 Minnesota men (mostly volunteers) fought, and 2,500 died. →

SAM BLOOMER

"I was left on the field all day as the shot & shells of both armies playing in or about there."

Samuel Bloomer of Stillwater served the Union Army as a member of Company B, First Minnesota Volunteer Infantry. Bloomer, who was born in Switzerland, was a twenty-five-year-old bachelor when he joined the army. He saved many of the letters he got as a soldier. One of the people who frequently wrote to him was Adda Cornman, a young teacher in Stillwater and the sister of Bloomer's best friend, Oscar Cornman. Adda Cornman filled in Bloomer on the town gossip. Judging from the tone of her letters, the relationship was platonic.

STILLWATER, AUG 31ST [18]62
Dear Friend Sam,
Yours of 23d was gladly received yesterday, and according to promise, I proceed to answer it immediately.

There has been a great deal of excitement in Minnesota for two weeks, the Indians have killed a great many white people, up about Fort Ridgely and other places, but I presume you will read all about it in the papers. The Stillwater people had a great fright last Wednesday night between 9 and 10 o'clock. There was a woman by the name of Ellis, (perhaps you know her) was sitting up working alone, (her husband having gone to bed) imagined she heard somebody walking around the houses. She called he[r] husband and told him that there were Indians round the houses. So he got up and they both slipped out the back door, and started for town. They came screaming that the Indians were out there burning houses, and murdering every body. They frightened all Holhomes Addition, and brought them to town with them. Mr. Boyden got on to a horse, and came up on the hill screaming Indians & bloody murder, men & women were frightened half to death. Old Mrs. Lyman was here visiting, & her & Mother and the girls went down town to Mrs. Crandalls. Ella went in her nightdress, but she put on her Gaiters [ankle-high shoes). Mother asked her the next morning what made her wear her gaiters, she said she was

After the Battle of Antietam, Maryland, September 17, 1862, the bloodiest day of the Civil War. *National Archives*

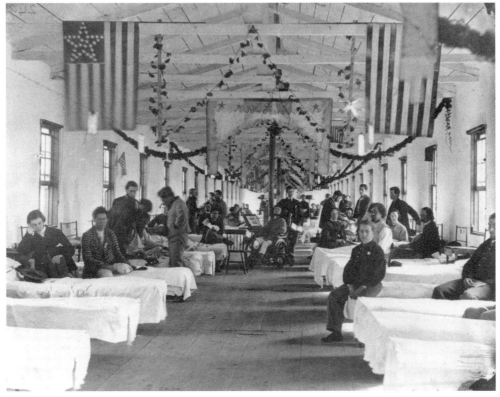

Wounded soldiers in a hospital near Washington, DC. *National Archives*

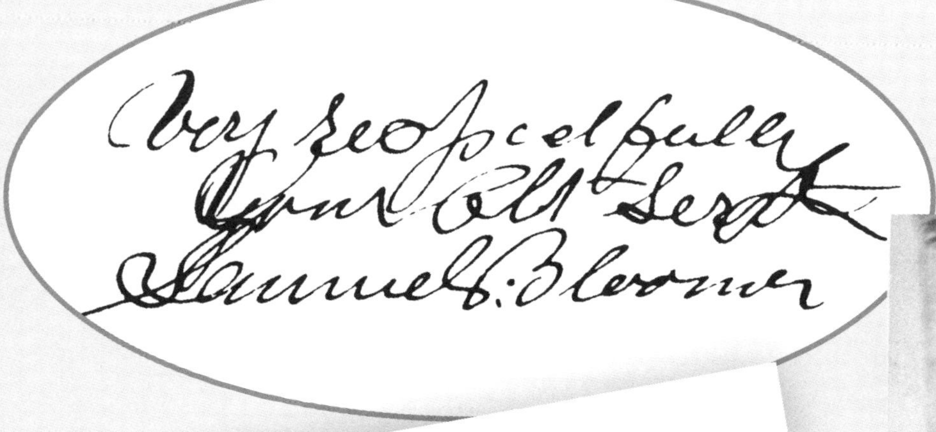

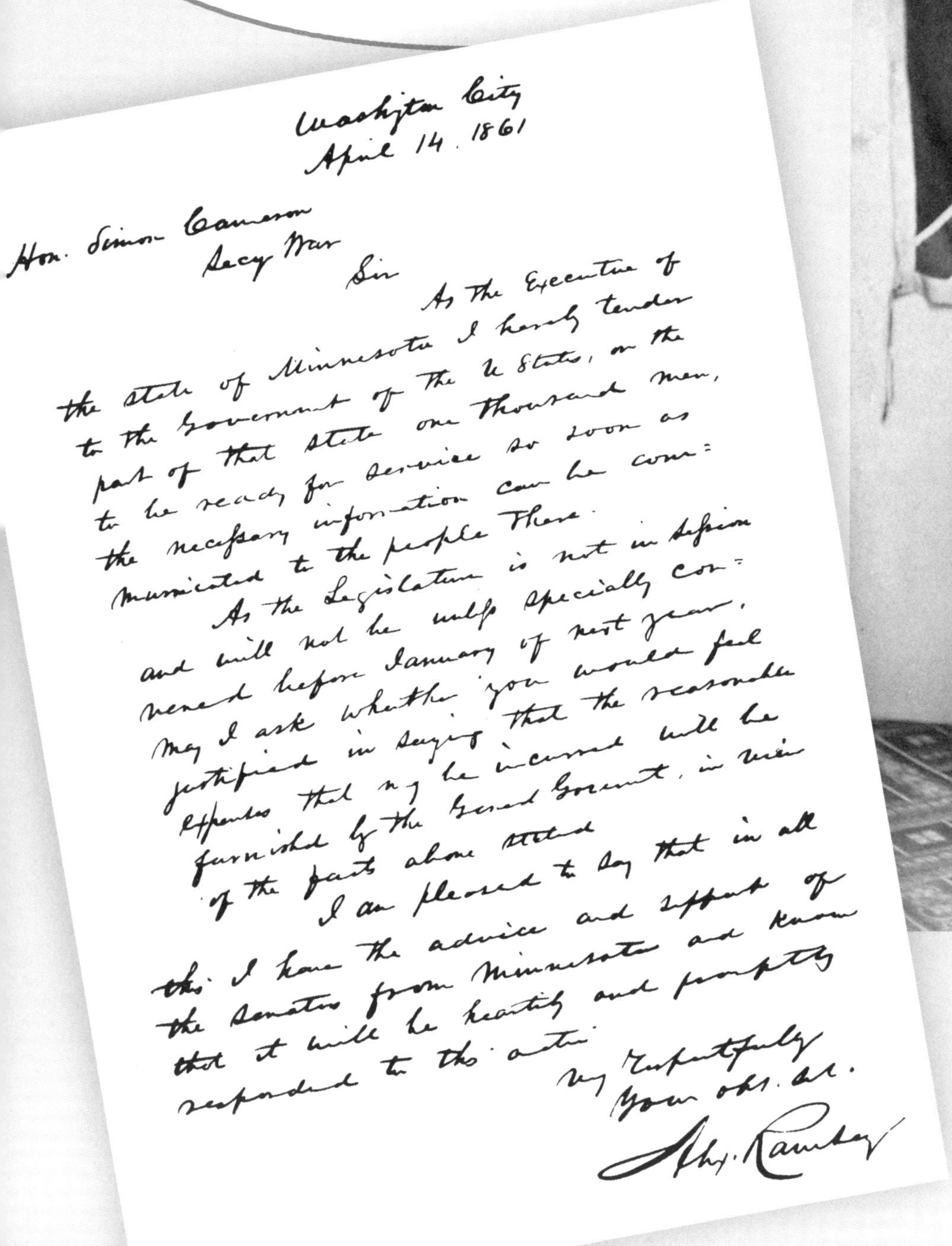

Very respectfully
Your Obt Sert
Samuel G. Bloomer

Washington City
April 14. 1861

Hon. Simon Cameron
Secy War
Sir
As the Executive of the State of Minnesota I hereby tender to the Government of the U States, on the part of that state one thousand men, to be ready for service so soon as the necessary information can be communicated to the people there.

As the Legislature is not in session and will not be unless specially convened before January of next year, may I ask whether you would feel justified in saying that the reasonable expenses that may be incurred will be furnished by the General Govent, in view of the facts above stated

I am pleased to say that in all this I have the advice and support of the Senators from Minnesota and know that it will be heartily and promptly responded to this action

very respectfully
Your obt. st.
Alex. Ramsey

Marshall Sherman of Company C of the First Minnesota Volunteer Infantry, in front of the Twenty-Eighth Virginia Infantry flag he captured at Gettysburg. *MNHS*

The governor's offer of a thousand Minnesota men to fight. *MNHS*

bound to have her best shoes if they burnt the house. Mother & Mrs. C. were standing out at the gate listening Pretty soon they heard Father & Judge McMillian coming along talking. They were bragging how courageous their Wives were they knew they would not run down town, just as Father was saying it, he came up to Mother, then the Judge had a laugh on him. Well the Judge went on some, but the house was locked & nobody at home. They [the women] had gone down town to Mr. Butlers, so Father had a laugh on him . . . but you will have to wait untill you get home to hear the laughable stories they tell about frightened people. I did not get frightened for I was not in town, & I am glad I was not. O! I tell you every body was glad it was a false report. I do not think the Indians will come here. The home Guard are going up to Snake River tomorrow to see if there is any danger.

Well I think I will close this subject and turn to something else.

Miss Emma Smith & Mr Melvin Clay were united in the holy bonds of Mat-ri-money last Thursday week. It was not thought of till two weeks or 15 days, before it was all over with. He starts for war tomorrow.

Uncle Dan is home now, but expects to start the fight with the Indians next Tuesday. He has not been very well and looks rather slim, he is the same Uncle Dan. Ed Armstrong is not going to war, his father would not give his permission. . . . No, there is not much patriotism about the Lyman boys, but I think they will have to go, for there is to be a draft in a few days. I am taking Music lessons of Mr Perkins, and expect to be a great player one of these days.

I close my school next Tuesday, (but I am not tired of teaching yet.)

Mr Bull expects to go to war as a Chaplin. May this find you in good health again, is the prayer of your friend as ever

Adda Cornman

[Adda's letter did not find Sam in good health. His tiny diary, a 4½-by-3-inch home-made notebook that he probably kept in his uniform pocket, tells what happened:]

WEDNESDAY, SEPT. 17 [1862] We were up very early. Got our coffee. It's about 7 o'clock. We fell in line, forded Antietam Creek marched about 1 mile, formed in line of battle & Advanced through fields, Woods & over fences & over the field where the Battle commenced early in the morning & which field was covered with dead & wounded of both sides. At last we halted at the edge of a cornfield by a rail fence, but still we were in the Woods. Had not been at the fence more than 15 minutes before the most terific fire was pour[ed] into the left of our brigade from the rear to front & which fire came quickly down the line to the right where we were. The firing was very lifly [lively] for a time. But I never had to go to the rear for I was shot in my leg just below the knee. I had just got behind a large tree when the whole line was ordered to fall back which they did leaving me behind. The advance of the Secesh [Secessionists, the Southern troops] soon made their appearance & passed by me but did not go a great ways further but formed their picket line about 40 rods in front of me & shortly their line came up & formed just where our line had stood, which left me about 7 or 8 rod in front of their line, a wounded prisoner. I was left on the field all day as the shot & shells of both armies playing in or about there all day cutting off limbs of trees & tearing up the ground all around me, & which made it a very dangerous place. But as luck would have it I got through safe, by that fence my pardner Oscar Cornman [Adda Cornman's brother] was killed & one of Co. A. Likewise some were wounded. & all this while the battle was raging terribly on our left. Secesh were quite gentlemanly toward me, but they took from me my sword which was a present to me from our

Lieut. Muller. Likewise two revolvers which I did not care so much.

SEPT. 18TH. During the night I slept considerable & was wake at day break by a noise at my head & found a Secesh pulling at my canteen stopper which he wish to take. Laid on the same spot all day. & my pardner's dead body lay in my sight all the time. About 6 P.M. 4 Secesh came with stretcher & took me up to a barn where there were about 100 more of our men. & there took our names intenting to perrol [parole] us in the morning. I for one slept but little last night for pain. During the night the Secesh skedaddled off for parts unknown to us & soon made their appearance, the first men out of our regt. that I saw was Cofflin of Co. 1. Then Capt. Pelecan gave me some breakfast, & soon my dear cousin came to see me About noon I was put in an ambulance & taken to Hoffman's barn Hospital & laid in the yard in the ground where I lay all night with most dreadful pain. There were in & around this barn some 5 or 600 wounded soldiers.

SEPT. 20TH. This day will long be remembered by me for about 8 oclock A.M. the Doctors put me on the table & amputated my right leg above my knee and from thence suffering commenced in earnest.

OCT. 29. To day I got up & stood on my one leg for the first time. But I was very weak. I had to have assistence of my nurse to hold me up to keep me from falling.

NOV. 22. Today I was up on crutches for the first time. I felt rather weak in my joints & could not walk around a great while. Weather pleasant, received two letters from Stillwater.

DEC. 5TH. Today the Doctors told me that I might start for home tomorrow so I spent the day in getting ready.

[By this point Sam was getting letters of condolence from the folks at home. This one is from a relative, who signed it L. B. J. and who urges him to get an artificial leg, made of cork, in the East.]

STILLWATER, OCT. 6TH, 1862
My poor boy:
I can give you no idea of the sorrow that filled our hearts when we heard of your misfortune. I should have written to you immediately if we had known where to write. Adam [Sam's cousin] wrote to let us know the fate of our friends, but he could not tell where you had been taken. When Adam wrote he thought you would get along nicely and would come home for a while. I thought, every time I heard a boat whistle that very probably you was on it and while we felt sorry for your wound which must cause you much suffering we were pleased with the thought that we should clasp you in our arms once more and have the pleasure of nursing you back to health. But in a few days the astounding news came that your leg had been amputated. We would not believe it until it came from the Dr himself, and then how many hard things we said of the Dr I cant begin to tell. We had felt so hopeful for you, from what Adam wrote, it did not seem possible that he could be so decieved in your case, but we are compelled to accept the belief, sad as it is, and even thank God that it is no worse and that your life is spared. We shall still have Sam, though he may not be quite as sound and active as he was when he left us. We hope and trust that his heart is unchanged and we look forward with impatience to the time when we shall see you make one of our circle as of old. Come home dear Sam, as soon as you can travel with safety. You will find a warm welcome from more than one heart and from more than one family. I wish you could go to an establishment where they manufacture cork legs and get one fitted to you before you come, it will save a great expense if you can. It

costs so much to travel back and forth. A leg you must have, cost what it may. If it can't be got now, we will have to wait a while that's all. You being in the hospital, I suppose do not miss Oscar as much as you would if you were in camp, or as you will when you get home. Poor fellow! We shall all miss him very much. His home is a very sad one. He is very deeply and tenderly loved by them all. His mother, Addie and Raymond have grieved themselves almost sick. They look dreadfully. They seem to grieve for you too almost as much as for Oscar. Addie is very anxious to find out where you are. She wishes to write to you.

You have one great consolation in your trial, it is that you lost your limb in the service of your country, and your friends will never love you less for your loss but ever feel a deep and tender interest in whatever concerns one who has given so much to help preserve the liberties we all enjoy. Keep up a good heart Sam, and get well and come home to us soon as you can. Rufus is sick in the hospital. I wish he could come home too. I have such a dread of the hospitals. I feel almost as if his doom is sealed, if he is very sick. I do not know if he is. I wish I did. Remember my boy, no melancholly to keep you from getting well fast as possible, and hasten to the arms of those you love you

L. B. J.

[And from Adda Cornman:]

STILLWATER OCT 26TH/62
Dear Friend Sam,
. . . O! Sam I know you have suffered everything and have thought of you continually & wished you could get home where your friends could take care of you.

My dear Brother Oscar will never suffer any more. O! Sam you don't know how hard it is to bear but the Lord gives us strength to bear all your trials and afflictions. It was a sudden blow to us all. We had not hardly thoughts of such a thing but that is generally the way, trouble comes when we least expect it. It is a great comfort & consolation for us to know that he was a good boy, & I believe a Christian, altho he never publicly professed still I think he was. Sam, we will never see him on earth again, but if we live as we ought we will meet him in Heaven. O! when we come to die may we be prepared to meet him there. . . . O! Sam it will be hard to see you come back without my dear brother but we must submit and bear it as well we can . . .

Sam I have not said anything about the amputation of your limb for I cannot bear to think of it. O! it is dreadful. I am glad you are resigned & cheerful with your great loss but we will talk this all over when you get home. May this find you improving in health & spirits rapidly is the prayer of your afflicted Friend.
Adda

[An 1863 letter from Sam Bloomer's cousin Adam Marty shows that Sam was active in pursuing women, one leg or not. Marty also was from Stillwater and a soldier with Company B.]

. . . From indications noted I should say that you were at your old tricks again, running after the Gals. Going to church pretty often, no doubt in good Fair Company. It would seem from all this that the dear creatures have not thrown off on you, but contrary that a man with only one leg stands the best show, probably because them kind ain't so common. (Now don't tear your shirt.) I wish you much joy & happiness. But mind if you get Married before I come back, I will track you & kiss your wife in the Bargain. I am not selfish but I want to be present when that happens. . . . If you do [get married] just send me a piece of your wedding Card, & a piece of Cake . . .

[Sam did go home to Stillwater, and he did marry in 1863. He must have missed military action, for he joined the army's Invalid Corps the following August as a second lieutenant. That corps, also called the Veteran Reserve Corps, was composed of partially disabled soldiers who guarded and staffed army hospitals.

He served in Indiana and Maine until December 1865. He had four children, lost his wife, remarried, and lived to age eighty-two. He outlived three of his four children.]

Samuel Bloomer papers, MNHS

MATTHEW MARVIN

"It will set one to thinking about home & the difference between sivel & millatary life."

Matthew Marvin was a Winona farmer who during the Civil War was a sergeant of Company K. He was wounded at Bull Run, Harrison's Landing, and Gettysburg. Here is part of a letter he wrote to his brother about the Battle of Bull Run.

Matthew Marvin. *MNHS*

Washington, D.C.
AUG. 1, 1861
Dear Brother,
. . . It was a great battle for our old solgers say that they never saw the like. There is an old solger in my own mess that I can depend on says that in the old country he fought 48 hours on a stretch 50,000 on a side he says the bullets did not fly as thick their as they was here. It was by a myrical that we escaped atall. . . . we attacked them at No. 5 after they had been driven from No. 7. They retreated in to the large circle in the bushes & to all appearance we had gained the day. But thanks be to god that we was to tired or that we did not follow them up. If we had we would eather of been taken prisoners or killed by a marked battery. We was 40 hours and only had eaten about 3 crackers and slept 5 hours and eather walked or run all the rest of the time untill we arrived at Washington. The nearest I came to being wound was after loading my gun & turning over on my left side. A Secesh bullet struck a stick about 3 feet from me & bounced & struck my thigh tearing a hole in my pants without inguring my leg atall. I had quite an number strike close by me in the ground & roll under me & stop. We shant have another battle with as many little bullets as their was their . . .

I never felt better my feet are all rite please write as soon as you can convienantly. My best respects to all inquiring friends.

Your brother
Matt

[On August 25, Marvin wrote this to his brother:]

The boys talk in a low voice consequently nothing breaks the quiettude but the birds singing & locusts and now & then the sound of canon in the distance. It will set one to thinking about home & the difference between sivel & millatary life. Crack comes a rifle ball within a few feet of me from the other side of the river. They are early fellows they will hit somebody if they dont look out Charley North [Northern troops] has sent his compliments to the one that shot this way I don't hear him hallow [holler] so I guess he did not hit him. . . . The secesh wimen think it very strange that we can be so wicked as to come down here & kill our own brothers I tell them it is kinder cool [cruel?] & a solem thing to think about but we have taken an oath to support the constitution & we must do it.

Matthew Marvin papers, MNHS

WILLIAM CHRISTIE

William Gilchrist Christie was thirty-two years old when he wrote this letter from Vicksburg, Mississippi. He was born in Scotland in 1830 and came to the United States sixteen years later. He had little opportunity for schooling. By 1856 he was farming in Olmsted County, Minnesota. In 1861 he sold his farm and enlisted with his brother Thomas in the Minnesota Artillery. After the war he married, bought farmland in Winona County, and had eleven children. This letter was written to his younger brother Alexander,

Fort Snelling, Civil War rendezvous of the Minnesota volunteers. *Harper's Weekly, A Journal of Civilization*

seventeen years old and back on the family farm. (The Christie family reappears in the 1880s portion of this book.)

VICKSBURGH, AUGUST 14TH 1863

Brother Alexander—do you think I am a surveyor or a topographical engineer, that you ask me to give you a full description of Vicksburgh and Vicinity, in every detail and point of view. Now I have not the least doubt of it you are what might be call[ed] damned HOT, as you toil in the Harvest field. But let me tell you we are a damn sight Hotter, as we lye dow'n here in the shade, [in] our tents with Nix Pantaloons, or anything else but our shirts. But after all I will try and give you a look at this City and surroundings. Provided you do not hurry me this remarkably warm day and just let me get a few minutes to wipe the sweat off of my Noble Brow. AHEM! Well Sir let me inform you in the first place that this part of Mississippi is very rough so that Vicksburgh might be set down as the city of many hills. It contains one courthouse which is as near to the centre of the city limits as you can think for. On this court house there is a town clock with four faces that showes the time of day to all that can read the signs of the times and this clock has a bell which strikes the Hours so that all may hear that are not deaf. . . . Folks of the South made many small caves to hide in so that they might be out of the way of the wrath that has come. And let me inform you that since they have come out of these burrows there are great numbers of them going to better and happier homes. At least let's hope so, seeing there mortal remains are being hid away in the bosom of old Mother Earth at a very fast rate.

Well, I am getting almost in the Notion of having a furlough sometime this fall, if things will permit, and there is not any likelyness of me being away from the battery when there might be a fracas with the Secesh. I am trying to persuade the Corporal to take one now if he can get it. He is as well as ever. But still I think it would be for his good to have the trip

Now mind don't strain your eyes looking for either of us, for there is NOT the very sure sign of either of us succeeding in getting away. The health of the members of the battery improves. Only one Capt. in trouble with ague [the flu]. A man of Wis. who has been in our battery all winter and this summer died a few days ago. Drunkeness, the cause. He is buried in the cemetry close by and I believe would not have had any better a burial if he had been in Janesville [Wisconsin] where he belongs . . .

Write as soon as you can. I will write to Sarah [his sister] in a few days.

Good by.

William G. Christie

[The glories of war wore thin to Christie. A later letter to his farming brother said, "Be thankfull that yours has been the victory of the harvest rather than the battlefield."]

James C. Christie and Family papers, MNHS

A page from an album of soldiers' pictures. *MNHS*

ISAAC TAYLOR

"We buried him where he fell."

Isaac Taylor of the First Minnesota Volunteer Infantry kept a day-by-day record of the war, starting several months after his enlistment. This is part of his diary from 1863:

JUNE 25. Some skirmishing between our cavalry pickets & Secesh cavalry this morning. Some Infantry sent out to look after Secesh troops who show themselves in a field at the base of a mountain. 1st Minn, ordered under arms at 5-45 AM. At 9 A.M. our column forms along the south side of Haymarket road & Flankers are thrown out. After waiting an hour & a half for the wagon train to get under way we move on towards Haymarket covering the train. Some cavalry appear on a bluff south of us & while the boys are earnestly arguing the question, "Are they our boys?" a puff of white smoke & the unearthly screech of a shell doses the debate & a unanimous decision is rendered in the negative. Shells fly about ears pretty briskly for a short time but

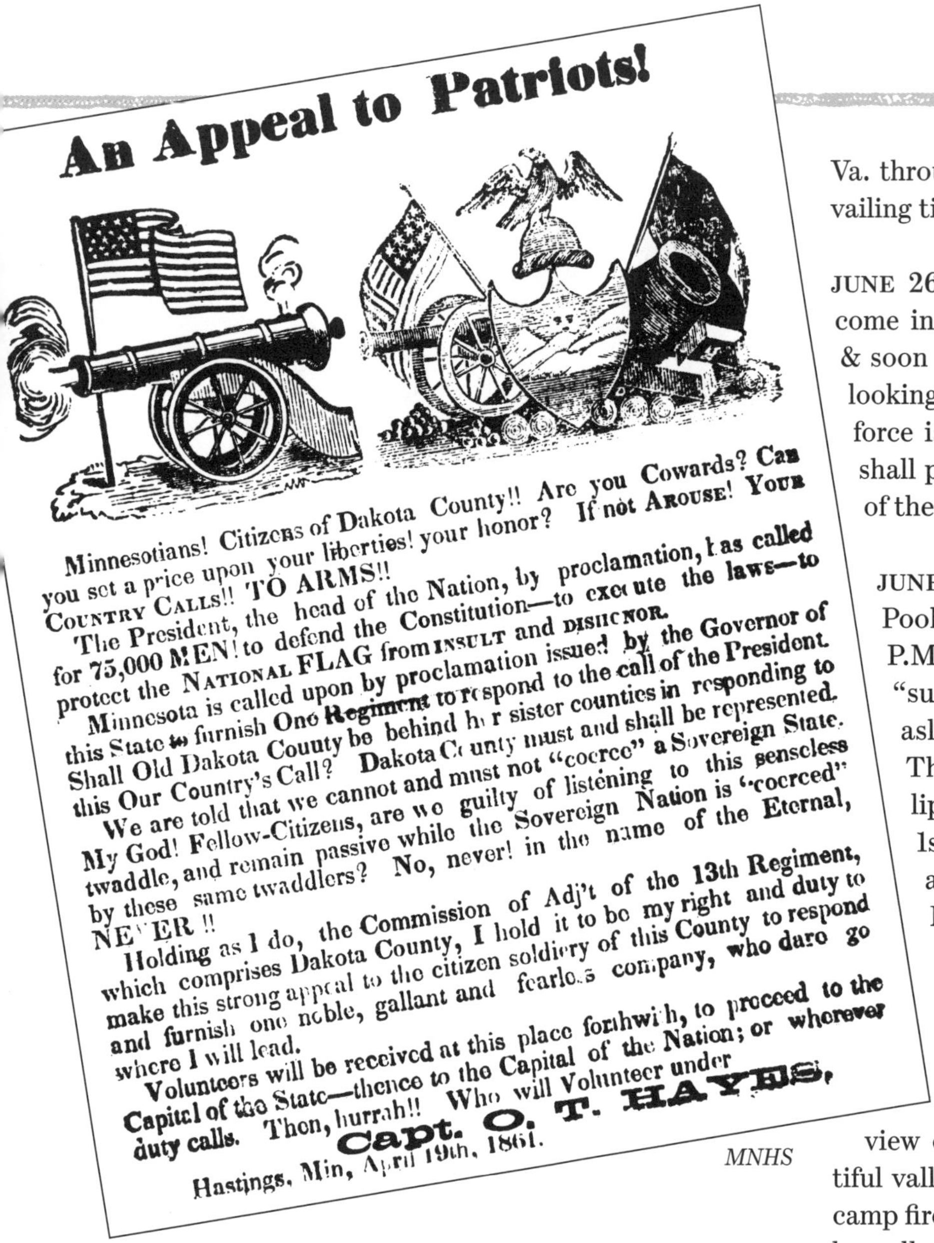

An Appeal to Patriots!

Minnesotians! Citizens of Dakota County!! Are you Cowards? Can you set a price upon your liberties! your honor? If not AROUSE! YOUR COUNTRY CALLS!! TO ARMS!!

The President, the head of the Nation, by proclamation, has called for 75,000 MEN! to defend the Constitution—to execute the laws—to protect the NATIONAL FLAG from INSULT and DISHONOR.

Minnesota is called upon by proclamation issued by the Governor of this State to furnish One Regiment to respond to the call of the President. Shall Old Dakota County be behind her sister counties in responding to this Our Country's Call? Dakota County must and shall be represented.

We are told that we cannot and must not "coerce" a Sovereign State. My God! Fellow-Citizens, are we guilty of listening to this senseless twaddle, and remain passive while the Sovereign Nation is "coerced" by these same twaddlers? No, never! in the name of the Eternal, NEVER!!

Holding as I do, the Commission of Adj't of the 13th Regiment, which comprises Dakota County, I hold it to be my right and duty to make this strong appeal to the citizen soldiery of this County to respond and furnish one noble, gallant and fearless company, who dare go where I will lead.

Volunteers will be received at this place forthwith, to proceed to the Capital of the State—thence to the Capital of the Nation; or wherever duty calls. Then, hurrah!! Who will Volunteer under

Capt. O. T. HAYES,

Hastings, Min, April 19th, 1861.

MNHS

our batterys soon get into position & succeed in quelling the disturbance. Col. Colville's horse shot from under him. Several of our Div. wounded & one of 19th Me. killed by our own artillery & buried by the roadside.

We take the road leading directly north from Haykt., then easterly to Sudley's Springs, thence north to Gum Spring where we arrive about 9 P.M. and bivouac for the night. We are obliged to halt frequently to allow the wagon train time to get out of the way. Our march today has been through a beautiful plain with gently undulating surface. It seems to be better cultivated & better supplied with apple & peach orchards than most parts of Va. through which we have passed. The prevailing timber is oak. Cloudy. Rain in P.M.

JUNE 26 . . . Between 11 and 12 oclock we come in sight of "old familiar hills" of Md. & soon after halt on the brow of a hill overlooking Edwards Ferry. Gen. Lee's main force is reported to be in Md. and Pa. We shall probably pay our respects to him one of these days . . .

JUNE 27. Leave camp about 4 PM. Reach Poolville at 5:45 PM. Barnesville at 11 P.M. Halt for the night at the foot of "sugar loaf" mt. Just as we get fairly asleep we are roused up to go on picket. The mild expressions that fall from the lips of the weary soldiers of the veteran 1st show that they are in no very amiable mood. The picket detail from 1st Minn is 160 men. Gov. Curtain of Pa. has called for sixty thousand militia to repel invasion. Cloudy & drizzly.

JUNE 28 . . . AT 4 P.M. encamp on the left bank of the Monocacy in view of the city of Frederick. This beautiful valley filled with troops, wagon trains & camp fires presents a scene that may certainly be called picturesque. The intelligence that "Fighting Joe" has been superceded by Gen. Meade fall on us "like a wet blanket."

JUNE 29. Leave camp at 7-45, cross and recross the Minocacy and at 2:20 P.M. reach the town of Liberty where we take a forty minutes rest. We pass through Johnsville, Muttontown, &c &c & at 9 Pm we encamp at Uniontown. . . . We have marched thirty miles today & find ourselves weary and foot-sore to-night . . .

JUNE 30. Light showers & sunshine alternate. Mustered for pay in A.M. In P.M. I go "out round" to farm houses & get bread, butter, milk & eggs &c. A good Union lady gives me a quart of apple butter. We live on the "top shelf" today; the boys are enthusiastic in their admiration of Maryland generally & the nice bread & nice girls in particular. Gen. Hancock issues an order complimenting us for our "vigorous exertions" in marching "full thirty miles" yesterday & saying that such a march was required by the Maj. Gen. commanding on account of "urgent necessity." Brig. Gen. Harrow issues an order reprimanding field officers, chaplains, surgeons for stragling.

JULY 1. The news that Gen. Meade has superceded Gen. Horker is confirmed. I shall hope for the best but I don't like the idea of changing commanders on the eve of battle. . . . Just after passing through [Harneytown], a citizen tells us we are in Pa. At Taneytown, we hear there has been fighting at Gettysburg today. At 8:45 P.M. we halt within a few miles of Gettysburg. Build a barricade of fence rails &c. The full moon occasionally appears from behind the clouds. Bivouac for the night.

[That was the last thing Isaac Taylor ever wrote. His brother, Patrick, continued writing in the diary:]

JULY 4TH 1863. The owner of this Diary was killed by a shell about sunset July 2nd 1863— his face was toward the enemy. He is buried 350 paces W. of the road which passes N. & South by the houses of Jacob Hummelbaugh & John Fisher (colored) & about equal distance from each & a mile South of Gettysburg, Penn. The following is inscribed on a board at his head:
I.L. TAYLOR
1st Minn. Vols.
Buried at 10 o'clock A.M. July 3rd 1863
By his brother
Sergt. P. H. Taylor
Co. "E" 1st Min. Vols.

[His brother noted, "We buried him where he fell."]

William Lochren and Family papers, MNHS
***
[A message against the proposal that Blacks be allowed to vote:]

The people of this country should not deceive themselves in one of the most important issues now before them. Negro suffrage as proposed by the abolitionists means much more than the simple fact of conferring the right of voting upon the released slaves of the South, and their little less enlightened brethern of the North. Their intention is to place them with you in the jury box, beside you at the table, along with you in bed—to make them your father-in-law, your brother-in-law, your son-in-law, your uncle, your aunt, your niece, your nephew—your equal in everything and your superior in patriotism, blackness and flavor. It don't mean that the privileges of Sambo are to cease when he shall march to the polls and offset your vote with his, but you must take him to your home, have your wife wait upon him, let him kiss your sister, set up with your daughter—marry her if he wants her, and raise any number of tan-colored grand children. You will be called on by the congo as a candidate for congress, the legislature, and all other offices of honor and profit. Negro suffrage is but the steping stone to universal equality in everything, even to the detestable and Godforbiden principle of miscegenation. In it is covered up all the hideousness of amalgamation. It is loaded with the foetid breath of mongerelism and carries with it the putridity that will blot from earth the white race of this continent.

Chatfield Democrat, August 19, 1865

US–DAKOTA WAR

Perhaps the most tragic event in Minnesota's history was the US–Dakota War. It left more than five hundred white people and an unknown number of Dakota people dead, much property burned and looted, a white population scarred by horrors, and a Dakota population driven from their homelands. The outbreak caught Minnesota by surprise, but it was long in coming. The Dakota had surrendered almost all their land in the treaties of 1837, 1851, and 1858. They were pushed onto two reservations—narrow strips of land along the Minnesota River that were not good for hunting. Dakota women were experienced gardeners, but missionaries and government agents considered farming to be men's work. They tried to get the men to farm, using methods that were foreign to them.

By 1862 the Dakota were nearly starving because crops failed and because the goods and cash owed them by the whites in exchange for land were several months late. The insensitivity of whites was represented by a comment of a storekeeper, Andrew Myrick. Told that the Dakota were starving, he said insolently, "Let them eat grass." Myrick was one of the first whites to be killed in the outbreak. His body was said to be found with grass shoved down its throat. →

HENRY WHIPPLE

"I resolved by Gods help to be the Redmans friend."

There were warnings to white officials that trouble lay ahead. Some of the most eloquent came from the Rev. Henry B. Whipple, Episcopal bishop of Minnesota, who came to the state in 1859. He was respected by both the Ojibwe and the Dakota, who called him "Straight Tongue." In 1861 he wrote to a new Indian agent for the Dakota, a political appointee who was unfamiliar with the problems on the reservation. Whipple wrote:

Bishop Whipple. *MNHS*

FARIBAULT APRIL 15, 1861
Hon. Thos. Galbraith
Hon & dear Sir
I trust you will pardon me for addressing you on behalf of an Indian Mission. My only excuse is in the deep sympathy I feel for a race whose cry of wrong has for long years ascended unto God. When I heard that you had received the appointment of agent for the Siouxs I felt that I might without any breach of courtesy write to you and tell you all I have in my heart. At the time of my consecration as Bishop of Minnesota, I found many thousand heathen in my Diocese. They were not heathen a great way off, where the picture could be tinged with romance: it was a dark picture of heathen at home. . . . I resolved by Gods help to be the Redmans friend—with His help neither man nor devil shall tempt me to give up effort for the Indian.

There are many reasons why we ought to help them. They were lords of the land—we have dispossessed them—we have taken his hunting grounds and unless taught a Christian civilization he must perish. His history with us has been one of robbery & wrong. Dishonest agents or careless servants have made way

OPPOSITE TOP: Dakota warriors firing at New Ulm, painted by Alexander Schwedinger, 1891. *Brown County Historical Society*

OPPOSITE BOTTOM: Dakota leaders associated with the uprising; Taoyateduta, or Little Crow, is to the right. *Frank Leslie's Illustrated Newspaper*

300   FRANK LESLIE'S ILLUSTRATED NEWSPAPER.   [JAN. 31, 1863.

Mah-pe-oke-na jin, or Cut Nose.   Ampetu Tokeca, or Other Day, the good Indian   Little Crow, the leader.

PORTRAITS OF INDIANS CONNECTED WITH THE MINNESOTA MASSACRE.—FROM PHOTOGRAPHS BY WHITNEY, ST. PAUL, MINNESOTA.

with his money, corrupt whites have polluted his home, wife & daughters & blasted his home by the accursed fire water. If the poison makes whites drunkards it makes Indians devils. But with all which makes philanthropists sad—there is a chance to work, the Indian is the only heathen who is not an idolater, he is naturally a brave man & has manhood, he feels the need of something & kindness will make him take our outstretched hands.

An American might blush to ask how it happens that the English govt, have not had an Indian war in Canada this century? how is it we have a new one every year? Why are our missions broken up? why does an English Bishop write that he has 600 Indian communicants on his side of the Border while ours is blackened by vice and death. The fault is our own. You have taken an office with scores of years of bad management against you. I believe you know all I can tell you—but you are permitted of God to represent the honor of our government & race and will answer to him for the trust. I could not tell you of the scores of men among the foremost of the nation who write to ask my cooperation for this poor race.

In humble faith in God, I have planted a mission & school among your Red children. It asks not a dollar of government—it has three as true laborers as Bishop ever sent forth. It depends solely on the offerings of men who believe in God. . . . Thousands will pray for you and stand by you. . . . If God will, I hope to meet you soon either at the agency or your home and tell you much I have in my heart for these people. Pardon my frankness & believe me

Yours Faithfully
H. B. Whipple
Bishop of Minnesota

Bishop Henry Benjamin Whipple papers, MNHS

Taoyateduta

A small incident provided the spark. On August 18, 1862, four young Dakota men hunting in Meeker County came across a hen's nest near a white family's cabin. Somehow the discussion of whether or not to steal the eggs led to dares, and one Dakota said he was not afraid to shoot the white man inside. He did. With the other Dakotas, he killed five settlers, two of them women. Realizing the severity of the action, they hurried back to the reservation.

That night, a council of Dakota leaders and warriors met at the house of Little Crow, or Taoyateduta, a political and diplomatic leader. They debated the issue of war or peace. Some wanted Little Crow to lead a war against the whites and regain Minnesota for themselves, but he refused. One called him a coward. In answer, he made this speech. Several versions were recorded later; this one was passed on by his son.

Taoyateduta is not a coward, and he is not a fool! When did he run away from his enemies? When did he leave his braves behind him on the warpath and turn back to his tepee? When he ran away from your enemies, he walked behind on your trail with his face to the Ojibways and covered your backs as a she-bear covers her cubs! Is Taoyateduta without scalps? Look at his war feathers! Behold the scalp locks of your enemies hanging there on his lodgepoles! Do they call him a coward? Taoyateduta is not a coward, and he is not a fool. Braves, you are like little children: you know not what you are doing.

You are full of the white man's devil water. You are like dogs in the Hot Moon when they run mad and snap at their own shadows. We are only little herds of buffalo left scattered; the great herds that once covered the prairies are no more. See!—the white men are like the locusts when they fly so thick that the whole sky is a snowstorm. You may kill one—two—ten; yes, as many as the leaves in the forest yonder, and their brothers will not miss them. Kill one—two—ten, and ten times ten will come to kill you. Count your fingers all day long and white men with guns in their hands will come faster than you can count.

Yes; they fight among themselves—away off. Do you hear the thunder of their big guns? No; it would take you two moons to run down to where they are fighting, and all the way your path would be among white soldiers as thick as tamaracks in the swamps of the Ojibways. Yes; they fight among themselves, but if you strike at them they will all turn on you and devour you and your women and little children just as the locusts in their time fall on the trees and devour all the leaves in one day.

You are fools. You cannot see the face of your chief; your eyes are full of smoke. You cannot hear his voice; your ears are full of roaring waters. Braves, you are little children—you are fools. You will die like the rabbits when the hungry wolves hunt them in the Hard Moon [January].

Taoyateduta is not a coward: he will die with you.

Minnesota History, September 1962

***

[The war escalated. The Dakota knew that many of the state's healthy young whites were off fighting the Civil War. Two hundred warriors led by Little Crow stormed the Indian agency. War bands spread into Brown and Nicollet Counties, killing German settlers. Two hundred white refugees poured into Fort Ridgely, most of them women and children. The whites held the fort, but three were killed and thirteen wounded. The fort was under siege until August 29. Meanwhile, the Dakota attacked New Ulm, eighteen miles from Fort Ridgely. They took many captives.

Here are a few of the verses of a maudlin poem called "Minnie-ha-ha!," written after the Dakota Uprising. There is no clue on the handwritten copy about the author's identity or if the poem is based on a true story.]

Minniehaha laughing water
Cease thy laughing now for aye
Savage hands are red with slaughter
Of the innocent today.

Change thy note, gay Minniehaha
Let some sadder strain prevail
Listen while a maniac wanderer
Sighs to thee his woeful tale.

Give me back my Lela's tresses
Let me kiss them once again
She who blest me with caresses
Lies unberried on the plain!

See yon smoke, there was my dwelling
That is all I have of home
Hark! I hear their fiendish yelling
As I houseless, childless roam.

Have they killed my Hans and Otto?
Did they find them in the corn?
Go and tell that savage monster
Not to kill my youngest born.

Yonder is my new bought reaper
Standing mid the ripened grain;
Even my cow asks why I leave her.
Wandering unmilked o'er the plain.

Faithful Fido, now they've left me
Can you tell me Fido why
God at once has thus bereft me
All I ask is here to die.

But the laughing Min-nie-ha-ha
Heeded not the woeful tale
What cares laughing Min-nie-ha-ha
For the corpses in the vale.

John A. Nelson papers, MNHS

HENRY HASTINGS SIBLEY

"We have inflicted so severe a blow upon the red devils that they will not dare to make another stand."

Henry Hastings Sibley, a former fur trader and the first governor of Minnesota, led an expedition to oppose the Dakota and end the war. Governor Alexander Ramsey appointed Sibley colonel of volunteers. Moving slowly up the Minnesota Valley, Sibley's forces fought the Dakota and pushed them west. Little Crow and his supporters fled to the Dakota plains, leaving the other Dakota to free the captives and surrender.

Sibley, like most other white Minnesotans, condemned the Dakota for the uprising and insisted on punishing them. The bitterness of the times are reflected in these excerpts from letters to his wife:

AUG. 21, 1862. Belle Plaine. Do not believe the thousand extravagant reports you hear. People are absolutely crazy with excitement, and credit every absurdity. Things are bad enough, no doubt, in the upper country, but I have no idea that the savages will withstand the attack of an organized force.

Henry Hastings Sibley. *MNHS*

Sarah Sibley. *MNHS*

Scene in prison in Mankato, with the Dakota awaiting the decision of President Lincoln

AUG. 22. St. Peters. All is quiet hereabouts, but murders continue to be committed in the region about New Ulm about twenty five miles from here.

AUG. 24. St. Peters. The poor people up here are being butchered by the score, with all the horrible accompaniments of fearful mutilation. One of my parties brought in three bodies at two o'clock this morning, those of an old man, and his wife, and a young woman, probably their daughter, all disfigured with wounds. The man was still breathing, but unable to utter more than a few incoherent words, and shortly afterwards expired. Oh, the fiends, the devils in human shape! My preparations are nearly completed to begin my work upon them with fire and sword, and my heart is hardened against them beyond any touch of mercy. We shall advance towards Fort Ridgely tomorrow, but as it is forty-five miles distance, we shall not reach it until the day following.

SEPT. 7. Fort Ridgely. You will have seen the account on my detachment at Birch Coulie and the lamentable loss we sustained. Eighteen men were killed, or have since died, and forty more or less seriously wounded. I went to see the latter yesterday, that lie in the hospital with ball wounds, and a pitiable sight they presented. I was the first man to enter the doomed camp, after driving off the

Executive Mansion,

Washington. December 6th 1862.

Brigadier General H. H. Sibley
St. Paul
Minnesota.

Ordered that of the Indians and Half-breeds sentenced to be hanged by the Military Commission, composed of Colonel Crooks, Lt. Colonel Marshall, Captain Grant, Captain Bailey, and Lieutenant Olin, and lately sitting in Minnesota, you cause to be executed on Friday the nineteenth day of December, instant, the following named, to wit

"Te-he-hdo-ne-cha" No. 2. by the record.
"Tazoo" alias "Plan-doo-ta." No. 4. by the record.
"Wy-a-tah-to-wah" No. 5 by the record
"Hin-han-shoon-ko-yag" No. 6 by the record
"Muz-za-bom-a-du" No. 10. by the record.
"Wah-pay-du-ta." No. 11. by the record
"Wa-he-hua." No. 12. by the record
"Sna-ma-ni." No. 14. by the record.
"Ta-te-mi-na." No. 15. by the record.
"Rda-in-yan-kna." No. 19. by the record.
"Do-wan-sa." No. 22. by the record.
"Ha-pan." No. 24. by the record.
"Shoon-ka-ska." (White Dog). No. 35. by the record.
"Toon-kan-e-chah-tay-mane" No. 67. by the record.
"E-tay-hoo-tay." No. 68. by the record.
"Am-da-cha." No. 69. by the record.
"Hay-pee-don or Wamnuonawanica-tah" No. 70. by the record.
"Mahpan-o-ka-na-ji" No. 96. by the record.

"Henry Milord" a Half-breed. No. 115. by the record.
"Chaskay-don" or "Chaskay-etay." No. 121. by the record.
"Baptiste Campbell" a Half-breed. No. 138. by the record.
"Tah-ta-kay-gay." No. 155. by the record.
"Ha-pink-pa." No. 170. by the record.
"Hypolite Ange" a Half-breed. No. 175. by the record.
"Na-pay-shue." No. 178. by the record.
"Wa-kan-tan-ka." No. 210. by the record.
"Toon-kan-ka-yag-e-na-jin." No. 225. by the record.
"Ma-kat-e-na-jin." No. 254. by the record.
"Pa-zee-koo-tay-ma-ne." No. 264. by the record.
"Ta-tay-hde-don." No. 279. by the record.
"Wa-she-choon." or "Toon-kan-shkan-shkan-mane-hay." No. 318. by the record.
"A-e-cha-ga." No. 327. by the record.
"Ha-tan-in-koo." No. 333. by the record.
"Chay-ton-hoon-ka." No. 342. by the record.
"Chan-ka-hda." No. 359. by the record.
"Hda-hin-hday." No. 373. by the record.
"O-ya-tay-a-koo." No. 377. by the record.
"May-hoo-way-wa." No. 382. by the record.
"Wa-kin-yan-na." No. 383. by the record.

The other condemned prisoners you will hold subject to further orders, taking care that they neither escape, nor are subjected to any unlawful violence.

Abraham Lincoln, President of the United States.

Lincoln's execution order, condemning thirty-nine Dakota and sparing hundreds. *MNHS*

savages, and as the [white] survivors emerged from the holes they had dug in the ground in and around the tents, a more delighted set of mortals I never saw. There lay 91 horses shot dead, and a very few hobbling about all wounded. The killed and wounded men were lying around, and as the warm weather hastened decomposition, the odor was sickening.

SEPT. 8TH. Fort Ridgely. I received a letter from Little Crow yesterday, by the two bearers of a flag of truce. He writes (his amanuensis [secretary] is an educated half breed) that the reason the war was commenced was because he could not get the provisions and other supplies due the Indians, that the women and children were starving, and he could get no satisfaction from Major Galbraith, the U.S. Agent. That he had many white women and children prisoners &c &c. I have sent back the men today with a written reply, telling Little Crow to deliver the captives to me, and I would then walk with him like a man &c &c. What he will do remains to be seen. The half breed bearers of the flag of truce, both of whom I know, say that the mixed bloods with their families are not permitted to leave the camp, and are virtually prisoners, as most of them are believed to sympathize with the whites. They assure me that the Indians are determined to give us battle, at or near the Yellow Medicine, and are sanguine of success. I sincerely hope they will not change their programme.

10TH SEPT. Camp near Fort Ridgely. We are still awaiting the result of my message to Little Crow, demanding the delivery of the white captives, and I expect a flag of truce today. This question embarrasses me very much, for if I should make an advance movement, two or three hundred white women, and children, might be murdered in cold blood. I must use what craft I possess, to get these poor creatures out of the possession of the red devils, and then pursue the latter with fire and sword. I am also in want of cartridges, hard bread, and clothing for the soldiers, which I hope will be forthcoming very soon.

SEPT. 12. Send me a fine tooth comb, a new toothbrush, and a couple of handkerchiefs by first opportunity. We shall be off in two or three days.

SEPT. 17. A civilized Indian came down the River in a canoe yesterday with his own family, two white women and eight children, whom he aided to escape from the Indian camp. One of the women, the mother of three of the children, is near her confinement [the birth of her child] and you may judge of the shock she received when she was informed that her husband named DeCamp, a very fine man by the way, had been killed in the Birch Coolie battle. She was dreadfully distressed of course, and as they lost everything they possessed, and she and her little ones had scarcely clothes enough to cover their nakedness, her case was a sad one indeed. The fugitives were kindly

Azayamankawin or Betsey St. Clair, a Dakota woman called "Old Bets" by whites, who helped whites during the uprising, 1867. *Minneapolis Public Library*

Tamaha, a Dakota man called the "One-eyed Sioux" by whites, 1862. *Minneapolis Public Library*

treated in the Fort [Ridgely], furnished with clothing, and made as comfortable as the crowded quarters would admit. They report that the brutes in human shape have fearfully abused their white captives, especially the young women, and the girls of tender age. I have written this while almost every body else is in bed, and as I have had a hard day's work I must close, and try to get a little sleep, after visiting the guard, as I shall have a busy time tomorrow.

SEPT. 19TH. In company with my scouts, we pursued a poor German or Norwegian today, supposing him to be an Indian, and when he saw that he could not escape, he attempted to cut his own throat to avoid being tortured by red skins, whom he took us to be, but he only succeeded in making an incision in the wind pipe, as his knife was very dull, and he will doubtless recover. So entirely are these people imbued, naturally enough, with terror of Indians.

SEPT. 23. A large force of savages attacked us this morning, and after a desperate fight of two hours, we whipped them handsomely, killed twenty five or thirty of their warriors, and wounded a large number, with a loss on our side of four men killed outright, and thirty five or forty wounded, more or less seriously. We have inflicted so severe a blow upon the red devils that they will not dare to make another stand. They sent in a flag of truce by a half breed, offering to surrender, if I would promise them immunity from punishment and would allow them to carry off their dead, both of which conditions were peremptorily refused.

SEPT. 27TH. Camp Release [the name given the area where the white captives were freed]. You will rejoice to learn, that after having beaten the savages so soundly, I moved up with my command to this spot, where is

located the large camp of Indians and half breeds, and to my in-expressible satisfaction, found most of the female captives and a few children safe therein. I went into the encampment, with a few of my officers, leaving a guard of a couple of hundred soldiers on the outside, and after a brief speech demanded the immediate surrender to me of all the white prisoners. They were brought into the circle, to the number of between a hundred, and a hundred and fifty, and a pitiable sight they presented. The poor creatures cried for joy, at their deliverance from the loathsome bondage, in which they had been kept for weeks, suffering meantime nameless outrages at the hands of their brutal captives. Most of them were young, and there were a score or more of fine, ladylike appearance, notwithstanding the ragged clothes they wore. They all clustered close around our little group, as if they feared their attempts would be made to keep them in custody. I re-assured them on that score, and when all were collected, they were placed in charge of the guard and conducted to my own camp near by, where tents, and other accomodations, had been provided for their reception. One rather handsome woman among them had become so infatuated with the red skin who had taken her for a wife, that, although her white husband was still living at some point below, and had been in search of her, she declared that she would not leave her "dusky paramour."

SEPT. 28. The woman I wrote you of yesterday threatens that if her Indian, who is among those who have been seized, should be hung, she will shoot those of us who have been instrumental in bringing him to the scaffold, and then go back among the Indians. A pretty specimen of a white woman she is, truly!

OCT. 5TH. You will notice that I have named this spot "Camp Release" to indicate the locality where the miserable captives were given up to me. Tomorrow a large number of Indians, occupants of nearly one hundred lodges will come in and surrender. Among them are many men who are the most guilty of the murderers and ravishers, who have caused such mourning and trouble to our frontier people. The military commission now in session have tried about thirty of the prisoners thus far, of whom twenty, including one negro, have been sentenced to be hung. I shall postpone the execution until I have secured all the other villains, and it is probable that a hundred or more, will soon pay the penalty of their misdeeds, at the same time. Keep these revelations to yourself, as it is not my intention to make them public for the present. The officers are most opposed to my leaving them, but I am so anxious about my business at home, which is suffering, that I must get away so soon as I have disposed of the Indians who can be reached, and who are coming in daily in small parties.

OCT. 13. I shall have about four hundred warriors in close custody. Some of them are probably innocent, but by far the greater part will be found guilty of murder, rape, &c. As they will all be sent under guard to Fort Snelling, in obedience to orders, my command will be deprived of the gratification of strangling the guilty ones.

OCT. 17TH. The Military Commission is still at work, and the Indian prisoners are being tried as fast as a due regard to justice will permit. I have to review all the proceedings, and decide the fate of each individual. This power of life, and death, is an awful thing to exercise, and when I think of more than three hundred human beings are subject to that power, lodged in my hands, it makes me shudder. Still, duty must be performed, and judgment visited upon the guilty. . . . I sent out a detachment on the night of the 15th

which surrounded thirteen lodges of redskins about fifteen miles from here, and when daylight dawned, the occupants were summoned to surrender, which they did without resistance. There were twenty two men, most of them desperate rascals who will be hung, and forty five women & children in the camp, all of whom were brought in. I have the former in irons, but the others have been despatched to the rendezvous below. I am sending out a strong party in search of another and larger number of the enemy, who are endeavoring to escape. The poor [Native] women's wailings when separated from their husbands, fathers, & sons, are piteous indeed, and I dislike to go in person to their lodges, when I give the orders for their removal, but in several cases, I have had to do so. The amount of plunder of different kinds recovered from the prisoners is very great. Many daguerrotypes of adults and children are found, with other momentos of affection. The fresh scalp of evidently a young girl has been brought to me, taken in one of the recent raids.

OCT 20TH. I see the press is very much concerned, lest I should prove too tender-hearted. I shall do full justice, but no more. I do not propose to murder any man, even a savage, who is shown to be innocent of the "great transgression," or to permit of the massacre of women and children. . . . The weather looks decidedly threatening, and I am anxious that my command shall move out of this wide, wild prairie before a snow storm overtakes us. The men are without sufficient tents and warm clothing, and many, myself included, gave their blankets to nearly naked white captives, and now suffer for the want of them.

I find the greatest difficulty in keeping the men from the Indian women when the camps are close together. I have a strong line of sentinels entirely around my camp, to keep every officer and soldier from going out without my permission; but some way or other a few of the soldiers manage to get among the gals—and the latter, I notice, take care not to give any alarm.

OCT. 28TH. You assert that I am becoming enamored with a military life. You mistake. I am far more so of a certain wife of mine, who I hope to rejoin. I believe I have discharged the duty devolved upon me as well as anyone else could have done, with the slender means at my disposal. I have, naturally, a desire that our children shall, in after years, have reason to be proud of the part their father has played, in the greatest Indian tragedy of the age.

NOV. 3D. Camp Sibley. After so long a sojourn in a wild country, fighting savages, an inglorious warfare at best, and living in a dirty tent, without sufficient covering to keep me warm, and living upon hard bread, pork, and potatoes, day after day, ad nauseum, it is not surprising that I long for one good home meal. Matters are working so that I think I can foresee a speedy deliverance, at least for a time, from the labors which have tasked both body and mind for more than two mortal months.

NOV. 12TH. Camp Lincoln. 1½ miles from Mankato. I have my force and my prisoners; and I am hourly expecting a decision of President Lincoln involving the fate of the latter . . .

In passing the town of New Ulm, the long succession of wagons containing each ten prisoners, flanked by a strong force of mounted men, was set upon by a crowd of "men," women and children, who showered brickbats and other missiles upon the shackled wretches seriously injuring some fifteen of the latter, and some of the guards. The assailants were finally driven back by a bayonet charge, and fifteen or twenty men who were among them, were arrested, and made to march on foot, twelve miles to the spot, where we encamped for the night, where after being reprimanded for the insult to the U.S. flag

committed by them, and their female associates. They were released and compelled to walk back the entire distance to New Ulm. I did not dare to fire, for fear of killing women and children. The Dutch she devils! They were as fierce as tigresses.

Henry Hastings Sibley papers, MNHS

[The captured and surrendered Dakota men were tried quickly; 303 of the 392 were sentenced to death. The hangings needed to be authorized by the president. Instead of quickly approving the executions, as Sibley and the others had hoped, Abraham Lincoln asked for the files on each of the condemned men. He was unwilling to hang men for fighting in the war. Only those with strong evidence against them of rape (only two) or murder were to die. Lincoln ordered that only thirty-nine be hanged. One received a later commutation. That left thirty-eight to be hanged in Mankato on December 26, 1862.]

Governor Alexander Ramsey. *National Archives*

THE EXECUTION OF 38 SIOUX INDIANS BY THE U. S. AUTHORITIES, AT MANKATO, MINNESOTA, FRIDAY, DECEMBER 26.—From a Sketch by W. H. Childs.—See Page 279.

The execution of thirty-eight Dakota at Mankato. *MNHS*

[A proclamation from the governor:]

PROCLAMATION TO THE PEOPLE OF MINNESOTA

Whereas, information has reached me that the public peace has been disturbed by the unlawful attempt of a large body of citizens to seize and put to death the unarmed and manacled prisoners recently condemned to be hung for their atrocious crimes, and now in the custody of the United States military authorities at South Bend awaiting the final order of the President for their execution—

And whereas, it is further represented that other combinations are forming with a view to a renewal of this rash and ill-advised undertaking, and thereby provoking a collision with the United States forces having the convicts in charge—

Now therefore, I, Alexander Ramsey, Governor of the State of Minnesota, with a view to avert the disastrous consequences of such a collision, and to preserve the public peace and the good name and reputation of the people of this State, do hereby call upon all citizens engaged in these disorderly demonstrations, to desist therefrom.

The victims and witnesses of the horrible

outrages perpetrated by the savages may consider their sufferings and wrongs, a justification of this summary and high-handed method of retaliation. But the civilized world will not so regard it. Enlightened public opinion will everywhere condemn the vindictive slaughter of these guilty but helpless and unarmed prisoners. The sober second thought of our own people will recoil from it with horror . . .

St. Paul Daily Press, December 7, 1862

Headquarters Indian Post
MANKATO. DECEMBER 17, 1862
Special Order No. 11
The President of the United States having directed the execution of thirty-nine of the Sioux and half-breed prisoners, now in my charge, on Friday the 26th instant—he having postponed the time from the 19th instant—said execution will be carried into effect in front of the Indian prison at this place on that day at 10 o'clock A.M. The Executive also enjoins that no others of the prisoners be allowed to escape, and that they be protected for the future disposition of the Government; and these orders will be executed by the military force at my disposal with the utmost fidelity.

The aid of all good citizens is invoked, to maintain the law and constitutional authority of the land on that occasion. The State of Minnesota must not, in addition to the terrible wrongs and outrages inflicted upon her by the murderous savages, suffer, if possible, still more fatally, in her prosperity and reputation, at the hands of a few of our misguided, though deeply injured fellow-citizens.

STEPHEN MILLER Col. 7th Min. Reg't Vols, Commanding Post

[Miller issued an order a week later that said in part:]

The Colonel Commanding . . . declares Martial Law over all the territory within a circle of ten miles of these Headquarters.

It is apprehended by both the civil and military authorities, as well as by many of the prominent citizens and business men, that the use of intoxicating liquors, about the time of the approaching Indian execution may result in a serious riot or breach of the peace; and the unrestrained distribution of such beverages to enlisted men is always subversive of good order and military discipline. . . . Accordingly, the sale, tender, gift or use of all intoxicating liquors by soldiers, sojourners, or citizens, is entirely prohibited until Saturday evening, the 27th instant, at eleven o'clock.

Eli K. Pickett papers, MNHS

ELI PICKETT

"One of them broke his rope and came down but his neck was broken still he was hung up again"

A Minnesota soldier, Eli Pickett, wrote this to his wife the day the Dakota were hanged:

INDIAN POST, MANKTO DEC 26/62
My Dear Phy [Philena],
Tis night, dear bright and lonely, and although I am somewhat weried with the long and tedious exercises of this day, long to be remembered by the citizens of Minnesota, and by the red race of the Continant, I will never the less try amid the nois of an excited crowd to drop you a hasty line—thinking that you would be anxious to hear from me, and know that I am still alive and well. Well now to the execution. I wrote to you yesterday afternoon since which time all has been confusion and busy, the constant arrival of waggons during the night rendered it almost impossible to sleep which would have been out of the question if there had been no nois, for we were obliged to take an other company in to our quarters, which was so crowded that to have got into a horizontal position would have been at the risk of being stamped on by the noisy and restless crowd, and the stench was so great that we were obliged to keep both doors open and even then twas to warm for comfort Twas a long and noisy night but the morning came at last and with it more nois and more duties—we were in arms at eight o'clock A.M. and soon the whole of main street was one soled mass of liveing human beings, there was part of three rigiments present under their respective officers and all of them under the command of Colonel Miller of the Minnesota 7th our company was placed at the door of the prison to gather with other companies which made a narrow passage from the door to the gallos they came out some looking pale and sorrowful and some jumping and laughing. Some of them were striped with paint and some were painted entirely red, some were gayly smokeing a pipe or cigars while others were seemingly deeply affected with the awful scene through which they were about to pass—among the number I noticed two who held each other tenderly and almost compulsively by the hand they walked or rather ran by twos through the lane to the scaffold and as they did so they commenced hooping and singing which most disagreeable nois they kept up untill the fatal cord was cut and the platforms droped from beneath them and they were left suspended between the heavens and the earth—there was 48 [actually 38] of them all told one of them broke his rope and came down but his neck was broken still he was hung up again—they were covered with a blanket and a white cap of coten cloth, which was drawn down over the face after the rope had been placed about their neck they were followed to the scaffold by the Catholic priest who had been with them several days—they were left to hang nearly an hour and then taken down and loaded onto wagons

and driven to the big grave—and their ends. . . . I have just mailed a [news]paper to you containing a better account than I can give. We are ordered to march to henderson tomorrow morning and so I shall not be able to write to you for a number of days. . . . I feel almost sad to leave the folks here that I have not got aqainted with and especially the Lodge and Sabbath school—but such is the life of a soldier . . .

Phy, I should be glad to fill this sheet but my eyes won't let me and the confusion is so grate that I don't know as you can read or keep the run of what I have allready written but you will excuse all mistakes and blunders so good night my derling Wife and presious Children.

From your affectionate husband and father.

Eli K. Pickett

Eli K. Pickett papers, MNHS

JOHN FAITH

"You should hear their tales of woe! It would chill you to the heart."

That the Dakota killed and terrorized whites is well documented. What is not documented are stories of atrocities. Probably the Indians committed few of the horrors attributed to them. The whites were scared senseless, and rumors picked up speed and intensity. Many letters like the following have survived. While they don't reflect the truth, they do show the strength of the whites' hatred toward the Indians. This letter was written by John Faith, a printer and a publisher of the *St. Peter Tribune*.

"Tribune" office
ST. PETER, MINN. OCT 8TH 1862
Cousin Alf: . . . Well, we have had some awful blue times, I assure you. You may think that you have learned a good deal by the newspapers, but I tell you, Alf, if your friends at the East never learn more of the realities of our Indian War, than that which they learn by family newspapers, they will not know one-half, and that which they do not read is the worst part by far. The war is now, we think, virtually closed—the savage leader, "Little Crow," not having more than 40 lodges in his camp (240 warriors), all the others having come into our camp with the words, "Me good Indian!" whereupon, instead shooting them upon the spot, they were allowed a trial. Some are now being hanged, and others are "excused." It is said that in one camp of the Indians, who have come in under the list of "friendly Indians," thousands of dollars worth of stolen goods have been found. Last night ten released white prisoners arrived at this place—mostly women and children and today 51 more. You should hear their tales of woe! It would chill you to the heart. One poor woman had her little babe nailed to a tree—crucified, and all of the women were subjected to the most inhumane treatment imaginable—ravished and whipped until life was almost extinct. One party, who went out to bury the dead shortly after the first murders of settlers, went into one house where they found father and mother killed by the hatchet and their three children nailed to the

Dakota boy at Fort Snelling, 1862. *Minneapolis Public Library*

wall!—dead. One white man who was taken prisoner, but subsequently escaped, says his captors had a young lady of about 18 years in their possession; and that two of the young Indians wanted her for their wife. They could not agree, however, which should have her, both wanting her. Finally, when they could not agree, and coming very near Fighting between themselves, they took her into a "teepee" and each one of them ravished her, and then led her out, when both deliberately shot her! and thus ended the dispute. Another woman laid upon the ground, her hands tied fast to stakes near the ground, while two Indians each with a rope around an ankle held her while fourteen other bucks satisfied inanimate lust as fast as they could throw themselves onto and off of her! The poor wretch lived only for a few minutes afterwards. . . . These which I have told you are only a few, but I have them on good authority, and am not disposed to doubt them. You know it is their style.

John Faith papers, MNHS

HENRY WHIPPLE

Bishop Whipple could not rest with the outcome. He investigated and wrote to another minister, Rev. E. G. Gear, of what he uncovered. The letter is dated November 5, 1862:

I spent several days in examining the books of the Indian bureau & my fears of dishonesty were all confirmed. The whole system is a bad one & in the hands of bad men as corrupt as it can well be. I had often heard the Indians complain of their wrongs but I hoped it was not just. In 1853 these Indians sold the Govt about 800 thousand acres of land. The lower Sioux's portion came to [$]96,000. A clause in this treaty states that these Indians shall go home & hold an open council & decide what shall be done with the money. . . . Although 4 years have elapsed since that sale, these Indians have never received a cent of that money. [$]880.58 is to their credit on the books of the Dept & all else has gone for claims. This created very great dissatisfaction among them. In May of this year they were told by traders that ½ of their annual payment had been taken for claims. They were very angry. In June they came for the payment. They waited two months and no money came—mad, exasperated, starving—at last the outbreak came & it desolated 200 miles of our border. . . . Deeply as I sympathise with our poor suffering [white] citizens, I do know that this war is justly due to robbery & wrong—and as I fear God, I will not keep silence. I have done all I could to arrouse public attention to this matter & hope to do more.

Bishop Henry Benjamin Whipple papers, MNHS

[War continued in the West for a generation after the Minnesota outbreak, but Little Crow was not there to participate. He reentered Minnesota in the summer of 1863. A white man and his son hunting near Hutchinson shot Little Crow. They received $500 from the state as bounty for the scalp of the Dakota leader.]

Concentration camp below Fort Snelling, 1862–63. *Photo by Benjamin Upton, MNHS*

Duck pond on Main Street, Alexandria, about 1875. *MNHS*

1870s

Minneapolis emerged as the world's flour-milling center. Inventions made possible the milling of good flour from Minnesota's hard spring wheat. Steam threshers revolutionized farming. Cattle production became important. In 1878 James J. Hill, the head of the Great Northern Railroad, laid the foundations of his empire. Thousands of miles of railroad were put down. Railroads made heavy promotions to attract immigrants. The state made health claims, boasting it was the "Florida of the North." But signs of soil exhaustion were seen in the wheat-growing areas. Some farmers went west in the 1870s and 1880s to the Red River Valley. Geologists found great iron deposits in the north's Vermilion Range. St. Paul started its streetcar line in 1872. The state's first telephone switchboard opened at the Minneapolis City Hall in 1877. →

GRASSHOPPER PLAGUE

"They have kept from starving by catching a few fish, the children going on the ice barefooted, and standing on a little hay while fishing."

In the early 1870s, Minnesota was trying to recover from the Civil War and the Dakota War. Then came another blow. In the summer of 1873, hordes of Rocky Mountain locusts arrived on a wind from the southwest. They ate everything, but especially enjoyed wheat. The following spring, the locusts' eggs hatched, and there were more grasshoppers than ever. Farm families lost everything.

There was little formal relief system. People tried to help their neighbors, but not everyone was taken care of, as these letters to the governor show.

GRANGERS versus GRASSHOPPERS   OR THE   IRREPRESSIBLE CONFLICT.

Cartoon depicting the grasshopper invasion. *MNHS*

Office of Auditor of Lincoln County

C. H. Goodsell, Auditor

Marshfield, Minn.

FEB. 15, 1877

Gov. J. S. Pillsbury

Dear Sir:

This county, altho ravaged by grasshoppers for three years in succession, has refrained from calling for aid, thinking that we could take care of our own poor. But there has just been brought to my notice a case that seems to call for more than ordinary sympathy. A family named Stone living nine miles north of this place, consisting of 5 children the oldest of which is 10 years old. The children are barefoot, and have hardly clothing enough to cover their nakedness. There are but two old blankets in the house, and they have a babe a few days old. They have no flour or provisions except potatoes and they are most gone. They have kept from starving by catching a few fish, the children going on the ice barefooted, and standing on a little hay while fishing. The case was reported to me yesterday and I have sent over flour and a few needful articles from private funds. Calls have been so frequent that our people are nearly taxed to their utmost limit and I write you, thinking that perhaps you still have something left from the donations that might be applied to the relief of this family. We, of this county, have not as yet received any outside aid. Anything that you may see fit to send, either money, clothing or provisions, will be properly distributed and put where it will do the most good. If sent to me I will give my personal attention to it.

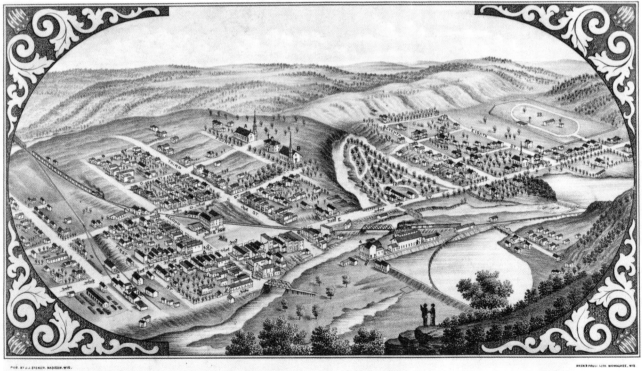

MNHS

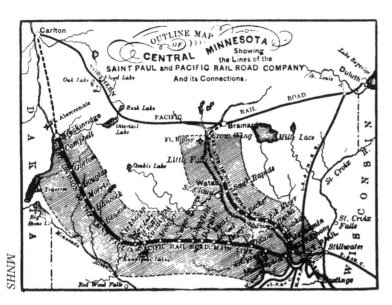

THE FIRST DIVISION
OF THE
ST. PAUL & PACIFIC RAILROAD CO.
For Sale, 1,500,000 Acres
OF
TIMBER, PRAIRIE AND MEADOW LANDS,

Along their lines of Railroad, as shown on the accompanying Map.
Land limits, 20 miles each side of the Railroad.

Prices range from $4 to $12 per Acre for Cash, or on long Credit, with
7 per cent. annual interest.

CASH PRICES ARE ONE DOLLAR PER ACRE LESS THAN CREDIT PRICES.

TOWN LOTS AT PRICES FROM $50 TO $300 PER LOT.

For descriptive Pamphlets and other information, apply to

HERMANN TROTT,
OFFICE AT ST. PAUL, MINN.   Land Commissioner.

For reference as to me personally see Sam H. Nicols, clerk of Supreme Court.

Respect
C. H. Goodsell
Hutchinson

JUNE 5TH [1877]
Mr Pilbury Dere sir I writ to you know if you will send me some cloths I am in the grass hoper regon money is so skerce that I can not get any I have four brothers bsids my self. I have no Mother nor father to take care of us And I can not see them go with out cloths from

Marvis Brown
Address
Hutchinson
Mcleod Co Minn

Windom Minnesota
MAY 19TH 1877
Mrs Gov Pillsberry
Dear Friend
Pardon the liberty I take in writing these, few lines to you while a strainger I am a Methodist minister with a large family on my hands to care for and five years ago we came to Minnesota to

138   "The Shakopee" of Minnesota Valley Railroad, about 1870. *MNHS*

Stereoscopic view of Mankato in the 1870s. *MNHS*

make a home for our boys and One Daughter of 16 We have passed through 4 years of hardship and suffering caused by the loss of all things by the Grasshopper scourge and last year we did not raise hardly a bushel of any thing & this winter has been the most difficult of all to support my family and I was expecting to go away to work this season to support my family but cannot for my wifes health is failing from a cancer on the side of her tongue the Physicians here advise me to go to Chicago or Cincitnati & have it cured or cut out but this will cost at least $100.00 and If I mortgage my last cow I could not raise over 70 or 75 dollars and where I am to get the money is more than I can tell if some kind friends would help a poor suffering yet patient afflicted mother & aid in trying to restore her to health again they would confer a great blessing upon her husband and helpless little ones

Hopeing your generous and sympathiseing heart may aid or assist in this matter or influence some kind friend to do so is the prayer of your

Afflicted Brother

Rev. H. H. Smith

PS. I am grateful for the small donation of meal & flour my family received during the winter from the governor the last bbl of flour and Meal and remedies I got for my wife I had to mortgage one of my cows to obtain

Yours

HHS

[The governor penned a note on the bottom of Smith's letter: "Send $10 to Hon. Mr. Smith of Windom (a state representative) to be paid to the wife. . . . She is a worthy woman and destitute the $10 was from collectors taken among the Sevrl Churches on Fast day."]

Nobles County Minnesota
JANUARY 20TH 1877
To his excellency J. S. Pillsbury, Gov. of Minnesota
Dear Sir:
I have not language to express my gratitude and grateful thanks to you for the generous and kind action you have taken in our behalf as sufferers on account of the incessant ravages of the locusts. Should we again have

the pleasure to cast our suffrages [votes] for the purposes of continuing his Excellancy in the Gubernatorial Chair no people will more gladly do so than those who have been so nobly sustained in time of need. Your private contribution while here to your humble servant will ever be held in grateful rememberance.

I would again submit for your consideration the fact that in less than one week I will again be destitute of provisions, excepting a few lbs of meat and that I am destitute of Clothing for myself and boys, especially underwear.

I herewith enclose a statement from B. F. Johnson. He himself is very destitute of clothing. He is in every respect worthy of any aid that may be rendered him. I would also respectfully recommend the names of the following families whom I know to be destitute of provisions, clothing and bedding. . . . Any requirements on your part to aid you in your arduous and burdensome task will be gladly performed by us. Hoping these lines may revive your kind consideration, I remain most respectfully yours

Frederick Bloom

Town of Alba, Jackson County
Gov. J. S. Pillsbury, Esq.
If you got any more Relief provision I wish you would send me some as I have none and I want to stay at home and put in some croap and stay and raise something for next winter there is not work to be had around here even at 25 cents a day. Now if you can't help those that wants to help themselves I think it is not wright to help thooes that never lost 5 dollar worth since they come on this pararie as it has been the case with a good many around here. There is some amount here that has been away all last summer and they got more help than thoose that stayed here and lost these croaps. Now I lost even $100 worth of seed last season have only 20 bushells of

wheat and a few potatoes and now if you cant send me what will keep us until I got through seeding I will have to leave my plase without any croaps I have 50 acres under cultivate we are 8 in the family the oldest of the children is only 10 years Six children in all. trusting you will help soon.

Yours truly,
D. B. Nab Hersey Station

Oscar Lake, Douglas County
MARCH 15, 1877
Please your Excellency!
A despairing wife asks mercy for her husband, who justly, but perhaps too severly, has been condemned to ten month imprisonment in the county jail at St. Cloud, for manslaughter 4th degree.

The jury was obliged to give their verdict according to law, and the judges were obliged to punish according to law; but if your Excellency would submit the trial of my husband to a kind revision, I am convinced that mitigating circumstances would appear to claim the attention of your Excellency. His crime was thoughtlessness of liquor. He had no intention of manslaughter but he precipitated his own into misery.

Now I have 2 children, for whom I have nothing to live of, because Grasshoppers eat everything last year, no grain to put in this year and nobody to put it in. Therefor the fate of a despairing wife and of two unprovided children depends upon a single word from your Excellency. Oh, say the word of mercy! The right of pardoning, is the noblest prerogative which your office bestows, and you will not leave it unused in our behalf, for which we will ever pray,

Dinna Clemetson
Wife of John Clemetson

Governor John Pillsbury records,
State Archives, MNHS

[Four years after the grasshoppers came to Minnesota, something remarkable happened. The grasshoppers flew right out of the state. By the middle of August, Minnesota was free of them. State farmers harvested the biggest wheat crop the state had ever had. Here's one explanation of why the grasshoppers left. "Honest John" refers to Governor John Pillsbury:]

HOW PRAYER STOPPED THE GRASSHOPPER
The farmers all remember the year of
    seventy-eight,
When Honest John was governor of
    Minnesota state.
When Rocky Mountain locusts flew from arid
    western lands
And covered all our prairies with their
    countless swarming bands.
They filled the air above us with their shiny
    silver wings.
And music of the zipping of the greedy,
    gobbling things.
For years the crops were ruined and the
    farmers could not pay,
And many saw the coming of an awful
    judgment day.
'Twas early in the springtime when the pests
    began to crawl,
And farmers knew that ruin surely faced
    them in the fall.
And sober were the people of this mighty
    northern state,
As hatching out the horror would foretell the
    farmers' fate.
Our lib'rals met in session, on an April
    Sunday night.
Proposing to the governor a Christians'
    praying fight.

Now John came from Puritans, and their
    fasting days of old
And faith in public praying was the iron in his
    mould.
The Tuesday's papers carried the iron
    governor's hand,
To proclamations scattered over all the
    northern land.
For summoning all the people, for fasting and
    for prayer
To God Almighty to destroy the hatching
    terror there.
The people filled the churches, and they
    prayed aloud to God
To kill the threatening pests and to spare the
    chastening rod.
The after-day, the warmest, sunniest of all
    the year,
So hatched the locusts' larvae as to cause a
    sudden fear.
But sturdy John, strong in his mother's faith,
    held on his way—
Believing earnest, Christian praying surely'd
    win the day.
The following day brought a northern,
    chilling, freezing blast!
The Christians' prayers were answered! The
    pests destroyed at last!

Roots, a publication of the MNHS, winter
of 1973–74

[Some people insisted the governor's day of praying and fasting banished the grasshoppers. Other reports conflicted with that. Some say a storm dispersed the hoppers, and others say the insects set out for a new supply of food.]

JOHN RIHELDAFFER

"Just now you and all the young men of St. Paul are under a peculiar pressure to give yourselves up to the excitement of the coming Winter Carnival."

John Riheldaffer was a Presbyterian minister who left an Indiana congregation to go to St. Paul in 1851. In 1868 he resigned from the Central Presbyterian Church to become superintendent of the Minnesota State Reform School in St. Paul. In the eighteen years he was there, the reform school became known throughout the nation for its fine work. He kept a little notebook in which he apparently required boys leaving the school to write a farewell note. Here are some:

JULY 3TH 1878
Dear Friends,
I come here June 4th 1877 I do not regret that I come because I think it has made a good boy of me.
Address
Elmer Stewart
Rochester
Minn

SEPT. 8TH 1871
Was sent here 10th of May 1869 and was discharged Sept 8th 1871.
Come here with the name of being a bad boy but leave with the name of a good boy. I hope I learned the shoe maker trade here & intend to follow it when I go home. I am very much obliged to Mr & Mrs. Riheldaffer for their kindness to me also to all the officers whom I was under.
John H. Lashalle
St. Anthony
Minn.

APR. 22TH 1873
. . . I know of no other way to express my gratitude to you than to endeavor to live an honest life. I hope that the past five years of religious instruction are not lost but that they may still take root and blossom. . . . I have been in this school so long [almost five years] that it seems hard to leave. I feal as if I was

John Riheldaffer. *MNHS*

Explosion at the Washburn Flour Mill, Minneapolis, May 2, 1878; an 1870s artist retouched the pre-explosion photo. *MNHS*

Washburn Flour Mill after explosion. *Minneapolis Public Library*

Eighteen men were killed and half the "Mill City's" milling capacity was lost.

MNHS

leaving a warm home and going out in to the broad world to labor for my self.

Frank F. Mooney
St. Paul

[While successful as a minister and reform school superintendent, Riheldaffer reveals in his journals a few failings. Keeping track of money was one.]

APRIL 4, 1877

For myself, I have never been able to keep up the habit of keeping an account of my income or expenses. I have never felt the necessity for so doing. And while I have admired the business like method of men, who living on a salary, keep a regular set of books, posting them at the end of each quarter & by striking a balance know just how much they have saved or lost. I cannot quite see the compensation

The result of a break in the tunnel under St. Anthony Falls, 1870. *MNHS*

for all this expenditure of time and labor, as it makes them neither better nor worse off. I arrive at the same result by simply counting how much money I have left if any. Or how much I am behind. This frees me from the perplexing effort to make my cash agree with my books, which I am sure it never would.

[Riheldaffer also failed at his grand idea of having his family keep a journal together. His family was not enamored with the idea. Many of the entries from his family are complaints about being forced to write in the book, referred to as "this neglected journal." Such as:]

APRIL 4, 1877. This poor book is sadly neglected, but everyone is busy with his own affairs, and I suppose we all feel we are not doing anything worth putting in a book.

DEC. 30, 1878. This year has been marked so far by no very striking events in our family. One would suppose so by noting the very few entries in this book.

JAN. 2, 1880. It is a year ago tomorrow since the last entry was made by Mary. Of course plenty of events have taken place but who can remember them all?

OCT. 8, 1880. I am quite astonished to find Kittie has written so lately in this book, [signed] Nannie.

MARCH 7, 1881. The book has not been in a very conspicuous place, so we have not thought of it. [signed] Mama.

MARCH 8, 1881. John has never written one word in this book and I think it would be safe to write secrets in here, but don't be afraid I won't. I mean secrets about John, [signed] Mary.

MARCH 28, 1881. I am afraid if I do not write in this foolish book I will be snobed by the rest of the family, for I can't sit down to read in the evening or have a quiet smoke without someone sticking this book at me with, "Now John, do write in it please" or "You never have written once in it yet" or "You are real mean." I have heard of some folks keeping a diary daily and recording how many rats they have caught or what was the matter the cat or dog each day—they write such foolish things of necessity, as something worth remembering does not happen every day. [signed] John

[Riheldaffer wrote these words of advice to his son, John, to prepare the young man, already married two years and a father, to resist temptation during St. Paul's Winter Carnival:]

JANUARY 23, 1886
My very dear and only Son:
Because I am your father, older than you and with more experience of the world, and because you are not only my son, but my only son, and because I love you with all my heart, and hope for so much from you, of comfort to myself, your mother and sisters, from seeing you living an honorable Godly life, I am impelled to write you. What I say, not because I have any reason to suspect your fidelity to the principles in which you have been brought up, but only as a warning and help to you in this time of peculiar temptation.

You are fond of healthful vigorous sports and I am glad of it. Just now you and all the young men of St. Paul are under a peculiar pressure to give yourselves up to the excitement of the coming Winter Carnival. It is in this connection that I want to say a few words . . .

Be yourself, stand by your colors like a good soldier. Never be ashamed or afraid to own your principles. Scorn the miserable toadyism which says, "When you are in Rome do as the Romans do."

Aim rather to lead others in the right way, than to permit yourself to be led by them in the wrong way. Always hold that you are at least equal in influence to your companions, use it for good. You are popular with your companions! Popularity gives power, they will be just as ready to follow, when you take a stand, as you might be to follow them. Never therefore condescend to be a milk sop or a mere echo of other people.

When there is liquor at the banquet turn your glasses bottom up and you will be past by out of respect to your temperance principles.

Do not permit this excitement of excursions wear you out and unfit you for home or religious duties. Do not neglect Church on Sunday because you want to rest up from the fatigue of an overdose of pleasure on Saturday night.

Do not be carried away by what is now going on, to neglect your health. Do not over exert yourself, or recklessly expose yourself to danger. No doubt more than one person will be injured or killed before these festivities are over. Therefore do not heedlessly put yourself in danger.

The best nest for the heart's best affection is home and kindness. Write on your heart the names of Sue [his wife] and the baby, in large capitals; under that Father, Mother and Sisters. These and the Church of God are the best refuge and safest home of the soul in its conflicts with the world of sin. I pray God ever to keep you and yours and to make you a blessing.

Your loving father,
J. G. Riheldaffer

John G. Riheldaffer and Family papers, MNHS

MARY CARPENTER

"Our cabin has a ground floor and we spread green grass over it for a carpet & change it occasionally. It saves sweeping & mopping."

Mary Carpenter, thirty years old and married to a Rochester-area farmer, wrote to her cousin Laura on August 18, 1871, listing what she had done the day before.

My hand is so tired perhaps you'll excuse pencilling. I'll tell you what I did yesterday. I am too tired to write but may have to delay a long time if I wait till I am rested. . . . You see we are right in the midst of harvesting, the great drive of the year. Now for what I did yesterday. I got up before four, got breakfast (we have a hired man), skimmed milk, churned, worked over the churning already at hand, did a large washing, baked 6 loaves of bread, & seven pumpkin pies, while I was baking put on the irons & did the ironing, got supper &c—besides washing all the dishes, making the beds, sweeping &c—Mamie [her daughter] was not well so she didn't help me much as usual. I was tired & lame enough at night, and feel miserable in consequence today. So you see I am giving you the dregs in writing today but this is the first gap in work I have had for weeks. We are now nearly through cutting the grain but it is all to be stacked & threshed. Then we may feel less driven I hope.

128 Main Street in Marshall, 1881, eight years after Mary Carpenter wrote from there. *MNHS*

Carpenter's letter. *MNHS*

Railroad building on the plains. *MNHS*

[Her life did not get easier. Here she is sick at heart—wanting sympathy, hinting broadly for handouts and money, ashamed of her poverty.]

MARSHALL, MINN. JULY 10, 1873
Dear Aunt Martha,
Your long and very acceptable letter came to hand last Monday. I had one from Mother the same day, also one from Mrs. Walker, an intimate friend in our old home.

Excuse my using pencil, as our ink is packed with goods we have not got yet. This paper is dirty and wrinkled but it is all I have at present, and no means to get more with. You kindly said that everything about our affairs would interest you so I'll try to tell you first how we are situated. Please tell Cousin Laura to take this letter as if written to her

also for I may not be able to get writing materials & stamps to write again soon.

We arrived here a week ago last Monday after a journey of two weeks. George and the children drove the stock on foot while I drove the load. George did not ride ten miles of the whole distance 200 miles. The older children took turns reading & driving. We camped in our wagon & cooked our meals by a camp fire. I was not romantic enough to enjoy it much, but endured it better than I feared. My health and appetite were very poor when I started. They have improved. I can work better than when I started. Our circumstances now are very discouraging. George is haggard & worn for his mind is ill at ease and he works very hard. The freight on our goods was nearly 50 dollars. Thirty of it is yet due, & we have no means of raising it. The goods are at the

Looking south from a hilltop in Duluth, about 1874. *MNHS*

Charles M. Hardenberg home, Sixth and Nicollet, 1871. *Minneapolis Public Library*

depot only four miles off & have been for several weeks but we can't get them. I am afraid they will be sold to pay freight. Most of our clothing &c is there. The bureau & large wooden cupboard & several barrels crowded full of clothing, household stuff &c. All my baby clothes are in the bureau. We have a horse we expected to sell but find there is no sale for horses. There is no chance to earn anything in this region. The grasshoppers have destroyed the gardens here so all we have is a few potatoes growing. We have everything to buy till we can raise something excepting our meat & potatoes for a while. And not a bit of money. Our appetites are good which seems rather unfortunate. No house but a leaky ten foot shanty. We expected to build something more right off. Mother said when we started "You are going there to freeze and starve next winter" I thought not, but George said today it might prove so. We have sacrificed considerable just to get here. It makes it

worse that I expect a confinement [delivery of a baby] in October. My health is pretty good now, & if we had a decent house & our goods here, it would look much brighter. George has learned to make brooms & if he could get a little money for stock he might do pretty well at that during the winter. Lumber is ten miles off & we have all the wood to buy before we haul it.

I try to trust in God's promises, but we can't expect him to work miracles nowadays. Nevertheless all that is expected of us is to do the best we can, & that we shall certainly endeavor to do. Even if we do freeze & starve in the way of duty, it will not be a dishonorable death. I laid awake almost all night, worrying about it but that didn't do any good. "Sufficient to the day is the evil thereof." We have a little to eat yet & perhaps some way will be provided for more when it is gone. We sold all of our cows but two & a young heifer. Our best cow was sick on the road & does not yet recover. She will be no dependance this winter. The other will give milk in a few days but we shan't have much butter to sell. The first two years here will be hard very probably. If we struggle through them, then we stand a chance to do pretty well I think. As to clothing we'll have to do almost without I guess. We came very poorly provided for in that respect. By the way, when you send Mother's box, if you happen to have any old things that you don't think worth sending, they would do us tons of good. I am adept in using old things up, have served a good apprenticeship . . .

We are not able to subscribe for any papers. It is lonely enough without reading. We left our books with Mother for fear they would be spoiled before we got a house. Perhaps you have some old papers to spare. They would be appreciated. Do you not think me a consummate begger? I'll run the risk of your thinking so. I am afraid you will not want to hear from me very often if I have nothing more cheering to write. Perhaps sometime it will be better.

Our cookstove stands out of doors with no protection. Isn't this roughing it? You [wrote that you] hope a double portion of the pioneering spirit descends to me. I am endowed with very little of it. My taste runs the other way to conveniences, elegances, comforts and all the paraphenalia of civilized life. The country here is very pleasant in summer. We have the [railroad] cars in sight for several miles. The children are well and hearty and all send love to Aunt Martha.

We had a good celebration of the "Fourth" [of July] at Marshall. Good speaking, singing &c. Mamie & I went down with Mr Ross' folks, our nearest neighbors. I took our team last Sabbath and Mamie & I went to meeting at Marshall. Congregational preaching in the forenoon, then S. School and Methodist preaching in the afternoon. Both sermons were good & the S. School interesting. My shoes were too poor to go, & I had no gloves which did not correspond with the rest of my

dress, but I put aside scruples & went. Geo. has no pants fit to wear, so he can't go. I have a number of things to fix over for the children, but can't do it because we can't get the goods. If I had fifteen dollars we could get all except George's machinery, reaper, horserake, plough &c. But fifteen dollars don't grow on any bush. Well, I mustn't worry. I should not have troubled you with all this only I could not tell you truthfully how we were situated without. Don't worry about it. I presume it is all for the best. "It is always darkest just before dawn." Mother's health is better than when I came away. She wrote that Father & Frank were feeling quite debilitated by the hot weather. Willie was well. Father thought he never should see me again when I started off. All the hindrance will be lack of means. It takes ten dollars to go there but a day and a half on the cars will take me there. I am owing Mother a letter, but am dreading to write for fear it will worry her . . .

Do you want to know what our carpet is? Our cabin has a ground floor and we spread green grass over it for a carpet & change it occasionally. It saves sweeping & mopping. But I would rather have a chance to do both. We brought a dozen hens with us, so we have some eggs. Our pigs could not travel so we had to sell them all except two which we brought in the pork barrel. I am not fond of salt pork but it is a good deal better than no meat. George desires to be remembered. He feels better to be on his own place than he did where we were before. If we can get through next winter, I hope we can do pretty well. With love from the children & myself to all & hoping to hear from you before long. I am

Your affectionate Niece
Mary E. L. Carpenter

Mary E. Lovell Carpenter and Family papers, MNHS

***

"Many females, by keeping a careful daily measurement of the neck, can always tell when they are pregnant."

[The title is *The Book of Nature, a Full and Explicit Explanation of the Structure and Use of the Organs of Life and Generation in Man and Woman*. It was published in 1875 in New York; a copy belonged to a Cottage Grove man. The book starts slowly—"Chapter 1. Vegetable Reproduction"—but goes on to quite frank discussions about such topics as venereal disease and masturbation, both of which were thought to result in eternal damnation and deformed children. Here are a few excerpts of the milder passages:]

Another important and remarkable sign [of pregnancy], and one the most to be relied on, is an increase of the size of the neck. This often occurs at very early period, and many females, by keeping a careful daily measurement of the

neck, can always tell when they are pregnant. Generally, the best age to marry, where the health is perfect, is from twenty-one to twenty-five in the male, and from eighteen to twenty-one in the female. As a general rule, marriages earlier than this are injurious and detrimental to health. Men who marry too young, unless they are of cold and phlegmatic constitutions and thus moderate in their conduct, become partially bald, dim of sight, and lose all elasticity of limb, in a few years; while women, in a like position, rarely have any bloom on their cheek or fire in their eye, by the time they are twenty-five.

The rich are qualified for marriage before the poor. This is owing to the superiority of their aliment [food]; for very nutritious food, and the constant use of wines, coffee, etc., greatly assists in developing the organs of reproduction; whereas the food generally made use of among the peasantry of most countries—as vegetables, corn, milk, etc.—retards their growth.

A male or female with a very low forehead should carefully avoid marriage with a person of like conformation, or their off-spring will, in all probability, be weak-minded, or victims to partial idiocy.

Plumpness is essential to beauty, especially in mothers, because in them the abdomen necessarily expands, and would afterwards collapse and become wrinkled. An excess of plumpness, however, is to be guarded against. Young women who are very fat are cold, and prone to barreness.

You [young women] may at times be unavoidably compelled to hear a vulgar word spoken, or an indelicate illusion made: in every instance maintain a rigid insensibility. It is not enough that you cast down your eyes or turn your head, you must act as if you did not hear it; appear as if you did not comprehend it. You ought to receive no more impression from remarks or illusions of this character than a block of wood. Unless you maintain this standing, and preserve this high-toned purity of manner, you will be greatly depreciated in the opinion of all men whose opinion is worth having.

Too much importance cannot be attached to cleanliness. Men may be careless as to their own personal appearance, and may, from the nature of their business, be negligent in their dress, but they dislike to see any disregard in the dress and appearance of their wives.

Nothing so depresses a man and makes him dislike and neglect his home as to have a wife who is slovenly in her dress and unclean in her habits. Beauty of face and form will not compensate for these defects; the charm of purity and cleanliness never ends but with life itself. These are matters that do not involve any great labor or expense. The use of the bath, and the simplest fabrics, shaped by your own supple fingers, will be all that is necessary. Those attractions will act like a magnet upon your husband. Never fear that there will be any influence strong enough to take him from your side.

HUGO NISBETH

"There was no Christmas tree, for fir trees are not yet planted in this part of Minnesota, but two candles stood on the white covered table and round these were placed a multitude of Christmas cakes."

Hugo Nisbeth of Sweden traveled in America for two years—1872 to 1874—and then wrote a travel book published in Sweden. "I intended principally to visit those parts of the country about which Swedish readers know little or nothing," he wrote.

One of those places was Minnesota. Here is part of his translated account of the 1872 Christmas he spent in a sod house on the prairie.

Much activity prevailed in St. Paul when I got there. The handsome stores were filled with newly arrived articles, which were tasteful and often rather costly, intended as gifts for the coming holidays. There was a brisk sale of Christmas trees in the markets, and those

streets along which the retailers had their shops were crowded with conveyances belonging to near-by farmers who were in town to buy gifts or delicacies for the Christmas table. It is not only the Scandinavians who celebrate Christmas here in America in a true ancient northern fashion, but even the Americans themselves have in late years begun to give more and more attention to this festival of the children and have as nearly as possible taken our method of celebration as a pattern. For example, most of them use fir trees with candles, confections, and other decorations, and so far as the number and costliness of the presents are concerned they often display a liberality that would amaze us Swedes. These Christmas presents are given in various ways.

152

MERRY AS THE SLEIGH-BELLS MAY THY CHRISTMAS BE!

MNHS

In the public schools, especially for younger children, the school officials usually arrange a huge fir, which stands for about eight days. On this tree the children's parents and friends hang small presents, which are distributed by the school-teacher. In the home the presents are sent with a message if the giver is someone outside the family, or they are distributed by a dressed-up Christmas mummer, who here goes under the name of "Santa Claus." Still another custom exists, although it is not used so commonly perhaps as the first two. If there is reason to expect presents, a stocking is hung up at bedtime in some convenient and

well-known place and in it in the morning will be found the expected presents. Not a trace of our traditional lutfisk and rice porridge is found. There is no special menu for Christmas Eve. On the other hand there are few American homes in which the customary turkey is not served on the following, or Christmas, day.

As I had planned to spend my Christmas Eve with some of my countrymen out on the prairie, I left St. Paul a few days before Christmas and went by the St. Paul and Pacific one hundred English miles northwest to the Litchfield station. Here, after some trouble, I was fortunate enough to secure a sled in which I set out over the prairie to the west. There was no road, of course. The level country which I entered first lay like an enormous white cloth spread out before my eyes, and the only guide I had for the direction I was to take was a small pocket compass and the blue smoke columns that here and there at a considerable distance arose from the log cabins. The way was not particularly difficult to traverse, for on the flat prairie the snow distributes itself comparatively evenly. But when, after twenty or thirty miles, I came out on the rolling prairie, I met with greater difficulties. In some places the snow had drifted in considerable quantitites between the hillocks, and had it not been for the hardy horses and the extraordinary strong conveyances that they have in the West, I should have had extreme difficulty in making headway.

Toward nightfall on the day before Christmas Eve I perceived far off the smoke from a human habitation, which, from what I could make out at a distance, should be a sod house. I was soon there and found that this, in truth, was the case, although it was one of the very best kind. That is to say, in this case, the owner had only half dug himself into the ground. Three tiers of thick timbers were laid above ground and over these there was placed a roof with a slight pitch. One lived, so to speak, half under and half above the ground, and thus is became possible for the occupant to get daylight through a small window, which was sawed out of the south wall formed by the three timbers mentioned above. About twenty paces from the dwelling house was the granary and, annexed to it, the stable, also a half sod house, which was occupied by two oxen and a cow. Only a little grain was on hand; that which was not necessary for winter use had been sold, as usual, during Indian summer. The sod hay barn, on the other hand, seemed to be well filled with cattle fodder. I had not steered wrong, for I had reached the house of the man I sought, Jan Erickson from Wermland, who had been in America for three years and for the last two years had been living on his large eighty-acre homestead. I was received by him and his friendly wife with that cordiality which I have been accustomed to find among my countrymen on the prairie. Nor did I need to put forth any request that I might stay over Christmas Eve, for I was anticipated in this by my friendly hosts, who simply but heartily bade me remain and help myself to whatever they had to offer. To the two children, a girl of seven named Anna and a boy of three, Eric, the visit of a strange gentleman seemed particularly surprising, but the sight of some packages I had brought along, which the dwelling's smallness made it impossible for me to hide, soon made us the best of friends.

Early in the morning of the day before Christmas my hosts were at work, and when I arose I found a huge ham already sputtering over the fire, while outside I heard my host's great ax blows, for he was busy getting the necessary Christmas wood ready. I hurried out and was met with a picture that was for me entirely new and particularly striking. The sun was about twenty degrees above the wavy horizon of snow and from the snow-clad tops of countless hillocks the sunbeams were thrown in a dazzling bewilderment all around. Yet, except for this tiny world in which I now found myself, I could not discern another sign of human presence than two columns of smoke, which arose, nearly perpendicularly, from the horizon, one in the northwest and one in the southwest. The first, explained my host, came from a sod house that was occupied the previous spring by the family of a German farmer who came from Illinois, where he had paid too much for his land and after two years of fruitless toil had been forced to leave everything with empty hands. In the other lived a Swedish family, a man and his wife and one child, who had lived there for a year and a half. After the wood was chopped

William H. Illingsworth, a photographer, and his family at Minnehaha Falls, 1870.
Minneapolis Public Library

and carried in, a task in which the two children took part with a will, the cattle were fed and watered, and a small sheaf of unthreshed wheat was set out for the few birds that at times circled around the house, in accordance with the lovely old Swedish custom.

With these and other chores the morning passed, and right after twelve o'clock we were invited in by the housewife for the midday meal. The cloth that covered the plain home-made table was certainly not of the finest, but it was whole and clean, and the defects of arrangement that a fault-finding observer would have been able to point out were plentifully outweighed in my eyes by the unfeigned, cordial friendliness with which I was bade to help myself to what the house had to offer. For the rest, one should have felt ashamed not to be satisfied. The bread that we dipped in the kettle was freshly baked and tasty [a Swedish Christmas custom is to dip pieces of bread in a kettle of boiling meat], and the fat chicken that was later served in a sort of stewed pie form, which awakened especially the children's delight, had clearly not fared ill during the short time allotted him to live. And so came the afternoon with its small arrangements for the evening meal and the Christmas table, for this could not be omitted. There was no Christmas tree, for fir trees are not yet planted in this part of Minnesota, but two candles stood on the white covered table and round these were placed a multitude of Christmas cakes in various shapes made by the housewife and such small presents as these pioneers were able to afford, to which I added those I had brought. Nor were lutfisk and rice porridge to be found on the table, but the ham which took the place of honor in their stead banished all doubt that the settler's labor and sacrifice had received its reward.

The meal was eaten in the happiest of moods and afterward the few presents were distributed to the children. The gifts were neither costly nor tasteful, but they were gifts and

that was all that was necessary. On the wooden horse I had brought, the little three-year-old galloped over the hard-packed dirt floor of the sod house with as much joy and happiness undoubtedly as the pampered child upon one polished and upholstered. All was joy and thankfulness, and when later the head of the family read a chapter from the Bible about the Christ child I am certain that from the hearts of these poor people there rose many warm thanksgivings to Him who smoothed their path and gave them courage and strength to conquer the hardships of the New World.

Outside the snow fell slowly and spread its white Christmas mantle over the endless prairie. Now and then a snowflake fastened itself on the single window of the sod house, its curtains faded by the summer suns, and quickly dissolved and disappeared as if its icy heart had melted with joy at sight of the peace that reigned within. And later, from the corner of the room where the housewife's kind hands had made my bed, I heard the small voice of the youngest child, still clutching his wooden horse, repeating after his mother, "Good night, kind Jesus." Then it was I realized in full God's infinite wisdom when He willed to apportion "the palace for the rich, but joy for the poor."

Roy W. Swanson, translation from *Minnesota History*, December 1927

***

[From the 1873 diary of a depressed Mrs. Ahira Richardson of St. Paul:]

SUNDAY, MAY 11. Cool in the morning a little rain in the afternoon. Clear at night. In church both morning and evening stayed for the holy communion and at Sunday School. The lecture this evening was interesting. O Lord forgive me all of my wrong thoughts for this day. Amen.

MONDAY, 12. Clear in the afternoon a little rain in the morning windy. In church in the evening. Mr. R. [her husband] cut two trees down in the front yard and I think it to bad. . . . Mr. R. went to the masons.

SUNDAY, 18. Cloudy and rain in the afternoon. In church in the morning and evening at Sunday School. I have been sad even Mr. R. only speaks to reprove me and how disagreable I must be people only stay to eat and sleep may God forgive me and may I put my whole trust in Him.

Ahira Richardson and Family papers, MNHS

***

[From the 1879 diary of John Purmort, who farmed at Bethel, Anoka County:]

CHRISTMAS. Stayed at home and ate chicken pie in the eving we went over to Mr. Greens to a dance had a very good time got home 4 AM.

DEC. FRIDAY 26TH 1879. Went and got a load of wood chored the rest of the day.

John E. Purmort and Family papers, MNHS

MARGARET KERR

"A settler's wife took a fancy to pay me an extended visit of ten days with 4 children under 7 years old and I had 5 under 9—and both families took chicken pox."

Margaret and Robert Kerr were married in Scotland in 1864. A Protestant missionary, he settled a colony of Scots in Wadena, Minnesota, in 1874. "I don't like to think of all the hardships I underwent that winter," Margaret wrote in a letter to her daughter seventeen years later. The winter was so rough, in fact, that they lasted in Minnesota only a year. The Kerrs accepted a call from a church at Mitchell, Iowa. In this letter, she told that she was miffed that missionaries' wives rarely got the credit for their endeavors.

My dear Annie,
. . . When your father went to Wadena, the city then was 16 straggling houses including the depot and water tank. The settlers in the country were widely scattered. The nearest minister being at Brainerd 47 miles off, no

doctor nearer either. Some people said that was the coldest winter since Fort Snelling was built. It was very cold from 15th October. We had snow till the last [of] April. . . . I usually hung my washing at midnight and took them in, ready to iron after breakfast— You know my time in the day was occupied in visiting the new comers—sometimes a team would come for me to tend to a sick one and often being up all night I had to walk home through deep snow then I would be sent for to teach a novice to make butter and this work was done when the thermometer was from 30 to 40 below zero. I sometimes walked down the track when the country got blocked with snow. I say country because then there were no roads to any dwelling—during this time your father was unable to go anywhere till we got a horse after we got the horse and sleigh he did

One of the first steam trains on the Minneapolis, Lyndale & Minnetonka Railroad.
Minneapolis Public Library

a great deal of travelling trying to get all the settlers to come to service—I did not blame many of them for not coming because none had horses and to drive behind oxen 4-5-6-7 and 8 miles through deep snow with the master of the house walking ahead to break the way for the slow going quadrupeds needed a great deal of grace as well as courage—and many [people] had not sufficient clothing to protect them from freezing—I don't like to think of all the hardships I underwent that winter—how all the few potatoes in the cellar froze and our fruit was frozen citron melons [watermelon-like fruit]—how we subsisted for 7 weeks on bread with weedy-tasting milk—the cow I bought had been pasturing in some slew—how a settler's wife took a fancy to pay me an extended visit of ten days with 4 children under 7 years old and I had 5 under 9—and both families took chicken pox—Just try to picture we two mothers every morning picking out each childs shoes and stockings besides the other garments—how all the bread had to be thawed out before we could cut it and how my pretty dishes were frozen and spoilt—how all my good bedding had many times to be spread out on the floor to accomodate men who were weather bound and had no money to pay hotel bills—I did not mind using them [the sheets] but I had an extra wash because they were not very clean (the men I mean). The greatest privation to me was the railroad getting blocked for two weeks and receiving no mail—the days seemed so long—how glad we were when the big snow plow came through and cleared the track—how I used to steam wheat to feed the horse and cow because we could get nothing else—how your father drove so carelessly that he struck a snag on a corduroy bridge, and preacher, horse and sleigh were turned over in the slew which was filled with snow. I often wondered how we lived because the people were all poor and struggling and instead of helping the minister I had to divide my flour

when they were unable to get to Parker Prairie which was about 30 miles away—before we went [to Wadena] they promised to break land and help with work if your father would only come here and stay there but escept a small garden patch they never did. Your father went to Parker Prairie to preach and there saw boys 18 years old who had never seen a minister nor a church, he said they were a rough lot—I traveled with the supply wagon belonging to a lumbering camp with six or 8 rough looking men but I heard not a swear nor unbecoming word from any.

The surface men on the track were very kind in taking me on the hand car—and would stop and wait when they saw me leaving my horse on the prairie—those men too were quietly polite to me—perfect gentlemen— even the Scandinavians to whom I could not speak a word were good about making a place for me on their big sleighs—I felt fortunate when a lady lent me a saddle—then I went everywhere on horseback—leaving the baby with your father—the horse could go often where a sleigh could not—one great blessing in that place was no saloons—no liquor—and I always felt safe because I was not any afraid of the Indians who came occasionally prowling around.

Sabbath (the day of rest) was just the hardest day of all the week the horse had to be fed & watered, the cow fed & milked then breakfast and feeding 20 hens—then wash & dress all the five children and myself and carry the baby to church service—at the close of Sunday school, after that we went home to start fires and often 3 or 4 men who were batching on the prairie would invite themselves to dinner with us and when Monday morning came, "The cupboard was bare." (With all our scarcity of food I never got into debt—got nothing at the store I could not pay [for]) . . .

When I think of those days I am puzzled to know where I got the energy because I had a voluminous correspondence to keep going at the same time and keep the children neat and clean. I think the missionary's wife on the frontier has the hardest time—she seldom sees any ladies—has to work at whatever has to be done whether she is fit for it or not—keep cheerful to be a companion to her husband and never complain—be ready to entertain all and believe [that] drudgery [is] amusement if she can—cut out [seamstress] patterns at the most inconvenient times for those who want them, know receipts [recipes] for doing everything and be ready to do them verily, her education and acquirements need to be wide reaching to be a successful helpmeet to the missionary and when we read of missionaries doing great things in different parts of the world, I think of the one not mentioned who made it possible for him to do great things. . . . I don't regret that experience—it widened my sympathies of all missionary workers—specially the poor overworked wives. I hope none of my daughters will ever be missionaries wives now I am done.

Your loving mother
M. C. Kerr

Robert Kerr and Family papers, MNHS

***

[The Bethany Home in north Minneapolis was founded in 1879 with the objectives of "the promotion of moral purity, helping the tempted, saving the fallen, and providing a home for erring women who manifested a desire to return to the paths of virtue." Contributions came from well-off people in the community. An annual report listed donations, including these:]

Mrs. Scott, nine napkins, one tablecloth, one sheet; Mrs. H. C. Webb, trimmed hat; Mrs. Mattison, 1 beaver cloak, 1 velvet cloak, 1 black cashmere dress, 1 gingham dress, 1 alpaca dress, 2 skirts; young ladies of Plymouth church, basket of grapes; a friend, underwear; Mrs. Oscar C. Griffith, package of choice baby clothes; Mrs. G. White, 25 cents; D. Morrison, 1 load hard wood, two loads pine; Mrs. Frank Holmes, 4 copies Gospel Songs; H. G. Milley, load of ice; Mrs. Clark, syrup can; W. A. Sampson, 10 pounds fresh fish; Mrs. Hirst, sauerkraut; Hon. William W. McNair, valuable legal services; Mr. Arnold, one peck of beans.

[The report, obviously written by a woman, also included this diatribe against the men who "lead these women into sin":]

Where are the men that make them what they [the women] are? Ah! where are they not? Go find them in our business marts, in drawing rooms, side by side with pure young girls; in churches; at all places of entertainment, and welcomed to the firesides of good women, who would avoid any contact with their sinning sisters, as they would the plague or leprosy. How many calls would have been made on New Year's day, if, before starting out with their gay teams on their merry ride, each man, young and old, had been required to furnish a certificate of his unblemished moral purity? Who will answer? We cannot tell, but over all, was the all seeing eye of the God of purity, that took account, and we may be sure. He will in no wise clear the guilty. But on that same bright day when nature rejoiced at the birth of the "New Year," there were, in darkened houses, and in private rooms in different parts of our city, women whom some of these may, it may be, had made outcasts, or had helped to encourage them in sinful lives, and rendered them unfit for association with their lady friends or any decent women. Of all the mean things that man has ever done, this outrage of womanhood is the meanest, the most dastardly. And yet these same men will talk, most eloquently, of how they dread to see women take any part in public affairs lest their delicacy and loveliness may be impaired. They do well to dread the time, for which God is surely preparing her, when woman shall have the right to aid in making and enforcing the laws that govern her, for just so soon will this wrong be righted, and this one-sided way of dealing with a two-sided crime will become a thing of the past.

***

[The following proves there really was an Ingalls family in Walnut Grove. The reference is to Charles Ingalls, father of Laura who wrote the "Little House on the Prairie" books. From the church records of a Walnut Grove, Minnesota, church:]

MARCH 3, 1879

Minutes of a business meeting

Met according to notice meeting called to order by John Ensign A Swanheim was apointed clerk pro tem church procede to the election of trustee Charles Ingalls was elected trustee for three years from March 3, 1879. moved seconded and carried that adjourn.

A. Smith, clerk

Congregational Conference of Minnesota papers, MNHS

***

The atmosphere in Minnesota in the winter is like a wine, so exhilarating in its effects on the system; while its extreme dryness and elasticity prevents any discomfort from the cold which is such a bug-bear to many. The extreme cold does not last but for a few days. . . . Why, laboring men in the lumber districts north of St. Paul perform their work without overcoats, and frequently, and indeed commonly, without a coat of any kind, simply in their shirt-sleeves; nor need this seem incredible, as in a dry, cold climate the body maintains a much greater amount of animal heat, and if exercise is had, a profuse perspiration may be easily induced, and a fine glow of health inspired; with the extremities warm, sensitive, and throbbing with life.

Minnesota, Its Character and Climate, 1871

Minnesota may be said to excel any portion of the Union in a healthy and invigorating climate.

State Board of Immigration pamphlet, 1878

NEWSPAPER CLIPPINGS

The state fish commissioners have stocked Lake Minnetonka with the young salmon furnished to this state by the government of the United States. The waters of the Red River valley and intermediate points have also been supplied. About one-half of the salmon-fry in charge of the commissioners have already been distributed.

St. Paul Daily Pioneer Press, June 1, 1875

A neatly painted barrel filled with ice water was yesterday placed in front of Gale & Co.'s, where all who desire may hereafter refresh themselves. The act is very commendable.

Minneapolis Tribune, June 5, 1875

Wild plums of the very choicest quality, almost equal to the favored tame varieties, are selling in this market at the reasonable price of a dollar and a quarter per bushel. This moderate sum should introduce this fruit into all of our families.

Minneapolis Tribune, September 2, 1875

A few weeks since Charlotte Elizabeth Dyring, about to become a mother, was taken to the Cottage Hospital, where at the earnest solicitation of one or two citizens, she was finally permitted to remain. Sunday last, Ole Olstrom returned from the pineries, at once visited the hospital, where to his surprise he found that he was the father of a bright baby, eight days old, which on that afternoon was to be baptized by Dr. Knickerbacker. After a little persuasion he concluded to marry the unfortunate girl whom he had so wronged, and the marriage ceremony was performed by Dr. Knickerbacker just previous to the baptism.

Minneapolis Tribune, June 8, 1875

One hundred and thirteen prairie schooners passed by the office of the Luverne Herald during five days of last week.

St. Paul Daily Globe, May 9, 1876

An emigrant passed through Worthington the other day with his family and effects, the wagon being drawn by three cows and a heifer.

Minneapolis Tribune, March 9, 1878

A company of German emigrants camped at Maple Plain on Wednesday night, and during the night a little child attached to the colony sickened and died. Yesterday morning the remains of the little one were deposited in the burial ground at Maple Plain, and the train moved onward to its destination.

Minneapolis Tribune, April 28, 1876

The Taylor's Falls Journal says there has been upwards of twelve thousand acres of land entered in that county within the last three years, for the purpose of raising cranberries.

St. Paul Daily Dispatch, April 12, 1875

A Frenchman, his wife and six children, ranging from two to eight years old, arrived at the St. Paul & Pacific depot night-before last. They were penniless and entirely unable to speak the English language. They children, all of which looked as near alike as two peas, slept on a piece of carpeting in the ladies waiting room during the entire night.

Minneapolis Tribune, March 21, 1875

Street Nomenclature. A committee of gentlemen from the City Councils, Board of Trade, with City Engineer Corson have had under consideration a plan for naming the streets and numbering the houses in the new city [Minneapolis], that is thought to embody the best features of that now in New York as well as Philadelphia. The streets are to be named according to the New York plan in the upper part of that city and the houses numbered on the plan adopted in Philadelphia. It is proposed to call streets running from the river, east or west, avenues, and those running parallel with the river, streets. The city will be divided as follows: All that part of Minneapolis (present) north of say Hennepin avenue to be called Northwest Minneapolis; all that south to be called Southwest. On the other side of the river, taking, for instance, Bay street for the dividing line, that part north will be Northeast Minneapolis, and that part south will be Southeast Minneapolis.

Minneapolis Tribune, February 15, 1872

Emigrant teams filled with women and children, and followed by large droves of cattle, colts, etc., are daily passing through this place bound west, where the best lands in the world are to be had at a cost of about $15 for a quarter section.

St. Paul Daily Pioneer, May 24, 1870

A party of thirty-one Finns, young and old, arrived over the Milwaukee road from Wisconsin, in this city last evening. They embarked on the train for Cokato, to seek their fortune. They look hardy.

St. Paul Daily Dispatch, May 20, 1874

The town of Marshall, started a year ago, has 12 stores, 3 blacksmith shops, 1 wagon shop, 3 lumber yards, 2 hotels, 1 livery stable, 1 printing office, a grist mill, and churches, a school house, and residences enough to number one hundred buildings.

St. Paul Daily Dispatch, November 3, 1873

Logjam on the St. Croix River, at Taylors Falls, 1884. *MNHS*

1880s

These were boom years. Heavy immigration consisted mostly of Scandinavians, Poles, Bohemians, Czechs, and Slovaks. Lumbering became a big business; lumbermen from the East were attracted to Minnesota. Steam power and machinery speeded up the exhaustion of the forests. Railroad lines to the Red River Valley made it easy for settlers to go west and for farmers to get crops to market. The Knights of Labor made efforts on behalf of unionism. The Pillsbury A Mill in Minneapolis became the largest flour mill in the world. The first iron ore was shipped in 1884; soon there was a proliferation of iron-mining companies. Diphtheria epidemics ravaged whole communities. A reformatory for young men opened in St. Cloud in 1889. →

C. J. BIRKEBAK

"The [Red River Valley] area is very, very thinly settled so that many times one cannot see a single human home."

When C. J. was born in Denmark in 1838, he was named Chris Jorgenson. His father was Jorgen Hansen, and tradition was to take the father's first name and add "son" to it to form a new last name. But when he came to Minnesota in 1874, he settled among Danes near Hutchinson and found an overabundance of people named Jorgenson. He was tired of being confused with other Jorgensons. So he changed his name to C. J. Birkebak, borrowing the name of the Danish farming community where he grew up. He was forty-three years old, a farmer, and the father of five children when he kept a diary in 1881. Here are some of his observations, translated from the Danish, of his train trip to the Red River Valley. The first page notes, "In each railroad car there is a sign which says, 'Beware of Satchel Thieves, and Pickpockets and Confidence Men.'"

On the first of December I left my home in the morning at eight o'clock to go to St. Paul, and from there by railroad up through the Red River Valley to look at the farm land there. I arrived at St. Paul that evening, at eight o'clock, but had to stay over until the next day's evening [until] eight-fifteen in the evening when a train would leave for the Valley. I had a free pass for this trip up there and I am right now on the train, ready to leave! We were in Fergus Falls the next morning at six o'clock. Here the landscape started to be level and flat, as flat as a pancake, so one could see far, far ahead! There were occasional huts that looked very much like haystacks and some looked like piles of dirt—or whatever it was. [He apparently saw sod houses.] Here is good farming land, if only they had something to burn [for fuel]! . . .

The man who lived near Glyndon, that I met on the train, had four thousand acres of wheat—one thousand acres on one piece and three thousand acres on another. I saw the land that lay right up to the railroad track and

C. J. Birkebak. *Danish-American Fellowship & Center*

it was very even, and without the least interruption. He had raised twenty bushels per acre, which amounts to sixty thousand bushels of wheat, and he sold it for $1.05 a bushel. He kept six men the year around at $25.00 a month, and in the harvest he had eighty men for two months for $2.00 per day. How many horses he kept, I did not find out because the time was short . . .

The 6th of December began as a very nice day but soon it began to snow and to snow real hard, and this was uncomfortable for me because today I planned to go out and look at some land, but it could also be useful to me to see how these snowstorms act up in this corner of the earth. I certainly hope that it soon will be good weather again, and it already seems to be tapering off with the snow. Last night I stayed with some Swedish people. The bed was not good, but the food was very

fine and cheap—only 60¢. Wages here about during the summer and in the spring months is $18.00 [a month], and during the harvest it is $35.00, and then from the harvest to winter it is $25.00 a month, and during threshing time the wages are $2.00 a day. The immigrants and other working people can hardly get off the train and walk across the street before there is someone after them that wants to hire them . . .

The area is very, very thinly settled so that many times one cannot see a single human home. We arrived at Hallock at about three-thirty so I took a walk to the north of the town, along the railroad. . . . The railroad tracks are for the most part straight, so one can see the train coming and going in a many, many mile distance. Yes, when one sees a train coming one may wait as much as a half hour before it arrives and one can see the tracks and the

Sod house in Lac qui Parle County, about 1880. *MNHS*

right of way and the telegraph wires so far until they both just disappear in the far distance. The land around here is, for the most, already been bought up, but about six miles to the east on what is a good high land with small woods on it that will give enough wood, at least this is what the agent tells me.

The drinking water here is very poor, and to all good luck the population here is mostly Norwegians, Swedes and Germans, and they will of course not drink water, but whisky and beer, so they do not notice the need of good water very much as sober people might do. I am lodging here in a saloon that is owned by a Swede whose name is Solberg. They drank and played very good but this did not give me any pleasure . . .

We reached Breckenridge at 11:30 P.M., which is a large town, a larger town than I had thought it would be. Here I must stop for the night. I had not thought I would have to do that. The town people here must be very rich because here a meal costs a half dollar and in St. Paul it was only 25¢. One would think that in Breckenridge the things that it takes to make a meal would be much cheaper than in St. Paul. A night's lodging and breakfast cost 75¢. Red River goes here, headed north and westerly, and of course surrounded with a rim of woods. I was down to take a look at the river and found it to be a very fast flowing stream, which was not even frozen at all because of the rapid flow of the water. . . . At 7:40 I was on the train again, on my way home with thoughts of what the iron horse can do. Breckenridge is a beautiful little town, although it is expensive to live in . . .

[Somewhere in the area of Morris or Hancock] Here there is a cemetery plot in this stretch. I cannot understand how in the world that they can find anybody to bury here for it is miles to any place where people live.

[Later that year Birkebak visited Chicago and wrote:]

It is large and majestic—buildings four to six stories high—such a concentration of wealth gathered in one place is shocking to think about. One must wonder about what men have done in such a short time. Chicago must be about one hundred years old, St. Paul forty-three years, and Minneapolis is certainly not over thirty years old, and now they are all large, splendid cities. St. Paul with a population of forty thousand people, Minneapolis with forty-five or fifty thousand, and Chicago has probably more than the aforementioned two cities. Cities grow out of the earth here in America.

[Birkebak wasn't far off. Official census figures from 1880: St. Paul, 41,473; Minneapolis, 46,887, and Chicago, 503,185. But Minneapolis inflated its figures; St. Paul was still the larger of the two.]

Danish-American Fellowship & Center, Minneapolis

THE CHRISTIE FAMILY

*"I can tell you that I am **determined** on having an education, and if I keep my health I will have one if it takes me ten years or more."*

James Christie was born in the industrial city of Dundee, Scotland, in 1811. He worked in the mills as a master spinner in Scotland and Ireland. Dissatisfied with what he could provide his family, he came to the United States in 1846 and settled in southern Wisconsin and later Minnesota. He lived with his son David in Minnesota's Blue Earth County from 1864 to 1885. He had five children (William, Thomas, Sarah, Alexander, and David)—and outlived three wives. He died in 1890. These excerpts follow the family from 1847 into the 1880s.

On February 3, 1847, the year after they came to America, James penned to his wife, Eliza, his reasons for the family leaving Ireland. Eliza was still on the east coast of the United States when he went to Wisconsin to clear their land:

I have always told you that it was for the sake of our children that I would take upon me the toils of a settler's life and if God spares them, how much easier it will be for me to die, knowing that they are independent. We will each of us have 40 acres of good land and my 40 will still be there when I am gone Not [as if] working in a mill, when you die it is likely that you will leave a legacy of debt to your children and the same eternal round of slavery which has been your own lot.

[In later years his sons Thomas and Alexander rejoiced that their father had made the decision to leave all that was familiar and the people dear to him. Thomas Christie wrote to his sister, Sarah, on September 29, 1901, after he visited Ireland:]

How much we owe to him for having brought us away from the Old world to the New! I shall never cease to be grateful to him for that. That was my chief thought when I visited the old mill in Ireland and saw the workers. "Thank God and the wise father, we were saved from this!" I could hardly breathe for dust in the "heckling" room [the room where

Sarah Christie, about 1861. *MNHS*

169

flax was finished by machine and by hand and which was filled with fine dust that caused lung problems], I wondered how father could have lived, day by day, year in and year out in that polluted air. He was such a grand and wonderful man, with a personal history such as none of his children have been called to go through. As the years go by I love and honor him more and more. With a thousand advantages and blessings that were denied to him, it will be well for us if we do half as good work as he did.

[And Alexander, working in Washington as a mathematician for the government, wrote to his brother David in Minnesota, April 17, 1881:]

Am I in favor of farming? My life here has made me realize the blessings of a piece of land, and independence. I tell you I never appreciated, before coming East, and I know you can not appreciate what Father and his brothers did for us all when they brought us out of bondage into the Wilds of Wisconsin. I tell you I see every day how the rich grind the poor, how men clothed with a little brief authority make their fellow men

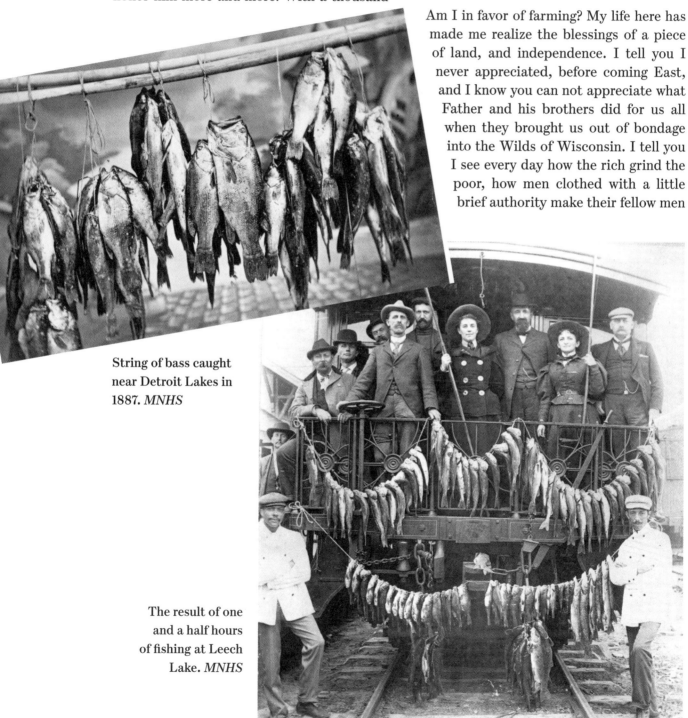

String of bass caught near Detroit Lakes in 1887. *MNHS*

The result of one and a half hours of fishing at Leech Lake. *MNHS* cringe and tremble for their bread. Even here in America—what must it have been in Britain and in Ireland? I am at war with my surroundings. I may say nothing, but I keep up a mighty thinking all the same. If I am of the fortunate few, who have little tyranny to bear, I am not at peace while the man at my elbow is under the iron heel. I would never advise that your boys look foreward to mingling in this mighty seething sea of struggling humanity. Let us give them education and a chance to see the world, but for Godsake give them land free from incumbrence and teach them how to keep it so and be contented.

[James Christie was not an educated man, but he read widely and passed on to his children a love of books and study. Here his daughter,

Bessie Stevens, Sarah Christie's daughter, in 1888 at age eight and a half. *MNHS*

Lake Calhoun, about 1889. *MNHS*

Sarah, a student at Fox Lake Seminary in Wisconsin, heatedly wrote to him about the value of education for women:]

FOX LAKE, WIS. NOV. 11TH 1862
My Dear Father,
Yours of the 15th came on Saturday night and now I sit down to answer it. In the first place I am well and enjoying vacation to the best of my ability . . .

You think that I cannot come [to college] any more than this term. Well if you cannot afford it I am agreeable to it—that I should come home. Though it will be very hard for me to leave my Studies here and all the Friends whom I have become acquainted with. But I know that you have spent more now on me coming here than you can well afford and a great deal more than I deserve. . . . The term closes sometime in January and then I will come home to stay, I suppose, and teach again in our District—if they will give me enough wages, for I want to get as much as possible, and I will then teach till I get enough to pay you, and to give me a start to come up here again.

I suppose that you will laugh at the Idea of me saving money to go to school with. But I can tell you that I am determined on having an education, and if I keep my health I will have one if it takes me ten years or more, to earn money for it. I will first take this College Course and then take a higher such as Appleton [Lawrence College in Appleton,

Stillwater, 1885. *MNHS*

172

Wisconsin] can give. It will take a great many years, I expect, and hard work too. But when I see the well educated Ladies and gentlemen here to be examined, Graduates from Appleton and the Eastern Colleges, I feel that the good which can be done with an education, not to speak of the pleasure which it gives to the possessor, will more than pay for the expense, time, and hard work expended in getting it. Education gives power for good which money can not give, and as God has given us these intellectual powers, it is our duty to cultivate them to their utmost extent and to use them for the means of doing the greatest good to our fellow creatures. I think therefore that it is my duty as well as the duty of others to improve as much as possible, and to cultivate my mind to be a Teacher to others. It is my highest ambition in this world, and if I keep strength and health, I am to have an education if I am thirty years of age before it is finished.

You speak of Algebra as being a "masculine attainment." I cannot see as it is any more that than a "Feminine attainment." Now I cannot see how it is that men will think that they are any better fitted for the duties of life than women and that their powers are stronger. They think that they are a little bit more elevated and look at everything from a higher place, and are, in fact, a few inches taller. But it is them who keep women where they are. It is the education which a woman gets and the false Ideas that are crammed into them, that keep women where they are. Now I believe that the weakness of women lies in their education. They have the same powers given them that is given to man and if they were cultivated and strengthened, in the same way and Direction, woman would be just as able to make her way through life as man is. To be sure, there would be a great many who could not. But let each have a fair trial and those who are not able for it, let them fall back to their old place. It really made me vexed

when you said that Algebra was a "Masculine attainment," like as if I could not learn it as well as any "Masculine" I ever saw and maybe a good deal better than some, without killing me either. It or any other study will only do me great good by disciplining my mind and developing it . . .

I guess that if the "Masculines" got the same teaching and the same ideas crammed into them which the "Femmines" get about their not being anybody, they would be just as helpless, weak, vain, miserable things as the generality of Females are. Once in a while you do see a real, true strong, independent woman, but it is very seldom . . .

I am glad that you are willing that Willie should give me money for the private singing lessons. I will write and tell him to send it to me when he gets his next pay. I have not time to write more as I have to write to Sandy and Dave. So I hope that this will find you all as usual. Give my love to Mother and the boys and to all Friends . . .

Your loving daughter,
Sarah J. Christie

[Sarah got her way. She finished her education and taught at Carleton College in Northfield, Minnesota, and Wheaton College, Wheaton, Illinois. She was single until she was thirty-five, when she married William Stevens, a widower with four children living in Rapidan Township, Blue Earth County. After their marriage, she was elected county superintendent of education. Part of William Stevens's October 5, 1878, letter to her told of a diphtheria epidemic:]

Since you left here they are having the Diptheria in Mankato and Vicinity it seems to be assuming a lighter form in the City there is a Family near Eagle Lake that seven died when the fourth one died the Mother left the house & has not been heard of since the People are raking the Lake for her boddy they think that her reason [her mind] must have been Dethroned & She drowned herself. I heard in Mankato to-day that Doctor Snow had treated over Sixty Cases Without loosing one Patient—that is a Feather in his Cap.

[Two years later, Sarah's brother William lost three of his sons to diphtheria in ten days of July 1880. James, seven, died on July 18; David, eleven, on July 25, and Thomas, six, on July 27. Their father wrote of it to his brother Alexander on August 25, 1880:]

I will now try to tell just how it is with us. We cannot forget our Boys, and as you say it seems to be an unfortunate thing for us that they have been taken from us. It may be selfish of us to think and feel about it as we do. But when all things are looked at in all ways in connection with their sickness, it makes me feel as though it were a loss time will never make ammends for. Although I know they are in just such a world as you describe, and cared for in Love and wisdom far superior to mine yet I feel as though we had been robbed of them in a way that will tell against us through all our earth life.

At one time I had despaired of getting my grain cared for at all, for we are yet "Taboo" by a great many of our nebors. . . . Indeed it is only since the wet time has set in . . . that I have been able to say I was capable of doing any thing like a days work. Mary [his wife] has too been in a rather poor way, and it is even worse for her than for me for she must be in the house and miss the lads more than I do.

The [other] Children are in good health, that is, gaining. Willie's mouth inside is pitted with the disease and he is yet unable to do much labor of any kind, he eats meat and everything he likes, such as beef, and cheese, rice and milk, bread and butter, and cooked fruit to an alarming extent and I suppose he may soon be strong again . . .

[William Christie lost another child to diphtheria in 1901. She was twenty-two-year-old Elizabeth. Family letters indicate that he never recovered from the depression of losing four of his eleven children to diphtheria.

Despite the losses, the Christie family grew and prospered. James reached his goal. His dream, he wrote to his son Thomas in 1885, "was to be no man's Slave, [and] I have attained it."]

James C. Christie and Family papers, and
Thomas C. Christie and Family papers,
MNHS

THE DOCTORS MAYO

Medicine in the mid-1880s was primitive, even compared with medicine at the turn of the twentieth century. In the 1850s few scientific procedures or instruments were available. The stethoscope was new. The clinical thermometer had not been invented. Infant mortality was so high that people could only hope that a baby would live. Surgeons washed their hands after an operation, not before, and their ability was judged by the speed they could saw through bones. It was under those conditions that William W. Mayo started as a frontier doctor in Minnesota in the 1850s. His sons, Charlie and Will, followed as physicians in the 1880s and turned the little town of Rochester, Minnesota, into one of the greatest medical centers in the world. The Rochester newspapers chronicled some of their advances:

MNHS

Dr. W. W. Mayo and young family. *Mayo Clinic Archives*

The Doctors Mayo: Charlie, W. W., and Will. *Mayo Clinic Archives*

Dr. W. W. Mayo, assisted by Drs. Bowers, Nichols and Sanborn, removed a tumor of a cancerous nature from the cheek of Mrs. J. Hickox, Wednesday. It was situated at the bottom of the right ear, and an artery ran through the base of it. The operation was a very delicate and dangerous one to perform, but under Dr. Mayo's skillful hands it was safely done, and Mrs. Hickox is doing well.

Rochester Record and Union, April 23, 1880

Dr. Mayo removed a tumor from the top of D. F. Wilcox's head, Friday morning. The tumor was eating through the bone, and had eaten through one layer. The operation was successful.

Rochester Record and Union, July 28, 1882

Of all the noble works of the charitable, none is nobler than the erection and maintenance of a free hospital, in which all in need of medical attendance may obtain it, and with it the best care and attention. The Sisters of St. Francis in this city are now erecting such an institution, and pushing it to completion as rapidly as possible. The basement is already completed, and the brick work has been commenced.

Rochester Record and Union, October 12, 1888

A son of Ole Nelson of Rock Dell, who has been studying medicine at the State University, was taken ill recently with inflammation of the bowels, and was very low, when an operation was performed by the Drs. Mayo, assisted by Dr. Witherstine. A gangrenous portion of the bowel was removed, and the patient is well on the road to recovery. This is the eighth successful operation of this character made by the Drs. Mayo.

Rochester Record and Union, July 26, 1889

Tuesday afternoon, Mr. Sumner Snow of Farmington, was kicked by a vicious stallion, thrown down and stamped upon by the brute, injuring him very seriously. The hoof struck him in the hip causing a compound fracture of the hip bone and cutting a hole into his abdomen. The Drs. Mayo were summoned, Wednesday morning, and reduced the fracture. The hip bone had to be wired together with silver wire as the muscles drew

A train with immigrants. *MNHS*

the sections apart. He was also badly cut and bruised by the stamping. He will recover.

Rochester Record and Union, August 16, 1889

There appears in the last number of the Annals of Surgery, the leading medical journal of the country, published in New York and London simultaneously, clinical reports of three surgical operations performed at St. Mary's Hospital by Drs. W. J. and C. H. Mayo of this city.

Rochester Record and Union, January 18, 1895

Of the work done at the great institution which has made Rochester famous throughout the world, Dr. Bernays [of St. Louis, a leading surgeon] says he is convinced that at St. Mary's hospital more than any other place, surgery is being done in an artistic way, and, on the basis of a more scientific ante-operative examination than at any other place in America. He states that his party witnessed 104 operations during the few days stay in Rochester, every one of which was successful. He says: "I have learned by observation that patients operated on by the Mayos scarcely ever die, and I know that the mortality following their work is getting lower year by year, until now it seems almost impossible to reduce it still further."

Rochester Post and Record, April 27, 1906

WORKING GIRLS

After the Civil War, increasing numbers of young, single women left home to find jobs, many of them in big cities. They wanted both money and independence. Minnesota's Bureau of Labor estimated that in the 1880s the average working woman in Minneapolis was paid about $3 or $4 a week. At the same time, the cost of room and board ran about $6 a week. The cheapest boardinghouses charged from $2.50 to $3.50 a week. Many of the working women rented rooms together to keep down costs. Some had to go back to the farm; some became prostitutes.

Average Weekly Wages of Wage-Earning Women [1888]

HOTELS		RESTAURANTS			
Dining Room	3.55	Dish Washers	3.83	Table Girls	5.10
Laundry	3.56	Laundry Help	4.00	Buttonhole Makers	7.05
Chamber Maids	3.71	Assistant Cooks	5.50		
Dish Washers	3.91			OVERALLS AND SHIRTS	
Cooks	4.37			Pressers	5.66
Assistant Cooks	3.33	BOOT AND SHOE FACTORIES		Finishers	5.17
Pastry Cooks	4.00	Stitchers	7.75	Sewers	5.16
Common Help	2.25	Machine Operators	6.50	Pant Makers	5.84
House Domestics	2.79	Fitters	5.84	Shirt Makers	3.66
		Vampers	8.50	Machine Operators	5.53
		Lining Makers	7.75		

Average Weekly Wages of Wage-Earning Women [1888] continued

BOOK BINDERIES
Copy Holders 6.50
Folders 4.72
Collators 6.75
Sewers 4.93
Gatherers 5.33
Binders 5.71

FURS
Sewers 5.61
Finishers 7.35

LAUNDRIES
Starchers 5.55
Ironers 5.47
Manglers 5.83
Washers 5.89
Sorters 5.83
Machine Operators . . . 6.20

CRACKERS AND CONFECTIONERY
Crackers Packers 3.87
Candy Packers 3.25

Candy Wrappers 4.10
Candy Rollers 3.75

CIGARS
Bunch Breakers 5.72
Bunch Rollers 8.00
Strippers 3.00

First Biennial Report of the
Bureau of Labor Statistics

[Prostitution was semilegal in Minneapolis from the 1870s through 1910. Prostitutes paid monthly fines to the municipal court and were allowed to work in certain districts. A newspaper reporter wrote of them:]

Not long ago I overheard a woman belonging to the large class of outcasts who swarm our streets. She and a companion were on a shopping tour, and their talk turned on the life of working girls. "I used to be a respectable working girl myself," she said. "I tried for three years to support life on the wages I was paid as cashier in a big store. It didn't seem as if anybody cared what became of me. The patrons of the store disdained to speak a kind word to me because I was a working girl. There were temptations on every side. So I gave up the struggle at last, and it always makes me shiver, to see a girl dying by inches in these stores. They call me unworthy of any decent person's notice now, but I don't starve and freeze since I quit being respectable," was her story and probably many others of her class could tell the same sort of tale.

In large stores I found the wages of cashiers to range from $6 to $8 per week. Of course, the absence of evening work makes their life more pleasant than it otherwise would be.

St. Paul Globe, September 2, 1888

[The Minnesota Bureau of Labor Statistics in 1888 interviewed people who employed domestic help and found a "spirit of general dissatisfaction." Opinions included:]

"Girls want to go out every night in the week, or else have a houseful of company, and I will not allow them to do either."

"Girls not cleanly."

"Some girls take as much interest in the management of a house as the mistress herself. I had one servant whom I could leave in charge of the house for a whole summer. She would see that everything was rightly cared for and in its place. She staid two years; I paid her $3.00 a week."

"Girls must prepare three meals on Sunday, and can only go out every other Sunday afternoon for a short time."

"Do not think a girl ought to be allowed to use the front door."

"Looking after the girls—I keep two—takes so much time that none is left for social duties."

"No girl seems willing to work for less than $3.00 per week. There used to be girls who would accept $2.00 and $2.50 per week, but they are disappearing."

"A girl broke a vase worth $15.00 and there was no way of making her pay for it. That is only one of many instances. Domestics spoil

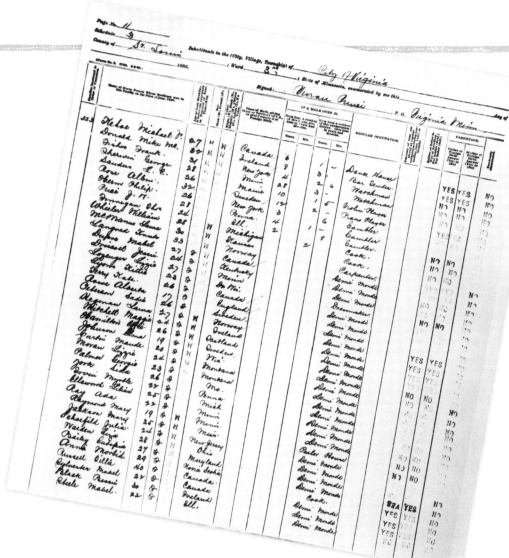

1880 Census of Virginia, Minnesota, address—apparently a house of prostitution—that included a bartender, violin player, piano player, gamblers, and demi-mondes (prostitutes). This is just part of the page, showing a few of the prostitutes. *MNHS*

and break costly articles, but their wages must go on just the same, and their employer suffers the loss."

"I think that many women would be more kind and friendly, but it spoils the girls, gives them false notions about their place."

"I don't think that employers always use girls fairly. I have had girls work for me who have been cheated out of their wages and starved and overworked by people who could abundantly afford to do what is right by their servants. When people treat girls in that way it's no wonder that girls are careless and hateful."

"I give the girls my old party dresses in addition to their wages. It keeps them in good humor."

First Biennial Report of the Bureau of Labor Statistics

The undersigned informs the public, that after a long illness, she is able to attend old and new customers, at her barbershop, next door to the railroad crossing on First street north. Having been for thirty years in the business she hopes to give satisfaction. Prices: hair cutting, 15 cents; shaving, 10 cents; 14 shaves for one dollar; children's hair cutting, 10 cents. Francis Shubiger.

Minneapolis Tribune, April 1, 1881

[On the length of skirts of "waiter girls" at a St. Paul restaurant:]

Some wear slippers and striped stockings, but most of them have plain, high-top shoes and mild-colored stockings. This last feature is more noticeable on account of the shortness of their skirts, which seem to grow shorter every

Bedroom of the Burbank-Livingston-Griggs house, St. Paul, 1884. *MNHS*

year. Probably the wearers are becoming more saving, and so purchase less quantity of cloth. When I first visited St. Paul several years ago the skirts were of regulation length. Year before last they had got up to their ankles, last year to the shoe-tops, and this year about an inch or two above the shoe-tops. So when a [female] waiter at a few tables ahead bends forward when reaching for a dish on the opposite side of the table, one finds it necessary to study the frescoed work on the ceiling. If the shortness continues to grow I will be afraid to venture here in a few years.

St. Paul Pioneer Press, January 31, 1887

Engaged Girls. Fashion has decreed a change in this matter. The engaged couples of 1881 are not commanded to hide their endearments under a bushel. They may even kiss in company if they are chaste about it. I saw a daughter of one of the wealthiest and most refined of our families touch lips with her husband-to-be before at least a hundred persons in a picture-room of the academy of design the other day. He had been out of town for a week, I was told, and their meeting here was by chance. She greeted him affectionately, but without ado, and put up her mouth in the most self-possessed way imaginable. He was not so cool about it; yet he gave her a smacking salute with a good grace, right in the presence of his future mother-in-law. The girl did not blush nor simper. Such a public kiss would have been scandalous in March 1880; but in 1881 it is fashionable, and therefore proper.

Minneapolis Tribune, April 3, 1881

[The First Methodist Church of Minneapolis had a women's group that had as its object "the relief of worthy poor." These were the days before public charity. Among the minutes of this Young Ladies Home Mission was this:]

DEC. 30, 1885
The attention of the Society was called to the case of a very worthy young man who met with a most unfortunate accident in falling from a

building, and at present is under treatment at one of the hospitals and has no money to pay his board which amounts to $4 per week. The Pres. stated that if the Society would agree with pay ½, provision could be made for the other ½. A motion was made & carried to give an entertainment in the near future for the benefit of the young man, and at present to take from the Treas. and replenish when the entertainment is given. Various kinds of entertainments were discussed, but nothing decided on.

Hattie Plummer
Sect'y

Albert Graber and Family papers, MNHS

JOHN McGAUGHEY

"To make industrial and moral worth, not wealth, the true standard of individual and national greatness."

When a workman was injured in the 1880s the government did not step in to care for him or his family. This letter is the closest thing there was to workman's compensation.

Chicago, Milwaukee and St. Paul Railroad
Special Agent's Office
J. A. Chandler, General Agent
ST. PAUL, SEPT. 13TH 1880
[To] C. H. Prior, Esq., Supt
Dear Sir:
The bearer, Mr. McGaughey, is the unfortunate brakeman who lost an arm on the Minn. Eastern last winter. He is now able to work (at anything that a man with only one arm can do)—has himself and a wife to support—and is entitled to consideration.

Can you put him in the way of earning an honest living?
Resp[ectfully]
J. A. Chandler

[John McGaughey went on to important posts in union work and was deputy commissioner of labor statistics for the state of Minnesota. Among his papers are demands from workers of the Minneapolis Street Railway Company, who struck in 1889 because their wages were reduced two cents an hour. The strike was violent; on one occasion a crowd of about ten thousand overturned streetcars and destroyed track. The demands included:]

We, the employes, ask the Minneapolis Street Railway company to put Closets [water closets, that is, bathrooms] at the end of each line where the City does not object to the same.

We, the employes, ask the Minneapolis Street Railway Company to sell the Regulation Caps to its employes at cost.

We, the employes, ask the Minneapolis Street Railway Company, to erase all black marks [for bad conduct] once each year.

[The streetcar company responded by demanding that employees sign contracts pledging themselves not to join a labor organization. The company eventually retreated from the stand (and thus recognized unionism) but the workers never got back their two cents.

McGaughey also saved the preamble to the 1893 constitution of the Knights of Labor, a national group that promoted unionism, took an interest in cooperatives, and worked for recognition of labor by industry and the public. Here are some of the goals:]

To make industrial and moral worth, not wealth, the true standard of individual and national greatness.

The prohibition by law of the employment of children under fifteen years of age; the compulsory attendance at school for at least ten months in the year of all children between the ages of seven and fifteen years; and the furnishing at the expense of the State of free text books.

The recognition, by incorporation, of orders and other associations organized by the workers to improve their condition and to protect their rights.

The adoption of measures providing for

Streetcar in Minneapolis, 1889. *Minneapolis Public Library*

the health and safety of those engaged in mining, manufacturing and building industries, and for indemnification to those engaged therein for injuries received through lack of necessary safeguards.

That a graduated tax on incomes and inheritances be levied.

That the government shall obtain possession, under the right of eminent domain, of all telegraphs, telephones and railroads; and that hereafter no charter or license be issued to any corporation for construction or operation of any means of transporting intelligence, passengers or freight.

And while making the foregoing demands upon the State and National Governments, we will endeavor to associate our own labors:

To secure for both sexes equal rights.

To gain some of the benefits of labor-saving machinery by a gradual reduction of the hours of labor to eight per day.

To persuade employers to agree to arbitrate all differences which may arise between them and their employes, in order that the bonds of sympathy may be strengthened and that strikes may be rendered unneessary.

John P. McGaughey papers, MNHS

***

LOST—Strayed from the banks of Lake Calhoun, a bay horse. A liberal reward will be paid for the return to Ensign's stable.

STOLEN OR STRAYED—From my farm at Lake Harriet, two red setter pups. Suitable reward for their return. Charles Reeve. City Bank.

Minneapolis Tribune, May 17, 1881

REES PRICE

"There has been suffering that no one will ever know on the frontiers for the newspapers will take good care never to mention for it would stop immigration."

An account of a miserable winter, from Rees Price, a homesteader near Tracy, Minnesota:

Tracy, Minnesota
APRIL 7, 1881
Dear Mother and Sister:
I received your welcome letter some time ago and I now take the opportunity of answering. Well I suppose you first want to hear how we got along this hard winter. It has been the severest winter on record, I think. I never seen it but a man could go out after a storm until this winter. It was impossible. Finally

we did get tracks broke to Tracy and the timber. I think snow would average 4 feet on the level and 20 in some places. I was lucky in having enough wood home to do me about two months but it was a job to get to it after all it kept one busy in shoveling wood out and hay. I had the same thing to go through every day it drifts so fearful here. I lost one cow. She was not doing well since last fall. One of my hay stacks I did not see since the 12th of Feb. I dug it out last week and had the misfortune of finding all spoiled. It was hot. I did not have any use of the cattle yard as it was out of sight. Therefore the cattle were allowed to run all over and [I] lay it to the cattle tramping the stack that spoiled the hay. There were lots here that did not have any track at all from their houses and were compelled to carry their fuel wood on their backs and hand sleds not far once or twice but I have known them to do it for near two months. I could not go to mill so I had to take wheat to a feed mill and have it ground into graham. There was not flour in Tracy only as they hauled it from Sleepy Eye. And the mail came by teams from Sleepy Eye in sacks it looked like loads of grain. Wood sold in Tracy at the rate of sixteen dollars per cord and hay ten dollars per ton. It was bad here but I don't think we have suffered half what they did in Dakotah. I don't know what is true but this I know Dakotah settlers depend on the railroad for fuel for there is no wood hardly in Dakotah and there has not been any train through yet from Sleepy Eye since 12th of Feb so you see they must have suffered for wood and provisions and I heard the way they were doing was two or three families would move into one house and burn their houses in turn. There has been suffering that no one will ever know on the frontiers for the newspapers will take good care never to mention for it would

stop immigration. There is lots of stock died out here, cows in general.

I had ten ewes come in in February. I had them in a warm place and some of the lambs were from a month to six weeks old doing fine when one stormy day I had an old sow loose and she broke into the sheep pen and killed five or six. Then she grabbed one of them out doors. So I had good luck and bad luck with my sheep. We have a pair of mare colts one 2 weeks old and one 2 days. They are just normal. I expect another mare in soon . . .

Well I must close hoping you have survived the hard winter all right. One thing we have had good health all through and that is half the battle. Hope you are all in good health and hoping to hear from you soon again. Our love to all we remain

Your Brother and Sister,
R & R Price

P.S. You wanted to know how many children we have, we have 5. W. D. is the youngest he outweighs Mabel who is 4 years old and he is 2 years, 2 pounds and a half heavier.

Personal collection of Rosalie Willford Weber, Ruthton, Minnesota, the great-granddaughter of the letter writer

EDWARD DREW

The diary of Edward B. Drew, a farmer near Winona:

Thursday, March 5, 1886. Haul one load of wood. Bundy came & got me to go to Winona & get load of lumber for him. It begins to rain soon after we leave town.

Friday, 6 March. Haul 8 loads of fire wood to day. Very poor sleighing. I went fast last night & going to day. Nicholas chops up trees & helps me load.

Saturday, March 7. I am compelled to

chronicle here the saddest event of my life. Nothing could have happened to me that would have been more so.

My wife was taken sick about midnight. About 6 oclk her child was born. About 9 she died. The poor child is alive & well.

O what a day—What is this world to me now. Were it not for my poor helpless motherless children. They must be taken care of.

Sunday, March 8. Lonely lonely day & dreary enough to me.

Monday March 9. Following dear wife to

184

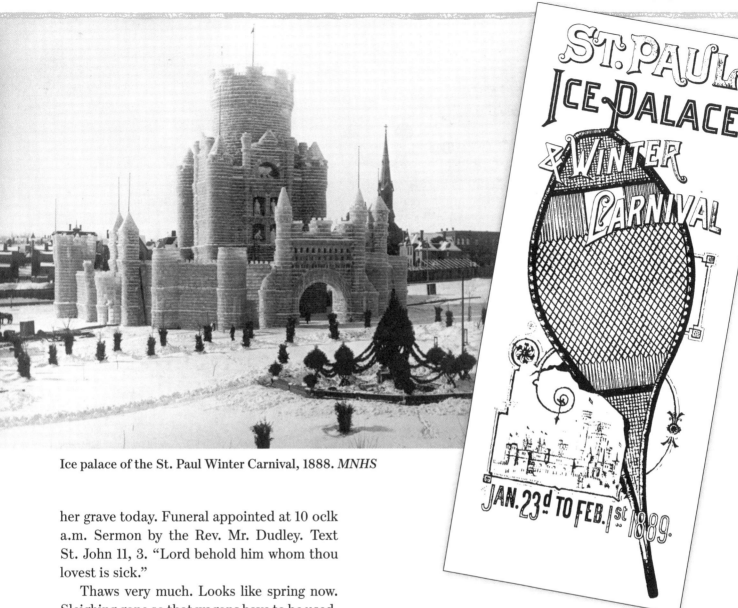

Ice palace of the St. Paul Winter Carnival, 1888. *MNHS*

her grave today. Funeral appointed at 10 oclk a.m. Sermon by the Rev. Mr. Dudley. Text St. John 11, 3. "Lord behold him whom thou lovest is sick."

Thaws very much. Looks like spring now. Sleighing gone so that wagons have to be used.

Tuesday March 10. Spring birds are flying over this morning. Froze quite hard in the morning but soon begins to thaw very much.

Haul big load of corn to the yard & Nicholas hauls it. I overhaul the harnass & shoulders again this second time. Cut up the meat. Get the Bsls & old meat out of the cellar.

Dreary time.

Wednesday March 11. Spring has come. Hear the prairie chickens for the first time.

James M. Drew and Family papers, MNHS

***

[From a Crookston newspaper of the 1880s, under the headline "LINTON HOUSE: Grand Opening Banquet To-Day":]

For some weeks past a large force of carpenters, painters, paper-hangers and like artizans have been at work in the Dobson Block, making alterations and changes so as to fit it up for hotel purposes. This labor having been finished the place was thrown open to guests to-day, by a grand banquet for a number of invited persons. Before the ceremony of sampling the viands took place, a number went on a tour of inspection through the different apartments. Entering from the street we find ourselves in the office, a handsome, light room, 20 x 22. Partitioned in one corner is the wash-room and all appliances for lavatory purposes. Opening off is the dining room, a large, attractive place, capable of seating sixty persons at one time. Back of this are the kitchens managed by W. N. Fox, as chef de cuisine. Mr. F. is an artist of fifteen years experience and has held sway in several prominent hotels at Boston and New York, and latterly was second at the exposition buildings in Milwaukee. A door at one corner communicates with a broad winding staircase, leading to the second floor. At the upper landing is situated the gentleman's reading room where guests may peruse the various journals at their ease. The hall leading by this terminates in the parlor, a

pretty room furnished with sofas, easy chairs, piano, etc. At the left is the bridal chamber. The guest chambers number twenty-five and are all neatly fitted up. The upstairs has three means of entrance—one between Lambert & Matthew's and Chiniquy's store, a passage between the two blocks used for the hotel and one through the dining room. Egress in case of fire would be easy. The papering throughout the house is done in the very best of style and that it was put on by T. N. Segar is a sufficient guarantee of its worth.

Promptly at one o'clock the guests filled the tables and ordered from the following:

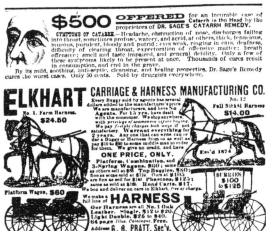

Northwest Architectural Archives, University of Minnesota

Bill of Fare
MENU

Oysters
Raw

Soup
Mock Turtle
Beef Broth

Fish
Baked stuffed Pickerell, a l'Italienne

Boiled
Leg Mutton, Caper Sauce.
Ham.
Corned Beef.

Roast
Sirloin of Beef
Ribs of Beef, Brown Potatoes
Chicken, Cranberry Sauce
Pork, Apple Sauce
Breast Veal, with Stuffing

Entrees
Fillet of Beef, larded with Mushrooms
Peach Preserves, Wine Sauce
Escalloped Oysters, a la Down East
Boston Baked Beans

Vegetables
Mashed Potatoes
Corn
Cabbage
Onions

Pastry
English Plum Pudding, Brandy Sauce
Apple Pie. Mince Pie. Cranberry Pie.
Vanilla Ice Cream. Assorted Cake.
Fruits. Nuts. Raisins.
Cheese

Coffee. Tea

[An unsolicited testimonial for Warner's Safe Medicines, written in a letter by the Rev. George Fish of Heron Lake to his relatives:]

My health has been very poor through the winter and the fore part of the summer, and so has it been with Mother. We have both suffered a great deal and I began to think that we would have to give up work altogether but I was induced to try Warner's Safe Medicines, especially Kidney and Liver Cure and his Safe pills. They have helped us both very much. Our healths are far better than they were one month ago. I think if we keep on using it it will make us as well as could be expected for persons of our age. I am nearing the 69th anniversary of my birth.

Personal collection of Neal E. Simons, Minneapolis

[Today few medical people recommend applying potato or carrot scrapings to a burn; simple cold water usually is advised. But a century ago, the treatment was complex. A first-aid lesson printed in the foreword of the 1886 American Diary included this tip.]

Burns or Scalds—Do not puncture the skin in case it is blistered, but cover with a piece of linen or muslin slightly coated with simple cerate or moistened with hamamelis. If the skin is broken and comes off, cover with cotton or some other light covering to keep the air out. Dress with beeswax and sweet oil, equal parts, or lime water and linseed oil, or scraped potatoes, or carrots, or sprinkle with flour. Warm applications are preferable to cold. Keep the air from the wound as much as possible.

Elias H. Connor papers, MNHS

***

ASHBY, MINN. AUG 4, 1880

To Hon. J. J. Hill, Genl Manager St. P M & M RW. [St. Paul, Minneapolis & Manitoba Railway]

Dear Sir:

Perhaps you would like to hear from this Place, the Farmers are all busy as beavers cutting their Harvest, the Crops are Looking splendid and I think the St. PM & MRW will have their hands full in about six weeks to handle all the freight along the Line.

by the way that material you sent up and built the Depot out of is Verry Poor quality the Depot Looks Like Hell Every time it Rains and Pasengers Complain Verry hard about standing in the Rain at night waiting for the Trains & any freight Retd or forwarded from here is in the same bad fix.

Your agent is so careless that he never attempts to Close a Door night or Day and it is actualy unsafe to Leave any Baggage or Freight in the Depot. I hope for the Good name & Reputation of your Road you will send a carpenter to repair the roof and that you will Please instruct your agent to be a little more Carefull. I know this to be facts by standing in the Rain to change the mail.

Very respectfully yours
N. Q. Puntches

James J. Hill correspondence, Great Northern Railroad papers, MNHS

***

[The Minneapolis Maternity Hospital opened in 1886. In its report the following year, the hospital at 2529 Fourth Avenue South, spelled out its mission:]

Maternity Hospital is a lying-in hospital for the confinement of married women, who are without means or suitable abode and care at

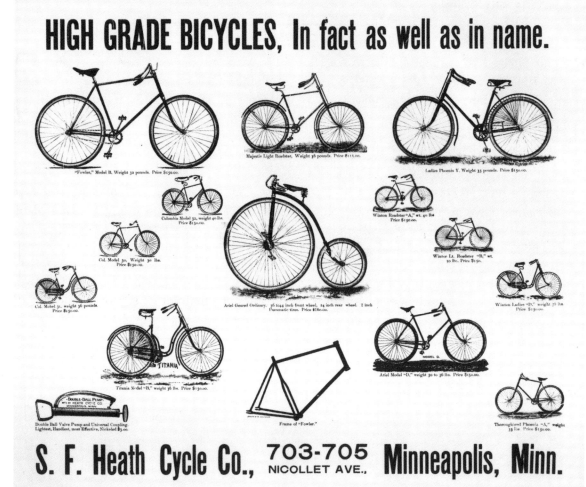

the time of childbirth. It also admits to its shelter unfortunate girls, who, under promise of marriage have been led astray. These girls are not of the vicious or abandoned classes; most of them are young women of good moral and religious training, and who cherish both virtue and reputation, but who in a moment of over-confiding weakness have fallen. No hospital in the city admits an unmarried woman for confinement, no matter what the circumstances may have been. It is obvious on a moment's consideration, that it is much better for these patients to have a separate hospital devoted entirely to such cases, than to have only a ward in a general hospital. There should be a distinction made between those who are living a life of shame, and those who are often "more sinned against than sinning." To the latter, Maternity Hospital opens its doors, cares for them in every way, and as far as possible watches over them after they have left us.

Maternity Hospital, Minneapolis, papers, MNHS

***

CLIMATE: Much has been said detrimental to Minnesota upon this point by irresponsible and designing persons. It is true the temperature two or three times during about two months usually reaches a low degree, but in these instances it is for but a few days at a time, while in the meantime a more pleasant climate could not be found. The air is dry and the rain and mud and chilly penetrating atmosphere, so disagreeable in warmer and moist climates, are not to be found here. Accompanying this steady and desirable condition of weather is most excellent health. No malaria, no ague and chills, but all enjoy the greatest blessing possible to mankind, clear heads and healthy, vigorous bodies. That Minnesota is the home of 1,500,000 people, and that St. Paul and Minneapolis contain 325,000 active, prosperous inhabitants, surely should for all times establish the fact that there is no climatic difficulty, and for once and for forever silence objections on this point.

"Minnesota As It Is," a pamphlet published in many languages by the St. Paul, Minneapolis and Manitoba Railway to encourage immigration, 1889

NEWSPAPER CLIPPINGS

Lemon-juice is said to be a sure cure for small-pox.

Stillwater Gazette, February 1, 1882

AMUSEMENTS. SNIDER AT THE MUSEUM.— Some months ago the papers contained an account of one John Snider who had become afflicted with a nervous disease which found action in walking. Snider was reported to find relief from his distress only by walking and the local physicians were baffled. Theories have been raised and several diagnoses have been made of Snider, but no cure for his strange malady was offered. He grew worse, and has for some time had but little sleep. He walks at a steady pace, although at times he will run and show signs of great nervous disturbance. A crowd watched him on his go-as-you-please journey at the Museum last night. He is said to be 52 years of age.

Minneapolis Tribune, March 29, 1887

An old Irish gentleman was making a speech last night at a political meeting, and referred to the fact that in his precinct there were 24 Democratic and 17 Republican candidates for alderman. He explained this great number by telling a story of a King who sought the advice of his prophet on the weather one day when he wished to go hunting. The prophet said it would be a fine day. On the road the King met a farmer riding on a jack-ass, and the farmer warned the King not to proceed, as it would surely storm. It did storm, and the King called the farmer to learn how he knew of the coming storm, and the farmer replied that his jackass told him. The King then discharged his prophet and put a jackass in his position. "And from that day to this," said the speaker, "every jackass wants an office."

Minneapolis Tribune, April 3, 1887, during a spring election campaign

A PECULIAR ACCIDENT—A Woman Saves Her Life By Her Grit—A very strange accident befel Mrs. S. K. Drown, of Western, on Wednesday last which, had it not been for her courageous conduct would no doubt, have proved fatal to her life. It appears she went on the top of a straw covered stable in search of eggs; the straw giving way, she fell through and landed on the head of an ox that was tied in the stable. At this unexpected presence the ox became greatly excited, hooked her and trampled upon her until her head was literally mashed and her face covered with blood. When consciousness returned she saw the alternative of death or a desperate struggle for release. She wiped the blood that was flowing freely from her temples, out of her eyes, and seizing the maddened beast by the horns, raised herself up and climbed back on the top of the stable, through the hole that had let her down. She then succeeded in reaching the house and lay there for two hours before any one discovered her condition. . . . A physician . . . found her head terribly mashed and that it was necessary to remove two pieces of the fractured skull. The doctor reports hopefully on her case. Mrs. Drown is 56 years of age, but she has enough grit to always take the dilemma, or ox, which ever it may be, by the horns and pull through. . . . The world needs more women of that type.

Stillwater Gazette, March 8, 1882 (Reported from the *Fergus Falls Independent*)

POLITICAL WIND. THE LABOR PARTY'S PLAT-FORM.—The Minneapolis Union Labor party in its platform makes the following demands:

1. We believe the power of railroads and telegraphs exercised over the channels of trade and distribution of products and their control of legislation, has become a public menace to free government, and therefore advocate government ownership and operation of railroads and telegraphs.

2. We demand laws prohibiting the employment of child labor; we demand sanitary laws and their rigid enforcement; we demand that convict labor shall not be put in competition with honest labor; we demand laws to arbitrate differences between employee and employer; we demand shorter hours of labor, and weekly payments.

3. We demand that a single tax upon land values be substituted in lieu of all others.

4. We demand the repeal of the national banking law, and that the government issue a currency direct to the people, making it full legal tender, and that the government establish and maintain postal savings banks as a safe depository for the people.

5. We demand that all civil officers of the government be elected by the people.

Minneapolis Tribune, March 22, 1887

The St. Paul Dispatch has ceased to be a newspaper, and is therefore a financial failure. Its publication would be suspended but for the pleasure its editor derives from throwing mud at Minneapolis people and interests. However, the latter are too high to be reached by the vile contents of the little squirt gun, and the Dispatch editor simply keeps himself under a backward falling shower of his own slop.

Minneapolis Tribune, March 3, 1882

Last night the sash factory of Messrs. Corlies, Chapman & Drake, on Eagle street, near the Seven Corners, was a scene of great attraction, and crowds of people were visiting the building for several hours. The attraction was the electric light these gentlemen have had put in their establishment. Altogether there were eight lights in different parts of the building, up stairs and down. The light was very steady, clear and bright, and was sufficient to enable a person to read fine print in any part of the room. Those who saw the electric light at Lake Elmo a few years ago, can form no idea of the superiority of this now on exhibition. It gives such a clear, pure, steady light, that it renders it impossible to make any comparison of it with any other kind of a light, or with the electric light referred to at Elmo. The exhibition was a great success.

St. Paul Daily Globe, February 26, 1882

Consideration for the Weaker Sex: At the last session of the legislature an ordinance was passed to the effect that all the stores that employ women as clerks, must furnish chairs to enable them to rest when an opportunity presents itself. In compliance with this, Commissioner Lamb of the statistical bureau, has warned all merchants who do not already comply with this ordinance, to do so.

Translated from *Svenska Amerikanska Posten*, a Minneapolis Swedish-language newspaper, July 30, 1889

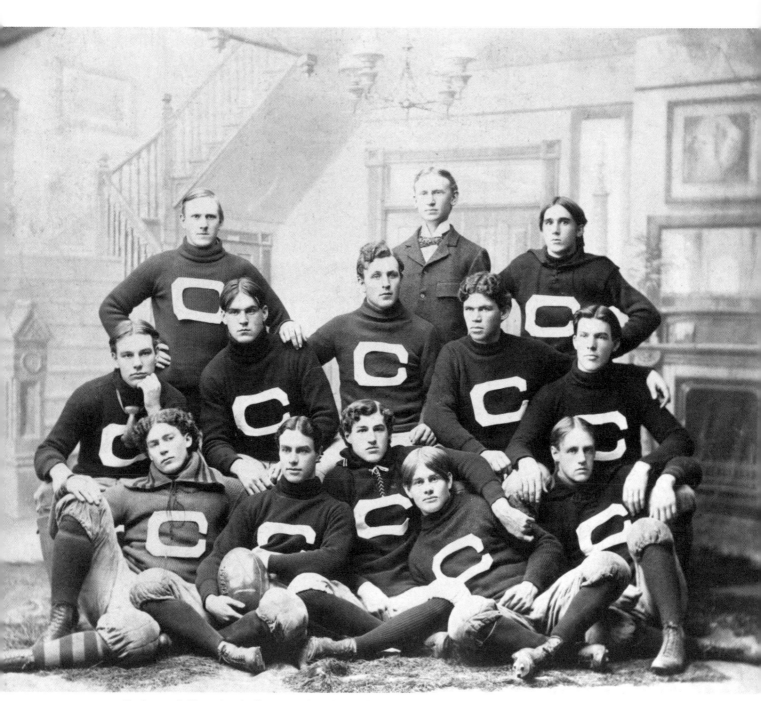

Carleton College football team, 1897. *MNHS*

1890s

The labor movement grew, with the State Federation of Labor working on behalf of child laborers and for shorter hours, better working conditions, and workmen's compensation laws. Iron mining was in high gear. Many of the decade's immigrants—southern and eastern Europeans—came to work in the mines. The dairying industry made major advances. The Hinckley fire was just one of the forest fires that ravaged a dry Minnesota. In 1890 Minneapolis for the first time had a greater population than St. Paul. Electric-powered streetcars were in many Minnesota towns. Thomas B. Walker invited the public in to see his art collection. →

WALTER T. POST

"I think Uncle Ned has treated me mean. . . . A man that will smoke cigarettes will do anything else as low."

Walter Teller Post was born in 1867 near Holland, Michigan. He worked on a farm with his father and took stenography and typing courses at a Detroit business college. When he was twenty-three, he went to St. Paul. He was an accountant and ticket agent in several railroad offices.

Post wrote often to his family in Michigan and told about his work, his struggles to get out of debt, the costs he incurred, his church activities, and his health. He had toothaches, stomachaches, migraine headaches, weepy eyes, and a nervous disposition. But he managed to enjoy much of his life, and he left letters revealing a great deal of life in St. Paul. He was twenty-three when these letters began.

St. Paul, Minn.
MAY 13TH / 90

Dear Bud [an affectionate family name for his mother]

I will write to you again, I suppose I will have to excuse you from answering for I know how hard it is for you to sit down and write.

Well at last I have good coffee, I make it myself, I was down town one evening and stopped in a coffee, tea and spice store, where they had a new process for making coffee in one minute; they have a special kind of coffee pot to make it in, the man made me a cup of coffee and it was real nice, the coffee is ground as fine as flour, it does not look much like coffee after it is ground, and you would not know it was, only by the smell, the coffee pot has a cloth filter in it and you put the coffee in it and pour boiling water on it and it is made I[t] was so nice that I bought a little coffee pot holding a pint, and half a pound of coffee, and now I make my own coffee . . .

Well, I have got a roommate now I do not like it very well, he seems to be a respectable man, but I know nothing about him, I

Walter Post, 1893. *MNHS*

White Bear Lake, 1894. *MNHS*

can change for a single room if I want to but the single room is so small, smaller than my room at home. Was no place to put my things, hardly room to turn around and it is only half a dollar less than this room. I have been looking around this morning at diffrent boarding places but did not find any thing suitable, I could get a handsomely furnished room without board for ten dollars per month, but I can not starve, and it would cost three dollars and a half per wk for table board . . .

Well, it is bed time, my partner has gone to bed already and is asleep. I hate to get in bed along side of him, I laid as strait as possible last night, the first time

Good night.

With love from your son,

Walter

AUG. 12, 1890. Last Saturday after noon I took the street-cars and went over to west St. Paul acrossed the river, and went as far as the end of the line then I walked out in to the country aways. I came to a field of corn the first I have seen this year, it was not very extra corn either, it was very dry and dusty out in the country, one thing I miss about the farms is Orchards, they do not have any of the kind around here and most of the farms are garden farms or dairy farms, I would like to get out far enough to see some large grain farms and where it would be less hilly so I could see beyond the end of my nose, but it is to far to walk and costs to much to hire a horse or ride on the cars.

AUG. 28, 1890. The chief Clerk in the passenger department of the Auditors office was

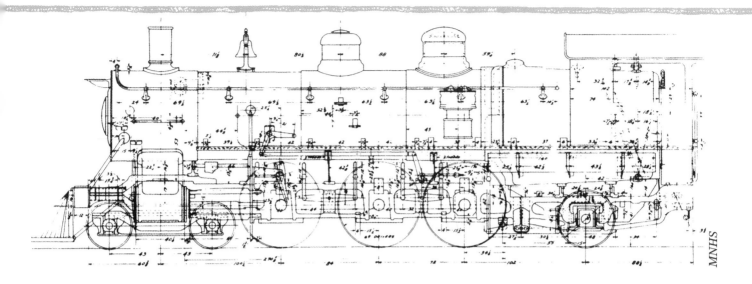

discharged last week he has been chief clerk but six months, the reason of his discharge was because he drinks and has nearly had the delerium Tremors, he would be examining the work, when he would suddenly start back and wave his hands and exclaim, "Go away! Go away!" He is a young man about thirty or a little over, he does not look as though he drank at all, his face is pale and his eyes are clear, so anyone that did not know he drank would not suspect it at all. He was a good worker and was smart.

They are hard at work getting the tracks ready for the electric cars, there is to be a line from here to Minneapolis, it won't be to long before horse cars will be done a way with, which will be a good thing for the horses, it is awful for them traveling over the rough stones and some times (quite often) they slip and fall on their knees, especially when they start to go after they have stopped.

SEPT. 12, 1890. This week has been a very gay and eventful one. it is Fair week. The state fair is being held here, and the Third Street is lined with gas gets [jets] all within six inches of each other and diffrent coloured shades over them making the lights all colours, they are in diffrent shapes, arches, semi circles, etc. the prettiest piece is a great dome over the intersection of two streets. . . . I was

invited by Miss Attwood and Mrs Powers to accompany them to the art exhibit where we saw some fine paintings, one picture was valued at ten thousand dollars, another one at twenty thousand. . . . So you see I have had a fine time this week. I haven't been to bed early a single night nor have I got up early, this morning it was quarter to eight before I woke up, so I have had only 3 quarters of an [hour] to get dressed, eat my breakfast and get in the office, and I did it too.

NOV. 28, 1890. [Typewritten letter.] I suppose you will be surprised to see this letter written in this style, and wonder how I happen to be writeing in this way: well I have bought a Type Writer; Mr. Attwood has taken the agency for the Hall Type writer, and I bought this of him, the regular price is forty dollars, but he sells them for $35, and he let me have this for $27 with three months to pay for it, what do you think of it?

JAN. 5, 1891. We were paid Friday morning, after paying my board, etc., I have only $4.50 left this month.

JAN. 12, 1891. As today is your [his mother's] birthday I will write you a few lines to let you know I have not forgotten it. I wish you a happy birthday and many returns of the day.

I would have sent you something only I do not have the money now to get any thing. You can call my Photo a birthday present I suppose you have received them by this time. I want you to notice the tie I have on, it is one I bought last fall it is real pretty a kind of silver blue, a rich color. I paid two dollars for it, you see after wearing the one Aunt Fannie gave me, I could not come down to a common one for winter. I will send you one of the proofs of the pictures, you see he took two negatives and as one was better than the other I had all my pictures taken from one, I will send the one so you can see the diffrence.

Post's letter. *MNHS*

Costumed group promoting a railroad to New Ulm, about 1891. *Brown County Historical Society*

Musical group at Lake Como, about 1895. *MNHS*

FEB. 17, 1891. [To his father] I received a letter from Aunt Anna Taylor last week tuesday. I believe she is now in a Hospital at San Francisco, she say[s] she is well cared for there and that she likes it better than she thought, she is very lonely, she has a room by herself, and has to pay $25.00 per month, though the regular price is forty she got it cheaper through the influences of friends of the doctors.

FEB. 17, 1891. [To his brother Charlie. Walter had gone skating with a Miss Bowie and seven others and then walked Miss Bowie home.] Maybe you would like to know who Miss Bowie is and what she is like, she is a school teacher, as is also her sister. I do not think her Father is living so there is only herself & sister & Mother, they are scotch Canadian, she is

small about Fannie's size and is a very pleasant jolly little body, dark hair and brown eyes and a pug nose though she is not very homily or rather one does not notice that she is at all homily as she is so pleasant and good her sister is quite pretty with lighter hair and blue eyes.

Well I am afraid you will think I have fallen in love with her if I say any thing more.

MAY 3, 1891. Well, I have bought myself a Bicycle the New Mail safety No. 2 the price was one hundred dollars. I paid thirty dollars down and gave six notes for the rest, one note payable next month for twenty dollars and the rest ten dollars notes, for the next five months after next mo. I asked Uncle Ned's advice about getting one and he thought very favourably about

An unidentified young couple, about 1895. *MNHS*

Hotel Dewey, Minneapolis; the old glass-plate negative is cracked. *Minneapolis Public Library*

it he said it would not be imprudent extravagance, as the exercise would be as good as a Doctor and I needed something of that sort being in the office so much after being used to an active life, then I went to Mr. Halfenstiens who works in the office and who knows all about bicycles and asked his advice about the kind of bicycle to get and he advised me to get this one, of course it is not the highest grade bicycle those cost $135 but this is a good strong one, I will send the catalogue so you can see, I got the wheel yesterday afternoon and had it sent up to the house so I have not had a chance to try it yet. Uncle Ned seemed so much interested in my bicycle when I was showing the catalogue out there as he would if I had been his son.

JUNE 18, 1891. I am at St. Anthony Park and you will wonder if I have gone there to live, well I have for the next two weeks or so. Uncle Ned and Aunt Hortense and the children left this afternoon for Portland, and as Uncle Ned did not want to leave the house alone he asked

me to come out here to sleep nights while he was gone.

JULY 21, 1891. I have not told any of you about our Railroad picnic which took place the 26 of June at White Bear Lake about fifteen miles from St. Paul on the St Paul and Duluth R.R. we left at nine o'clock on a special train they had, several of our new parlor coaches attached, by "our" I mean N.P. [Northern Pacific] coaches, they had not been used

Northfield High School football team, 1894. *MNHS*

before. They are real handsome coaches with elegant plush seats with high backs so one can rest his head against the back. We had to pay one dollar for the tickets to the picnic including the dinner which was served at [a] pavilion. It was rather a high price, and there was a good deal of kicking about it.

AUG. 14, 1891. I have not been very well lately one day I had a neuralgic headache, last Saturday I had three of my teeth filled and I took cold after that and that is what caused my head to ache, then one of my teeth have been aching considerable, to-morrow I have the rest of my teeth fixed one of them together with a false one that they will put in where I had one pulled will cost thirty dollars the one they fix will have a solid gold crown as it is to far gone to fill.

AUG. 17, 1891. Yesterday Frank Oakes one of my S.S. [Sunday School] boys and I went out to Lake Harriet, in the after noon, we took the Electric over to Minneapolis, and got a transfer there to another line that goes out to Lake Harriet. Lake Harriet is a pretty little lake, all fixed up nice with drives and walks around it. We did not stay long at the Lake but took a walk off into the country, and then went back and took a car for home, it was quite a pleasant trip.

OCT. 8, 1891. Now I am boarding at what is called the "Miner" it is a boarding house run by Mrs Miner, she had two houses in the same row and both of them are full, she sets a splendid table claimed to be as good as at the Ryan Hotel. I have a fine large room on the ground floor finely furnished, it is what would be the dining room if the house was occupied by a family, it is lighted by gas and heated by a furnace. She charges for the room and board twenty five dollars per month, but I get it for twenty two per month, as I told her I could not

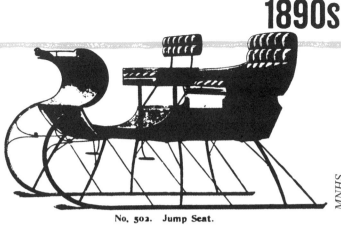

No. 502. Jump Seat.
Well finished and trimmed in crushed plush; easily changed from two to one seat; roomy seats and high backs; shafts.

MNHS

afford to pay more than that, so I was going to look elsewhere but she said if I would get a room mate I could have it for $22 per month, so I took it on those terms, and I have found a room mate, a friend of mine, Peter Johns is his name. I got acquainted with him at the Y.M.C.A. he is a very nice fellow he has not moved here yet but will next Saturday and we have already planned to attend a Chataqua (if that is spelled right) this winter.

OCT. 31, 1891. Last Friday evening Mrs. Miner the lady I board with gave a Progressive Euchre [a card game] party to her boarders and their friends there were about thirty present, she served refreshments which were very nice, sweet crackers, cake and chocolate Ice cream and Grapes and plums, it was after twelve when the party broke up.

NOV. 14, 1891. I am not at work today as I am going to have an operation performed on my eye. my eyes have been troubling me lately so I got an order on Dr. Fulton one of the company's oculists, he has a big reputation and if I had to pay for his services it would be a big price, he is going to fix my eye so it will not be weeping all the time, he gave me some medicine to put in my eyes three times a day also some salve to rub on the eye lids at night. . . . [After the operation] I will try and finish the letter though I do not know how it will look for I have but one eye to use. [Continued later that day] I went to the doctors at ten oclock and he told me to be at St. Josephs Hospital at twelve o'clock so I was there on time. "St Jo's" Hospital is a Catholic institution. I had to wait nearly half an hour for the doctor to come. When he came I went with him to the operating room where I had some kind of medicine injected in the eye lid. then I had to lie on a table and the doctor cut the place where it had grown together and took a couples of stiches in it so as to draw the lid apart, it hurt considerable but I did not stir only to

Chester S. Wilson, age one year, 1897. *MNHS*

Donald and Ruth Wilson with parasols, about 1895. Young boys often wore dresses. *MNHS*

201

Child's sled made from wooden packing crate, about 1898. *MNHS*

Young boy, about 1895. *MNHS*

draw one foot up. one of the sisters was there and while it was hurting the worst she took my hand for an instant in sympathy. there was another young man from the office there to have his eyes operated on. I guess he was going to have them straightened, they were cross eyed, he had to have chloroform administered to him. I guess I will not try and write any more just now. Love to all.

MARCH 2, 1892. [To Charlie, his brother] You ought to be more careful, Charlie, in your spelling. I am not finding fault, but how many misspelled words do you suppose I found in your letter?—15. . . . You see I speak about it because if I want to show your letter to any of the folks out at the Park I cannot if there is so many mistakes in spelling, for they will think you do not know anything. [This from a man who consistently spells "different" as "diffrent."]

SEPT. 20, 1892. Bert Chamberlain is one of the sneaking thoroughly bad boys, he is over sixteen years, smokes cigarettes, reads dime novels and goes to low theatres. . . . One evening I ran across him and Fred and they both were smoking cigarettes, after Fred had left here, I gave him a good talking too for giving Fred cigarettes, he promised he would not give him any more, but how well he kept his promise I do not know. I noticed he took Fred down town nearly every Saturday night, so I followed them one night and he took him to a low dime museum [a collection of sensational curiosities, monstrosities, and freaks, exhibited for a low price of admission]. This summer he was out at the lake camping and Fred went out there two or three times. I discovered that he had got Fred to reading dime novels and it has made an awful change in him. his sisters know about it but they cannot do much, he promised them he would not read any more dime novels but I do not think he is keeping his promise as I discovered he had one today, and that he spent a good deal of time in the water closet [bathroom] at the office reading them.

NOV. 5, 1892. Last Wednesday was pay day. My check called for fifty nine dollars & fifty cents ($59.50). So you see I got another raise and am now getting sixty dollars per month. . . . I have had a tight squeeze [financially]. I had fifteen dollars to pay the dentist for the tooth the horse kicked out, then I had to have two pair of pants which cost me $18.50, and then I had to finish paying for my typewriter. Last month I had to borrow fifteen dollars from Uncle Ned to help me out.

APRIL 18, 1893. I enclose a clipping from the paper in regard to the Catholics and the A.P.A. [American Protective Association]. If you will notice you will find in the papers from time to time little articles like that in diffrent parts of the country. I have just joined the A.P.A. which is a secret society of no political party but who are sworn to vote for no Catholic to any office what ever, to employ no Catholic when a Protestant can be got, also to enter in no agreement with a catholic to strike, we swear to denounce Roman Catholicism, and the Pope. It is not even known to but few out side of the society that there is such a society in the city and members are sworn not to tell the names of any member, we work in secret, as we are not strong enough to come out openly, but expect to be strong enough to make an effect at the next municipal election, do not mention this out side of the family. The Catholics are doing their best to get control of all the offices in the city, nearly all the police force and fire men and the heads of the several city depts. are under the control of them now. a good share of the school teachers are Catholics. The fifth of next Sept, has been fixed by

the Pope in his Encyclical letter as the time when all Catholics will be absolved from the oath of Alegiance to the U.S. and then they are to fall on the Protestants and will be doing God['s] service by killing them right here in this city they are drilling and have arms and ammunition stores in the cellars of their churches, these are facts, the A.P.A. have had detectives watching them and several things have occurred to confirm their suspicions. one was a mysterious explosion in a Catholic store.

JUNE 10, 1893. [Apparently Walter's father disagreed about the Catholics.] I was out at Uncle Ned's yesterday after noon and had quite an argument with him on the Catholic question, he thinks about as you do that is he don't believe in it. but I do not see any reason not to believe in it when all the evidence goes to show it. and the only reason they join with the protestants on the temperance question is just as a policy of theirs to blind and fool the protestants.

JUNE 25, 1893. Well I don't get a vacation of any kind this summer. They are not going to let any one have a vacation. I asked Uncle Ned about it tonight. I even tried to arrange to have them let me off without pay and have some one take my place but Uncle Ned said they could not get any one who understood the work enough to keep it up and it would take about as long as I would be gone for them to learn, so that it would be practically the same as having no one do it. The trouble is that the road is getting in such bad shape that they are cutting down expenses all around and have reduced the force in our office and Uncle Ned said that there was more likelihood of a decrease in force than an increase so that the work has got to be kept up and not let fall behind.

JULY 21, 1893. There is a rumor around the office that the salarys are to be cut down 20%.

I do not know if it is so or not but the N.P. [Northern Pacific] is a bad fix now, if they do I shall look for another place.

[Post's letters in this collection don't mention a fiancée, but suddenly he wrote home about a pending marriage to a woman named Lillie.]

JUNE 23, 1894. I will tell you how I am to be dressed. I will wear a black coat the shape of the one I had when I was home only longer, light trousers, white vest, a white silk bow tie with small blue figures in it a couple of shirt studs solid Gold with genuine Ruby settings. I got them with a pair of cuff buttons of Fred Harm, he let me have them for $4 the price was seven dollars. I will wear patent leather shoes. Fred made me a handsome gold Wedding ring considerable heavier than the one I had on when I was home, for $5. then for a wedding present I got Lillie a handsome diamond ring which Fred set for me and sold to me for $35. the diamond had a flaw in it but only a diamond expert could detect it otherwise it would be worth $75 unset, as it was it was worth $60 but Fred let me have it set for $35. I wish some of you folks could have gotten down for the wedding.

JULY 11, 1894. I am hunting for a house. Lillie and I have decided that it will be much nicer to go to housekeeping than to board and probably be cheaper or anyway as cheap we have to pay $35 per month for board besides washing and street car fare, it cost us 50¢ a Sunday to go to church and S.S., 40¢ for st car fare, and 20¢ for collection. We want to get a house for about $15 or $20 per mo. it will take $314.25 to furnish a house. I went down to the New England Furniture Co. and we went right through from kitchen to parlor and I got the price of every thing that would furnish the house finely. With Brussels carpet in the parlor and ingrain carpets in dining room, sitting room and bedroom, the carpets would be madr. [manufactured], lined and laid. I could pay ⅓ down and the bal [balance] in ten months, but that would make it so that I could not send anything home during that time.

[Post then wrote out a description of his wedding, as it appeared in the newspaper of Peru, Indiana, where they were married.]

"A charming wedding was celebrated last evening at the home of the bride's parents, Mr. and Mrs. Martin Carl, 77 W. 7th St. The marriage of their daughter Miss Lillian to Walter T. Post occurred. At six o'clock to the music of Mendelsohn's March the happy couple entered the parlor and proceeded to the northwest corner, when, surrounded by a number of relatives and friends, they were united in the holy bond of matrimony by Rev. E. E. Neal, the Methodist minister.

"The bride wore a beautiful dress of cream chine silk, trimmed in deep silk lace, and carried La France roses. Shortly after the ceremony the guests, about forty or more, were seated to an elegant supper. The menu consisted of the choicest delicacies of the season. Rev. E. E. Neal, Mrs. J. B. Wallace of Indianapolis, and the bride and groom were seated at the bride's table.

"The bride, well known to all Peruvians, possesses the many womanly virtues so necessary to brighten the house and lighten the labors of a dutiful husband.

"Mr. Post is a worthy young man of good family. He is employed in the accounting department of the Northern Pacific railway at St. Paul, which speaks well in his behalf as an honest, upright and industrious gentleman. The happy couple were the recipients of many useful and costly presents. They left last evening on the ten o'clock train for their future home in St. Paul.

"Among the guests from abroad were Charlie Post, South Bend, Miss Mary Miller and sister Mrs. John Wallace, Indianapolis, Miss Jackson, Wabash, Mr. and Mrs. West and Miss Sadie Alspaught (cousins) of New Waverly and Mr. and Mrs. Wanasmith of Mexico."

AUGUST 15, 1894. We have to get up at six o'clock every morning so I can get off to work in time I leave for the office at quarter to eight it takes just ¾ of an hour to walk to the office. I come home to dinner [at noon] as it is just as cheap to pay car fare home & back as it to buy lunch down town and I get more and better food to eat. Lillie knows how to cook as good as the best, it takes a little more than an hour to go and come and eat but they do not mind if one is a few minutes late under those circumstances.

We had quite a nice little shower a few nights ago but not enough to more than lay the dust, people are having to water the large trees around their places to keep them alive, the leaves are all dying and falling off so that it looks like fall instead of summer.

AUG. 31, 1894. Lillie has an Aunt that lives at Winona, Minn, she expects to come up to St. Paul during the State Fair and will visit us. I suppose I will have to sleep on the floor while she is here and let her sleep with Lillie. Some day we expect to own an other bed so that when folks come we will be fixed for them.

SEPT. 12, 1894. I have had so much writing to do at the office the last day or two that my hand is so tired I can hardly hold my pen and also my arm has been quite lame lately. I have plenty to do when I get home from the office, putting ice in refrigerator, and after supper I generally help Lillie clear up the table and wash dishes. I also help her cook, she thinks I do every thing so nicely. Last week we had callers every day of the week.

OCT. 4, 1894. I spent most of my evening piling wood and getting a place ready to put coal in. I have my wood in the celler. I bought a cord of Maple the first of last Month 4 foot wood and had it sawed & split when I bought it I have over half left. I expect to get a Ton of coal tomorrow coal is $7.25 per ton but I get it for seven dollars as the Lehigh Coal Co came to the office and had a paper passed around agreeing to sell any amount of coal delivered for cash at $7.00 per ton during Sept Oct. Nov. & Dec to the clerks that signed the paper so I put my name down for 3 Tons.

DEC. 6, 1894. [To brother Charlie.] I have time this noon to answer it [Charlie's letter], I am taking my lunch with me so I have plenty of time at noon now I take my lunch so as to save st [street] car fare, which amounts to $3.00 per month when I go home to dinner. I am gradually getting my debts paid up and hope soon to be free from them. I owe $40.00 on my furniture yet and $15.00 for my stove besides some small matters and what I owe you.

JAN. 10, 1895. I think that the sooner I can get out of this office the better it will be for me, of course this will not make any difference [he finally spells it right] in my salary but I cannot stand that kind of work. I think Uncle Ned has treated me mean. . . . A man that will smoke cigarettes will do anything else as low. I would like to get out of the R.R. business entirely it is getting played out. I wish I could find something down in Michigan or Indiana to do it would make it ever so much nicer for Lillie.

FEB. 21, 1895. There is not much news to write about from here, it is the same thing over and over again, get up and go to the office come home and go to bed, it seems as if I was hardly at home any length of time, when it gets pleasant weather so we can go out more, we will have more of a variety.

FEB. 22, 1895. How did you manage to pass the winter? was the house as cold as ever so that you had to keep close to the stove and roast on one side while you froze the other? our house is not as warm as it might be and our bedroom would get awful cold as it is only heated with a drum.

MARCH 4, 1895. I was home all of Thursday, Friday & Saturday, with what I took for neuralgia in my head and eyes so that I could not use my eyes at all, I went to the office Sat. afternoon to let them know why I had not been down and also to get my pay, that being pay day. I get awfully discouraged about my eyes they hurt me so much of the time, but I have to keep on using them or lose my job. I hate to be off so much of the time too. but I do not know what else I can do, it is like looking for a needle in a hay stack, to find anything to do now days especially when one wants to choose something that will be the best for his health care . . .

I suppose you wonder why Lillie does not write an answer to your letter to her, she is afraid she cannot write an interesting letter and also she does not like to write letters anyway, she is awful anxious to see you all though, she thinks you write such good letters. Maybe I can get her to answer you after a while. I know you will all like her when you see her, which I hope will be before long. She is a lovely house keeper as neat and clean and quick as can be also a good cook, the only fault I find with her is that she is apt to worry and look on the dark side not all the time of course but she gets spells of being blue, one reason is when she was home she did not have to think about where the money was to come from as she has to now, though she never was extravagant and is even more economical than I would be if I didn't let her have her say.

APRIL 25, 1895. There is a rumor at the office of another reduction in salarys that seems to be well founded. . . . I would give anything if I could get out of the office in to something better, it is bad enough to live on the salary I am getting with out having to get less I wish I could get something that would be worth while in Holland [Michigan] so we could live nearer our folks. If one had the money to start in to some kind of a business that would pay!

MAY 28, 1895. In regard to Jim Hill [James J. Hill, the railroad owner] and the N.R [Northern Pacific Railroad] you cannot go by what that clipping states. . . . Some of the stockholders and bond holders might rejoice that he is going to take hold of the road but you may be sure none of the employes are rejoicing. Jim Hill pays his men the least wages of any road here and have kept cutting them down all the time . . . his wealth represents immense Steals that he has schemed. . . . If Jim Hill takes personal control of the Northern Pacific he will cut down the force & salarys, consolidating it as far as possible with the Great Northern. Jim Hill is the wage earners worst enemy.

[Walter then told his father of his animosity toward his brother Charlie.]

Of course you would stick up for Charly you always did think he was the most wonderful boy, but I say that considering the chances Charlie has had he has not done anything to boast of at all of course he has done first rate but hundreds of other boys have done the same in the first place Charlie had a good education to back him up and that counts every thing, then you let Charlie start out when he was but a boy and he had lots of time to learn in. You have Very often in your letters sung Charlies praises to me until I am tired of hearing them, it would look as if you were giving me back handed hits, when you know you never gave me the privileges you gave Charlie. I had to stay at home until I was of age, and I did not get as much schooling as Charlie did, and when I came out here and went into the office I had not the slightest knowledge of business of any kind and had to learn after I was 23 years old, and now I have got to stay in the Railroad business all my life I suppose as I could not without either Money or experience get a paying position in other business, and as I have said before a person working for a large corporation like a railroad office never does stand a fair show of advancement as he would working in a small firm there is always injustice, favoritisim & jealousy in a large RR office that keeps them back. Now here is Charlies position, he went to South Bend to work for Mr. Westerfelt to drive the wagon & deliver goods for a business that was run down from lack of attention. Charlie was working for one man and he had taken a fancy to Charlie, there was no one else there to draw away from Charlie any favor that Mr. W. might bestow on him. Charlie paid attention to the business as he should have done consequently it responded to the attention and picked up. . . . As I said before I do not want to run Charlie down but I say he has not done such a wonderful thing as it looks to folks living down in a little place where most of the people are asleep, in big Cities his case could be matched by hundreds. I would jump at the chance to get out of the RR business and get into something where I could be more independent, railroading has run to seed there are to many at it and it is getting worse, after a man has been at it a few years he is good for nothing else and has to poke a long at the same thing all his life and if he is fortunate enough to get an official position he does not know when his head may be cut off especially if he gets a Jim Hill to be his boss . . .

Well it is nearly half past ten. Love to all. Your son, Walter T. Post.

JULY 8, 1895. [To Charlie] Well Charlie, you might begin to call yourself "Uncle" for practice, for I expect in not so very many more months you will be one. About Dec or Jan. What do you think of that? I am tickled to death nearly. We want to have Bud [their mother] come and take care of Lillie while she is sick [recovering from childbirth], I wrote and asked her yesterday & I hope she will.

NOV. 28, 1895. [To Charlie] It has kept me awful busy since the baby was born so I could not get time to write to you before I told Father to write and tell you about it. You see I had to do all the writing to Lillie's home beside to Father. So I was kept busy at that during my spare time while I was not waiting on Lillie. Baby was born two weeks ago yesterday morning Nov. 13th at 2:45 A.M. Lillie had an awful hard time of it the Doctor had to use instruments and take the baby away it was too large for Lillie, she was placed under the influence of chloroform, but the Dr commenced to use the instruments before she had gotten under its influence the pain made her scream awfully, she was in terrible pain every once in a while from about 9 oclock till after the Dr got her under the influence of the chloroform which was about 1 o'clock A.M. When the baby was born the Dr. said he did not think it was alive after all, that the heart had stopped beating but he worked hard breathing into its mouth till finally we were delighted to hear it give a sigh then commenced to cry. it was hurt considerably by the instruments which made a few sore places one side of its forehead also hurt one of its eyes so that for a while it was swollen shut its face and head were pulled awfully out of shape, he looks ever so much better now as he is getting all straightened out now he weighed between 8 & 9 lbs when he was born we did not have a chance to weigh him till afterward when he had lost ever so much Bud says he weighed all of eights lbs if not more. We have to feed him on the bottle as Lillie did not have enough milk for him, she did not know it at first and the Baby got awful thin, he is doing finely now. Lillie is getting along nicely she got up yesterday for the first time. I did not go to work till the next Monday after Baby was born I had to stay home and help nurse Lillie since then I have had to go and come from the office when I could sometimes it would be nine or half past before I would get down, they have been working every night for the last two weeks and also Sundays . . .

Baby' name is Carl Teller after Lillie's maiden name & my middle name. How is Business down there? I will not write more this time. We all send love.

Your brother,
Walter Teller Post

JULY 1, 1896. [To Charlie] Yours of the 27th received this A.M. I am very sorry to have to disappoint you about the balance of that money but I can not possibly scrape enough together for a couple of months yet to settle with you. I am as anxious to settle with you and get it off from my mind as you are to get it. If you are at your wits ends I don't know what you would call it in my case, for I have to do some awful close figuring to make ends meet and then they dont meet. Why actually we don't have enough to clothe ourselves. I don't have a suit of clothes hardly decent to wear to church and both Lillie and I are in bad need of shoes but cannot get them yet. Of course I don't expect it to be so always but we have so many expenses this spring & summer, it has just kept our noses to the grindstone. I still owe $9.00 on the Dr. bill & $2.50 to the dentist. I have to make them wait as well. You see out of a salary of only $56.50 per month a person cannot save anything above actual living expenses, here is a list of what I will have to pay out this month.

Rent 12.00
Groc &c. 19.75
Ice 2.00
Fuel 2.75
T & coffe & c. 2.20
Milk & cream 3.00
Baby food 3.12
On sew. mach. 3.00
Laundry .76
Total $48.58
Sal. 56.50
minus 48.58
7.92

Which will show you that I will have only a bal. of $7.92 for incidental expenses. I am sorry it is so and will be only to glad to get the matter settled but you will have to use the patience you have hither to kindly shown (and which I appreciate) until I am able to pay it which will be just as soon as possible.

Your brother,
Walter T. Post

SEPT. 6, 1896. [To Charlie.] Your letter was received sometime ago. We have been having a very busy time of it for the last two weeks. Lillie was quite sick for nearly a week. We had to have the Doctor then she took a bad cold she is about well now and has gone to church this A.M. I had to remain at home with her while she was sick and so all the house work, take care of her and the Baby . . .

You will probably be surprised to hear that I have lost my position at the N.P. to take effect the end of this month, it came as a surprise to me though I was afraid if more reductions were made I might have to go. they notified 14 in our office yesterday, the letter said it was not on account of any fault in the character of our work but only solely to a change in the methods of work. You know the road has

Martin Newman, his son Art, and an unidentified woman on their front porch, location unknown. *MNHS*

just been reorganized and the new company took charge the 1st of Sept, the rumor is that changes will take place among the officials and from the Gen Manager down they are all quaking. This places me in a bad position and I have not the least idea what I shall do it is like looking for a needle in a haystack to find work here. I wish you would see how it is in Indianapolis and let me know I would take anything I could get.

JAN. 19, 1897. [Postcard to Charlie] You have probably wondered why I have not written before, but I have not felt like writing and did not have much to write about. I have not found anything yet. I went to Holland

[Michigan] to see what I could find there but it was duller than ever there I had quite a visit there & enjoyed myself that way I went to Grand Rapids and inquired at the RR office there with the same results as elsewhere. . . . When I got home I found both Lillie & baby sick with colds.

[That's the last communication we have from Walter T. Post. Relatives said he later lived in South Bend, Indiana, and died in 1930 of Bright's disease. Lillie died in 1944 in Indiana. Their son, Carl, served in World War I, trained in Salvation Army work, and rose to the rank of captain.]

Walter T. Post letters, MNHS

EMILIE WILHELMINA NYMAN

*"He bought a black suit for the wedding and paid 100 marks for it.
He only wore it twice and now he'll wear it forever."*

Frans Nyman was born near Turku, Finland, about 1850. His father was a blacksmith. As a young man, he learned to tune organs and later to build them. In 1880 he emigrated to St. Petersburg, Russia, to work in an organ factory. It was there he met a young woman named Emilie Wilhelmina, who spoke six languages. They immigrated separately to Minneapolis in 1891. He found work in an organ and piano factory. They renewed their friendship and were married. Her letter to his mother in Finland tells the rest of the story.

Dear Mother:
With this letter, dear Mother, I want to inform you and share with you the heavy burden of grief that has fallen upon me since our dear heavenly Father in his all-knowing wisdom called to Himself my dear husband and your son, Frans Johan Nyman. He became ill in January with tuberculosis and suffered from it for 6 months until the 19th of this month, when at half past five in the evening he quietly slept away. He was buried last Wednesday.

Frans wrote to you last winter telling you he was getting married and so it happened. Our wedding was on the 30th of April. A week after the wedding he became ill and was home from work for 2 weeks, then he returned to work for a short time but his illness continued. Finally he was simply too weak to work. For six months he was sick and I nursed him as well as I could. We tried doctors and drugs and Frans got everything that he could have wanted, but it was too late. On Saturday morning he said to me, "Listen Emilie, I'm healthy again. It doesn't matter if I'm thin. Muscle can grow back onto bone." This is what he said that morning—and that evening he died. We've lived for this entire time with my parents. Frans didn't leave much money but enough so that we gave him a proper burial. The casket, wagon and gravesite cost 235 marks, not including the clothes that he wore. He bought a black suit for the wedding and paid 100 marks for it. He only wore it twice and now he'll wear it forever. There were many mourners. His co-workers from the factory brought a wreath that cost 25 marks.

I would have written earlier about Frans' illness, but he wouldn't let me. He said the news would only make mother sad and, who knows, he might get well yet. On Friday the 18th, a day before he died, he said that "everything else is fine, but I didn't write to mother." I said I would write. "All right—that would be fine," he answered. We hadn't been married but 6½ months and now I'm already a widow at the age of 18. A thousand greetings from me and my parents to you and also to all relatives and friends. May the good Lord see to it that these few lines find you in good health. Good-bye and good health to you— that is my heartfelt wish.
Emilie Wilhelmina Nyman

P.S. Please forgive me for my poor Finnish. Also please write to me as soon as you can.

University of Minnesota's Immigration History Research Center, which also supplied the translation

***

[Mary Brown left a list of her expenses for Thanksgiving dinner to serve eleven people in 1890. Two days before Thanksgiving she bought:]

Steak .34, fish .08, potatoes .25, cherries .18, bread .05, c. beef .38, butter 1.25, turkey 1.44, squash .15

[Then on Thanksgiving Day she bought:]

Cream .15, oranges .30, candy .15, graham .20, cakes .15, celery .15, sugar .25, sage .05, salt .08, oil .10, gelatine .18, steak .30, bread .10, sugar .10, milk .25

[Some of these items were staples and some were for other meals. Mrs. Brown noted that the Thanksgiving dinner for eleven cost $4.50.]

Edward Josiah Brown papers, MNHS

***

[J. H. Morrison was a general contractor working in Everett, Washington, in 1892. His wife went to visit her family in St. Paul and was about to take the train west again when he wrote a letter that started:]

My Dear Little Pet,

I am beginning to hope the days will be few till I can take you in my arms once more & give you a real Washington hug, one such as would make a girl's heart go flipety-flop, a widow think there was something still to live for and a sweet little runaway wife glad to get home again, I hope.

Agnes Morrison Park and Family papers, MNHS

Unidentified men displaying fur coats. *MNHS*

DAVID FREEMAN

"Sometimes I have a notion to start down the track and never look at the place again."

The summer of 1894 was hot and dry. Only a little more than two inches of rain fell in the northern woods between May and September, compared with an average then of seventeen inches. Settlers battled sporadic fires. But the fire of September 1 could hardly be fought. It destroyed Hinckley and several smaller communities and killed more than four hundred people. A train managed to get out with 276 people; five minutes after it crossed a bridge, the bridge collapsed. Here is a letter written by a survivor of the fire:

OCTOBER 8, 1894
Dear Brother,
I received your letter and your five today. You may be sure I was glad to hear from you and get the money. I was wondering why you didn't write. I thought you must be offended at something I had said while you were up here. It has been awful lonesome since you all went away and I wish that I had went while I had a chance to get the money from Will [his brother-in-law]. . . . I got some lumber today to build a shack with. I gave my note for it. My insurance knocked me out of getting a house from the [relief] commission. And the Lord only knows when I will get my insurance. As you say it is awful discouraging to start in here again. Sometimes I have a notion to start down the track and never look at the place again.

Hinckley will never be to me what it was before though it is growing quite fast now and begins to look like a town. It has four saloons running now, one store, one barbershop and one blacksmith shop. I expect Will up here this week. I got a letter from Millie today and one from Mother Saturday. I hadn't heard from home since you left and could not think what was the matter. They all want relics, something Kate [Kate Grissinger, his sister] had. I had not thought of it before. I might have saved lots of them. It has all been picked over by strangers so now I do not think I could find much.

I found out how Kate went on the day of the Fire. And who she went with over to Strombergs (the family in my house) and they all went over to Ginders and tried to get them to go along but Ginder laughed at them and said he was not afraid of his house burning and would not go.

So they went through Ginder's garden and up to the St. Paul and D.R.A. You know I said they must have crossed the wagon bridge when you were here. It seems they did not. They could have seen the headlight of that train standing up the track about a mile and that was where they were going. The oldest Stromberg boy carried Mabel part way and until he became scared and then he left her with Kate and ran for the train, him and all his folks and Willie reached the train.

Kate must have given up reaching the train and turned to the right towards Curriers which brought her over on that road that crosses the bridge where she was overtaken by the fire.

When the train had burned so it could go no further the Strombergs all got off and ran straight up the track. The oldest boy happened to think he had left the satchel on the train and started back to get it. He could not get to the train nor back to his folks. In the morning he found them all in the pile of the dead. How he saved himself he didn't say. I only had a few minutes talk with him when he came down from Duluth. It was lucky Willie did not follow the Strombergs. I do not know what Kates chances would have been had she reached the train. This was some satisfaction to me to learn what she done and where and who with and explains how Willie came to be on the train.

Well I will close. I could write a book about Hinckley tonight but I never seem to have finished so I break off anywhere.

Now write soon.
Love to all the family,
Your brother David Allen Freeman

Hinckley Fire Museum, Hinckley, Minnesota

***

[Minnesota's governor appointed a Minnesota State Commission for the Relief of Fire Sufferers, which received and distributed

Minneapolis letter carriers. *Michael A. Carroll*

more than $165,000. Here is one of the applications for aid:]

Surname? Hanson.
Given name? Mrs. Henry.
Born at? Sweden.
Number of children? 6.
Names with ages? George 8. Frank 6. Harold 5. Walter 3. Hilda 2. Baby 10 months.
Are you helping to support others? No.
Were any of your family hurt, and how badly? Husband burned to death.
Where were your dead found, if any? At Hinckley, near his house.
By whom identified? John K. Anderson.
Residence at time of fire? Hinckley.
Length of time lived in Minnesota? 13 years.
Occupation? Husband worked in saw mill.
Business for himself? No.
Owns his home? Yes.
If mortgaged, for how much? $100 to man in Pine City.
What property was destroyed by the fire? House & barn & contents. House $900, contents $300.
Had insurance? Fire? No. *Life?* None. *Accident?* None.
What property left and its value? Two cows. $50.
Have you property elsewhere? No.
Address of relatives and friends? Brother-in-law in St. Paul. A Johnson. Uncle in North Branch. Father & Mother lived in Hinckley and were burned out.
Can you expect help from them? No.
Do you want to go to them? Yes.
If not there, where? North Branch, Minn.
Have you an income of any kind? No.

Pension? No.
Have you any pressing debts? What? About $35 store bills.
Needs? Everything. Wants a small house to keep family together, can decide where to locate after seeing father & mother who are at North Branch.
What do you think you need the most? A home.

[A note at the bottom of the form says Mrs. Hanson was provided "clothing enough for all winter" plus "transportation to North Branch for lady and 6 children." But "6" is crossed out and "5" inserted. What happened to number six wasn't noted.

The government helped some. Private persons and individuals donated money. Records show these contributions to victims:]

The people of Gardner, N.D., $40.
Aurelius Bros, grocers, 920 Rice St., St. Paul, $5.
People of Excelsior, Minn., $153.30.
Citizens of New Ulm, $172.
Women's Union Missionary Society of Glenwood, Minn., $28.41
Hutchinson, Minn., Leader, Burt W. Day, Proprietor, $122.60 ("This is a slight token of the sympathy felt here for the people who lost their all in the terrible fire.")
WCTU, Almon, Minn., $5.
Swedish Society of Portland, Ore., $38 "to be distributed to the Swedish sufferers by the late fire."

Governor's Commission for the Relief of Sufferers, State Archives, MNHS

***

The University of Minnesota asked students to keep detailed records of their expenses for an academic year. The results were published in the 1899–1900 *Bulletin*, the university course catalog, to help prospective students budget their money. The most frugal student was a freshman woman in the college of science, literature, and arts who spent $159:

Board, room, fuel and light	$75.21
Clothing, besides that brought from home	32.63
Railroad fare, street car fare and cartage	9.32
Stationery	2.16
Books and fees	32.26
Y.W.C.A., fraternity and amusements	7.50
Totals	$159.08

A senior man spent the most:

Board, room, laundry and fraternity dues	$208.75
Clothing	74.25
Class dues	8.25
Books	29.10
Stamps	3.41
Church donations and amusements	24.90
Railroad fare	16.25
Street car fare	4.95
Incidentals	27.23
Totals	$397.09

"Home management" was taught at the University of Minnesota at the turn of the century. The 1899–1900 *Bulletin* described it:

This includes both housekeeping and home making, and the teaching of the subject naturally falls into three divisions, household work, sanitation and family life. The instruction is based upon the belief that housekeeping is as important as it is difficult, and that home making is the noblest form of human endeavor. The points in detail in the preparation of food, the making of clothing, the care of the house and household belongings, and plan for home management. To start the student in the correct way of becoming mistress of the business of housekeeping is the end sought. It is believed that for one who knows the reason for the doing there is no drudgery. Therefore students are taught the specific danger that lurks in dust and dirt, in order that they may understand the dignity of the unceasing war which the housekeeper makes upon these forces. The practical benefit to be derived from the knowledge students have gained in the cooking, sewing, laundering and dairy classes is emphasized and shown in its relation to an adequate plan for the daily program for the home. While the science of family life has not be formulated, yet some of its fundamental principles are recognized and may be taught.

NEWSPAPER CLIPPINGS

ANNIE HEDSTROM stood before the court last Wednesday charged with having broken the laws of this city [St. Paul] by appearing in male attire. She passed under the name of Charles Parker and did a man's work at a farm in the vicinity of St. Paul for a period of more than a year without her true sex being discovered. Her employer, however, discovered the circumstances accidentally, and informed the police who arrested Annie. She said she did not know that it was unlawful to be dressed in man's clothing. She disliked house-work and furthermore was able to earn more money as a man. She was dressed in rough working clothes, a dirty flannel shirt, slouchy felt hat and heavy shoes, and said she intended to go to a lumber-camp this winter. Judge Twohy tried to reason with her and admonished her to act as it befitted her sex, but Annie said she had had to support herself ever since she was 7 years of age and that she had done pretty well at it. The judge then dismissed the case against her under the provision that she would dress in women's clothing. Annie Hedstrom formerly resided in Minneapolis, and is about 22 years old. She has been in trouble with the police several times. In Minneapolis she is known by the name "Cowboy Pete." She is an excellent equestrian and used to ride through the streets at a reckless gallop dressed in so called cowboy clothes. It was this which revealed her sex when she landed at the police station. After having been arrested and reprehended repeatedly in Minneapolis she was finally ejected from that city and took up residence here.

Translated from *Svenska Amerikanska Posten*, a Minneapolis Swedish-language newspaper, October 17, 1893

Mr. Herman Harms, a modern Rip van Winkle, has awakened. He awakened three months ago and has stayed awake ever since. During the past 20 years he has slept, and has only been awakened in order to be fed, once each night. He appears to be but skin and bone. Even the greatest specialists have been unable to give the reason for this phenomena, but it is believed to have been caused by an injury to the brain. Harms, who is very poor, lives with his family on a farm between Quincy and St. Charles.

Translated from *Svenska Amerikanska Posten*, January 15, 1895

A new invention has been made by a Swede, by name Per O. Elliot, 905 Washington Ave. So. It is a simple little apparatus designed to aid in attaching the postage stamp to a letter thus making it unnecessary to fumble around with big and clumsy fingers in an attempt to afix it. As soon as the inventor receives the patent papers he will sell his invention preferably to a Swede. Several prospective buyers have already contacted him.

Translated from *Svenska Amerikanska Posten*, May 21, 1895

A blood-curdling murder occurred at Wells [Minnesota] on Wednesday. Henry Ringer, owner of a meat market was stabbed to death with a huge butcher knife by a man in his employ named Korr. Briefly told Ringer suspecting improper relations between Korr and his wife, came home clandestinely and secreted himself under the bed, and was discovered by Korr who supposing him to be a burglar killed him instantly. It is a sad state of affairs in which a wife's infidelity seems to have been the inciting cause.

Martin County Sentinel, September 15, 1893

The Scandinavians Ignored!—The Scandinavian members of the republican party were the recipients of another "slap in the face" at the state convention, held in St. Paul last Thursday. Not one single Scandinavian was remembered [in the choice of delegates and presidential electors], but a negro Frederick L. McGhee, who claims to represent a handful of his race, was elected to the most responsible and most honorary position which the convention has at its disposal. . . . But the Scandinavians, which comprise one-fifth, and perhaps even more, of the state's most law-abiding citizens and the republican party's most loyal supporters, were completely ignored . . .

It is a shame that our newspapers won't take up this thing. But they are in the most cases republican and presumably ruled by the Irish rings and content themselves with quiet agreement or even in some cases defend the party for its shoddy treatment of the Scandinavians. Are our countrymen going to stand for such treatment? Are the Swedes going to vote for these Irish bums forever? These bums who openly and boastingly and everywhere refer to the Scandinavians as "voting cattle!" When a political party which for its very existence in Minnesota depends upon the Scandinavians, treats them in such a manner, then it is simply our countrymen's duty to chastise the "bullies" at the ballot-box. And surely thousands of Scandinavians will know how to avenge such insults this fall.

Translated from *Svenska Amerikanska Posten*, May 10, 1892

RESTORED MANHOOD
Dr. Mott's Nerverine pills
The greatest remedy for nervous prostration and all nervous disorders of the generative organs of either sex, such as Nervous Prostration, Failing or Lost Manhood, Impotency, Nightly Emissions, Youthful Errors, Mental Worry, excessive use of Tobacco or Opium, which lead to Consumption and insanity. With every $5 order we give a written guarantee to cure or refund the money. Sold at $1.00 per box, 6 boxes for $5.00. De Mott's Chemical Co., Cleveland, Ohio. Sold in Duluth by Smith & Smith, 101 West Superior Street.

Duluth Evening Herald, November 10, 1894

The leading citizens of St. Cloud played baseball last Sunday. This violation of the Sunday law so angered some of the ardent church people that they made a list of those that participated in the game as well as the attending fans. The list includes the mayor, the chief of police, the county attorney, the chief of the fire department, most of the aldermen and 40 of the leading business and professional men of St. Cloud. These are now to be arrested and charged with violating the Sunday law. The only thing that troubles the collective minds of the law enforcing church group is; who is going to do the arresting and the prosecuting?

Translated from *Folkebladet*, a Minneapolis Danish and Norwegian publication, June 4, 1890

1900s

Lumbering reached its peak in 1905. The population in the federal census was 1,751,394—seven times that at the close of the Civil War in 1865. Wheat was a major crop, but diversification was obvious. Flour and milling were still 46 percent of Minnesota's invested industrial capital. The railroads built in almost every direction from the Twin Cities. About a dozen automobiles were in the state in 1902 (and one man was arrested for exceeding Minneapolis's ten-miles-per-hour speed limit). By 1909 the state had licensed seven thousand autos and four thousand motorcycles. The Minneapolis Symphony was organized in 1903. →

Charles Munson, about 1908. *Albert Munson photo, MNHS*

HORACE GLENN

Your Son Horace

"I am looked upon as a sort of stuck-up dude because I wash my feet once a week and use a handkerchief."

Horace H. Glenn was twenty-one when he headed north to the lumber camps to make money. His letters show he was well educated and considered himself vastly superior to the Irish, Swedes, Norwegians, Russians, and almost every other logger. Glenn, of Scottish-Irish ancestry, wrote to his parents in St. Paul. His father was a railroad conductor.

Two Harbors, Minn.
Nestor State Camp 1
JAN. 6, 1901
My Dear Parents,
Received your letter yesterday, also [news]papers. I am always glad to get papers as literature of any description is very scarce in camp. Once in a while a police gazette gets into camp & the jacks crowd around it like a lot of children around a toy, especially the Irish which abound here. . . . I brought several magazines in with me & one of them picked one up last Sunday & looked at it & said, "Oh, I guess it's only an advertisement" & laid it down. They had never seen a magazine before & didn't know what it was. They are the most utterly illiterate uninformed savages I ever encountered. They work for six months without hearing a thing from the outside world, go into town, spend every cent in a few days & go to work again. That is the program of 9/10 of them & they have followed it from early childhood. Of those who come from Canada, about one in ten can read & write, & of those from Michigan about half. As you might imagine, the conversation of such people is highly edifying and instructive. In the cook shack no talking whatever is allowed during meals for the simple reason that most of them cannot utter the simplest sentence without beginning, ending and interspersing it with the most disgusting, blasphemous and useless profanity imaginable. I am looked upon as a sort of stuck-up dude because I wash my feet once a week and use a handkerchief. In the evening they all chew tobacco to excess, spit on the

Horace Glenn and his family, 1909. *Glenn Family*

Washing clothes in northern Minnesota, 1907. *MNHS*

floor & when they go to bed, take off their socks & walk around in it to the stove to hang up their socks & back again to bed.

I can honestly say that I am the intellectual superior of the whole lot of men in this camp by a large margin, laying all vanity or conceit aside. I also have the cleanest feet. It is needless to say however that I make no boast of these facts around camp. Their sole ambition and only idea of recreation is to drink whisky and blow their stake in the shortest possible time. In the spring they herd into town like sheep to the slaughter, you might say. About 3 drinks of whisky sets them crazy drunk, a few more & they are laid out and the saloon man goes through them & they go out to work again in the morning & tell of what a time they had. They log here in the summer a good deal as well as winter. I saw lots of them in town Christmas & know whereof I speak. I now realize more fully than ever the value of a good bringing up and schooling. If I

ever become a legislator or statesman I shall see that a rigid compulsory education law is enacted & enforced in the back woods.

But in spite of these drawbacks of association I believe I enjoy the work better than any I ever did before. Sawing to my notion is the best job in the woods, the time passes quickly and although it is very cold, from zero to 30 below so far, you don't notice it as so much in the timber and what I eat at home would be scarcely a light lunch for me here. There is no boss over you while you work, you go into the woods & saw all day & give in your logs at night. We saw from 80 to 110 according to the size of the timber. There are three men in a gang, an undercutter & two sawyers & you are alone all day. The undercutter notches the trees, measures them when down & cuts off the top & all you have to do is saw. It is steady but if you know how to saw & have a good partner it is not hard. There are 9 gangs going here now & one man does nothing but saw files, fix

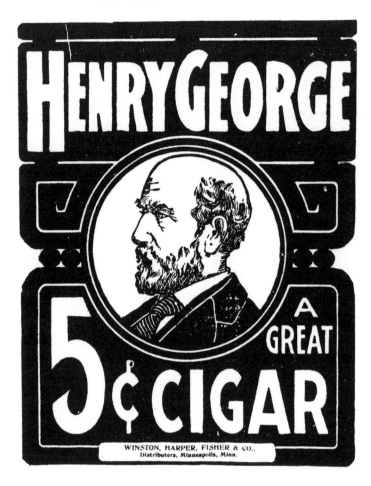

without working, being careful to make camp at meal time & then leaving or perhaps working a day or so. There are lots of men who do nothing else all winter long & make their board without any more work than walking. I went up to Allen J.C. [Junction] & worked three days, I didn't like the place so I didn't stay. I have put in 7 days here & like the camp.

The Duluth & Iron Range is a great Railroad for a country like this, it is nearly all double track & they are grading the rest of it for double track as fast as they can & at the same time reducing grades. The principal traffic is in logs and iron ore. Rockerfeller owns great iron mines at the northern end of it and all the ore is shipped to Two Harbors and then by the lakes east. There is also logging the entire length of it and there are 40 & 50 trains a day when they are hauling both ore and logs. The logs go to Duluth. They of course employ a lot of railroad men & Two Harbors is a town of about 3000 made up of but little else.

. . . One thing I am positive about if I ever was positive about anything, and that is I am going to save every cent I can from this on for next winter. Next winter I am going to have enough laid by so that I can stay at home all winter & take music lessons and improve my mind. I am going to buy a violin & take lessons on it and the piano, guitar and mandolin. Every time I think of the home I have and its advantages & then consider the way I am living and among such savages I can come to no conclusion but that I am a hopeless lunatic. I have talked like this before and nothing came of it but I have never thought so earnestly over it as I have lately.

We are having good weather & am in the best of health & never ate more in my life.

Your son,
Horace

[And on to his opinions of the Swedes, written from Smith's camp in Marcy, February 24, 1901:]

wedges, etc. You use a saw but one day & bring it in & get a new one. If I stay till April 1st I get $.30 per month & if not I get $26.

I have no way of sending money here so I wish you would send 23 cents to the St. Paul Dispatch & have it sent here for 1 month. As soon as I draw any money I am going to send most of it home. You stated in your letter that they had not found Ray Tennant. It would be of interest to me to know what they are looking for him for. Be sure & tell me in your next letter.

Your son,
Horace

[In February of 1901, Horace wrote to his folks from Smith's logging camp in Marcy, Minnesota:]

. . . After quitting Ulstar's [logging operation] I went on what they call here a camp inspecting trip, that is I travelled from camp to camp

9/10th of the men are Roundheads [immigrants] & the most disgusting, dirty, lousy reprobates that I ever saw. I want to hit them every time I look at them. I licked one last week & kicked him bad & I get so mad sometimes I could whip a dozen if I had to. There are probably 15 white men here to 60 Swedes & those 15 keep them so they don't dare to say their soul is their own. Every time a Swede gets gay [lighthearted, carefree] he is promptly squelched & it is done so quick & decisively that he don't try it again. It is getting worse every year & soon there will be nothing else up here. The idea is that the poorest wages & board in this country are so far above anything the Swede ever dreamed of that he is contented with anything here & therefor makes a first class scab. In any labor requiring a degree of skill he cannot be used, however. In all the camps I have been in I have never seen a Swede cant hook man & only one Swede teamster & he got fired & they are none too good at anything else. When I get out of here I never want to see a Swede again. . . . If

Enjoying a summer day, location unknown. *MNHS*

I had my way with them I would have them carroled & made to take a bath & instructed in the use of a handkerchief at the point of a bayonet . . .

[Same camp, March 10, 1901:]

My Dear Parents,
Today is my 22nd birthday but I feel like a kid of ten. I have always enjoyed the best of health & spirits but never I believe in such a degree as lately. My supply of animal spirits seems inexhaustible. I can work hard for 12 hours & feel as fresh as a daisy with the morning dew on it. The perfect spring weather is partly responsible for it I suppose. It is only evenings when I am forced to associate with these beasts they call Swedes that I get depressed, but as soon as I get out in the morning I forget them, forget that I am lousy [have lice] & enjoy myself & nature. I am the first man out in the morning

because walking 2 or 3 miles behind a string of Swedes is something impossible to a person with a delicate nose. The only smell which I have encountered which approaches it is the odor of a lot of Russians on a [railroad] hand car when well warmed up. It is an odor which could only come from generations of unwashed ancestors & no man can hope to acquire it in one lifetime without the aid of heredity. It also reminds me of times when I have been out hunting & have come unexpectedly to the windward of a dead horse. It gives the ravens the same idea for wherever there is a bunch of Swedes working there are always buzzards or ravens perched around in the trees.

There is an art other than logging which has received an exalted degree of perfection in this section of the country and that is use of profanity . . . I am swamping for a teamster who is adept and when once thoroughly roused he can swear continuously for 15 minutes without the repetition of a single word. He is very impartial about it and nothing seems to escape his profane attention, the logs, the team, the chain, the weather & the general management of the universe all receive their due share and he does it with an accuracy & perfection of detail worthy of a much better cause. But in spite of his profanity he never cursed the swampers and is a very good man to work for . . .

My swamping partner is a Norwegian of a little better grade than the average and my precepts and practice have worked wonders with him. I prevailed upon him to wash his feet after three months total abstinence from water. He differs from the others in that he is not averse to adopting American customs and learning the language. He has a great respect for me & he confided to me yesterday that when I first came he sized me up as a different & superior type from other Americans here. Now he in the course of time will probably marry & encourage his children to adopt American ways & in the course of a few

Load of logs, 1899. *Carlton County Park Commission*

generations they may hope to eradicate that distasteful foreign odor & become good citizens and my humble influence will have had some affect. I might formulate a proverb out of this that "there is more patriotism in teaching a Norwegian to wash his feet than in fighting Filipinos" or something like that. [This letter was written during the Spanish-American War.] But as a rule, precept or example are pearls before swine in these back woods and I have not bothered myself in scattering many of them, besides I have a few beams to cast out of my own eyes before I bother with my brother's motes.

If I had studied zoology more diligently when at school I could derive considerable satisfaction from the study of the human louse this winter and I would never be at a loss for specimens. I never realized before what a complicated creature he was in fact I never made his acquaintance till last fall on the railroad. They are of all shapes and sizes & varied colors, some can run fast & some can scarcely wiggle but they all multiply very rapidly & they all bite. Nothing but boiling water will kill them, the most intense cold does not affect them. Some [people] seem to derive a certain satisfaction from them which is embraced in a saying very much in vogue here. It is "Blessed is the man who is crumby [who has body lice] for he knoweth the benefit of a scratch." I think it deserves to be ranked among the other beatitudes. If I had David Griffith's address I have thought of making a collection & sending them to him in the interest of science. I found an entirely new species this morning with no legs on it.

Smiths Camp
Marcy, Minn.
MARCH 24, 1901
Today is Sunday & there is considerable excitement in camp. There is a dance & a poker game going on. We have a fiddle in camp & we always dance on Sunday nights [sometimes with women but more often with the other loggers].

[And so we leave Horace Glenn, lice and all. He married in 1906, started law school at the St. Paul College of Law in 1911, and graduated first in his class in 1914. He practiced law in St. Paul.]

Andrew W. Glenn and Family papers, MNHS

***

Orphaned girls, ages three and four. *MNHS*

Same children, after adoption. *MNHS*

Clara and Mary Radinty three and four years of age. Born in Haygatta, Minn. Dependent upon the public for protection and support The mother is insane and confined in an asylum. The father is cruel and brutal, so as to imperil their lives.

'Out of earth's elements mingled with flame, Out of life's compound of glory and shame, Fashioned and shaped by no will of their own, And helpless, into life's history thrown, Born by the law that compels men to be, Born to conditions they cannot foresee"

Admitted to the State Public School Aug. 17. 072. Picture taken on their arrival

[These little girls were the victims of extreme cruelty and neglect. Their mother, a native of Switzerland and a good woman, was unfortunate in her second marriage, as her husband proved to be brutal and cruel in the extreme. Under his constant and continued abuse, she became insane and is now in the hospital at St. Peter. The little girls were rescued from the brutal father's custody and brought to the school in the condition shown in the first picture. The rest of the children, a little brother and an older sister, were afterward taken from him and brought here.

These girls proved to be pretty, attractive children, and Clara, the younger, was selected by a gentleman, a member of the legislature, who visited the school during the session of that year. Mary was soon wanted by another good family.

We now add [another picture], and a letter from Clara, which shows how she is progressing.]

"Dear Mr. ——, I received your letter and the book with my picture in it, for which I thank you. It doesn't seem possible that I was ever such a ragged urchin as that. I feel very glad that some one found me and put me in a good home.

"I shall be ten years old next Sunday. I have had ten birthday presents already this week. I will tell you what they are. Papa had my picture taken. Mamma had the dressmaker make me a nice new winter jacket. She also gave me four new aprons, three hair ribbons and a new school hat. Our school begins the fourth of September. I will begin in the fifth grade this year. I attended school eight months last year, but hope to be able to go every day this year. I shall have a splendid teacher this year. I have only missed five Sundays since Christmas. I learn a verse from the Bible every week, and repeat it to my Sunday school teacher. I have been quite busy through vacation helping mamma. I am learning to work. Papa says I am getting to be quite a nice housekeeper. I will close with love."

Eighth Biennial Report of the Board of Control and Superintendent of the Minnesota State Public School for Dependent and Neglected Children, 1900

Stone arch bridge, Minneapolis, about 1900. *Library of Congress*

POLLY BULLARD

"Bring your warm clothes; for 35 below zero means it is cold, of course."

Polly Bullard was a high school student when she kept this part of her diary. Her family lived near Irvine Park in St. Paul.

THURSDAY [IN APRIL 1897]. Mrs. Martin came in to spend the day. She told us all the news from the park. One of her confidences to Mama was about Ned Parker. Mama told me afterward. Mrs. Todd told her that Ned was in the habit of swearing sometimes, and this troubled them both. Mrs. Todd didn't like to speak to Mrs. Parker about it, because her own boys are very far from reproach. Mrs. Martin thought about it, and worried for some time and finally she wrote a note to Mrs. T. asking if she might speak to Mrs. Parker about it for she thought she ought to know. Mrs. T. answered that she must do as she thought best. So finally she told Mrs. P. about it. Well, one night Mrs. P. was in the kitchen alone, when Ned walked in. Her mind was so full of it that she could not keep still any longer. "Ned," said she, "are you ever profane?" She needed no answer, for she saw in his face that the accusation was true. "Yes," said he. And then she talked to him for over an hour. How he was her oldest son, and how, now that his father was dead, he was the head of the family and what a responsibility rested upon his shoulders, so he quite melted down and became very penitent. After she went to bed, quite late in the night, Ned came into her room; "Mother," said he, "you may be very sure I will never do so again."

Friday . . . I had a very lovely birthday, and a very happy one, accompanied, of course, with many appropriate remarks about "sweet sixteen." Grandma and Papa compared notes about Grandma's visit to Elgin [Illinois, where Polly was born] when I was five months old—about squealing and kicking, and how Grandma cried when she left after a long visit, never expecting to see me again, much less to sit down at my sixteenth birthday dinner-party. Grandma and Uncle together gave me a very pretty rocking chair for my room, Mama gave me a very handsome brown leather belt, Marjorie a black satin hair ribbon, and Elizabeth a very fine pencil, with a compartment at one end for lead, and one at the other for a pen and an eraser. Best of all Papa gave Marjorie and me tickets to the Carreno Concert for Monday evening.

Monday . . . In the evening we went to the concert which was, of course, magnificent. Madame Teresa Carreno is, without exception, the finest woman pianiste in the world, and some say the finest of either sex. The second number on her programme was Beethoven's Moonlight Sonata, which Miss Mott plays, and of which I have attempted to play the first two movements. . . . She played it so tremendously fast that one had hardly time to appreciate the full beauty. Then she played five numbers of Chopin, which so inspired Marjorie that she completely changed her opinion of his music. She and Mama have had

Stereoscopic view of open-pit iron mining at Hibbing, 1906. *Library of Congress*

Dancing in the woods, about 1900. *MNHS*

a most unpleasant dislike to it, which they have heard mostly under my playing, which is indeed a poor sample.

Sunday, May 30. Today I have not stirred out of the house, for the weather is bleak, chilly, with a raw wind whistling around the corners and rattling the windows. . . . This afternoon Papa is asleep on the sofa downstairs, with Mama's old red shawl over him, while she and the children have gone up to see Grandma and Dana. So I have had the house to myself, and enjoyed it too. Have been reading essays.

[Polly Bullard went to Eveleth to teach school in 1908. The village was just beginning to change from a primitive mining location to a promising Mesabi Iron Range town. The original townsite was platted in 1893, but by 1900 miners had discovered that there were rich ore deposits under the town and the village was moved a little to the east. The first letter here was written to Polly in 1908 by a friend, Rita Kendall, who arranged for Polly to work in the Eveleth school.]

Dear Polly,

Mr. Greening is writing about when to come— and this is merely a supplement about the things you wished to know. Considering the fact that everything in town is atrociously ugly, expenses are very high—but that seems to be a condition which has to be endured in silence. The room you will have if you live at

Fourth of July party in St. Paul, about 1908. *MNHS*

Mrs. Samuelson's is very small—contains a bed, a table, a bureau and a chair—and has one window. The rug on the floor you will wish to exterminate immediately. Moreover, she is very loath to get anything more for the room. So, if you want to be happy and comfortable on that score, you would be wise to bring with you a rug from home. All of us have done that, and have also brought what extra pieces of furniture we felt we should want. A writing desk is a valuable acquisition. The walls in the room are a noncommital bluish gray, so if you want any color schemes they will not interfere. If you want curtains at the window of anything but white, you would better get it there; for those things are most difficult to get hold of here. And for the privilege of occupying this room, you pay $7.00 monthly. The board for the most part is very good, and that costs one $22.00 a month. We girls are paid every four weeks, and these expenses are due every calendar month. We who are at the house have rented an extra room at Mrs. Samuelson's and fixed it up for a sitting room. That helps to make the smallness of things more bearable. The house is heated by stoves; but we manage to keep very comfortable. There is a good big bathroom, with hot water nearly all the time, which is one of the greatest blessings the house affords. There are also electric lights throughout the establishment.

With regard to clothes, for my own part, I do not feel the cold here any more than in St. Paul. It is true that the mercury drops a few degrees lower, but it doesn't seem to make an appreciable difference. However, bring your warm clothes; for 35 below zero means it is cold, of course.

I think Mr. Greening is going to ask you to come up Thursday so that you may visit some third grade work, and see for yourself what the work is before you begin. Let me know what train you come in on, and if I can I shall meet you, or send someone down. Please don't look for a great deal, for you will be disappointed,

Scenes of Minneapolis, 1900 to about 1908.
Top: MNHS; middle and bottom: Minneapolis Public Library

but be exceedingly humble in your expectations, and you will be much safer.

Very sincerely,
Rita Kendall Eveleth, Minn.
Nov. 2, 1908

[Polly's first letter home to her parents in St. Paul:]

Eveleth, Friday night
NOV. 6 [1908]
Dear Mother,
I got here safely and comfortably this morning at 10:30 and Mr. Greening met me at the station. His wife was with him. They are both young, and seem to be a very good sort. I sent my trunk and suitcase to the house and had him take me to the school. The building I am in is a very good one and quite new. The teacher in charge of the 3rd grade at present is a large buxom young woman, very good natured, and very kind about giving me all the necessary points of information. I went over to the other school building at noon and met Rita and came home with her and one of the other teachers, Miss Sherman, a charming girl from Marquette, Michigan. There are five girls living here, and about fifteen people take their meals here. My room is not bad—larger—about twice as large as my new one at home—has a double bed which I have not yet tried—and very few covers, so I shall have to have a good thick comforter, I think.

I went back to the school this afternoon and am to visit on Monday also, and then I think that by Tuesday I can take charge of the work without any trouble.

This is certainly a strange place. It makes me think of the weird scenes in Paradise Lost. You can see for miles in every direction—the land undulates in low hills covered with stunted pines or fir and the mines and their machinery are very much in evidence. The children in this 3rd grade belong to the foreign population, with the exception of one child.

They say there are 10,000 people here, but only about 2,000 civilized folk—of the others the Austrians and the Finns are the majority. The house would amuse you, or rather, alarm you, with its unpromising exterior, but it is comfortable within.

The bathroom is almost as large as Betty's room and has a stove going in it all the time, so it is entirely comfortable. The plumbing is modern & white enamel. My room is over the kitchen so the floor is warm & a register from the kitchen, just outside my door, gives heat, so I am entirely comfortable now, though it is quite cold outside. If I want more heat I shall get a little kerosene stove. The school is likely to be over-heated, if anything. I shall have a good walk in the fresh air going to & from school—about eight blocks, I believe.

The girls in the house are ever so nice, nothing extraordinary, but thoroughly nice.

I think this will have to do for a first installment.

Love to all
P.C.B.

[Another letter home, the next week:]

EVELETH, NOVEMBER 12TH [1908]
Dear Mother,
. . . The ride up here was most interesting. The types of people, the configuration of the land, and the arrangement and general appearance of the towns all along the way are entirely different from anything I had seen before. At Duluth the train ran for some time along the lake shore, and the view was truly wonderful. The sun was just rising as we pulled out, and shone through the lake mist and glanced back from the water like a painting of Turner. Away out, apparently rising right out of the water, were great high cranes & derricks & a revolving bridge, and up from the shore ran miles & miles of elevated track with hundreds of little ore carts standing on them. . . . From one window of our school we can look nine miles

away. I have never seen such a sweep of sky anywhere excepting in midocean, and ever since I have been here it has been filled with great gray &. silver snow clouds rolling and sweeping along. The town itself straggles over the hills. Most of the houses are little yellow & blue things but there are some very comfortable residences. . . .

Mrs. Samuelson [the landlady] is a strange creature. Her Finnish name is Mikki Koukkari. She is a rabid Socialist and all the Socialists who come here to speak stay at her house. One came Saturday night and they had a grand to-do down in the kitchen till two in the morning. Socialism is rampant here among the miners . . .

On Tuesday all the teachers gathered in Miss Maudeville's cooking room, in the basement of the Fayal School, & had a cooking lesson. We made lobster, souffle & coffee, and then had a feast. It was such fun that we are to get together and make corn fritters . . .

As to school, I have a funny little room, with the leavings of several rooms in it—quite a handful therefore. They are Italian, Austrian, Finnish, Swedish & Irish—only one American, I believe, & some of them have only been in this country a year or so. Most of them are good children, but I have two or three need a good deal of squelching.

I see that my Teacher's Certificate has expired, so I shall have to have my diploma, or else get some kind of certificate of my B.A. degree at the University. I think my diploma is in my box in the attic. If you can't find it let me know. & also have Marjorie ask at the Registrar's office what they can do for me about it.

Lovingly,
P.C.B.

Polly C. Bullard papers, MNHS

RECIPES

"Do not stare around the room, nor ask questions about the price of the furniture."

Around the turn of the century, ladies' church groups raised money by publishing cookbooks. They differed from today's versions. Examples:

GLOVE CLEANER—For gloves or grease spots on any kind of clothing. One quart of deoderized benzine, ¼ ounce chloroform, ¼ ounce coral of ammonia, ¼ ounce sulphuric ether. Mix.

Family Friend, Ascension Church, Stillwater, 1893

CALF'S HEAD STEW—Remove the brains and boil the head until the bones drop out; then cut the meat in rather small pieces, and have ready 6 hard boiled eggs, chopped; stew the brains separately and add ½ teacup of butter; pepper and salt to taste, 1 clove. Put all together and stew 10 minutes. Just before serving, flavor with Armour sauce or walnut catsup.

Family Friend

TOAST WATER FOR INVALIDS—Slices of toast nicely browned without a symptom of burning; enough boiling water to cover; cover

A confirmation class in Fillmore County. *MNHS*

closely and let steep until cold; strain and sweeten to taste and put a piece of ice in each glassful. If the physician thinks it safe, add a little lemon juice.

> *The "Central" Cook Book*, Central Presbyterian Church, St. Paul, 1900

FINE BREAD—THE FOUNDATION OF GOOD MEALS—There is nothing in cooking more important than bread making. Bread is a daily necessity. It is on our tables three times a day, seven days in the week and if properly made is always eaten with relish. Every woman should so thoroughly understand the principles involved in its preparation as to eliminate luck and always have perfect bread as a result of her time and labor expended, and the good wholesome food materials utilized in its preparation.

> *A Cook Book*, compiled by the Ladies of Dayton Avenue Presbyterian Church, St. Paul, 1892

[A book called *Sloan's Handy Hints and Up-To-Date Cook Book* was published in Boston in 1901 and made its way to Upper Midwest homes. Dr. Earl S. Sloan used his book to point out the value of his remedies: *Sloan's Linament Stops Pain for you or Your Horse*. Here are some of his hints:]

SOME POINTS ON ETIQUETTE—If you want your children to feel at ease at the grandest tables in the land, carefully teach them the small points of etiquette from childhood.

Never use the knife to carry food to the mouth. When through using knife and fork, lay them both diagonally across the plate, with both handles toward the right hand. Well-trained waiters understand this to be a signal to remove them with the plate.

Keep the mouth shut closely while chewing the food. It is the opening of the lips which causes the smacking that is so objectionable.

Chew your food thoroughly, but do it silently, and be careful to take small mouthfuls. Do not clatter your knives or forks upon your plates; use them without noise. When you are helped, do not wait until the rest of the company are provided; it is not considered good breeding.

Take soup from the side of spoon, not from the tip, without any sound of the lips; do not suck into the mouth audibly from the end of the spoon.

Do not give your arm, in the daytime, to a lady who is not your mother, wife or sister, or an elderly or invalid lady.

Never salute a lady with a gesture of the hand; take off your hat.

Never apologize when you shake hands with your gloved hand.

Do not take two ladies upon your arm except for their protection.

Do not stare around the room, nor ask questions about the price of the furniture.

Addressing people is no reason or excuse for touching them.

Whispering in company is not nice.

Your napkin is intended for your lips and beard only, not to wipe your face with.

Do not cleanse your nails, your nose, your ears in public.

HOUSEHOLD HINTS

Boil 3 or 4 onions in a pint of water and apply with a soft brush to gilt frames, and flies will keep off them.

To rid a room of mosquitoes, burn a piece of gum camphor about the size of a walnut on a plate.

In making coffee observe that the broader the bottom and the smaller the top of the vessel the better the coffee will be. Never let coffee or tea stand in tin.

To prevent the smoking of a lamp, soak the wick in strong vinegar, and dry it well before you use it; it will then burn clear and bright.

To prevent a scale or crust forming inside a teakettle, place a clean oyster shell in it.

To kill ants, bedbugs, cockroaches, etc., put alum into hot water, let it boil until it is all dissolved; then apply the solution with a brush to all cracks, closets, bedsteads and wherever insects are found. If you will use Sloan's Linament though a syringe, you get this advantage; that while it kills every insect in its path, the place where applied will not be again invaded.

Ants may also be exterminated in the following manner: wring out a sponge in sugared water and place on a plate in the room infested. When covered with ants plunge into boiling water. Continue the process.

Sloan's Handy Hints and Up-To-Date Cook Book, 1901

VICTOR MYLLYMAKI

"They say this America is the land of the free but that's a lie."

A Finnish American miner in Eveleth found himself caught up in the Mesabi strike of 1907. Here is his letter home, translated into English.

Eveleth, Minnesota
AUGUST 5, 1907
Dear Brother:

I just returned from the post office and got your letter. I decided to answer it right away conveying my heartfelt thanks for it. I have kept in good health which is what I hope for you there in my homeland. Now I'll describe a bit what the conditions are like over here. There is a great strike going on. There are many of us out of work. I don't know how long the strike will last. It's only been 2½ weeks since it started and this isn't a very pleasant time at all. There are a 100 stooges with guns paid by the mining companies harassing the workers just like some animals. A worker can't peacefully walk down the street anymore. People are jailed everyday. They say this America is the land of the free but that's a lie. A week ago Finnish socialists in Michigan had a large summer festival and they used some old flags in the festival procession just like the custom is in Finland. About 100 of them began the march to the festival site. But the local police and their accomplices met them, took their flags away and beat up 13 marchers and threw them in jail, from where they were later taken to the hospital.

You wrote that Kalle would like to come here. I'll sure send him a ticket, but not now.

I myself might have to leave here if this strike lasts very long. The workers have decided to strike for a year if their demands aren't met. They are asking for $3.00 a day and an eight-hour day. If we win the strike. I'll send Kalle a ticket right away.

Greetings to everyone in my homeland.
Your brother,
Victor Myllymaki

University of Minnesota's Immigration History Research Center, which also provided the translation

***

[Immigrants, facing tremendous pressures to adjust to new societies, sometimes reacted by drinking heavily. Temperance societies were established to help relieve the addiction.

These minutes are from a 1906 meeting of the Pohjan Leimu (Northern Flame) Temperance Society of Soudan, Minnesota.]

It was announced that the following members had broken their pledge: Heikki Mutka. Eli Myllyla and John Heikkila. Art Kuosmonen and John Jaanus resigned. It was reported that John Hajari had broken his pledge. Also in question was his wife's eligibility for membership, but it was felt that she couldn't be removed from the society before the investigating committee looks into the matter and renders a decision. Then it was reported that Nestor Wainio had admitted taking a certain medicine for his rheumatism and he wondered if it was against the society's rules. The

matter was discussed and it was decided that he would continue to be recognized as a member. Then Heikki Oja announced that he had taken some cholera drops for his diarrhea, but this also wasn't considered to be against the society's rules.

[Backsliding to the bottle was frequent. In a quarter of a century, the Ely temperance society had 862 violators among 2,104 members. Violators were forgiven; the Hibbing group allowed a member to fall from grace three times in three months before imposing a sentence of three months.]

University of Minnesota's Immigration History Research Center, which also provided the translation

***

[The Minnesota Automobile Association published an *Automobile Hand Book* in 1908 that included scenic routes. An example:]

Route No. 26
Minnetonka Beach to Excelsior
4½ Miles
By Index Speedometer
Via Narrows, Tonka Bay and Wildhurst

You enter the village, Minnetonka Beach, on its east side over a long bridge; continue on main Boulevard a few rods in straight direction, then turn left to the Lake, then right along bluff road (Lafayette Club on right) keeping always to left near lake (at the end of village a sign reading "Excelsior 4 miles" will direct you). Continue a few hundred rods to cross roads, turn sharply to left here (good sign will direct) and proceed straight to ferry, which is large flat boat, capable of holding four machines and perfectly safe, and easy to run onto without leaving machine. After crossing ferry (no charge) continue on main road which is quite winding but level, bearing to right ¾ mile from ferry (road to left leads to Tonka Bay) continue on main road across railway (be careful) past Wildhurst station, which is on the right, thence some distance on same road over R.R. tracks at Manitou Junction, to where it runs into an interesting road; turn left here, thence into village on Oak St., turn left on William St., one block, then right on George St. one block (conservatory on corner) turn left on Water St., and proceed across tracks to drug store corner Main and 2nd St., which seems to be about the center of the village of Excelsior.

***

[How a dead man won a baseball game:]

Around the turn of the century, two crack semi-pro teams from Minnesota had won the attention of the baseball world. When these teams met, one from Willmar, one from Benson, fans came from hundreds of miles to witness the battle.

For nine innings, those teams battled without being able to score a winning run. In the first half of the 10th, Benson scored a run. Willmar went to bat, grim and determined to better the score. Thielman, the Willmar pitcher, cracked out a single, giving them a chance. Next up was O'Toole, who smashed out a terrific drive into the outfield.

The crowd roared in a frenzy of excitement, for here was the game if both Willmar players could score.

Thielman, utterly exhausted by the tension of the tight game he had pitched for 10 innings, gritted his teeth and ran as fast as he could. He touched second and legged it for third with O'Toole's spikes pounding behind him.

Benson's outfield had not yet retrieved the ball. Thielman rounded third—and then collapsed. O'Toole rounded the base close on his heels. Unable to pass him on the home stretch, O'Toole picked him up and carried him, throwing him across the home base ahead of his own home touch.

Not until then was it discovered that

A couple posing with a deer head in Morrison County, about 1900. *MNHS*

A ninety-five-pound, six-foot three-inch sturgeon, about 1900. *MNHS*

Broke Jail!

Escaped from the Morrison county jail, Tuesday evening, Aug. 2, 1904, Frank Harrington, held for trial for horse stealing.

DESCRIPTION:—Age 24 years; height 5 feet 8½ inches; blue eyes, black hair, brown moustache; well dressed. Wore dark clothes, black soft hat, light shirt with dark stripes, red necktie, lace shoes. Second and third fingers on right hand injured, claimed in coupling cars. Scar on back of neck below collar, and on point of right shoulder. Weight, about 160 pounds. Light complexion. Wire

E. S. TANNER,

Sheriff Morrison County, Little Falls, Minn.

Wanted for Bastardy.
ADOLPH FRANSON.

DESCRIPTION

Height, 5 feet, 9 inches; age, 38 or 39; weight, 150 to 160; dark hair and mustache; complexion fair. Has one stiff, crooked finger. Is shoemaker and harness-maker by trade.

Arrest and wire all information to

WILLIAM FORSBERG,

Sheriff Marshall Co., Minn.

Dated at Warren, Minn., August 5th, 1903.

Thielman was dead of heart failure. But stranger than that, the umpire allowed the two runs, giving the game to Willmar, and making this the only baseball game won by a dead man!

[Nice story, but not true. The story was a figment of the imaginations of a Kandiyohi County railroad man and an umpire. They sent it out on the telegraph wire and told it so many times that people began to believe it. For decades, the Minnesota Historical Society gets inquiries about the baseball game won by a dead man.]

The Centennial History of Kandiyohi County

***

Linwood, Minn.

NOV. 11TH 1902

Dear Uncle John,

I will write to you and thank you for those skates, on my birthday. I am seventeen today. Papa went up country hunting, so I have everything to do all alone. I got the rest of the spuds in the root cellar, making in all about 1300 bu. It has been raining all day. I got one duck to day and one yesterday they make fine eating The folk said you were coming over, but have not seen anything of you. All are well here but me, my eyes are bothering me yet. I am going to the Dr. one of thies days. Well I will have to close, with love to all. Your loving nephew.

Walter B. Shorrocks

John E. Purmort and Family papers, MNHS

***

[Henry Smith was editor of the Mantorville, Minnesota, *Express* for thirty-three years. He also wrote poetry, especially about his wife, Jennie. For their fiftieth anniversary in 1916, when he was seventy-two years old, he copied into a notebook all the poems he had written about her and called it "A Lifetime's Love Rhymes." He wrote that "a pencil is used in this transcription because of my inability to use a pen steadily." The introduction begins:]

Five years my sweetheart, fifty years my wife.
For five and fifty years my joy in life.

[Before their marriage, he wrote in 1865:]

Jennie loves me, this I know.
For has she not told me so
Time and time again?
And is this not proof enough?
Ah! the knowledge of her love
Makes me the happiest of men.

[In 1872:]

The cottage seems lonesome tonight,
The good wife is gone from home,
And hearth and lamp though warm and bright
May not dispel the gloom.

The wind shakes window and door,
The rain beats loud above,
And listening to their mingling roar
I think of my absent love.

[On their twenty-fifth anniversary he wrote, "This latest year the happiest." And for their fiftieth anniversary, he wrote "Love Song of Old Age."]

In youth's glad days (what words could tell
How glad they were?) it so befell
I made a song of love to her
The one girl who was lovelier,
Sweeter (to me of greater worth)
Than all the other girls of earth.

In glad old age (let angels tell
How glad) I still a love song swell
To her who yet remains, life long,
The inspiration of my song;
O loyal heart! of greatest worth
To me of all true hearts of earth.

Henry A. Smith and Family papers, MNHS

ROLAND REED

Roland Reed, a Minnesota photographer who spent most of his adult life compiling a pictorial record of North American Indians, wrote about getting this 1908 photograph he called "The Hunters":

By the time I am ready to take these pictures, the Indians actually wish them taken; they are imbued with the very spirit of the subject I am trying to depict and they pose in all earnestness.

The Indians' makeup leaves something to be desired in the matter of imagination. This was particularly impressed upon me while I struggled to obtain my picture, "The Hunters." Two Chippewas, in full hunting regalia, monotonously paddled a canoe back and forth over the blue waters of a lake in northern Minnesota. I had the bow Indian stolidly discharging an arrow at a certain buoy each time the birch bark passed it. "More life to it, Yellow Face," I cried. "You wouldn't shoot a deer in that fashion!"

"I am not shooting a deer, Big Plume," he replied. "I am shooting a tree." "Imagine a deer," I rejoined. "Think you see a deer

Roland Reed's "The Hunters." *Kramer Gallery*

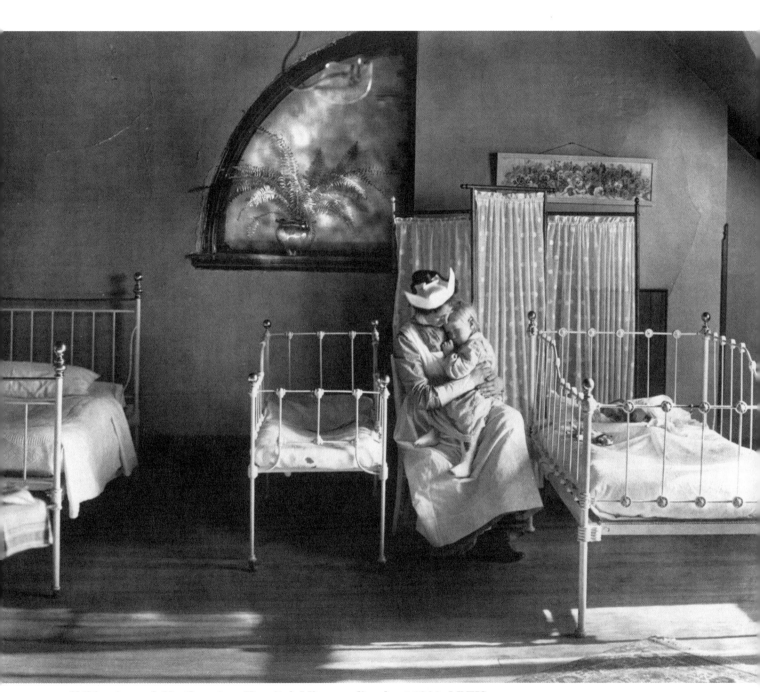

Children's ward, Northwestern Hospital, Minneapolis, about 1900. *MNHS*

swimming, trying to get away." "How can I see a deer when there is no deer, Big Plume," he quietly came back at me.

To this there was no answer. The afternoon light was growing yellow, but the shadows and reflections in the shining lake were at their best. I had been paying these Indians a regular wage for three days in an effort to get this one picture. Suddenly I drew out a handful of silver dollars and stuck them targetwise in the crevices of the tree bark.

"Make one more round, Yellow Face, while the light lasts," I shouted, "and listen. Shoot at these silver dollars as you pass the buoy. Every one you knock down is yours." On the next round the archer's eyes blazed with a savage light, his body quivered with all of the thrill of the hunt as he centered five silver dollars with seven whizzing shafts. When it was over and the air still hummed with the twang of his bowstring. I was out five dollars, but I had one of the few very animated Indian photographs in existence.

Private papers of the Kramer Gallery, St. Paul

***

[A product that never made it:]

Mothers: Children grow healthy and robust on YUCO, the new wheat food. They eat it with increasing appetite for breakfast, dinner and supper. YUCO is rich in the elements that

St. Paul, 1904. *Library of Congress*

the growing body demands—it is a complete food for young and old. YUCO is the perfected product of entire wheat scientifically prepared in the most cleanly manner in the largest mill in the world, thoroughly sterilized and packed while hot and in its purest, most healthful form. Made by Washburn, Crosby Company, Minneapolis, manufacturers of the celebrated Gold Medal Flour.

Minneapolis Tribune ad, May 4, 1900

***

[The downtown Minneapolis YMCA offered classes in 1901 that were billed as "Education for Busy Men." A pamphlet read:]

OUR EVENING CLASSES

ARE FOR YOU, who at an early age have been compelled to leave the school room to earn your own living. Until now you have had little or no chance to fit yourself mentally for the place in advance of the one you occupy at present.

ARE FOR YOU, who have had a good chance for such training, but have neglected it. The fault was your own. You regret the mistake now, and are glad of an opportunity to improve yourself.

ARE FOR YOU, who want special work. You are interested in Business, Mechanical or Electrical Engineering, Drafting, Economics, etc. We can help you.

ARE FOR YOU, who have been pursuing a certain line of work and wish something more advanced. Our advance courses are a feature this year.

ARE FOR ANYONE who is ambitious; who is willing to sacrifice some of his leisure time out of working hours for his own advancement. Positions of responsibility and trust are hard to fill. So few young men can qualify. A prominent bank cashier of Minneapolis says, "Many times we are asked to recommend a young man to fill some responsible place in business and are unable to find one." Chances for advancement all the time. No young man can afford to put off longer the important question of better preparation for life work.

Richard Chute and Family papers, MNHS

***

[Ad in the *Rochester Post and Record*, April 27, 1906:]

The parties who stole chickens from College Hill are known, and if the fowls are not returned they will be prosecuted.
Margaret Alseth

[Unfortunately for Margaret Alseth, on the same newspaper page was a news story about the chicken theft. It not only misspelled her name but also spoiled her bluff.]

Thieves broke into the chicken coop owned by Mrs. Olsett on College hill Thursday evening, and stole about forty chickens. It appears that the rogues went about it systematically, drove up with a horse and buggy, procured the poultry, and then drove away with their ill-gotten fowls. No clue is to be had as to their identity. Should the rascals be caught they should be dealt with as they deserve.

Rochester Post and Record, April 27, 1906

***

[Pollution problems, revealed in the 1899–1900 report of the Minnesota State Board of Health:]

The Lac qui Parle river, at Dawson, is another "eyesore" example of rural sanitation. It is a dirty, weed-grown stream, about sixty feet wide, and about five feet deep. All the town rubbish is dumped along its banks. Three private sewers discharge their foul contents into its waters. A nasty stock yard stretches and stinks to the river's edge. Here refuse from the slaughter-house, including heads, entrails, etc., are fed to the hogs. A dirty livery barn has unceasingly dumped the manure from some twenty-four horses on the inclined shore, until a great mass has accumulated, the base of which is lapped by the Lac qui Parle waters. Several other piles of similar proportions and locations assist in the pollution; all of which does not include the numerous outhouses on the shore. This highly polluted river is then used as an ice supply for the town of Dawson! Furthermore, ice is shipped out of Dawson to supply the towns of Madison and Boyd. These conditions were presented to the consideration of the local health officer, and he thoroughly agreed with us as to the necessity for energetic measures. Unfortunately such measures would, without doubt, arouse the enmity of many people on whose patronage the doctor's very living depends, and it is too much to ask a man to sacrifice his practice and make endless enemies in the service of a community which does not appreciate his work. The doctor, therefore, requested action from the state, and the matter was referred to the secretary of the state board of health.

NEWSPAPER CLIPPINGS

New Ulm people, who were interested in the last wrestling match at Mankato, will no doubt appreciate the fact that the Mankato athletic club has been able to bring the two greatest men in the wrestling game, John J. Rooney, of Chicago, and Bob Faulkner, of Guelph, Canada, together once more. The date of this next match is fixed for Monday evening, February 26th, at the Mankato opera house, and preparations are made to handle a big crowd. All roads offer reduced rates, when ten or more persons buy tickets at any one station.

Brown County Journal, February 17, 1900

COMMERCIAL ARC LIGHTS.
Linemen in the employ of the New Ulm Electric Lighting company have been busy this week stringing a line of wire along Minnesota street which will enable the merchants to burn arc lights in their stores. These arcs for commercial lighting will be enclosed and in other cities where the light has been used it has been found to be satisfactory.

Brown County Journal, November 22, 1902

The honor of raising the banner crop of potatoes for this section belongs to Emil Bethke, the well known New Ulm gardener. From a plot of land containing 2¼ acres he secured 600 bushels.

Brown County Journal, October 18, 1902

There is a likelihood of a large shortage of men in the pineries during the coming winter. At the present time there have been only a few men sent north to work in the logging camps. It is estimated that there are about 1,500 men employed in the pineries each winter, and up to the present time only about one-fifth of that number has been shipped.

Brown County Journal, November 15, 1902

THOUSANDS JOIN IN CELEBRATION. —Just as the Most Rev. John Ireland held aloft a silver trowel, preparatory to spreading the mortar over the cornerstone of St. Paul's magnificent $2,000,000 Cathedral Sunday afternoon, the downpour of rain that had earlier started ceased as if by a miracle, and the sun burst through the dark clouds overhead, in a benediction of warm, pure glittering rays upon the churchmen and laity, gathered thousands strong, at the Cathedral site.

Fully 60,000 visitors were in the city, and fully 30,000 men marched in the monster parade, which started shortly after 2 o'clock.

St. Paul Daily News, June 3, 1907

First airplane over Minneapolis, 1913. *MNHS*

1910s

The 1910 census showed that 71 percent of Minnesotans were either foreign-born or the children of immigrants. Milling declined after 1915. Prohibition began in 1919. Transportation was transformed by gasoline-powered automobiles and early airplanes. →

FRANK GEDDES

"There is strong talk of a RR in a year or so and if we get that it will be a great country soon."

Frank Geddes spent the first fifty-four years of his life on Indiana farms, then went to northern Minnesota in 1912. His nineteen-year-old son, George, had filed a claim near Frontier, Minnesota, fifty miles west of International Falls. George told his father that the soil looked rich for farming and suggested that they cut and sell timber until the ground was cleared enough to sow crops.

Frank Geddes. *MNHS*

This part of the state was still a frontier at the turn of the century. Homesteading did not begin until 1904, and Koochiching County was not carved from its parent Itasca County until 1906. Frank Geddes got to International Falls in April 1912 and filed a claim to 160 acres on April 19. There was no railroad to get him to his land on the Minnesota side of the Rainy River, so Geddes took the railroad from Fort Frances, Ontario, to Stratton, Ontario. He recrossed the Rainy River to the remote western part of Koochiching County and walked eight miles to his land. He wrote to his family in Indiana:

APRIL 28, 1912

Dear ones at Home,

I got my receipt from the land office last night. My file was accepted and now it is up to me to make good. My claim is one mile long and . . . ¼ mile wide. One 40 lays alongside of George's facing [the] sec[tion] line. We will build close together, about twice as wide as across the street, and live turnabout in the houses.

We have George's house most up to the square now. We cut spruce poles or logs—not very big ones, as we are doing it all ourselves. We peel off the bark, and they are nice and clean, and get the cracks as close as we can. Then we take moss like they used to sell in Starke [County, Indiana] and cork the cracks, and it is tight and warm, too. The roof we

Northern Pacific engine, 1916. *MNHS*

make in log cabin style, only we split poles and peel the bark off and lay them on the roof as close as we can and then lay moss or birch bark next. Then [we] put about three inches of dirt on top, with all the cracks corked with moss so you have a clean looking house inside. I don't know how we will roof ours yet. Maybe we will split some shingles, but we will have to double the roof some way.

This is a wild country yet. Some seven or eight shacks [are] in here in all, and a slew or muskeg [bog] with water now boot-top deep for two miles when we go out. But they have petitioned for a road out and they think they will have one next year—a corduroy [a road made of logs laid side by side]—but you can then get out at any rate. There is no use for a wagon in here. You have no idea the roots are so thick and the road so rough. There is now only one horse in here and that will go out before the bog thaws out. We got the horse and hauled some lumber from here that the man left where we stay about a mile from where we are building. We had seven hundred feet and we made four loads on a sled like we used to have to haul logs in the mill yard.

The ground is covered everywhere with moss, and the roads are just cut out of the timber by the homesteader without pay, but there is a good many trails open. Our land where we are building is somewhat higher than the most of it and is easier to clear around the house than most of it.

Oh yes, I must tell you how we got the trunk in. I hired a man [to] get it across the river and bring it three miles in on his horse. [He had] the only team out at the river on [the] Stratton road. George took Mrs. Carney's one horse and the sled and ax last Sunday morn and started about five miles after it. I went in [the] afternoon and met him at the muskeg and we got home about five o'clock.

We are living fine. George had some grocrys brought in before the snow went—150 [pounds] of flour, 50 of sugar and some other things. But we haven't got enough it looks as if we were in for carrying the rest 8 mi. We have no windows for the house yet. George has some cooking utensils, enough to start with, I guess. The man we are staying with [Johnnie Dahlstrom] is a pretty good cook, and I wash dishes and learn how. We have canned milk,

But the Grocer has more — Thank Goodness.

oatmeal, rice, peaches, and most everything we need at present.

We cut the logs close to where we built and got one horse and dragged them in. When I build I will have to get a ox, I reckon, as that will be my only chance. It looks pretty tough to me here, but I am glad I come as George was bound to stay and prove up his claim and I might as well have one, too, if I stay. The land is good—surely the best—and the trees just set on top of the ground. They don't sprout when cut down and in three to five years you can take them out easy. But meantime when they cut it off and just burn the moss off you can sow timothy and it grows just like weeds. There are a few stone scattered around, but I don't think very many. The soil is gravelly clay and sand loam. There are some big rocks, though, high as my head and some of them cover ¼ of an acre.

Mr. Carney told me there had been about $1,500.00 of timber cut on not more than six acres of his land and if he were to cut it clean it would make a thousand more. But ours is not quite that good, though I have some just as thick but [not] so valuable.

Over at Stratton a man told me that clover was a weed there. Their land is like ours, only they have got more cleared and they burn it off in dry weather and that helps to get it ready sooner. But we don't dare to set fire in a dry time on account of starting forest fires that would ruin all the timber.

There is strong talk of a RR in a year or so and if we get that it will be a great country soon. And then we can sell everything and get a better price as it is only the cedar poles and tamarack piling and ties [that it] pays to haul to the river, and then you have to look out or they beat you.

I do hope that Esther [his daughter] will get stout and that you all get along all right. I suppose Ralph [his son] is a carpenter by this time, but I hope he will never have to build a log house as I don't like the job myself. But we will have to build two houses and a stable before we get through. We want to clear two or three acres this summer so as to get some hay started. I guess this is enough for once. Love to all from your

PaPa

Find some cedar leaves enclosed.

F. M. Geddes

[Frank Geddes didn't survive the wilderness experience. He died in August 1913. His children in Michigan were sent a telegram saying, "Frank Geddes had stroke paralysis Sunday, died Monday, buried Tuesday." The burial was quick, and his son George explained later, "It was August, we didn't have an embalmer and it was hot."]

Personal papers of Jane Geddes Griffin of Shaker Heights, Ohio

***

APR. 15, 1910

HOME OF THE FRIENDLESS

Entrance fee to residents of St. Paul, $300.

Entrance fee to non residents of St. Paul, $600.

None taken under 65 years of age. All old ladies enter on a six months trial. If at the end of the six months they do not like it they are at liberty to leave and the whole of their money is given back to them except board for the six months at the rate of $3 a week. If, on the other hand, they have objectionable habits or are so cranky they cannot get along happily with the others, their money is given back to them on the same conditions.

Most of the old ladies furnish their own rooms and have their own belongings around them. Occasionally friends or the Church people have helped to pay the fee or to furnish the room. If they have money of their own, or friends, relatives or Church people to help them with clothing, so much the better. If not the Home will provide for them. The amount of the entrance fee covers all expenses until death.

The capacity of the Home, 18, with 6 employes, including a matron, making a family of 24 living in the Home. There are 9 old ladies on the waiting list at the present time. There are few restrictions in the Home, no regular visiting hours and but few rules. The ladies are at liberty to have their friends call upon them at any time and may invite them to a meal, for which fifteen cents is paid.

The Home is pleasantly furnished, the dining room and kitchen particularly being large and airy, scrupulously clean and attractive looking. There are large porches and very pretty grounds, and as the property is on a hill there is quite a view . . .

The building is a frame building and the fire escapes are wooden stairs. It is the hope of the Board to build a large, fire proof building before long, but they are waiting until they can do it as they wish to.

Amherst H. Wilder Foundation records, MNHS

Edward Brewer, his wife, Mayme, and son, Edward Lucien, St. Paul, 1910. *MNHS*

E. J. BROWN

"Now you rotten old skin flint if you think you can get anything out of me by starting a suit, hop right to it."

A Minneapolis doctor, Edward J. Brown, practiced the art of responding to nasty letters from patients. Here's a letter from a man from whom Brown was trying to collect, and Brown's response.

MARCH 26, 1915
Dr. E. J. Brown
525 Syndicate Blk.
Minneapolis
Dear Sir:
I have been notified by the National Law & Adjustment Company that you have filed a claim against me for professional services.

Now in the first place I do not nor have I ever owed you one single penny and if your memory is real good you will remember that my father took me to your office when I was a boy and you agreed to cure my deafness and he at that time paid you for this service.

Now you rotten old skin flint if you think you can get anything out of me by starting a suit, hop right to it. You ought to be glad I am not suing you for damages for the way you cut me up and at the same time knowing that you were not nor had any hope of doing me any real good. Now as I said before, start your suit and I will give you and your lawyer also the court a chance to find out what I think of you and your snide treatment.
Yours very truly,
Don. G. Sheldon

MINNEAPOLIS, MARCH 27, 1915
My dear Mr. Sheldon:
Your very emphatic letter is a great surprise to me. Your father was a gentleman and I had no suspicion that one of his sons could be capable of such a letter. You are evidently laboring under a mistaken conception of various things. My notes do not indicate that I ever promised to "cure" your deafness, and as a matter of fact I never made such a promise to any deaf patient. The operations and other treatment were entirely legitimate and I think were performed with reasonable degree of skill. The account was placed in the hands of a collection agency because you took no notice of a letter which I wrote you long since.
Very truly yours,
Dr. E. J. Brown

[Another of Brown's letters, to a Miss Anderson on January 2, 1906:]

I have just received your very foolish letter. The headaches or something else must have robbed you of your senses or you would not have written such a letter. . . . I am sorry you are having trouble with your ears and head. It is probable that you are in need of the attention of a physician, and I would advise you instead of abusing the one who has already tried to treat you kindly and skillfully, to put yourself in the care of some one whom you are willing to trust and let him see what can be done for you.
Edward Josiah Brown papers, MNHS

NOTICE
TO YOUNG WOMEN AND GIRLS

Do not go to the large cities for work unless you are compelled to. If you must go, write at least two weeks in advance to the Woman's Department, Bureau of Labor, St. Paul, or to the Young Women's Christian Association in the city where you want to work.

They will obtain for you such a position as you ask; tell you about wages, boarding places and whatever you want to know.

Two days before you leave home, write again and tell the day and hour when your train will arrive and a responsible woman will meet you at the station and take you safely to your destination.

Do not ask questions of strangers nor take advice from them.

Ask a uniformed railway official or a policeman.

This advice is issued by the State Bureau of Labor and posted through the courtesy of the Railway Officials of this road.

Mrs. Perry Starkweather,
Assistant Commissioner
Woman's Dept.

W. E. McEWEN,
Commissioner of Labor,
STATE CAPITOL, ST. PAUL

Christmas, 1912. *MNHS*

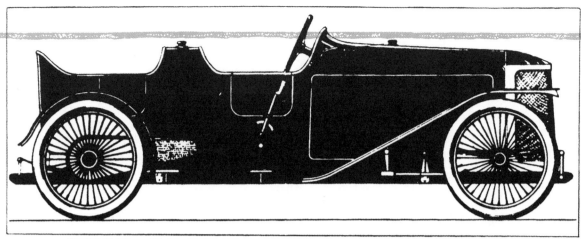

THE PRIDEMORE CYCLECAR

Two-seater built in Northfield in 1914. *MNHS*

***

PEOPLE IN A PANIC

Duluth is fortunate indeed that the small panic that started in a local vaudeville theater last night isn't responsible today for many houses of mourning and many beds of pain. But that fortunate outcome seems to have come from the fact that it was easy to get out of the theater rather than because the audience showed any better sense than audiences turned mobs usually have. The spectacle of a crowd in a panic always makes the most ardent admirers of humanity a little ashamed. Last night, for instance, the occasion for the alarm was a burst of flame which was part of the performance, and which almost anybody should have been able to see was a part of the performance. Yet some hare-brained idiot yelled "Fire!," there was a rush for the doors, and the house was emptied in a few seconds. Had there been fewer exits, or had some of them been closed, a terrible calamity could hardly have been averted.

Nor is it always women who are the chief offenders in such cases. It was a man—so-called—who raised the silly alarm, and according to a reliable eyewitness it was men who scrambled most energetically for the exits. The incident should be a lesson in the value of cool-headedness. It is fortunate indeed that it cost so little.

Duluth Evening Herald, January 25, 1910

J. M. DREW

"He says it is a disgrace to the state to have such doings right on the edge of the campus."

J. M. Drew, on the staff of the University of Minnesota's agriculture school, wrote to his daughter Helen on September 25, 1915, about a surprise party in honor of the Drews' twenty-fifth wedding anniversary:

Your mother and I celebrated the day yesterday by going to Minneapolis on a shopping tour. We took lunch at the Glass Block [Donaldson's department store] and got home early in the afternoon. Margaret [their daughter] was to get dinner all alone. She told us it would be ready at 6 oclock, and warned us to be dressed by that time. Your mother put on her wedding dress by making some allowances and using pins instead of the original fastenings. Margaret told us to let her know when we were ready as she wanted to play the wedding march for us to come down stairs by. When we got to the bottom of the stairs and were making the turn toward the dining room, your mother said she saw someone at the front door. When she went to the door she met Mrs. Green, Mrs. C. P. Bull, the other Bulls, Mr. and Miss Kelley, the Saltzmans, the Reeves, three Stewarts, the Mackintoshes, Mrs. Andrew Boss (Mr. Boss came later), Dr. and Mrs. Hause. They brot all kinds of baskets and dishes with them, and all hands marched around the dining room table and took what they wanted, cafeteria style. You can imagine we had a jolly time.

After the eating Mr. Stewart, the spokesman, produced a box and handed it to us with a little speech. We unwrapped it and found a silver baking dish with a big D engraved on the top. Of course we had to do a little talking then and they made me tell about the wedding of twenty five years ago and what led up to it.

[The great oleo (margarine) issue emerged in 1918. Drew wrote to Helen November 23:]

Our friend Arthur McGuire is much exercised over the fact that Mrs. Marshall is selling more oleo than butter. He says it is a disgrace to the state to have such doings right on the edge of the campus. The other day he heard that they were using oleo in the school dining room, and he went to the dean with blood in his eye, and asked if the rumor could be true. The dean said he knew nothing about what the students were being fed, but supposed the

Lake Calhoun, Minneapolis, about 1911. *MNHS*

home economics teachers who had charge of it this year were managing the table in as economical a manner as possible, and if the students wanted oleo in place of butter in order to keep down the price of board they ought to be allowed to do so. He said he would look into the matter, and if they were using oleo he would suggest that they be allowed to vote on the question, and have whichever product they preferred. This morning we heard that the vote had been taken and that 40 voted for butter and 180 for oleo.

[Drew's letters to his daughter over the decades included a little of everything. To skip ahead a few decades, here are his comments on newfangled electric razors, written February 7, 1937:]

If any one asks your advice about getting an electric razor, give him the advice that Josh Billings gave the very young couple who wanted to be married. He said: "Don't."

The electric machine is too slow. If it would do as good a job as a lawn mower by going over the ground but once, perhaps it might save a little time over the old method, but in order to get all the stubbles it seems to be necessary to cover the surface several times. I think I shall take it back and trade for an old-fashioned razor that I can sharpen when it gets dull. Razor blades for safety razors are all now made so that they cannot be sharpened in the ordinary way.

Helen Richardson papers, MNHS

A Minneapolis streetcar, 1911. *Wayne Blesi*

Buffalo Bill making his last circus appearance in Minneapolis, 1912. *MNHS*

NEWSPAPER CLIPPINGS

DEAR SIR:—The Current News club have for some time felt that the window displays of corsets and the moving picture show advertisements of like nature have had a harmful influence on the young people. It is noticeable that the people who look at these exhibits are the men and boys, the ladies not wishing to stop on the street to examine them.

We, the Current News club, therefore, kindly ask you to use your influence in preventing such window displays and such slides being used in the moving picture shows.

Yours respectfully,
CURRENT NEWS CLUB
Brown County Journal, May 3, 1913

THREATEN TO ARREST THEATRE MANAGERS ANNOUNCEMENT THAT 'LIVE BABY' WOULD BE GIVEN AWAY AT THE 'GEM' CREATES SENSATION. EXCITEMENT PERMEATES LOCAL SOCIAL CIRCLES. One of the most sensational stunts ever attempted by a moving picture theatre in New Ulm was pulled off by the management of the Gem theatre last Sunday evening, when they advertised that a 'live baby' would be given away at that popular place of amusement free. The glaring announcement of this striking feature in a large advertisement in last Saturday's issue of the Journal and on glowing billboards created such a high pitch of excitement that it furnished the subject for conversation and gossip among our citizens of both sexes. From one end of the city to the other, the matter was discussed. In some instances with grave faces, in others the subject was spoken of more as a joke. Nevertheless, the event drew one of the largest crowds in the history of the Gem theatre.

The baby was a very "handsome young creature," dressed in the very latest, effete Parisian mood, being gowned in a lavender silk "dress," and several yards of light green silk ribbon hung in a large, graceful bow from its chubby neck. It was "simply too sweet for anything," as one of the young ladies present remarked excitedly . . .

WINNER OF THE BABY. Henry Nevwirth, the popular and comely night clerk at the Dakota house, was the young man whom fate had ordained as the recipient of the baby. As he walked up to aisle to where the announcer stood, he was accorded a monster ovation by the large audience, and when the Gem man held up the baby so that all could see the coveted prize, the crowd went wild with applause, when it realized that the prize was a husky baby pig.

Brown County Journal, January 4, 1913

NO "UNSEEMLY" CONTORTIONS. THEY WERE BARRED AT OPERA HOUSE DANCE LAST FRIDAY. When a young couple departed from the staid old way at the Opera House hall last Friday evening by dancing the hula-hula the management and those in attendance were awe-stricken at their audacity. The manager rubbed his eyes to make sure that his vision had not become veiled and after he was thoroughly convinced that it must be one of those much-talked of contortion dances he politely informed the couple that no more such exhibitions would be tolerated and that if they could not conform to the more modest style of dancing they would have to leave the hall. The male participant became rather indignant and couldn't understand why the people in this city were so far behind the times. His entreaties, however, were of no avail and the management put any further exhibitions of that character under the ban. Such dances as the turkey trot, bear dance, bunny hug, toad hobble, hula hula, crab crawl, gaby glide and Texas Tommy will not be tolerated. While these dances are public the management feels that certain restrictions are necessary and those attending must adhere to them.

Brown County Journal, September 6, 1913

A loyalty parade in St. Paul. *MNHS*

WORLD WAR I

The state fair in 1914 carried the anti-war slogan "Flour barrels are better than gun barrels." But the United States entered the war, and the Minnesota Legislature gave the Commission on Public Safety near-dictatorial powers. Anti-German feeling was extreme. Slogans abounded: "Eat onions to finish the fiendish Hun." Many a Minnesota soldier who had never been out of his own county found himself abroad. →

PHILIP LONGYEAR

Love to all Philip

"Well, I have finally seen all the war I want to and my curiosity and desire for 'sightseeing' are entirely satisfied."

Philip Longyear was rich, well-educated, and handsome when he went off to fight World War I. He was not a typical soldier—many American young men who went overseas then had never been out of their own towns or counties—but he wrote well about the serviceman's lot. His father was E. J. Longyear, mining engineer and a developer of Minnesota's Mesabi Iron Range. When the war broke out, Philip was a twenty-one-year-old junior at Williams College in Massachusetts. With other young men from the college, he joined the US Army Ambulance Corps. American ambulance drivers were sent to France before American soldiers were sent. Here are segments of Longyear's letters to his family.

Allentown, Pa.
JUNE 28, 1917
Dear Mother:

I am sending a telegram in a few moments which will reach you before this letter. We missed our connection in Pittsburgh and didn't get here till this morning. It is certainly interesting here. There are about three thousand nine hundred men here and it looks like a regular war camp. Everything is all bustle and excitement. Everywhere you go you hear bugles, see men drilling, etc. We are quartered in the old fair buildings and have one of the stock buildings. Each of us has half a stall to himself. We have gold medal cots. The camp is fitted up in fine shape. Right next door to us is the shower building, which is merely a stock building with double rows of showers rigged up down the middle. We all eat in one big room underneath the grandstand. It looks like a whole army in there. They are all a fine-looking bunch of college boys, and treat newcomers as if they were old friends, and help them to find their places. When we

Philip Longyear, student. *Williams College*

Off to the war, St. Paul. *MNHS*

National Archives

My Daddy Bought Me a Government Bond
of the
THIRD LIBERTY LOAN
Did Yours?

Dinner for the 36th Infantry at Fort Snelling. *MNHS*

arrived, everybody shouted at us, "Hello, boys, where are you from?" Some Amherst boys grabbed our suitcases and showed us our quarters.

That is the whole spirit here. Everyone feels good and anxious to work. We have not been definitely placed yet and are classed as "casuals," and have to do all the dirty work of the camp. So far to-day I have been digging a sewer. Just now we are waiting to be inoculated and I am writing this in the Y.M.C.A. tent. This Y.M.C.A. is a great thing. They have magazines, writing material, etc., movie shows every night in front of the big grand stand, have gotten up an inter-unit baseball series, and such things.

It looks as though we would be here two months or more. Why don't you plan on taking your tour with Robert out here? There is some great scenery in Pennsylvania and this camp is mighty interesting. They say there were five thousand visitors out Sunday.

My address, as you found in the telegram, is care of Williams College Unit, U.S.A.A.C. (United States Army Ambulance Corps). Will you please send on my writing pad (left in auto), a couple old shirts, a bath robe. I will send for other things as I find I need them.

I see we are ready for the doctor next. Will write more later.

Lovingly,
Philip.

The Stars and Stripes Forever *MNHS*

1776

1917

1812   1861

1846   1898

" With firmness in the right, as God gives us to see the right." —LINCOLN INAUGURAL ADDRESS

Family with soldier. *MNHS*

ALLENTOWN, PA., JULY 2, 1917

I am taking a lot of pictures and will send them on as soon as they are done.

This morning we started in on regular drill. It is certainly good to get away from the hard work we have been having. You can find a schedule of the day's work in the camp paper I sent you. We have just gotten through our morning drill and have nothing till lecture at eleven o'clock. I have been out without any shirt on and my shoulders are getting started with a good coat of tan. You see some of the funniest costumes here. Some wear derby hats with the rims cut off. Others wear rims without the tops. I saw one fellow with an old silk hat with no brim and all stuck up with poster stamps. Everyone who has a numeral or letter sweater wears it around. You see every letter from A to Y. Some fellows wear just a bathing suit and some only half a one. They are as brown as Indians. As soon as we get our uniforms, though, we have to wear them. We expect ours pretty soon now.

They expect three thousand ambulances here by the middle of July and we will each have our own. There is a rumor that a bunch of the sections have sealed orders to leave now within a week, and that a big liner is fitted out ready to carry about 1500. I rather doubt it, though.

ALLENTOWN, PA., JULY 5, 1917

We are getting well settled in camp now and it begins to seem as though I had always been here. I have gotten used to my cot and sleep well. I slept through reveille this morning and had to appear at roll call in my pajamas. We feel like old timers and sit in the shade and josh the new-comers who have to do all the dirty work. We really have quite a little time to ourselves and it sure feels good to sit back and think there is nothing to do.

I took my first Ford lesson yesterday, and got by my exam the first thing. They let anybody who can drive a Ford take the exam

Walter W. Tritchler of the 6th Regiment Band, 1918. *MNHS*

right away and not go through the course. It was very simple. I just had to drive around the race track a couple times, reverse, start the engine, stop it, answer a few simple questions about what the carburetor and magneto are for, etc., and put a tire on a rim. I am through now till we get over to France, where they put us through a stiff road test. We will probably have to drive our own car from Bordeaux to Paris in a certain time. The ambulances are chain drive and geared very low. They won't go over thirty. The rear axle and wheels are very strong. The front part is a regular Ford chassis. A bunch of them are arriving every day.

They had a chance to use one yesterday. We had an inter-unit track meet in front of

June 2 1918

Dear Mother:—
    It is a long time since I have written but we remained so long at the last place, that I was waiting for something to happen worth while writing about. But enough has happened the last two days, and I am so tired and sleepy, I can hardly see the paper. The trouble is, most of it is of military value and I would give away where we are, but will do my best. We got orders to move to here about four o'clock on the afternoon of May 30 and were off by seven. I might say we are away off at the another part of the line again, even further than where we were when we took our first big jump. But we took a new route so have seen

Longyear's letter. *MNHS*

the grandstand in the afternoon. I never saw such a crowd in my life. It looked like the auto races at the Minnesota Fair. The grandstand was packed, and it is nearly as big as the Minnesota one, and people were packed inside the track. The meet was won by U. of Michigan. We won the first place in the broad jump. In the five mile race, one of the runners fainted after about three miles and somebody in khaki rushed out with one of the new ambulances and picked him up, to the great applause of the visitors. After the meet, the

ambulances gave a parade, and then the camp got together and sang the new army songs for the audience, which was greatly appreciated. They are a good peppy bunch of songs, mostly about "Kaiser Bill" and what will happen to him when "Uncle Samee" gets over there.

ALLENTOWN, PA., JULY 9, 1917
We just had our second dose of inoculation a few minutes ago. It was funny to watch the way some of the men took it. Four men fainted while I was waiting my turn, which cheered me up considerably. One man fainted before they even touched him. I didn't mind it much, although it seemed they squirted a couple quarts of stuff in my arm. I feel kind of groggy now and my arm is getting sore. We got one more inoculation and then a vaccination and are supposed to be disease proof.

    A large bunch started on a hike this morning after shipping all their extra stuff home. No one knows where they are going. They sure looked neat in their nifty rain coats and kits. We gave them a great send off. There were about twenty sections. Our lieutenant says we ought to get our uniforms and equipment this week.

ALLENTOWN, PA., JULY 16, 1917
There are a fine set of people around here. Every-where you go they will do anything for anyone in uniform. We were passing one house, mopping our brows, and a lady invited us in and gave us some lemonade. I am getting used to my uniform and don't feel so conspicuous walking around. Nearly the whole camp has them now and it looks a good deal better. They won't let you outside the gates now, without a full uniform on.

ALLENTOWN, PA., AUG. 4, 1917
I am still in the kitchen and nothing much of importance has happened. I will sure be glad when Monday comes and I will be through. The work is far from pleasant and I have

entirely lost my appetite from hanging around with all the grease, flies, etc. I have met a fine bunch of fellows and we try to get as much fun out of it as we can. We usually get away with about half the officers' mess, when the chef isn't looking. Last night I swiped a big piece of steak off the stove and five of us had quite a meal. We fried some potatoes and hooked some watermelons while one of us was keeping the chef busy. It was a meal fit for a king!

DEC. 27, 1917

I am down here at the Allentown Y.M.C.A., getting a shower, swim and a little warmth. For the first time in my life I am thankful that Christmas is over. I hope I never have to put

in another like it. I finished my week in the kitchen on the 24th and then had the bright hunch of doing another week of it and escape going on guard. . . . I had made plans to go to the big military ball on Christmas night in

MNHS

MNHS

the same building and was looking forward to it. I didn't know any girl to bring but a lot of the fellows I was working with in the mess hall promised me dances. I thought Christmas wouldn't be so bad after all.

Christmas noon they gave us a wonderful turkey dinner and I was just getting off for the afternoon, when our sergeant came around and said he had a special order from headquarters to release all in our battalion from various detail work they were on to go on guard at 3:30!! I nearly expired right there. I wouldn't have minded so much if I hadn't made plans for the afternoon and evening. They only succeeded in rounding up 38 men out of our whole battalion of 5 sections, when 55 are supposed to mount guard. So we had to double up the shifts and work over time. I was on guard 12 hours out of the 24. I was on from 4 to 6 at the solitary confinement cell. I had two prisoners in there and was supposed to see that no one talked to them. One of them was in for two years at hard labour without pay, for beating up the military provost guard sergeant one Saturday night when he was drunk. The other was in for a worse offense. From 8 to 10 I was on guard at the gate which leads into the dance hall, from 10–12 was back with the prisoners, from 4–6 a.m. and 10–12 a.m. in the same place and from two to four at the regular guard house with ordinary prisoners.

My post at the dance hall was the worst. I was right where I could hear all the music and watch the couples come in. I must have looked particularly despondent or something because all the girls as they passed in would say something to try to cheer me up. One girl went so far as to bring me out some refreshments. But they only made it worse, and I got lower and lower. The U. of California section furnished the music and were awfully good and nearly drove me wild. I started dancing with my club to keep my feet warm and nearly bumped into the officer of day making a round of inspection. This caused great merriment

among a group of girls outside who didn't have invitations but wanted to get in. They took revenge on me and tormented the life out of me.

Then I had to go back to my cheerful companions in the cell. One of them gave me the jim jams every time I looked at him. He would sit on his stool near the bars, grip hold of them and peer out at me for a half an hour at a time . . .

I got about two hours sleep that night and we were sure glad to be relieved yesterday at 4 o'clock. We got passes till 11:15 tonight. I went to bed early last night and didn't get up till 11:30 this morning. I had a bad cold in my chest and a head ache but now that I have had a good shower I feel better. I go on the kitchen again tomorrow until the 31st when I expect to get a five day pass. . . . Don't think I am particularly low, although I admit I was Christmas night. But now that it is all over and I have slept off the gloom I feel better. I can imagine now that I must have looked almost humorous kicking my heels in the snow outside the dance, though it didn't seem so then.

Lots of love,
Philip

Somewhere in France
APRIL 6, 1918
Dear Mother,
At last we are here. I supose you have already heard by various ways that I am here.

We have just had the censorship rules read to us and I am quite discouraged as to what I can write, but will do my best. You will have to use your imagination as to what I omit.

We left Allentown amid considerable excitement of course. My barracks bag had an accident going down to the train in the truck and was ripped open. I heard about it and managed to locate it. I changed everything to another bag but found quite a little missing— mostly candy—nothing of much value. We were as lucky as we could be in the boat we got for a transport. I can't tell you her name but it is one which everyone knows. I can't tell you much about our trip as everything of interest pertains to our precautions against submarines. We had fairly rough weather most of the way but I felt fine all the time except for about a half hour when I wished I was dead.

I wish I could tell you about our daily routine and some entertaining incidents. Of course we were jammed in like sardines. I wonder there are any soldiers left in the States at all. If you ever want to see a miracle find some one who is about to sleep in a sailors hammock which we had! They couldn't possibly be more tippy. I thought it was funny at first, watching the others fall out, but when I woke up the first night on the floor, I gave up and spent the rest of the night on the mess table underneath, without slinging my hammock. I enjoyed the trip in itself though, altho it would have been much pleasanter to be an officer up in the first class cabins. We had services on board Easter Sunday in the main smoking room, but it was so crowded I had to stand out in the companionway and hear only the music. I guess everyone was making one last effort to redeem their souls as we were about due to enter the danger zone. We finally arrived on this side and are now in camp, sleeping in tents, ten men to a tent.

The most interesting part of the trip was in getting here, but that would probably tell where we are. This is the most beautiful and picturesque country I ever saw. The grass is a bright green, the trees are all coming out, and it is as warm as summer. Yesterday, when we arrived here, it was a perfect day. We are near a large town, and as we marched through it on the way to camp, I had a good, close-at-hand view of the French people. They sure are interesting.

A whole army of little children ran along side of us jabbering away, and asking for pennies. I happened to have my pack filled with a lot of chewing gum, which I found lost out of my barracks bag when we left. . . . I had a dollars worth of gum, but found it stale so started passing it out to the children. I immediately became as popular as Santa Claus. Gum costs ten cents a stick here and they were crazy for it. You would have laughed yourself completely sick seeing this huge mob of little boys and girls completely surrounding me, hanging to my coat tails to keep up with the pace. I happened to be the only one near who could speak any French at all and this also pleased them. One little girl in particular ran along with me for a long ways, holding onto my finger. She had the prettiest little face I ever saw. I should say she was six or seven. She had a bright colored, quaint dress on, a huge pair of wooden shoes and a funny lace cap on her head. I was quite surprised how easily I understood her when I got her slowed down to about a hundred words a second. She was very bright and answered a lot of questions I managed to say in French. I let her ride on my shoulder for quite a ways and she had the time of her life. When I finally put her down, she said, "J'aime les Americains tres bien! Au revoir," and ran off with her wooden shoes clicking on the pavement. The whole company was greatly amused over the performance. All the women and old men (I didn't see a single man eligible for service) came to the doors and waved at us, and showed off their one or two words of English. A bunch of little boys started singing "Oh Johnny!" which a soldier had taught them. They had half the words wrong and probably hadn't the slightest idea what they meant . . .

I am feeling fine and much pleased with the prospects of what we are to do. I certainly am glad to be here and delighted with this whole French atmosphere. I haven't had a chance to get out of the camp yet and talk with the people except on the march yesterday. I would have been dead tired last night if it wasn't for the American food, plenty of it, although of course the meat is all canned. Had some good wheat cakes and oatmeal without milk for breakfast.

I have to do my washing now while there is room. Will write again soon.

Love to all,
Philip

APRIL 26, 1918
We left this morning at about 9 o'clock with our ambulances, trucks, field kitchen trailer, etc. We couldn't make very good time with such a convoy and had to keep stopping to keep the bunch together. We finally arrived here at our destination in time for supper. This is probably our last stop, it is another French camp, and we get our final orders here. We are now only 30 kilometers (19 miles) from the front. We can hear the guns here now for the first time. They are hitting it up pretty good just now. Sounds like someone drumming their fingers on the table, "rat-tat-tet-te-tat." We can't show any lights here at all tonight. There are a lot of ruins in town from air raids, and it looks like the pictures you see in the war zone.

It is getting pretty dark and I will have to stop. We may be in here some time, as we just wait here till ordered to relieve some section in this sector. Of course I know what sector we are in, but don't know just where we are going. Will write again as soon as anything turns up.

Love,
Philip

MAY 7, 1918
I witnessed my first shell fire day before yesterday, when the French artillery broke up a would-be aero raid on their town by three Boche [German] aeroplanes. I was lying out on the grass in back of my ambulance, reading a Sat. Eve. Post, when a French "75" gun, about a quarter of a mile down the road, began to suddenly talk. I had walked by the place a dozen times and never seen it. Some other guns around began firing too. I couldn't imagine what it was till I looked up in the air and saw a lot of white puffs which looked exactly like cotton balls. Then I noticed three tiny aeroplanes in the midst of it all. They must have been ten thousand feet up. It certainly was a pretty sight to watch these fluffy balls of bursting scrapnel suddenly appear and remain motionless against the blue sky. The nearest aeroplane meanwhile was zig-zagging and dipping to change the range and disappeared toward the firing line, after about five minutes firing. Then I noticed rising after him from the nearby aviation field here a flock of French machines. I counted twenty-six of them. They looked exactly like a flock of mosquitoes. The other German machines escaped some other direction. It was our first sight of any action and we were considerably interested.

JUNE 14, 1918
Well, we have gotten to work at last, and this is the first time in several days, I can't figure out how many, that I have had time to do anything. I have seen enough wounded to last me for the rest of the war, as far as curiosity goes. I have just gotten through cleaning the blood out of my car and it was hardly a pleasant job.

We were suddenly called, from the place where we were quartered in the old chateau to this place, which is about five or six kilometers back of the lines. We had no idea what we were going to do, expecting it to be one of our accustomed fruitless moves. I was not here fifteen minutes when I had a load of "blesses" [wounded] bound for an evacuation hospital. That was five in the afternoon, and I drove steadily for twenty hours, carrying the wounded from the field hospital here back to various other hospitals 15 or 20 miles in the rear. We are only doing evacuation work and are not hauling from the advanced posts. We have not been attached to a division yet and are only doing this temporarily to help out in the rush which is a result of some big action on this front the last two or three days. We kept making one trip after another, stopping only for a cup of coffee or to load up with gasoline. We took turns being relieved by the assistant drivers, snatch a few hours sleep, and go at it again. The action has quieted down up front now, and no more wounded are coming back. We got our last load out last night, and have nothing to do now but wait for further orders.

The hospital we took the wounded from was certainly a sight. It consists of a large private residence set in the middle of a park. They had several times as many patients, on a whole, as they had capacity, and the whole park was almost literally covered with

stretchers containing wounded waiting to be hauled back, and in all stages of wounds. I was surprised how little I was affected by the sight of so much blood. The thing as a whole was what affected me. To see these hundreds of wounded, groaning, waiting for hours for their turn to be taken away, and I would wonder what was the use of it all. To be sure, the French had gained a little ground by their counterattack, but was it worth it?

My program was to drive in the front gate, stop, open up the rear, let the stretcher-bearers load in three couches [men lying down], two below and one above, take an "assis" [assistant] on the front seat with me, get a kind of

Farewell to the 151st Regiment Field Artillery, state fairgrounds, St. Paul. *National Archives*

hat check for each patient, and start off for some hospital I had never heard of. At the evacuation hospital, hand my checks to the man in charge, have some bearers unload the patients, get three empty litters to carry back, and then back again as fast as I could go.

I am glad my first trip was before dark, as I was a bit shaky from all that I had seen, and the artillery was banging away on all sides and making a terrible racket. It certainly is a thrilling experience to start out with a load, headed for some new place in the middle of the night. It is really amazing how you can drive so far without hitting anything, when you can hardly see the radiator cap. I think it is a kind of sixth sense. I have had some mighty close escapes from collisions. We have not seen any enemy shell fire as yet, at least not very close. I think it is a very good thing we have had a chance to do this evacuation work before we get up to the advanced work where it is more dangerous. This is exactly the kind of work we will be doing when we get attached [to a regular unit], only minus the shell fire and gas shells, and shell torn roads.

The most interesting part of it all is to watch the fire display from the lines at night. The country is flat and open here, and on the return trip I could watch it all the way back, watching it get closer and closer till I seemed to run right by it all. During the heaviest of the bombardment the sky was continually lit up by the artillery fire and it was very bright but dazzling to drive against, especially when they sent up a star shell. At times I would have to stop entirely till my eyes were used to the darkness again. In the day time, coming up from the rear, one can trace the trenches for miles and miles by the row of observation balloons. Where we are quartered here now, one of the balloons is directly overhead, and I can just make out the man away up there in the car when I look up. A while ago a German aeroplane suddenly appeared overhead heading for the balloon, but was driven off by the

anti-aircraft fire. The sky was just filled with soft, white balls of the bursting shells. He got away without being hit. Yesterday while I was snatching a bite to eat, we saw an aeroplane over the trenches, being fired at and suddenly fall in flames and a lot of black smoke. It was too far to tell whether it was Allied or German.

Things are very quiet now, only an occasional artillery shot. There is a big "210" right across the street from us, which speaks up once in a while and nearly makes my pen jump out of my hand. We are quartered in an entirely deserted village except for the hospital at the edge of town. Every building is barred up and there is not a sign of life. The town has not been shelled since there is nothing here of military value, as far as the Germans know, but the hospital. We have our ambulances parked in an old abandoned court yard and are sleeping in the surrounding buildings.

I had a puncture last night about midnight, on my way back from my last trip and didn't get it fixed before one thirty. It was pitch dark and I had to do it by feel. My pump was out of commission and I spent about half an hour on it before I managed to stop a French truck driver who didn't see me and nearly ran into my car before he could stop. He lent me his pump and I got in about 2:30 A.M. I have been lucky with my car and that is the first trouble I had had at all except the first night when I broke a fan belt and came steaming in like a locomotive. But I have been taking pains with it and have kept it well oiled and cleaned up, so it didn't fall apart when the rush came.

JUNE 28, 1918
This has been the most exciting day I have had yet and I am nearly deaf. The reason I didn't close my letter yesterday was that I knew this French attack was coming off today and thought there could be something to write about. I had better not say much about the attack itself or the results except it was

satisfactory. I wouldn't have missed being up here and seeing it all for 3 months pay. The "poste" is situated right where I could watch all the preparations and I was immensely interested. It started about five o'clock this morning with a most unearthly artillery bombardment. I never realized such a racket was imaginable. The noise was a constant roar and it was hard to distinguish the individual shots. My teeth nearly shook down my throat from the vibration, down in the dugout, so I piled out to see the show. Pretty soon the Germans began replying with what might have seemed pretty concentrated fire, but was nothing to what the French were putting over. One couldn't distinguish the exploding shells from so much noise, but here and there large fountains of earth would rise up, or branches from trees would go sailing off in the air for no reason at all apparently. They soon stopped their fire and I emerged from the dugout and

Philip Longyear, serviceman. *Williams College*

Equipped with gas masks and helmets, near the frontline trenches. *MNHS*

"Inasmuch as ye have done it unto one of the least of these"

HELP YOUR RED CROSS

Some of the poor fellows I carried were pitifully torn up and mangled, but I have stopped trying to put myself in their place every time I go over a bump and it is much easier. If I paid attention to all the gruesome sights and sounds I had to witness today I think I would be a nervous wreck tonight.

The Boches have just started an artillery concert in preparation for a counter-attack, according to a Frenchman. Sounds like a bowling alley or roller skating rink overhead.

JUNE 29, 8:30 A.M.

I take back what I said last evening about not being a nervous wreck. I came as near being one last night after an experience I had as I ever hope to be. I was just getting to sleep about 12 o'clock in the dugout here at the second dressing station, where I wait till the other car comes down from the poste de secours [dressing station]. An artillery officer came rushing in, saying he wanted an ambulance at once to haul in five wounded, he didn't say where or how. So they sent me out with him alone for a guide. He led me up some wild unused road toward the front about 1 kilometer. Right in the middle of a terribly steep hill facing the lines was the most terrible mess. An enemy aeroplane had seen the artillery train moving along the road and had dropped a bomb square on one of the guns. Three of the horses were strewn all over the road and I had to run over one to get by. They had carried the wounded to one side of the road. I then had some job on my hands. The men were just as they had been hit, and had no first aid at all. The artillery men were quite wrought up and knew nothing about handling wounded and I had to dig in myself to get them on the stretchers. For once I was able to use a little knowledge gained at Allentown, as to various methods for picking up a wounded man. They were in bad shape and it was impossible to move them without them yelling. When we finally got them all in,

found the road directly in front of where my car was parked blocked with part of a stone wall blown in. About seven o'clock the wounded began to come in, and from then on till just a little while ago we surely had our hands full. They were coming in faster than our two cars could handle them so we had to get two more. We finally got the place cleaned out this afternoon. My first trip this morning I had a little difficulty in keeping from running into some big new shell holes and branches lying in the road, but that was soon fixed up.

I was quite gory and thoroughly sick at my stomach and shaky. We got nearly to the top of the steep hill, when the car was at such an angle that the gasolene wouldn't flow to the carburetor. We stopped dead and the emergency brake wouldn't hold it on the grade, so I got my eye on a big rock and hopped out and pushed it under the wheel. Luckily we always carry 15 extra liters of gas in our side box so I dumped that in and it was all right. The Germans were doing considerable shelling near where I was. They didn't land very close but it was sufficiently interesting. Also I could distinguish a Boche aeroplane motor which was snooping around close somewhere looking for more prey. It was bright moonlight and I was certainly thankful for the big red cross which we had recently painted on top of our cars.

I finally got my motor started, hopped in and found the low speed wouldn't take hold so I had to tighten up on the set screw. You can imagine the state of my nerves fussing around all this time with the infernal racket, and one of the blesses inside with a shattered leg, yelling like a maniac, because the angle of the car was throwing his weight on his leg. Then to finish the whole thing up, after I had discharged my load and was backing my car into the little shed near the post, a German shell knocked a hole in the wall of the farm house constituting the poste de secours. I practically fell out of my car, ran for the dugout, found

Women workers in 1918 replacing men at the Minneapolis Steel and Machinery Company, later Minneapolis Moline. *MNHS*

Men of the 105th Machine Gun Battalion
in France, firing at German troops. *MNHS*

I had forgotten my gas mask, and had to go way back for it. The sticks and dirt were still falling from the explosion and I heard several tinkles on my helmet. One doesn't dare go for a minute without a gas mask here as they may send gas shells at any time.

JULY 24, 1918

Well, I have finally seen all the war I want to and my curiosity and desire for "sightseeing" are entirely satisfied. I am afraid I haven't written for a long time, but will try to make up for it this time. I would give anything to have the censorship rules lifted so I could tell you all I have seen and gone through the past week. It is mighty hard to write anything and I know where to draw the line.

We were called up to a new port in preparation for an Allied movement six days ago. I was lucky enough to be one of the three cars to go up first. We started at three A.M. just before it began to get light. At [censored] o'clock, the time for the action to start, the sky over the trenches was filled suddenly with hundreds of signal lights. At the same time the artillery opened with a roar. It certainly was an impressive sight. Our post was a few hundred yards from the lines and I was the first car out with a load of wounded. By the time I had unloaded at the hospital and returned, the advance had so progressed that the post was moved up the road, the other side of "No Man's Land." I saw some sights on the battle field I won't forget till my dying day. Every little while the dressing station would have to be moved ahead.

I started at three o'clock that morning and drove steady for 38 hours without hardly stopping my motor. I ate one meal in all that time, besides snatching a slice of bread and jam every trip while my car was being filled with gas and oil. I was relieved for a few hours, got a little sleep and was at it again. We kept that up five days, managing to work in two or three hours sleep a day, sitting on the front seat.

Yesterday we were called back here for two or three days rest and repairs, and then expect to be back in the thick of the fight again.

I had many personal experiences I could tell about, but they were most of them of such a nature that they are censored. We aren't allowed to tell what kind of troops we were working with and that is where the whole difficulty of writing lies. At one point I had as good a view of the battle as anyone could wish. I climbed on top a pile of rocks, which were recently a church, while waiting for my car to be loaded and had a view of the whole battlefield. I could see the [censored] troops advancing in open formation through heavy German artillery barrage. Once in a while a shell would land directly on the line, and after the smoke cleared away there would be a hole there and a few forms lying in the rear. Everywhere you looked shells and shrapnel were bursting, not excluding our immediate vicinity. It was a wonderful sight, if you didn't believe that every shell you heard coming was headed directly for you. One big 210 knocked a boulder across the road right in front of my car, which I had to dodge while it was still rolling. I drove through two gas shells, which set me sneezing and eyes smarting for some time. A gas shell makes more noise coming than an explosive shell, for some reason, and one of them nearly scared me off my seat. I was sneaking along pretty slow, crawling out of a big shell hole which had recently been made, when I heard the familiar screech of an approaching shell. It got louder and louder, and I thought, "Here is one with my name and address on it." It landed about 15 yards directly off the road and burst with a ridiculous little "P-f-bl-uup," the way gas shells do. I saw the hazy gray vapor come piling out, and didn't even know the next few shell holes had bottoms! Luckily a strong wind was against me, or my lungs wouldn't be in such good shape just now. I finally arrived at the post and found it about as hot a place as I ever want to get in. It was temporarily a little ravine about 30 feet deep and 50 feet across and was almost a natural trench, only it was at right angles to the Germans. They must have thought an artillery battery had been posted there from the way the shells were dropping. I could see the fountains of dirt rising on all sides as I drove up. Just as I was piling out of my car, I heard a terrible whizz-z-c-r-ash! right behind me and clods of dirt went whistling past my ears and plastered the side of my car. I managed to reach the ravine in one jump or so and did a Charlie Chaplin slide to the bottom, much to the detriment of my breeches. But I saved my skin (or most of it). Down in there it wasn't much better. Everybody was jumping up and down like a bunch of jumping jacks. Everytime we heard one coming, we would all flatten out on the ground, get up, look around to see if all were there, and then duck another one. It seems that about fifteen minutes before I got there, the lieutenant of another ambulance section, who was working the same post we were, was killed standing along side one of his cars up on the bank. I was decidedly relieved, about ten minutes later, when the entertainment suddenly stopped, and I got a load. After getting a close view of some of those big shells and seeing what they can do to a piece of hard ground, I have a wholesome respect for them, and will give them the right of way any time!

But at that I didn't mind the shells and gas, as much as I did the sights and smells I had to go through. After five days, during which they had no time to care for the dead, the battlefield was hardly appetizing! I became so sick and disheartened at times, when I was almost too tired to drive, that I would have given anything to have been safe back in Rose Farm, away from all the revolting sights. It all seems so futile. At times I would have been willing to get a job in a morgue, and call it cheerful. We Red Cross don't get any of the excitement and enthusiasm which keeps the combatants

going. I hauled one young fellow in on my front seat, from St. Louis, slightly wounded in the leg. In the rear were three pitifully mangled couchees, groaning, begging me to stop, etc. etc. The young fellow had been in the advance three days, had had hardly anything to eat, but thought the whole thing was a big game and was anxious to get back. The noise in the rear of the car finally calmed him down a bit, and he said he didn't see how the Red Cross men could stand such sights and said he wouldn't have my job for the world. But it is a great work, and when one sees how much just a little time will help the sufferings of the wounded, it is much easier to keep it up when he is too tired to see the road.

The bad part of the whole affair was the amount of traffic on the road. I thought I had seen the road filled before, but this surely beat it. I talked with a [censored] man who was at the battle of Verdun and he says the traffic there was not nearly as congested as it was here. There was on an average, three moving lines on the road, two going towards the front and one away, always, starting and halting. One trip took me four hours to reach the hospital. I had three serious blesses, to make it worse, it was the middle of the night, and for fifteen minutes we had the worst driving rainstorm I ever saw. I was absolutely drenched, chilled, worn out and discouraged. I didn't reach the post till after daylight again.

The villages which have been retaken are certainly in ruins, hardly a wall left standing. I got a lot of good German souvenirs in the German dugouts, but lost most of them in the confusion we have been in. I wish some of our Government officials or whoever is responsible for our various war delays could see what I have seen this last week, and they would delay no longer in bringing this war to an end by hastening our troops over here as they certainly are needed. It was a pitiful sight to see the less serious wounded walking back the long distance to the hospital for lack

Camouflaged ambulances in France. *Committee on Public Information, Washington, DC*

of ambulance space. Nearly every trip I have started out with what should have been a full load for a little Ford and I would pick up a couple more limping along, just able to move along. It was little short of criminal to pass them by. The last couple days, though, it was better managed and they finally had enough to relieve us a couple days.

As to the military action itself, of course I can't say anything, but you can't help but know what it was from the date of my letter, and probably know more about the results than I could tell you from here, anyway.

I guess I have told you enough gloomy news and will try to say something more cheerful. It may interest you all to know that I won a "Croix de Guerre," in the little action we had

here about three or four weeks ago and which I wrote such a long letter about. I don't think myself that I deserved it, but will not refuse the citation very strenuously, if they want to give it to me! I think I wrote about everything I did in that letter and you can judge for yourself. Three of us got them at that time. The official citations haven't been given yet, but I guess there is no doubt but what they will go through. We have just heard that four more are to be given for this present big action.

NOV. 1, 1918.
[Letter to sister, Margaret] I forgot to tell you a great thing has happened to me. I have become engaged to a nice young French lady who has reached the magnificent age of nine

(9) summers, or winters, or both for all I know. She lived next door to one place where we were billeted. I spilled the beans by taking her for her first auto ride down to the river for the romantic task of washing my car. Then I started teaching her English, telling her about the U.S.A. and showing her pictures of it, till she got so excited I had to promise to come back in ten years, when she was grown up, marry her, and we would "partirons ensemble en Amerique." [He probably means "leave for America together."] I get the funniest letters from her. She seems to remember every English word I taught her, but doesn't know how to spell them and usually gets the meaning twisted. I have to take a day off and rest up after reading one. So, I guess it is all up with Miss Butler, or Beatrice, or Bee or whatever I am supposed to call her.

NOV. 15, 1918.

Well, the great event has happened at last, and none is more pleased than I am. I can imagine what must have been going on in any town in the States on the night of the eleventh and would have given anything to be there. But the jubilation and excitement over here was about as great as it could be. The people were nearly wild. About nine o'clock, when the news of the signing of the armistice came in, all the whistles and bells began blowing and everyone rushed out on the street. Inside of an hour every house, nearly, in town had one or more tri-colored [French] flags out and a good many had the old Stars and Stripes too. Then everyone got out a bunch of firecrackers and rockets from somewhere and made our Fourth look like a Sunday school picnic in a convent. In the evening, for the first time in four years, the street lights were lit. You can't imagine how strange it looked after being used to seeing absolute darkness in the towns. It made me quite homesick.

That evening they got up a dance right out in the main square of the town, which was a riot. The first dance since the war started, and they acted like it. I made one stab at it until I got dizzy from being whirled around so much by my energetic partner, and my feet got sore from being stepped on by so many wooden shoes. Besides, the boys were taking great delight in throwing fire crackers into the center of the mob. One lit in my hat and went off. Give me the front any time, where you know when they are coming (usually)!

Then a bunch of us decided to walk down to the next town, where they were having a real dance in a regular hall, and a real American band. That turned out to be the worst riot I ever hope to get in. Before the music started the floor was simply packed so you could hardly move, and then the band started up! Everyone grabbed the person nearest and tried to dance. The first dance I got hold of an old man about eighty years old, so drunk he couldn't tell his hand from his foot. He cut the most extraordinary capers, dancing up and down waving his arms and legs without noticing who was next to him. Next dance I was nabbed by a "buxom lassie" who was about as wide as high. She whirled me all over the floor, knocking people right and left as if they weren't there. I would like to see her on a football team! Everyone laughed and whooped till the tears came and they were hoarse.

[Telegram from Longyear May 23, 1919:]

DISCHARGED TODAY STOPPING OFF BOSTON WILLIAMSTOWN AND GRASSLAKE PHILIP.

[Longyear made it home. He was married and had a daughter. He died in 1931 at age thirty-five near San Jose, California, when the glider he was piloting crashed. The *San Jose Mercury Herald* reported, "Scores of golfers at the San Jose Country Club and residents of the east side watched his easy glides for 70 minutes and then saw with horror the fatal plunge."]

Edmund J. Longyear and Family papers, MNHS

WAR HYSTERIA

"You are advised that disloyalty is quite a common fault among Ministers of the Lutheran Churches."

A commission with near-dictatorial powers operated in Minnesota during World War I. Created by the legislature and called the Public Safety Commission, it was supposed to suppress disloyalty. Some historians say that if a large hostile army had landed in Duluth and was about to march on the capital, a more powerful commission could hardly have been created. The commission controlled many aspects of daily life: It prohibited "aliens" (noncitizens) from hunting game and teaching school, ordered all males over age sixteen to "work or fight," encouraged people to turn in "suspicious" neighbors, regulated the liquor trade, published a blacklist of German books, barred strikes and lockouts.

This was a time of superpatriotism and paranoia. In 1917 about 70 percent of Minnesotans had either been born in another country or were children of foreign-born people. Almost all were loyal to the United States, but rumors and suspicion flourished. Following is a sample of the letters the commission got and sent, reflecting the war hysteria.

[From the US Department of Justice's T. E. Campbell, special agent in charge, to the Minnesota Commission on Public Safety on February 15, 1918:]

I am in receipt of your letter of Feb. 14th, enclosing slips of paper with the wording

National Archives

"Kill Wilson Traitor" on one side and "Hurrah for the Kaiser" on the other side.

I regret that there is no evidence who the party is who left these slips at the Capitol, and if you commit possession of any clue that would lead to the detection of the party,

I would appreciate if you would immediately furnish me with the same.

[Another from Campbell to the commission, this one of March 4, 1918.]

I am in receipt of your letter of March 2d, enclosing communication from L. F. Diddie of Marshfield, Wisconsin, in which you mention the pro-German attitude of Reverend Nauss of Milaca.

You are advised that disloyalty is quite a common fault among Ministers of the Lutheran Churches. We will investigate Nauss at the earliest opportunity.

[From H. J. Loud, a Bemidji lawyer, to the commission, June 27, 1918.]

I desire to ask whether or not moving picture operators, having no other employment, come within the provisions of Order 37 [the Work or Fight order].

There are two young men here in that class, who do nothing whatever except to drive around with young girls in "Flivers" all day, and turn a crank for an hour or two in the evening.

I am one of the peace officers appointed by your body, and desire to assist in all ways in the enforcement of your orders.

Liberty Loan drive, St. Paul. *MNHS*

St. Paul Minute Men, who sold bonds and encouraged patriotism. *MNHS*

[From the secretary of the commission to Mrs. Frank Warren of Minneapolis on May 7, 1917:]

A matter has come to my attention which may interest your Committee now planning for women's employment. I believe I am addressing one of the ladies who called at this office some days ago.

A young woman called here, explaining that she had land in Dakota, formerly broken, that she is now in St. Paul Law School and will be at liberty June 1st, that she has taught and can return to teaching, that her present resources are practically exhausted, there being an unexpected dentist bill which disarranged her budget. She would like to plant beans on five or ten acres, she wishes to have the undertaking financed by a crop loan. Apparently she would have no bankable security to offer. This young woman is as big as a

house and apparently as powerful as the average two men, she wishes to do something for her country and assures me she will blow up if she has to sew or do any work of that sort. She is apparently best fitted to lead an amazonian band through a corn field.

Obviously this office has no machinery for dealing with such a proposal but assuming her statements are to be taken at face value . . . there is offered an opportunity for public spirit to put her in the way of doing what she can do best.

[To the commission on February 13, 1918, from Pearl J. Berg of Elbow Lake, who enclosed a two-layer postcard picturing the empress of Germany.]

I received by mail Enclosed Pichure and as I ame suspicius what is under that stuffing, I send it to you, so If You find it advisable to

Nurse in stormy weather uniform / Red Cross nurse / War nurse in uniform. *MNHS*

have it analised to find out If it should contain any Poisonouse Germ.

[From George A. Franklin, superintendent of School District 6, Itasca County, to the commission on February 18, 1918:]

The question is raised whether having basket ball games without making an extra fire to heat the gymnasium is violating the order sent out recently. We, of course, have to use the electric lights.

It was decided that social dances could be held at our village, and the boys think that high school athletics are of more benefit than dances. We burn wood in our heating plant, but it is not necessary to keep an extra fire for the games. I will be glad to have your advice in this matter as our school owes other schools some games.

The answer was, "I do not know of anything that would prevent the use of the school gymnasium."

[From C. H. Cooper of Carlos, Minnesota, to the commission, March 20, 1918:]

Jentlemen,
As chairman of the safety Commission here I would like A little advice,

There is a young man here sixteen years of age and in good health; who refuses to work.

His father has a large farm and is depending on him and A younger boy for this years help.

When the father tries to get him to work He swears at his father.

and tells him he cant make him work or Lick him either.

the Boy has always had good clothes and was never refused money to spend nor asked what he wanted the money for.

I will withhold the Kids name in hopes of getting him to work by showing him A letter from the Commission,

which I hope You will write.

[The response:]

Replying to your communication of March 20th. If you are unable to influence the young man you mentioned to go to work and do his share to the end that the Allies may be victorious in the present war,

The Commission will be obliged to take drastic action in this matter as it does not propose to have able young men idle when the necessity is so great.

If you furnish this young man's name I assure you no delay will be lost in bringing him to time.

[From Sam Dilley, age thirty-four, from New London, Minnesota, to the commission, August 19, 1918:]

I am writing you in regard to the 24th July as i have been reported to you as not having a useful occupation. I wish to say I have been working all the time when the weather was so I could but it has rained so much but the harvesting is all done now thrashing has begun and all the farmers are changeing hands, so I thought I would write and ask you if fishing and catching frogs was a useful occupation as I am a married man with quite a large family, and Im not what you would call a able bodied man if you come right down to it. Im writing this as i think every Pound fish and every crate of frogs I ship to the city and to Chicago it saves that much meet for our boys in the army, hoping you find this Letter all right and a early reply from you.

[From the local safety commission in Leroy, Minnesota, October 17, 1917:]

On Oct. 16th a transit drove into our garage, a Maxwell Roadster, bearing license #129549 Wis.

We, trying to do our duty to our country, pasted a Liberty Bond advertisement on his windshield, in the lower right hand corner. In the morning the driver came into the garage, and seeing same pasted to his windshield, made the following remark, "Who in Hell pasted that God Damn thing on my windshield? I don't want that Damn thing on there."

We found he registered at the Hotel as Roy R. Dalton of La Crosse, Wis.

We consider him a "slacker" and believe that he should be taken care of.

Headquarters for the Girls Liberty League, the W. D. Washburn house, Minneapolis. *MNHS*

Meter maids, Minneapolis General Electric Company, 1918. *National Archives*

[From the commission to Fred Hauslen, St. Paul, October 22, 1918:]

It has been reported to us that you are not engaged in a regular occupation.

You can appreciate at a time like this that no one should be idle. There is work for everyone to do.

I would be glad to have you advise this officer whether or not you are employed and if so when you entered your present occupation.

[To W. P. Lemmer, postmaster, Belgrade, Minnesota, from the commission, October 7, 1918:]

The following is a copy of a letter received today from Carl J. Troelstrup, whom you reported under Order #37 of this Commission:

"I am working and real hard labor too handling 150 lb. potato sacks and other stuff. I was just enjoying a 3 weeks vacation, having quit the Post Office after eleven months service. Sure a man deserves a 3 weeks vacation after working 11 months and not a day off. It was only spite work of some one whom I have been trying to Americanize, one of our pro-German friends around here. But just the same I am willing to work I am called for exam, at the Local Board next Friday. I have a grandmother partial dependent on me but I claim no exemption, willing to fight."

Will you kindly advise us whether or not his letter is correct.

[From James H. Hall, Lyon County Attorney, Marshall, Minnesota, to the commission, October 12, 1918:]

I have had several complaints regarding three young men who live at Galvin, Minnesota, and who have refused to work all summer and who are now without employment. All are within the draft age, but none have been called so far.

Ben Lindberg is the worst offender. He is a married man with a family. He has not worked a week for six months. He has made a little money boot-legging. We caught him a few days ago and he paid a fine of $100.00 and costs.

The other two are brothers, Oscar and Dewey Smith. Both have refused to work when women and girls have had to go into the fields to save the grain and to keep the threshing machines going.

I wish you would write them good strong letters and inform them that they have been reported to your office and see if we cannot get them started. Especially give Lindberg a good strong one.

[From the commission to the US Department of Justice office in St. Paul on March 6, 1916:]

The following is a copy of a letter received today from Henry Engebretson, Kent, Minnesota:

"Franz Rieber a farmer residing in this village has been making a lot of disloyal remarks about this Government, such as: his boy is not getting enough to eat at the training camp also that he do not get sufficient clothing therefore suffering unnecessary hardships also that he could make a better living in Germany than here. This party has been talking about the Government ever since the war started and will keep it up, therefore I am sure it would be a good idea to make an example of this party as it would put the scare in a few other pro-Germans we have in this territory." When you have a man in the vicinity of Kent, will you please investigate this report.

[From William O'Donnell of Mound, Minnesota, on August 8, 1918:]

There is a man residing here by the name of Joshua Bowers who I would judge to be about 40 years of age apparently fit for any manual labor, I believe he is a carpenter by profession who is in the habit of sitting around the post office here from morning to night only leaving it when he goes home to dinner and supper returning just as quickly as he gets his meals, he has an old father and mother but does not appear to assist them at home preferring to hang around the post office rather than stay at home and help the old folks.

Red Cross war fund parade, St. Paul, 1917. *National Archives*

It seems to me at the present time when there is such a demand for men in almost all classes of labor that he should be compelled to get out and hustle for himself and do all he can do win the war even though he is a Hun.

[The commission wrote to Bowers:]

We have been informed that although you are a carpenter by trade you are not at present engaged in a useful occupation, but spend your time loafing around public buildings in your town.

I beg to call your attention to Order #37 of this Commission attached hereto and unless you immediately engage in a useful occupation it will be necessary to start prosecution under this order.

Trusting that it will not be necessary to take any immediate action but that you will immediately go to work.

St. Paul store window. *MNHS*

War parade, St. Paul.
*Ramsey County War
Records Commission*

[Some people went out of their way to avoid links with German heritage. Aimee Fisher of the commission's women's auxiliary wrote August 17, 1917:]

The check just came. Thank you for it. Will you please correct my last name by leaving out the "c." I am of English descent and not German. Thanking you for your trouble.

[From the commission to the Department of Justice on August 7, 1917:]

It is reported to us by Rev. Amandus Norman of Hanska, a member of our organization in Brown County, that Joseph Steel, of Scarlet, Brown County, Chairman of Cottonwood Township, is a vicious man who should be dealt with promptly.

He is reported to have declared that neither of his two boys would be taken from his farm except over his dead body.

It is represented to us that he is a proper person of whom to make an example.

[From the commission to the US Department of Justice, March 25, 1918:]

We have an anonymous letter in the office calling attention to the Columbia Hotel, 109 Nicollet Av., Minneapolis, and in particular to one Pete Miller. It seems this is a congregating place for a number of Germans who spend their time in criticizing the Government.

[From Dwight E. Woodbridge of St. Paul to the commission on April 27, 1917:]

I notice in a telegram from Minneapolis that the board has decided to close the saloons in the Bridge District in Minneapolis, also at Fort Snelling. If, in the Bridge District in Minneapolis, why not in the Bowery District in Duluth? and if you are closing saloons why not close such places as pool halls, etc., where a lot of kids, who need nothing so much as army duty and army discipline, are wasting their time and forming bad habits? If all these kids could be rounded up and given the alternative of going to work or joining the army, I imagine there would be quite an increase in enlistment.

We, the women of the Jefferson School Club, Fergus Falls, Minn., desire to express our confidence in the President of the United States in the stand he has taken in the war. We desire to pledge our utmost loyalty and patriotism.

WHEREAS We are asked to encourage enlistments of our sons in the defense of our country; therefore, be it

RESOLVED, That the members of the Jefferson School Club strongly urge the army department to take immediate steps to rid the army of the saloon and the prostitute. We believe in taking this stand we express the sentiment of the mothers of the Nation.

[This song was called "Swat the Kaiser" and was sung to the tune of "There's a Long, Long Trail." It was written by Dr. A. E. Spalding of Luverne, Minnesota.]

While our boys across the river, struggling
    for the right,
Are enduring all the hardships in this
    dreadful fight,
We'll be ever mindful of them, treasure in
    our heart
Thoughts that we'll be always with them
    and will do our part.

Chorus
It's a long, long way to reach the Kaiser,
Into the land of his dreams,
But we'll show him that we'll get him
And will block his schemes,
For his heartless acts are rousing
The blood that courses our veins
We will rush him, crush him, down him for
    his bloody stains.

We through age or other reasons have to stay
    at home,
Must do something for the cause by taking
    Liberty Loan.
We have got to swat the Kaiser, show we have
    the vim,
So plank down the silver dollars and we're
    sure to win.

God bless the women of the Red Cross for the
    work they've done,
They'll not shrink from any duty till Bill is on
    the run.
So he'd better look "a leetle oudt" for he has
    no right to win,
Time has shown man's chance is very slim
    when the petticoats get after him.

[An ad in the *St. Peter Free Press*, December 29, 1917:]

[A telegram from the federal government to the state capitol, St. Paul, November 2, 1918:]

PLEASE GIVE WIDEST PUBLICITY TO THE FACT THAT MORE THAN TEN THOUSAND ADDITIONAL NURSES WILL BE NEEDED FOR THE ARMY NURSE CORPS BY JANUARY FIRST STOP ANOTHER TWENTY FIVE THOUSAND WILL BE NEEDED BY JUNE ONE STOP AN IMPRESSION THAT NO MORE NURSES ARE NEEDED IN MILITARY HOSPITALS HAS GONE OUT STOP THIS MUST BE KILLED IMMEDIATELY STOP

The Hoover Pledge

We are hearing so much about economy of food now-a-days that some of us are getting a little touchy. And yet, it seems, there are still many of us who do not understand the present meaning of the word. We think of it, as we always thought of economy—in terms of dollars, and Mr. Hoover is asking us to think of it in terms of food. It is not for the sake of our pocket books that he is making his campaign, but for the sake of making the food go around.

When we sit down to the family dinner, we do not expect the head of the house, because he does the carving, to help himself abundantly and skimp the rest of us. Uncle Sam now sits at the head of the World Dinner Table—and the table is not too well filled. Mr. Hoover is asking him to apportion the dishes so that all his children shall get a square meal.

There is not enough meat and wheat in the world for everybody, if we waste a bit or if we eat more than our share. So don't be selfish—not on account of your bank account, but because you want the boys at the front, our boys, and the brave men of brave France, almost bled white and fighting our battles, to be well fed. There is the same necessity with fats and sugars.

So eat perishable foods here at home in order that the grains and meats that will bear transporting, may go where they are more needed. And eat the things that grow near

you, because trains are needed to carry men and war material and we have no right to ask them to bring us luxuries from afar when the very safety of the world depends on efficiency in other directions.

Food conservation, then, is not a matter of personal choice. It's a world matter, in which every one ought to do team work.

Is it fair to our men at the front, who are offering their lives for world democracy, that women should fail in helping to feed the world democracy?

But it is not only a woman's problem. Although 90% of the food eaten is served in homes, remember that while mother prepares it, father and the children eat it. Women must keep in mind the world necessity and the world program while they are getting dinner, but the rest of the family must cheerfully accept the changed menu and learn to like war breads.

ALICE AMES WINTER, Chairman National Council of Defense, Woman's Committee, Minnesota Division

[In order to save wheat for the fighting troops, potatoes were pushed at home. Some of the potato ads:]

The Potato is a native American. Enlist it to fight against the Kaiser.

The Potato is a good soldier. Eat it, uniform and all.

Wait! Don't eat that slice of Bread, have another Potato instead.

Make your motto: "To Berlin, via tubor."

The newest fighting corps, the potatriots: Join the ranks and spud the Kaiser.

World War I conservation papers, State Archives, MNHS

[An ad run in many state newspapers:]

Minneapolis Soldier Under Fire
"We have had several brushes with the enemy since reaching the trenches here, which I am sure I would not have reached had it not been

for Mayr's Wonderful Remedy. It has entirely cured me of indigestion and awful gas in my stomach; Army food now digests as good as mother's used to." It is a simple, harmless preparation that removes the catarrhal mucus from the intestinal tract and allays the inflammation which causes practically all stomach, liver and intestinal ailments, including appendicitis. One dose will convince or money refunded.

[A wartime investigation of immorality:]

SPECIAL SURVEY OF THE MORAL CONDITIONS SURROUNDING GIRLS & YOUNG WOMEN OF MINNEAPOLIS & ST. PAUL

The following investigation was conducted by two National Secret Service men and made possible by two public spirited women, one of Minneapolis and the other of St. Paul.

[An example:]

Case 542C
Investigator #16
Minneapolis, Minn.
SEPT. 4, 1917
Continuing up on this case today, Inv. #7 and I again visited the balcony of the West Hotel, where we found conditions the same as on our previous visits. Many young girls were seen coming and going, most of them entering the ladies' room, but we saw no flirting.

At about 4:00 P.M. we took the car to Lake Harriet. As many couples were out on the water, we also hired a boat. Many soldiers and sailors were in the boats with young girls. . . . In a number of cases we saw several couples lying in the bottom of their boats. The girls did not appear to be over 14 years of age.

After leaving the boat we walked around the lake and Pavilion. We found soldiers and young girls lying in the grass and sitting on benches, spooning [kissing]. We heard several people remark it was a shame the way

the young girls were carrying on there. We remained there until 9:00 P.M. at which time we returned to the city, and covered Nicollet and Hennepin Avenues from 5th to 8th Streets. Here we found conditions very bad. Prostitutes walk the street soliciting every man they meet. Here also we overheard people talk about the bad conditions. These street walkers all seemed to be over 20 years of age. Inv. #7 and I were solicited a number of times. In one instance, we were solicited by two girls who had spoken to a policeman just a few minutes before. One of the girls said her name was Ruth and the other Irene. They were 22 years old. Ruth said she was from Iowa and here for easy "Fair Money." That the girls were getting $5.00, but that included the room. I asked her to what hotel she would take us and she said the Atlantic. We promised to see her at midnight and asked where we could find them. She said on Nicollet between 6th and 7th Streets.

In the next block we found conditions the same. We were solicited a number of times, the prices ranging from $2.00 to $5.00. The girls said they would take us to either the Gruenwald or the Atlantic Hotels.

We discontinued for the night at 1:00 A.M.

Time, 1 day $8.00
Meals. $1.55
Necessary Incidentals $1.25
Total $10.80

[His partner, #7, reported the following day:]

After dark we strolled through the park and found couples lying about in grass and behind bushes and in all dark places. Most of them were only spooning, but we passed two couples who appeared to be in actual intercourse. We were unable to overhear any part of their conversation.

Public Safety Commission papers, State Archives, MNHS

OPPOSITE: Return of the troops, St. Paul, 1919. *MNHS*

Bobbing for apples. *MNHS*

1920s

This was the Jazz Age, the era of the flapper, the speakeasy, and crazy fads. Industrialization increased rapidly. Lumbering petered out. Organized crime moved into the state. Women were given the right to vote in 1920. The Panic of October 1929 became the worst depression in United States history. →

Those who desire to dance the "shimmy" will have to confine their activities to some other place than Hibbing, says Mrs. Pritchard, policewoman who posted regulations in all the public dance halls of Hibbing this week.

Neither will cheek-to-cheek dancing be tolerated, the policewoman says.

With the notices posted were photographs of the correct position, at least the only position to be tolerated in the dance halls of Hibbing. This means that dancers must hold their partners at a distance.

Proprietors of public dance halls are authorized to eject all intoxicated or immoral persons from their halls. Neither will any minor under 18 years of age be allowed to frequent the public dance halls according to the notice.

The strict regulations are the result of the many public dances held in Hibbing during the past year to which any and all persons were allowed to attend. There was no restriction as to age, and it is claimed that girls are young as twelve years were frequenters. In many cases, there were no regulations as to the method of dancing, and cheek-to-cheek—sometimes even closer—was the rule, and not the exception.

Hibbing Daily Tribune,
February 23, 1922

THE FLAPPER GIRL

NOVELTY FOX TROT

Words and Music
by
"Vi" Stensrud

Paramount Publishing Co.
Minneapolis, Minn.

Fiftieth anniversary party. *MNHS*

[The *St. Paul Pioneer Press* ran a list of rules for young women trying to attract the opposite sex. They included:]

First of all, remember that there is just one thing that every human being, including men folks, hates, and that is Egotism. Hence, if you want to push young men from you, be egotistic.

If you want to be popular with the boys don't be Selfish. Selfishness, of course, is a form of Egotism. You may have charm enough to get away with it at first, but by and by selfishness always spoils love.

Speak low. Remember that the low voice is "an excellent thing in woman." Do not talk loud nor laugh loud. And for that matter do not dress loud. The kind of men that immodesty makes a hit with is not the kind that you want to know.

Be Good. I am not mentioning this from a religious or moral point of view, but merely as a lure for the opposite sex. Maybe you don't know it, and maybe you know it and resent it as an injustice, but no man loves a girl unless he has an idea that she is better than he is.

Don't try to shock the boys. Shocking them may make a sensation and attract attention to yourself, but it costs more than it comes to. It is always a losing game for you. Don't tell risque stories. Don't smoke cigarettes.

Be Chaste. What I mean is, guard your modesty and cling to your self-respect. Don't snicker at remarks that are off color. Don't let a boy put his hands on you. Remember, that very last defense and your principal charm is the sanctity of your person.

Be a Good Sport. By this I mean do not be a prude, and do not look for affronts where they are not meant, and do not see them when they are meant. Be in favor of things. Be a good pal.

Be Healthy. Be an outdoor girl. Boys are attracted to girls who are not only feminine but vigorous and strong. The kind of man that wants the clinging vine usually develops into a tyrant. The right sort of man wants an equal and a friend.

Above all things be Cheerful. Keep the sparks in your eye and the corners of your mouth turned up. Be optimistic, be enthusiastic. Be positive. Everybody likes sunshine and men take to it as a monkey takes to sugar. The average boy is apt to be tragic, and the girl that appeals to him is the one who is not tragic.

Don't be sensitive. If you are sensitive don't show it.

And if you keep all these rules and cannot attract the boys, don't blame me. I have done the best I could.

St. Paul Pioneer Press, April 25, 1922

Threshing, about 1920. *MNHS*

Prize-winning grain, rutabagas, turkey, and mushrooms, state fair, 1926. *MNHS*

MNHS

MNHS

Easter egg hunt, Logan Park, Minneapolis, about 1923. *MNHS*

University of Minnesota girls archery team. *MNHS*

St. Paul Daily News delivery trucks, 1922. *MNHS*

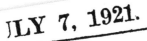

JULY 7, 1921.

MOTOR CARS.

AUTOMOBILES FOR SALE.

OLDS—Six, touring, like new, seven tires, spot light, motormeter. Cash or easy time payments. 233 Iglehart.

OVERLAND—Touring, $300; $150 down, balance terms. Dale 2232 or 921 Scheffer. Dale 8124.

OVERLAND—Roadster; $75 takes it; needs repairs. Dale 2232 or Dale 8124.

OVERLAND—Country Club, model 90, for sale, cheap. Tower 3211.

PIERCE ARROW—38, 5-passenger, cord tires; make splendid speedster. $495; terms. 408 Main. Garfield 2114.

PAIGE—Larchmont, model 6-55, five wire wheels; will sacrifice. Call Elkhurst 4878 for appointment.

PULLMAN—5 passenger; will sell for $175; a bargain; good running order and repainted. 1431 Sheldon. Midway 8154.

PAIGE—Five-passenger, good condition. Dale 9435.

REO—5-passenger, splendid condition; easy terms. 408 Main. Garfield 2114.

STUDEBAKER—1918, cheap, $200; 5-passenger; must be sold, as we are going to leave the city, or will sell lot and garage, $600. 1875 Helen street. Hazel Park.

STUDEBAKER—Roadster, 1918, 6-cylinder. $800; $200 down, balance terms. Call Dale 2232 or Dale 8124.

STEVENS—Roadster; also Overland Chummy; cheap. Dale 8262.

HUDSON SUPER SIX $1,050
AUBURN, 5-passenger, demonstrator...
CADILLAC, 7-passenger, 8-cylinder.....1,200
GARDNER, demonstrator 1,300
PIERCE ARROW, fine shape 1,000
PIERCE ARROW, 5-passenger 400

These cars are all in fine condition and are priced below market value.
TERMS OR CASH.

B. F. POWERS MOTOR CO.,
47 WEST FOURTH ST.

C. F. COLE COMPANY

20 high grade used car bargains; coupes, touring cars and roadsters. See us first ...

TOP: Hessburg Brothers truck. *MNHS*
BOTTOM RIGHT: Automobile of the
St. Paul fire chief. *MNHS*
BOTTOM LEFT: Boy and pets. *MNHS*

Hanging around a Minneapolis employment bureau. *Library of Congress*

1930s

Business failures and unemployment were common experiences. About 70 percent of Minnesota's iron range workers were jobless. Farm prices fell. Wheat production sank to new levels. Several cities were nearly bankrupt. Prohibition was repealed in 1933. Of the many labor strikes that occurred in Minneapolis during the 1930s, that of the truck drivers was the most influential in making the city a "union town." Charity, formerly a matter among family and neighbors, became more a function of government. →

LINDA BENITT

"Electricity is close to being a reality with us, tho the current is not yet turned into our place."

Linda and William Benitt began farming near Hastings in 1930, the start of a decade marked by sagging crop prices and drought. The Benitts had been married eight years when they started their "Apple Acres Farm." Both had extensive educations: William, a law degree from the University of Minnesota; Linda, a graduate degree in public health from Harvard and the Massachusetts Institute of Technology; both, postgraduate work in agriculture at the University of Minnesota. Linda wrote these letters. Most were to her sister Cornelia and to her friend Nellie Hubbell, whom Linda called "Hubby."

MONDAY, OCT. 13, 1930
Dearest Cornelia—
It is late afternoon as I write at our desk on the farm, the smells of roasting mutton and potatoes filling the room and Puggi scratching his fleas close by. The meat smells have roused him from his perpetual slumbers. William is at the University Farm where he goes every day now, tho I hope soon he will stay there overnight. It is too long a drive every day and leaves him too little study time. Outside is the continual sputter of the gas engine of the well drillers who have been at work a week trying to get rid of a rock in our well so that it can be deepened. Until we get water we can't have stock so we are naturally interested in their progress.

We have spent a hectic two weeks moving from Hills Edge [in St. Paul] here, but are now settled enough to think again and live. . . . After the violent day of cleaning here we followed it with hydrocyanic acid gas fumigation, finishing the airing of the house at 12 midnight the morning we moved. We were nearly dead but drove back to get what rest we could before the van should appear. I think the gas got every living thing in the house

Linda Benitt, 1938. *MNHS*

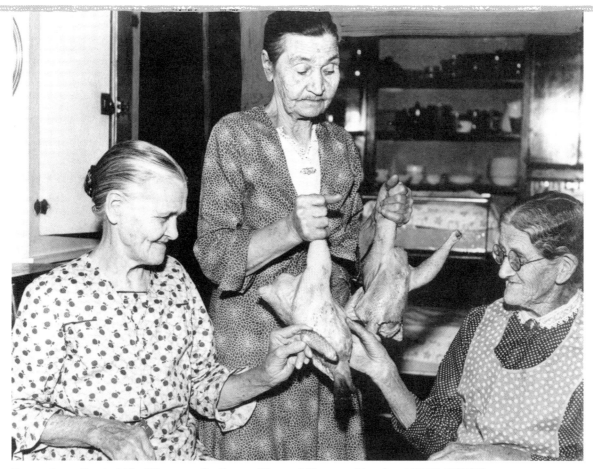

Preparing a feast at the Ebenezer Lutheran Home, Minneapolis, about 1935. *MNHS*

and when we opened the windows (from the outside of course) I could feel death flowing out them. The dead flies made a polka dot pattern over all the house floors. Rats, alas, have again found their way to us as I saw one slip under the porch a few days ago. Control of them is, however, a perpetual warfare with H.C.N. gas and poisons as they are very migratory. Some day when we have more time we shall campaign against them all over the farm. In the meantime they must be endured.

But as I glance out of the windows to the north and east I see only the beauties of the great views in the sunset lights, expanses that put rats where they belong as a minor factor in life! These views are very restful and changeful. To the south of the house lies the rich black soil all plowed and harrowed for the winter's seeding, the promise of our future livelihood. We have about 3 days of plowing

yet left to do. There is nothing like turning over those furrow slices for days at a time to sink one's roots into the soil of home. Plowing can either be an art or a job—like most things in life perhaps—but as an art it is very fascinating. It is a step in a sequence of events, a link in a chain; if well done, all that follows benefits, if ill done, all suffers—including profits. One must think of many things as he plows and adjust his work to attain his ends . . .

The well drillers have gone for the night, the sun has set, and I must get supper ready for William's return. Tomorrow he takes a day off to go to an auction near here where he hopes to find valuable junk—a Jersey cow, I believe, among it! We have not seen any of the stuff, however. Much much love to all the dear ones . . .

Your little sister, Linda

MON. NIGHT, DEC. 9, 1935
Dearest Hubby—
It is a little after 9 p.m., and I sit alone at our desk while the wind is howling thru our big trees and it is trying to snow. Wm. is at a meeting of the Amer. Farm Bureau Federation in Chicago, which Pres. Roosevelt addressed this morning. Wm. left yesterday noon and will not be back until Thursday. In the meantime I am farm boss—& miss him terribly.

We had a heavy financial misfortune befall us about 3 weeks ago when I discovered that we had a case of chicken pox in our flock. We have had carpenters and painters repairing the poultry house this summer, & we think the disease must have come in on their feet from some other flock. There is a considerable epidemic of it in Minnesota, most of it in the small farm flocks going unrecognized. We at once established quarantine measures and vaccinated the 1000 birds—which took 4 of us two whole days to finish. Between the disease

and the "takes" our birds have dropped their production to 20% of normal—now when eggs are at their peak price for the year! However, it was fortunate we caught it when we did, for ½ the flock showed no signs of the disease at the time we vaccinated. I think we are thru the acute stage now, & from now on we shall devote ourselves to feeding the birds back to production. They have to be pampered just like people. The experience has been a forceful lesson to us about letting anyone into the poultry farm. If tuberculosis ever gains entrance there! Disease is the great enemy of the farmer, be it of plants or animals. We have always had certain sanitary precautions in force for those who work around and with the poultry, but someone must have disregarded orders, probably thought they were foolish! And we pay the price! The loss is only financial, however, and Wm. and I still have each other. What does the rest matter?

Wm. has been working frantically to organize Wash. [Washington] Co. for utilization of federal funds in building electric lines to the farms. He has been rewarded so far by a large general meeting. . . . Now they have to get 1500–2000 members (who have paid their dues) before they can proceed farther . . .

That we should welcome you both [Hubby and her ailing mother, whom Linda invites to live on the farm] with open arms goes without saying. Your coming would of course greatly enrich our lives. I am confident that the farm could yield us all a comfortable living, tho we would never any of us get rich. But, oh, the blessedness of independence & the security of the soil!

[The invited guests did not move in.]

JUNE 23, 1936
From dawn till dark he [William] drives himself. Right now especially, when we are trying to finish cultivating & haying before we go. It is so dry this summer, with burning days &

freezing nights, that the crops are maturing very early. One sometimes wonders whether this vast Mississippi basin is doomed to become a desert. Montana & the Dakotas are nearly that now. Those sod prairies should never have been put under the plow, and it looks as tho it was too late to return them to sod, as not even grass can grow in those parched states. We are working our land on the contour lines in an endeavor to hold in the soil whatever rain may fall, & are also putting into hay crops all the land we can spare. Barnyard manure, too, we apply, constantly, as that holds moisture also. Even so, the grain looks wretched this year, tho corn is all right so far. But weather is not ours to control so we do not worry about it.

APRIL 25, 1937

A heartful of love to you, dear Hubby, & to your anxious and tortured mother. Remember the telephone always connects us in time of need. To me that is a comforting thought. Must go now to the chicks to put them to bed. Goodnight, dear girl, & love always.

Linda.

MAY 15, 1937

Two girls had driven up with me to buy shoes for graduating exercises. Their excitement brought back to the days of our own commencement at Central [High School in St. Paul], and the colorful exercises at the Auditorium. We were fortunate to have had so small a class that we knew each other as individuals and not as a mass. That was true of

Slot machine destruction in Minneapolis, 1932. *MNHS*

the University also. If I had children to send to school today I should be much puzzled about a college. I've seen my own nieces and nephews go to every sort of place, according to the parents' leanings, and which has had the richer experience it is hard to say. Youth seems much more critical of teaching methods today than we ever were. We swallowed a college curriculum hook, sinker and line, with perfect satisfaction. Not so the youth of today. We were of course conservatives, trained that whatever was, was good. Today young people are in a ferment of unrest, their minds are chaos as are ours, too, for that matter—and a cut & dried, question & answer type of teaching does not reach them at all. A teacher today has a thrilling challenge before him if he will but attempt to interpret the modern world to young people. They are not left free to do so, I suppose & so make botch of it.

It is raining hard here, is cold, and spring seems held in abeyance. Night before last we had a hard freeze; the night before that a windstorm which destroyed several farm buildings near us. Such is Minnesota weather.

MAY 18, 1937

Farming is a perpetual battle against all rodents and harmful insects, a battle which has no end in sight. Weather we are absolutely at the mercy of, but these others we can—and do—fight always. Farmers have killed off the natural enemies of these pests, like hawks, weasels, owls, snakes, etc., & we are all paying the penalty now.

JUNE 28, 1937

The eastern trip has fall thru for us because of a truck drivers' strike in St. Paul. The strike makes our egg deliveries too hazardous to leave in inexperienced hands. So our little visit will have to be postponed & Helen C. will have to be married without us. Too bad. I am hoping for a letter from you this Monday morning. I am with you so much in spirit that it would seem as tho letters were unnecessary, but how eagerly they are watched for.

SEPTEMBER 6, 1937

We have been desperately busy on the farm—due to lack of both male & female help—that letters have lapsed sadly. My carefully built structure for preparing the eggs for market (cleaning, grading for size, & candling) has completely crumbled, due to school ambitions, vacations & home needs. Man help is as extinct as the Dodo bird for the farm because the federal government is clearing trees off river bottom lands above Red Wing, lands to be flooded by a new dam. They pay 50¢ an hr, for an 8 hr. day, pay which would leave a farmer with a 12 to 14 hr day broke. You know we figure our own labor brings in from 5-15¢ an hr depending on the work we do & that labor might be classed as skilled! Cutting down trees is plain manual labor. So the farmers are meeting the situation by helping each other out & nearly killing themselves doing it. Crops are rotting in the fields for lack of help, & yet they will not compensate for $4 a day labor. The labor times are sadly out of joint for the farmer.

A good part of my week is given up to the egg work, & what is left goes to canning, jellying, pickling.

Farm boys with groceries, near Northome. *Library of Congress*

NOV. 7, 1937

At last I have a woman to help me with the housework and eggs, and what a relief it is. She is 42 years old, of cheerful disposition & a regular "hog" for work—a real blessing to us. I spend most of my time now in the orchard, tho I still candle the eggs two half days a week & make the Friday deliveries.

FEB. 10, 1938

I am just about to go to St. Paul with William who has sent a truck load of pigs to market, whose sale at the stockyards he wants to watch. They are a beautiful lot of pigs according to Wm.—very smelly according to me!—but good eating anyway. People who like pork

Linda Benitt, about 1940. *MNHS*

should never live with pigs. They might prefer beef thereafter.

MARCH 8, 1938

Our life here is a busy round of farm tasks, varying from week to week with the seasons. There is a feel of spring in the air today tho the ground is white, but the sun is high and the birds are singing their spring songs and the crows have arrived. So also we have our first 1000 chicks, darling balls of yellow fluff, scratching so happily in the ground corn cobs in their brooder houses at 95 degrees on the floor. In that temperature Wm. and I worked for 3 hours on their arrival, toe punching each chick for later identification. We were scarlet when we finished.

The egg business is rather discouraging this spring, tho we feel that if prices drop low enough, the in-and-outers in the business will conclude to be out next winter. Over double the pounds of frozen eggs in storage for this time of year is proving a very depressing factor to storing of eggs now by commercial cold storage concerns. This method of storing the opened eggs has caused a supply far beyond the demand for the product by bakeries, restaurants, etc.

Perhaps you would be interested to know what the labor earning of myself and W. were for the past year on this farm. After allowing ourselves a 6% return for our equity in the farm, & equipment & animals, and after deducting everything of a personal nature, like the house, food from the farm, clothing, etc., our earnings for the labor we two have expended all year amounts to exactly $80.38. It is easy to see why young people are drifting to the cities, & why farmers are losing their farms in such number. And yet last Sunday, at Helen's, Clifford said most positively that one thing was sure—food was too high! I have never heard him say a word about the cost of gasoline, or the endless expenses incurred in running an auto. Our sense of relative values

Shanties along the river in Minneapolis, 1936. *MNHS*

seems to have run all amuck, and where shall we end? Farm tenancy—a most unhealthy situation for all concerned & death to the land—has increased from 26% in 1880 to 43% today of all farm operators. At the same time the percentage of our total pop. that is on farms in the U.S. has dropped from 46% to 25%. No wonder our economic order is becoming top heavy in the Cities. Cutting cost of food is not going to better the situation, nor will decrease of production except as an emergency measure in a hopelessly chaotic time all over the world. The Roosevelt administration has done much to help the farm debt situation, but the tax situation is still a bad one. And always unsolved is the price situation for the farm products.

I did not intend writing at such length about the "farm problem," but I thought the earnings of this particular farm might interest you. There are other earnings of a farm besides money, and these are what keep the most stubborn of the farmers on the land. First among these is the feeling of security. Food & shelter are his for at least a year after foreclosure, & foreclosure approaches gradually and can be met better than the troubles subsequent to loss of work in the city, with rent to be paid, food bought—all with cash and no cash to pay with. Living close to nature, cooperating with the great natural forces that make our universe, has a strong appeal to all farmers. No city lives can equal the lures of nature as one sees them in farm life. The ceaseless ingenuity & skill make the rather orderly city life seem dull in comparison. And idleness is unknown!

MARCH 13, 1938

Electricity is close to being a reality with us, tho the current is not yet turned into our place. Our farm wiring is not quite complete. We look like a factory town with wires all over the place. But for the present we must remain content with lamps & gasoline stove. Electric appliances are pretty costly & they will have to be added gradually, for the installation of the wires was a stiff cost to begin with.

MAY 27, 1938

Rain is closing in on us again, after torrents of it this past week which tore out railroads, roads & bridges, & flooded the bottom lands of the river. Cold rains, mist, & cold winds are delaying our spring & things are growing slowly and all watery in texture. Dear sun, come out again.

SEPT. 28, 1938

I have driven over with William to an electric show of the R.E.A. [Rural Electrification Administration] in Dakota Co., and, while he contacts the people he has come to see, I seize the chance to write to you. It seems as tho all our thoughts and hearts these days are absorbed by the European crisis. When I am at home or candling in the poultry house I have the radio going steadily, and thus keep in close touch with each new development as fast as it happens. Chamberlain's speech yesterday addressed to the world at large was the most moving one I have ever heard, truly as great a speech as Lincoln's Gettysburg address. Tomorrow Hitler, Mussolini, Daladin [Daladier] & Chamberlain meet in Munich. What will come of it? By the time this letter reaches you we should know whether it is peace or war in the immediate future. And war in Europe means war for us, too. Let us not delude ourselves about that. As individuals we can do little, but we can live the agony of suspense of every European each hour that passes. We shall truly pray that Hitler's enormous egotism may feel a check in the world disapproved of his militant methods & empirical aims.

In the meantime we go on living our lives of daily routine while we hang on the edge of the abyss for our civilization. Hens lay eggs, Hitler or no Hitler; crops must be harvested when ripe and the weather permits; little pigs eat & grow; children must go to our democratic schools, etc. So we cut our corn, shock it; cut hay and stack it; grade our eggs & market them; kill a fine beef for our own table & put it in frozen storage for use during the coming year; and all the time we draw nearer to the brink.

William A. Benitt and Family papers, MNHS

DEPRESSION LETTERS

"Maybe next year we would have a better crop and things would pick up so we could make our payments regularly."

The desperation of Minnesotans during the Depression is reflected in these letters to the governor, who, unfortunately, could do little.

[Received at the governor's office, August 12, 1932:]
Hon. Governor Olson
Dear Sir:
With fear and trembeling I am going to ask a favor of your Honor. I know you will think me forward, but dont think to hard of us as you can't realise how hard it is for us old folks to give up our home. We took out a Federal Loan eight years ago for $5000.00 and we paid faithfuly for 6 years then everything went down and we could not pay any more so they forclosed and this year we rented our home we paid $40.00 cash and we still owe $200.00 on our rent our crops were a compleat failure. Now since we cant pay I suppose they will put us off. If we only had a chance to buy it back for what they are offering our home to others we would be so happy. My husband does not drink we are law abiding people. There is no display of luxury around here, we live in a little log house bare floors worn badly and the roof leaks, but we would be content if we just could live here. Maybe next year we would have a better crop and things would pick up so we could make our payments regularly. Would you please speak a kind word to the Federal Loan Co. so we would not need to move. If it

is not asking too much. We will work so much harder and save every cent we can to make our payments if we can make an arrangement to buy it back. Thanking you very much for your kind answer in the future.

I remain.
Yours very truly,
Mrs. Nick Kiser
Underwood, Minn.
Excuse my pencil writing I have no ink and pen in the house.

[The governor's response was not saved with the letter. We don't know what became of the Kisers.]

[William Haas of St. Paul, a forty-nine-year-old contractor, filled out an application for a federal job in 1934. He listed his talents:]

Know something of building construction.
Know something of bridge construction.
Know something of dam construction.
Know general municipal and highways construction.
Know sewers.
Expert on pavements particularly asphalt.
Know costs.
Can organize
Can tell the other fellow what to do and how to do it. Know if he is doing it, whether the water boy or the engineer of civil science.

[And he listed his experience, including being the $400-a-week superintendent of a construction job in 1926–27 in Chicago and subcontracting road construction from 1926–30 in Arkansas and Oklahoma. His resume ends:]

December 19, 1930. A Christmas present. Ruptured appendix. All of 1931 not able to work.

1932–33. Begging for a chance to work. The hardest work I ever did.

ST. PAUL MINN 9/22/35
Gov. Floyd B. Olson
St. Paul Minn.
Dear Gov. Olson:
Supposing you were forty three years of age, out of work, a wife & child to support and a mortgage foreclosure about to be put on your home. What would you do about it? I'm writing you, as the head of our state government, to give me some advice. I've combed this town over & over for work. I've written Mr. Christgan, as you suggested to me when I wrote you from Frazee, Minn., but its of no use. Seems like when you get about forty years of age, you begin to lose a foothold & start slipping. I can work hard at anything if only given the chance. I'd like to prove to myself as well as others that I can come back, but as I say its discouraging when you try day after day to find work only to be told "nothing doing." Now I'm a good pharmacist & if you know any member of the State Board of Pharmacy that can assist me in locating a job I would be thankful. Maybe theres an opening in the State Liquor Dept. I know Mr. Blake, state liquor investigator, quite well. Maybe theres an opening anywhere, doing anything, all I want is a chance to make a living. I'm not going to bore you with anymore details about myself. If you can assist me I'm sure you will, if you cannot I'm thanking you just the same for your patience & forebearance in the past.

Again thanking you I remain
Yours sincerely,
Fred G. Sundberg
363 S. Warwick ave.

SEPT. 24, 1935
Dear Mr. Sundberg:
I am in receipt of your letter of recent date and am very sorry to learn of your difficulties. However, I regret to advise that I cannot be of further service to you in obtaining employment. I can only suggest that you keep in touch with the Re-Employment office in

St. Paul relative to securing work on WPA and PWA projects.

Regretting my inability to be of assistance to you at this time, I am

Sincerely yours,
Floyd B. Olson,
Governor

Detroit Lakes, Minn.
OCT. 13—1933
Governor Floyd B. Olson
St. Paul, Minn.
Governor Olson:
Dear Sir: You are much too busy to bother with small farmers like me nevertheless I am taking this opportunity of writing you, regarding this farm loan that is supposed to benefit us fellows.

Why is it a loan is so impossible to get. They took my money all right, said the appraisors would not consider an application unless $10.00 accompanied it. But that's the last I've seen or heard of the $10.00 or any one else.

I bot a small 40 acre farm last fall, fixed up the house which was not livable, build fences, cut brush, and got about 10 more acres ready for cultivation. Now when theres no money to meet the payment they say get out. We've always made our own living without help from anyone but if we have to get out now some-one will have to take care of us, as we've put all our money into this place and there is no possible chance of getting work. The way things are now we had to sell some of our chickens in order to buy more feed, we got $10.76 for 56 chickens that cost us $23–52 to raise now how is a person going to meet their bills when things sell like that? I would appreciate an answer to this letter.

Very truly yours
Oscar B. Dahler
Detroit Lakes
Rt. 3. Minn.

Farm children near Northome, 1937. *Library of Congress*

OCTOBER 17, 1933

Dear Mr. Dahler:

This will acknowledge your letter of October 13th.

I am very sorry indeed to learn that you are having difficulty in making a federal loan. I should like to be of some assistance to you in this connection, but as you probably know, this is a federal agency over which we have no jurisdiction.

I assure you, however, that I am doing everything possible both through State and Federal agencies to assist the farmer.

Sincerely yours,
Floyd B. Olson
Governor

EVERYBODY WANTS A KEY TO MY CELLAR

BY ED ROSE
BILLY BASKETTE
AND LEW POLLACK

Honorable Floyd B. Olson
Governor State of Minn.

Dear Sir.

If I may be permitted to offer my idea of a solution to the employment situation I would suggest that the six hour day is in my humble opinion the best solution for the following reasons. In this age of Automobile transportation and modern machinery it stands to reason that there cant be 8 hours a day work left for all the people that have to work for a living, any emergency appropriation to furnish work . . . will simply make matters worse in the future and why should ¾ of the working people be required to work 8 hours a day and support the idle ¼ with what they make instead of everybody working 6 hours a day and all supporting themselves.

We know from experience what a holler there was when we changed from 10 to 8 hours lots of people said it was ridiculous, but it worked and worked fine so why not progress . . .

One more thing we all know to be true if more people have jobs more money will be spent more merchandise bought and more work created for instance if 100 people earn $150.00 a month they will put nearly all of it back in circulation while 50 people earning $300.00 per month might salt away nearly half of it thereby taking it out of circulation by this I do not mean that wages would be cut, that would be a calamity. Prices must be kept up or our whole house would come tumbling down. So lets hope that this 6 hour day gets a tryout soon.

Yours very respectfully
L. G. Anderson
726 Queen Ave. No.
Minneapolis

Dear Mr. Anderson:

I have your letter of January 17, containing suggestions with reference to the relief of the unemployment problem. I want to thank you

Gas station on Washington Avenue, Minneapolis, late 1930s. *Library of Congress*

for your interest in this matter, and to assure you that I am giving the question of unemployment my earnest consideration

Yours very truly,
Floyd B. Olson
Governor of Minnesota

Minneapolis, Minn.
SEPT. 18 [1931]
Mr. Olson
Dear Sir—
I wish to plead with you to give the position every married woman holds (that has a husband well and able to work) to a man or unmarried woman.

I can tell you of married women that I know that work in offices and earn up to 250.00 a month and their husband also brings home a good sized check. ('Taint fair.)

Instead of cutting the working hours

please try my idea first and you'll find that thousands of jobs will be then waiting for a man, now jobless.

Thank you.
Yours truly
Irene Anderson

Frazee Minn
11/27–31
Hon. Gov. Olson
A few words in short. I am in destitute circumstances for the winter. I worked 3 months for nothing through haying and harvest, and now winter coming on, and no work to be gotten here now, and nothing to live on, Your honor, will you please lend me $100.00 till next fall, to tide over winter, when it opens up in the spring, and I get a job I will pay you back, I have a sickly wife and Two small children to take care of, and clothe so please do me this

favor, you can't get a pleasant look from the banker here.

Please, by Dec. 1st

Yours truly

John B. Beckstrand

PS. I will appreciate this kindness very much.

Dear Sir:

The Governor has your recent letter and regrets that he is unable to be of assistance to you, in the manner specified. He receives so many requests of this nature that he has found it necessary to decline in each instance. I am sure you will appreciate his situation. Very truly yours,

Secretary to the Governor

Bowlus, Minn
Rt. 2 Box 32
11/2/31
Gentlemen—

As the times are hard. As we all know, we will have to ask governor olsen for some help, we have plenty to eat but we have no cloths 3 children are going to school But as we can't buy any cloths so will have to keep them from school we can't let them freeze on the way to school they have 2½ miles to go if there is any way out we would be very thankful

Your thruly

Wm. B. Bieniek

Coffee party in south Minneapolis, about 1935. Seated here are Ethel Anderson, Mrs. A. L. Anderson, Mrs. Axel Black, Mrs. Charles Brink, Mrs. G. Carlson, Mrs. J. A. Jacobson, Mrs. A. R. Johnson, Mrs. R. Johnson, Mrs. Sven Johnson, Mrs. E. Liedstrom, Mrs. G. Malmquist, Winnifred Malmquist, Mrs. M. Nelson, and Mrs. G. Schroeder. *MNHS*

Dear Mr. Bieniek:

I have received your letter of recent date, and am sorry to learn of your destitute circumstances.

I regret that there is nothing that I can do to help you. I would suggest that if you are in need, that you apply for aid to your local welfare agencies or to your Board of County Commissioners. They may be in a position to help you.

Yours very truly,
Floyd B. Olson
Governor of Minnesota

Bemidji
NOV. 6 1931
Governor Floyd B. Olson
Dear Sir:

Pardon me for writing to you but i don't know your house adress so i can write to your wife but will you please give her this letter i have thought so long i was going to try and get up enough nerve to write and ask for a littel help its so hard for me to do such a thing i hate to let anybody know how bad it is now i will tell you we are my husband myself and litel boy 9 years old and its so hard to get any work but the Lord has been good we havent had to ask for any help but my husband gets a few days work now and then and we had a nice garden so we have enough for food and we try and get cloths for the boy to go to school and dady says overaals is good enough for him. but there dont seem to be anyway so i can get any cloths or shoes and its been 2 winters now i havent had a coat and now we are worse of before and i cant even get a days work so i can get me a coat i am getting worried i haven't had a thing to wear now would you please help me to get a coat a dress and shoes, them are the things that are empasebel for me get of course i am out of everything in the line of cloths and shoes now i don't ask for new things they could be used and i am handy to make over things, please will you do it i would be so glad, a coat lasts me for many years, i haven't even got a hat didnt have one last summer and now its getting cold and i am to proud to let any-boy know and i have thought if our Governor knew he would help me, or i am sure if there is a Mrs Governor Olson if she would please help me to get this things i need so bad as anybody ever did, in case you would, i will tell you my size of coat is 44 and allso in dreses i am 5 feet 5 inches high 45 years old, and i wear a no 5 shoe wide widts, for anything on head, large size. Please Mrs. Olson if you can or any of your freinds have any used cloths that would fit one would you please send them to me and i would be so glad and thankfull and love you allways for its so hard to me to ask for help but i just have to i have nevr been used to much but we allways had food a cloths that is the cheapr kind but now its so bad as it can be i cry myself to sleep many nights i cant hardly go downtown its getting to cold with out coat and i just have a light percale dress i can go out with, if we can spare anything i get it for my boy and my husband thats got to be out. well hope you will help me just this once my best wishes to you and Gods blessing allways, my adress is

Mrs Margit Lampman
Bemidji
Minn.
Rt.#1

PS sometimes when i know you are here i will come and speak to you

Dear Madam:

. . . There are so many requests for help that it is impossible to comply with them. Each community is taking care of the wants of its own residents, and you should be taken care of through some used clothing center, some Church or other private organization, or your county or township officials.

I trust that you will be taken care of properly.

Yours very truly,
Secretary to the Governor

Mpls Minn
Jan. 26—1931
Governor Floyd Olson.

Dear Sir.

I am going to plead with you knowing your heart is good Now Mr Olson could you do any thing in the line of work for my husband Mr Chase has in all work 5½ days since last June. We are 3 in family i would be willing to work but cant find none, the Public Relief gives us $4.00 per week, you know how that goes, but we dont ask for aid only give us work, our girl Lucile is 15 year and if we cant get help as she has gone so fare in school, but everything is worn out no shoes or stockings, we are no spendthrifts, as for shows ore drinking none of the same, now please see what can be done for us. And may the greatest Blessing be with you. and in all you undertake in your office. God Bless you and yours.

Mrs. Wm. Chase
2213 22 Ave South, City

Governor Floyd B. Olson papers,
State Archives, MNHS

Free milk at Jefferson School, St. Paul, 1938. *National Archives*

Milk station at Lincoln School, St. Paul, 1936. *National Archives*

JOHN F. D. MEIGHEN

"Not a good year financially, only moderate, but kept excellent health and have enjoyed life, the election campaign and my hobbies."

John F. D. Meighen, a lawyer in Albert Lea, kept diaries for decades. Those that cover the Depression years show that money continued to come in to him and that life continued pretty much as usual. He was born in Spring Valley, Minnesota, in 1877; was graduated from the University of Michigan law school in 1900, and began his law practice in Albert Lea the next year. In 1917 he married Katherine Morin, a widow with two children, William and Richard Morin. John and Katherine Meighen had no children. Meighen was a district judge from 1921 to 1923 and always was active in Democratic politics. What made his diaries different from most was that he seemed to be writing for posterity. Here are pieces of his diaries, starting with the year of the stock market crash (of which he made no mention).

1929

Nov. 16. Watch Michigan defeat Minnesota, seven to six.

Nov. 19. Young Gillrup takes my order for a heater at less than $30 to heat Ford.

Dec. 6. Hoover says 72¢ of every dollar spent by Fed Government during next fiscal year is for "past wars and preparedness for future wars."

Dec. 22. S.S. [Sunday School] and Church. Parson Barnes notes the miraculous part of the story in Luke. "Peace on Earth and Goodwill etc."

In evening have chow mein at Chinese Restaurant and then the talkies, "The Sap," who makes money in grain by buying when given a tip to sell and selling when given a tip to buy.

Dec. 31. Again the book [diary] closes [for the year], I shall not keep awake to hear the New Year come in, too many things left undone must promptly be done. . . . Katherine

John Meighen. *MNHS*

and I are too fat, yet enjoying life. Really a comfortable situation all around. No marked gain this year, nor no marked trouble.

1930

Jan. 14. Attend bank meetings.

Jan. 24. Spend forenoon with R. N. Klass of Cedar Rapids, on Wittmer insurance matter. We determine to divide earnings between our two offices, share and share alike.

Feb. 2. Attend 1:00 p.m. meal at B. O. K's [his law partner]—a delightful meal charmingly served; then spend an hour in office work.

Feb. 16. After Sunday school, wife and I get some hot hamburgers in a box, a few doughnuts and a thermos bottle filled with coffee for a picnic dinner, which is later consumed about seven miles east of Austin on the road to LeRoy.

Feb. 22. We plan an enlargement of our office by partitioning off a part of the hall and installing an additional clerical worker to handle an intercommunicating phone system.

March 10. Silverstone, the accountant, asks $60.00 a week for a 5 day week.

April 19. Finally get inventory in fair shape. Looking backward my real estate investments seem foolish. In banking my choice was good. Was lucky to get out of Albert Lea State. In Industrials my guess was good on Enderes and poor on the others. A. L. Farms was

Ukrainian National Chorus of the Twin Cities, 1933. *MNHS*

unfortunate, like all the other real estate. For me, 5% municipal bonds would have been a better bet. My life insurance was well chosen, no failures there.

June 12. Speak to St. Paul College of Law graduating class of 42 tonight.

Rather dramatic in several particulars

1. Husband and wife take law degree together.

2. One Negro.

3. Three women.

4. One man, whose Mother had brot him by wheelchair to each session. She was present.

July 7. In afternoon drive to Duluth with Judge and Mrs. Norman E. Peterson in the Jordan along with a lot of luggage, some on the running board. The view by night of electric lighted Duluth as we approached on #1 was a delight. . . . The concrete freed us from dust, so it was a comfortable drive.

Aug. 25. Golf for 9 holes. Norem . . . 63, Wilby 61 and Meighen 57.

Sept. 18. Very attractive day for the four hundred women who come out to house for the afternoon reception. . . . Tea was poured on east side of home. I supicion that to keep flies from bothering outside, they were all let into the house. Chamber of Commerce handled transportation nicely and the lake behaved beautifully. Katherine looked her best. She handles such matters delightfully.

Sept. 26. Dick [his wife's son] writes of the birth of Joan Purdy Morin at American Hospital Sept. 10, 1930, Paris. I place letter in my safety box to be handed her at 18 years—Sept. 10, 1948. Wonder what the world will then be like? Which ones of the family group will be living?

Sept. 30. Purchased 100 shares of Northwest Bancorporation at 42 3/8 and a commission of 15¢, a total of $4,252.50.

Nov. 28. Visit Tom Sawyer, Huck Finn and aunt Polly via motion pictures. Excellent.

Dec. 1. Bank may declare 20% dividend this year.

Dec. 29. [Part of train trip to California and Mexico.] Dirty Tia Juana with its many beer saloons & drab houses contrasted greatly with the green, well-kept hotel grounds.

1931

Feb. 19. See Greta Garbo in Inspiration. Do not motion picture and fiction producers rather overdo suddenness of love between masculine "A" and feminine "B"? They leave development thru acquaintance, education, out of account.

March 7. Spend entire day at residence, resting in effort to shake off a bad cold. Listen to Amos and Andy and many other

Family waits for truck to be loaded, 1939. *Library of Congress*

radio broadcasts. Andy made a mess of the cross-examination, thinks this is the worse "picklement" yet.

April 26. Prosperity is just around the corner. Whose corner?

July 3. Uncle is plainly troubled by the general agricultural depression and the high land taxes.

July 4. [The Meighens begin a two-month trip to England and Europe.] My bank balance at leaving is $1,451.00 in deposit checking account.

July 7. Our [ship's] cabin is steady and with very little vibration, #520. an outside room with a large porthole. . . . Do not find anyone that I know in passenger lists. The heavyweight champion, Schmeling, is in first class.

July 10. One of the interesting helps to First Class passengers on this ship is an electrically controlled . . . plan board. If you want to find the shooting gallery or the swimming pool, you press the button labelled "swimming pool" or "shooting gallery" and the path to the place . . . is at once shown electrically.

Sept. 7. 5 a.m. Train arrives [back in Albert Lea]. Taxi is on hand and takes us to house, where a welcome light shines in maid's room.

Nov. 16. Hiler calls re bankruptcy, but he has a car we must get rid of somehow. To be sure, one can point to the trouble with the above—living too well when times were easier, not providing for a day of rain and gloom.

1932

Jan. 2. Dow-Jones Average 40 bonds. Week ending Jan. 2, $77.77. Week ending yr. ago. $95.99.

Jan. 5. Home again [from California] about one o'clock in afternoon. Everything running smoothly at the house and at the office.

Jan. 11. The outlook for financial recovery is still poor. The bond prices are lower than ever. And stocks, I doubt your obtaining $5.00 a share for Am Gas now, once $42.00.

March 6. Dinner at Chase home. Take movies inside [house] of baby, with supersensitive film. Try some at 8 frames and some at 16 frames.

March 28. [A newspaper editorial he wrote, taped in his diary] An incompetent [county] board can spend 20 percent more than a competent board, without any trace of grafting or illegality, merely by exercising poor judgment. Last year the five dispensed over $500 of the county's money every day, including Sundays and holidays, for roads and bridges and averaged over $550 a week, winter and summer, for the poor. They checked out nearly $100 more each week for stationery, blank books and such supplies.

May 5. There was a general slowing down of endowment income [for Hamline College, where he was a trustee] due to depression.

There is a element of suspicion rather natural in business.

May 21. [Anniversary of] Lindberg[h] landing in Paris, 1927. After 5 years the first woman makes the solo flight—Amelia Earhart Putham.

June 11. Buy new Ford [deluxe] coupe and pay $500 difference, plus $14.05 for license. It is an 8 . . .

Delivery price with metal tire cover . . .	$672
Allowance on Model A	172
Net	$500

June 19. Morning waffles and sausage on Lake Ripley at 9:15 in Ed and Dorothea Kopplin cottage. . . . Splendid dinner at hotel. Drive home during afternoon.

June 26. 10:45 a.m. Take "Democratic Special" from St. Paul, on Burlington route, for Chicago convention. [1932 Democratic National Convention; Meighen is a delegate.] Have reserved a Pullman seat. Round trip is $21.41. Arrive at Chicago 8:45 p.m.

July 1. From 9:00 P.M. last night until after four this morning we have a flood of nominating speeches and marching demonstrations. Then three ballots. [And Franklin D. Roosevelt is nominated.] The morning sun pours thru the upper windows of the stadium upon wilted collars, deep lined faces, and wrinkled clothing.

Sept. 13. [Joke] What would you do if you have all the money in the world? Apply it on my debts as far as it would go.

Sept. 26. At loan committee meeting, things are growing more bleak. People cannot pay and are using their brains to avoid payment.

Oct. 21. Suppose Hollandale Bank will close unless Marketing association saves it.

Dec. 21. Purchased . . . Chrysler . . . 1928 4 Dr. sedan. . . . Owner Samuel Bybee, 526 College St., Albert Lea, Minn. Made purchase at lien foreclosure sale.

Riot during the 1934 truckers' strike, Minneapolis. *MNHS*

1933

Jan. 5. The depression is not lifting. Coolidge dies of Heart trouble this forenoon.

[Meighen at times practiced foreign languages by writing his diary entries in them. He lapsed into German in 1933. We rejoin him when he went back to English.]

1935

July 24. Law business is unusually quiet. No drainage improvements, no marked movement in lands, mort. foreclosures lessening, no active movement in liquidating banks.

The farmers have prospect of good crops at good prices and sale of farm machinery has been active.

But banking business is astoundingly slow and the law business is rather quiet along every line.

No night work and plenty of time for reflection.

Aug. 29. Told Dr. Pace today that Hamline could have $5,000 when needed from me for a capital investment, in cash.

Dec. 8. Anne [his granddaughter] seems interested in radio—the new five band General Electric.

Dec. 10. During evening hours have a pre birthday dinner for Dick. A remarkably good dinner—domestic duck. Sweet potatoes with marshmallows above.

Joan is in quarantine in her room [scarlet fever] and wistfully looked from her bed thru the doorway at the untieing of the presents.

1936

Jan. 9. Many less families than 2 years ago on government furnished work.

Feb. 12. Do my state and federal income tax and mail reports. Using my heavy loss on Banco (if allowed) brings me to zero.

Did not mention my allowable $2,500 (Fed) and $2,000 (state) deductions—the legal reward for being married.

Meighan's diary. *MNHS*

May 12. Claus [Anderson, a farm tenant] begs grace on monthly payments.

May 17. See "Mr. Deeds Goes to Town" with Gary Cooper, as a tuba player from a small town, given twenty millions and then beset by scheming persons who wanted his money.

June 23. [Democratic] Convention opens [in Philadelphia], The amplifier facilities are not good. Our seats are in a space where noise, but not words, can be sensed. The result is that [it] is much more difficult to keep delegates quiet than in Chicago. Another difficulty is the presence of so much harmony. There are no thrilling questions for determination. [FDR renominated.]

Aug. 21. What a flood of people want jobs.

Oct. 6. At five o'clock learn that Roosevelt is coming to St. Paul Friday.

Oct. 9. Roosevelt visit was a success. Excellent weather. He arrived on time and met all sorts—rumpers, regulars, Farmer labor, etc. Among them the widow of Governor Olson [he died on August 22].

Nov. 13. Have a fitting for new suit and obtain a new camel's hair overcoat.

Dec. 11. Fran Mayor told how Edward made wine, by having wife gather and prepare the grapes, the maid weight the sugar, and then Edward put in 6 gallons (instead of 6 quarts) of water, much to everyone's dismay.

Dec. 30. Carl Jacobson says he made $12,000 out of his Austin hotel last 12 mo. after liberal depreciation.

Dec. 31. Carl Jacobson buys the Harm apartments [in Albert Lea] for $31,000 of which 6,000 is paid down and balance is payable 250.00 a month at 5%. What a shock to the spirit of the builder! Think he spent far more in the 3 and 4th floors alone.

Dividends = $602.58

$5,983.16 misc. income—rents, interest, etc.

1937

Jan. 1. "The March of Time" is a current regular broadcast. Last night I listened for a half hour and it dramatized the outstanding events of the year. No. 1 was Mrs. Simpson and the king, which proves that human interests have not changed much since Cleopatra and Antony were the gossip around the Great Sea.

No. 2 events were more modern—namely Roosevelt and conventions.

The final 1936 message of the Pope, the drouth of 1936, Mussolini, Hitler, Chiang Kai Shek and Stalin received mention with one or two minutes given to the Rust mechanical picker.

Feb. 7. Around home in afternoon except for 2 hours at ski slide as a spectator. Camille in evening—Greta Garbo.

March 8. $5666.23 is earned income for partnership for 1936, a slump because of politics and Kiwanis; perhaps because of lessened litigation as people are more prosperous.

May 23. [New Lincoln Zephyr]

New car. Motor No. 3936287	$715
Radio	35
Heater	.17.50
1937 License	12.46
	779.96
Allowance 1934 Ford	349.25
	$430.71

June 5. Hair cut. New bifocals from Benson Optical Co. for $20.00. How do ordinary workmen obtain glasses for families? I furnished the frames and I must pay Folken for the prescription.

June 10. Katherine and I dine at Country Club. About 60 there. Mrs. Hayek at my left chats of county welfare and about son John having his first girl. Ed delights to tell of his tonsil removal operation—not so happy when first effect of local anesthetic wears off. Mrs. Geo. Wolf speaks of new "Book of the Month" book on U.S. Constitution. Howard Eastwood has an attractive appearing girl friend, whom everyone else save Katherine and I seemed to know.

June 12. Lota E. Tasker—56 years—butcher with Wilson & Co. since 1923, at $1.00 an hour, 32 hours guaranteed and William W. Tasker, 508 St. Thomas Ave.—20 yrs.—single—testing and repairing scales at Wilson & Co., 2 years—$24.00 per week ($23.56) net want to purchase a house foreclosed today, paying $350. down and balance thru 10 years.

Disgruntled farmers marching on the capitol, 1933. *MNHS*

Rooming house residents, St. Paul, 1939. *MNHS*

Wonder how those wages will sound 20 years from today? They seem rather good.

Nov. 4. We Rotarians all attend the Roland Wolgamot funeral . . . I wonder how many people have any definite conception of the God they worship? How many have clear notions about an after life? Of course, they can repeat the words of catachism, but that is about all. Are there punishments and rewards, or are such things mere efforts to stimulate or repress humans?

Nov. 5. He [Wolgamot] had $25,000 debt when Hollendale [bank] crash came. Now including insurance he leaves $51,000 and no debts.

Nov. 6. Jobs! So many want them. Glad that I am not working for some employer. Many are out of work because of the employer's mistakes or wastefulness.

Dec. 31. Too much politics this year, too many conversations, too much wasted time. But health has been splendid. Losses, very small. Income, all I deserve. To me a happy, contented year.

1938

April 2. [On trip south, at Hotel Kendal in Kendalville, Indiana] Food is excellent for a moderate price—75¢ for dinner & 25¢ for breakfast.

April 17. [Jokes.] "James," says F.D.R., "run out and buy a paper and see what Mother is doing today."

Re deflation and inflation: They are removing "In God we trust" and substituting, "I hope that my Redeemer liveth."

May 23. Miss Foley [office worker] asks whether marriage will cancel her job. I say "No." . . . Why this outcry against married women working outside their homes? Strikes me it leads to . . . living together without any ceremony of marriage.

June 3. The M.E. Church, as usual, is closing its year in difficulties. Rev. Main is troubled. At meeting, I suggest publishing the

budget for next year, also pledges above 25¢ per week.

Aug. 18. Katherine and I "Ford" it from A. Lea to parking lot behind St. Paul hotel in 2 hours, 22 minutes.

Sept. 20. Lunch on pancakes, brown sugar, and hash at home. Bad combination for my 175 pounds.

Sept. 23. Dick plans new home. Like modern persons generally, he pays little attention to the financed debt, and worries only over cash to be paid right now.

Sept. 25. [His 61st birthday] Life begins at 60. Most of one's enemies are dead and those remaining are growing tame. One is past the dangerous 40s . . .

At 60 life insurance salesmen commence to let you alone, let you live in comfort.

By 60 you have acquired a measure of balance. I read yesterday that 129,000,000 Americans would not be killed or wounded by automobiles in 1938. That observation probably came from a person over 60. . . . At 60 you appreciate good food, for you have known some bad food. You appreciate sunshine for you have known darkness.

Sept. 26. New ties, new socks, new woolen shirt, new phonographic attachment for radio use—all as a result of a birthday yesterday.

Dec. 17. At 9:10 A.M. we wheel out of Albert Lea on our road to Mexico via Mason City.

1939

June 21. Ordered space, twin beds, at Hotel St. Paul, self and wife $5.50 per day. . . . During evening we see "Ecstasy" at World Theatre, a Czecho-Slovakian play with Austrian actress. Unusual. We ask ourselves "What is it all about?"

Aug. 22. In evening went out to Hollandale. Warehouses have developed greatly. The farmers are becoming more stable, fewer firebrands.

Sept. 4. Self interest says "Keep out of

war at any cost." Another thot is "uphold the right" and most Americans think Poland is in the right.

Oct. 2. B. M. L. is against "our boys fighting overseas." I suggest I am against "our boys fighting," but if war comes, I would rather have the fighting overseas.

1940

Jan. 1. What will 1940 bring, peace or war? Finland is still battling stoutly, but for how long? Where will China be a year from now?

Jan. 2. Home all day. No fever, but a very husky throat, worst I have ever had.

How radio has changed staying at home! You are in touch with the world while nursing a cold in bed. [Radio station] KATE tells you what the merchants are pushing, what articles have been lost, what is at the movie houses, the hog prices, the news from the war and this country.

Other stations lecture and entertain.

Even the evangelists convert you by radio.

Jan. 3. Listen to F. D. R. speak to Congress on state of the nation. What a thrilling, clear radio voice.

Jan. 6. Dick and Delores take these Philadelphia guests to Austin for the train.

Strange as it may seem, Albert Lea no longer has a sleeper for Chicago.

Feb. 28. 15¢ lunch at M.E. Church in evening is so excellent that Katherine and I pay quarter each.

Feb. 29. Mrs. Shipstead told story of darky insisting Roosevelt is superior to Jesus. The latter said, "Come freely and take." The former "Stay right where you is and I'll push it up to you."

March 5. My guess is that our low earnings were quite common among lawyers.

May 1. The bank meeting shows our time deposits are going down in total amt, but not in number of depositors. Our savings accts are decreasing in total, but about the same in number of depositors.

July 15. Chicago Democratic Convention. I am not at the convention; thanks to not being a follower of Moonan [Ray Moonan, Minneapolis lawyer and active Democrat]. The radio is almost better than the convention from many angles—not so hot—seats are softer—meals more regular.

Oct. 30. Radio speeches are more and more the center of campaign activity. Motion pictures—talkies—take rather long to prepare, but have considerable use.

Wilkie has had a remarkably well advertised campaign. He has promised much—far outpromises Roosevelt and along the same lines.

Nov. 19. Not working much these days, but manage to put in the time. There is surprising little to do. To keep the stenographers busy we are giving them much work not very essential. Looks like a very poor year in our business. The excitement of a war does not help the law business.

Dec. 24. Rather hectic—cards and last minute gifts being mailed and received. . . . Watch Dick dress the Xmas tree and place the gifts.

In the background for all adults is war. We listen to the news broadcasts and speak of Albania and Libyia as of Iowa and Missouri. We speculate on when Hitler will commence his invasion of England.

The Leuthold home on Shoreland Heights shows a great Santa coming down the chimney. It is floodlighted. How electricity has added to Xmas!

Dec. 31. Closing a year again. Eventful in world affairs, not unusual in my personal life. Not a good year financially, only moderate, but kept excellent health and have enjoyed life, the election campaign and my hobbies.

1941

Jan. 1. New Years Resolution: Only one and this is less coffee. Shall cut down to three cups a day and see if any improvement results.

Feb. 28. Watch C. D. Darrigrand do steaks in his fireplace. They turn out splendidly. Katherine succeeds in eating hers, even with store teeth, and I finish two servings with enthusiasm.

March 14. This is a buckwheat cake winter for me. We are having excellent ones for breakfast in the new kitchen. Quite a change in meal formality since the maid left.

April 1. We are not yet at war, although Germany and England have had a state of war since September 1, 1939. But so many [here] are in training. The armory has become a much used place. Tribune has many notices from boys in camp.

Horatio Kellar's son goes on a battleship building in Philadelphia as ensign. Buzz is in Marines at Philadelphia. Dy. Sybilrud is away from divorce troubles and in Marines in California. Many Freeborn County men—200 perhaps—at Camp Claiborne near Alexandria, Louisiana.

April 22. Visited Ben Musser plant at Wells. It would make a good story for Life. 33 trucks take eggs from, and take poultry products to, farmer customers. Hatch chicks, feed them a week or 10 days in a remarkable machine fashion. If temperature changes ¼ degree in incubator, light comes on and bell rings.

May 24. Having few meals at home. No maid in residence bothers folks who desire to telephone.

June 17. [Joke] A local defense volunteer in a lonely spot cried "Halt" to a man in a car, who promptly halted.

"Halt!" said the L.D.V. again.

"I have halted," said the motorist. "What do you want me to do next?"

"I don't know," said the L.D.V. "My orders are to say 'Halt!' three times and then shoot."

July 11. Lunch with Paul Christopherson, who insists that for some years after war U.S. must support (thru loans or purchase of areas at high prices, or in some other way) Great Britain. Suggests that we may have a common currency. Canada may become part of U.S.

July 14. Attempt to pull in some garden hose at Mrs. Meighen's command, and break my glasses. Shall now confine myself to law, politics, Methodism, and golf.

Nov. 7. In evening M.E. church holds a Trustees Meeting. Pastor is kept paid up this year and debts are decreasing.

Nov. 20. In looking at income from law practice, it is down—very much down—this year, to date the figures are $4,000. On the other hand interest on investments has been promptly paid. For some reason court trials to jury are decreasing in number. In this country, the probate business has become the most profitable.

Nov. 21. Pug Lund, former famous Minnesota football player, told some amusing stories of his sudden decline from fame. Spoke highly of coach Bierman and commented on complexness of his training.

Dec. 7. Japan attacks Pearl Harbor. We

Saturday night in a saloon, 1937. *Library of Congress*

anticipate declaration of a state of war by U.S. tomorrow morning.

News hazy about exact damage done, but probably heavy as attack came without warning.

Katherine is glued to Radio until retiring time. We learned of the attack about 5:00 p.m. as we came out of Broadway Theatre.

Dec. 11. More declarations of war. Everyone jittery in the extreme.

Dec. 31. We close another period. I open my diary of 1902. So many of the actors of my life then are dead. Christmas that year I took a new Edison 2 minute cylinder record

phonograph to Red Oaks as a present. Father, mother, Tom—all passed on. . . . How dead the litigation seems now that thrilled me in 1902! How changed the work of the law office. No worry then about federal taxes. . . . No war, no radio, few automobiles. But the same kind of people, some cards, food, dancing, reading.

[Meighen kept up his diaries as long as he lived. He died in Albert Lea in 1957, at age seventy-nine. His wife died in 1968 at the age of ninety-five.]

John Felix Dryden Meighen and Family papers, MNHS

[The firm of Salkin & Linoff, Minneapolis, operators of fourteen stores in Minnesota and the Dakotas, bought a shipment of gloves in 1933 that turned out to bear the label of a German manufacturer. The owners didn't want to support merchandise produced under Hitler's rule. Part of the correspondence on the matter was this letter to the supplier:]

H. H. Schmidt Glove Co.
432 Fourth Ave.
New York City
Gentlemen:
We have your letter of September 2nd in which you state that you see no good reason why we should refuse acceptance of merchandise simply because it was made in Germany.

There is no need of going into a lengthy explanation and giving you reasons why we cannot use gloves, or any products for that matter, made in Germany.

It is very true that we ordered the gloves in good faith, not knowing that this merchandise was manufactured in a country of Hitlerism.

We have no grievance against your firm and we do not expect you to lose anything by this transaction. Therefore we are returning the gloves to you prepaid, thereby taking care of the transportation charges both ways.

As soon as a spark of justice will awaken the hearts of the German leaders, and they will cease their inhuman treatment of a people simply because they are Jews, then we shall resume buying German-made products.

At present our conscience does not allow us to display Nazi-made goods on our counters.

Please accept the shipment and credit our account.

We sincerely thank you for this favor.
Yours very truly,
Salkin & Linoff Co.

American Jewish World, a Twin Cities publication, October 13, 1933

SARAH BERMAN

From a January 30, 1936, letter by Sarah Berman, a Jewish woman living in Minneapolis:

At the present time, we are slaves of Jack Frost. The weather man has decided to leave me no regrets at leaving Minneapolis [she was about to go to California]. So he is feeding me a good taste of what it means to be imprisoned in a cold house with the outside so cold that one has qualms about running over to Jennie's house to thaw out. I am affectionate by nature, but I rebel at hugging radiators all day, for even while we get thoroughly baked at bottom we remain raw on top. No, for hugging purposes I have definitely decided, radiators leave much to be desired. Then again, who has time to be romantic? I have to sit at the phone all morning expatiating on the excellencies of the American Jewish World [which she was selling by telephone], and the desirability of its presence in every Jewish home, regardless of said home's lack of interest, of English, of money or brains, or in spite of brains. It is too bad that I have such an open receptive mind myself, that the counter arguments have now almost convinced me of the worthlessness of the paper, and how much more necessary are the hundred and one things that people need rather than a Jewish newspaper, and that most people "have too much paper already." However, sordid self interest keeps me chained to the cold telephone with the chill draughts from the imperfectly closed doors of the sun room freezing my feet and chilling my ardor. In spite of it, all I am managing to earn is enough to pay my way for the time being. I still hope for something better to "turn up."

Private papers of Dr. Reuben Berman of Minneapolis, Sarah's son

NEWSPAPER CLIPPINGS

THE MINNESOTA BIRTH CONTROL LEAGUE STANDS FOR THESE THINGS

Not fewer children, but more better born children.

The spacing of children to protect the health of mother and child.

Sterilization of those mentally unfit to bear children.

The giving of contraceptive advice in its own clinic by a physician of highest standards to every married woman whose health requires it, but who cannot afford the advice of a private physician.

An end to the menace to health and life in abortions, especially those self inflicted, by mothers made desperate at the prospect of the birth of additional children into homes too needy to care for the children already there.

The right of a man and wife to normal, happy marital relations, and to as many children as can be safely carried, safely born and adequately reared.

The Minnesota Birth Control League is supported entirely by private subscriptions.

Jean M. Wilcox papers, MNHS

ECONOMY IN SHOE REPAIRING

Money spent for shoe repairing is a better investment now than ever before. Repair prices have been sharply reduced. Several grades of leather are available at different prices. The best leather however is the cheapest for it will wear longer. Cheap shoes, resoled with good leather, will have their wear tripled. Save by having your shoes repaired with the best materials.

H. Henrichs

Worthington Globe, January 5, 1933

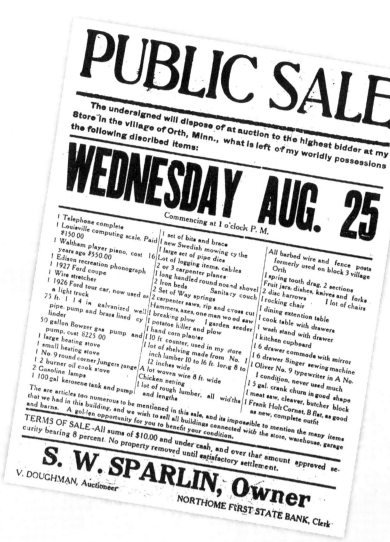

CARE OF THE POOR

What is to be done with the poor of the county is one of the major problems confronting the people at the present time. During January in the Worthington district alone the cost was nearly $2,000. There is little hope that despite economies it can be reduced materially. From a minor expenditure two years ago, present conditions have seen it increase to a point where last year the county spent $32,000 and it seems probable that it will spend even more this year unless some radical change can be effected.

The commissioners are adopting every economy measure which appears sound and will eliminate those who are not actually in need. But despite this the demand is increasing to offset the economies.

Worthington Globe, February 16, 1933

The family of Captain Richard Watson while he was on home leave in Minneapolis after accompanying a planeload of wounded men to the States, 1945. *Richard Watson*

WORLD WAR II

Young men joined the National Guard for monetary as well as patriotic reasons and ended up seeing the world. The war made heavy demands for iron ore; Minnesota mines surpassed all previous production levels. Duluth was a center for shipbuilding. Farmers produced record crops during the war. More than 300,000 Minnesotans served in the war. About 6,000 died. Postwar legislation for veterans made college educations and home ownership more widely available. →

RICHARD WATSON

*"Should I ever become dissatisfied when I am back in America,
I will merely turn off the fire and wait til the house gets, say,
46, and try to get warm by a cigarette lighter."*

Dr. Richard E. Watson of Minneapolis was a twenty-nine-year-old air force captain when he was ordered to England late in 1943. He was a flight surgeon assigned to the 9th Air Force's Pathfinder Group, which dropped parachute infantry into enemy-occupied France in advance of the main invasion forces in June 1944. Watson was stationed with Pathfinder at various locations in England before the invasion and on the continent afterward.

These are excerpts from almost daily letters he wrote to his wife, LaVonne. When the letters began, she was expecting their first child and was living in Minneapolis with his parents.

JANUARY 18, 1944
England
My darling wife:
This is another epochal day. I have told you about how our mail comes in bunches—nothing for days and days and then the deluge. Well, today the deluge deluged again. I will tell you about the mail I received first, then I'll go on to other things. I received another battered insurance advertisement sent to the wrong Lt. R. E. Watson at Lemoore, Calif. On the envelope are the addresses of all my army stations since I set out that warm July evening in 1942. Now it finds me in England. It is interesting to see my travels on that piece of paper, thinking how it has made most of the travels I have, muse over your coming to Fresno, of our happy Fort Stockton days, that god-awful stretch of heat and study in San Antonio, and all the rest. I am back at my travels again. I have long since been to Scotland and tomorrow I am going to Ireland, and in a week or so I am going to London as I have had all of this place [he could not specify where he was stationed, for security reasons] as I can stand for awhile. In due time I shall tell you as much as I can of these things . . .

Richard Watson. *Richard Watson*

London after a bombing.

From you, baby, I got 13 letters. . . . Mail is of tremendous importance to us. My day— my week—is now all right. . . . All the time you spent six weeks ago, faithfully posting a daily letter into the void, was not wasted. It has made this cold and dark English day not cold and dark any more . . .

Love, Dick

8:30 p.m.
19 JANUARY 1944
England
Dear Darling:
. . . Right now I am in my usual room, the blackout is at its blackest. Now, I have mentioned the blackout before and said merely that it was very, very black. Well, dear, you cannot know how black it is unless you have been in it. First of all, all windows, cracks, doors, are completely covered so that even the tiniest pinpoint of light is shut out. Secondly, assume that there is no moon. Now, at home, this usually leaves some starlight which here makes quite a difference. So thirdly, imagine a heavy fog which of itself obscures vision so that it, if it were daylight, would cause one to almost bump into other pedestrians. Since it gets dark at 5:30 p.m., there is no light reflected back to the earth from cloud banks. And, still, vehicles are so far and few between that they don't count. When you do see one, it has "blackout lights"—minuscule bulbs

"Hollywood Victory Caravan" in St. Paul to support the war effort, 1942. Celebrities are, left to right, Merle Oberon, Rise Stevens, Charles Boyer, Claudette Colbert, Jimmy Cagney, Frances Langford, Cary Grant, Olivia de Havilland, Marie McDonald, Joan Blondell, Joan Bennett, Eleanor Powell, Katherine Booth, and Alma Carroll. *MNHS*

"GOOD WORK, SISTER
WE NEVER FIGURED YOU COULD DO A MAN-SIZE JOB!"

AMERICA'S WOMEN HAVE MET THE TEST!

obscured with black paint; they can be seen only a short distance.

Now, if you can imagine such Stygian darkness, let us go out in it. At first, after closing the door, you see nothing—absolutely nothing; just like being blind-folded. You wait for your eyes to become dark adapted—you just keep on waiting because nothing happens. If you have your "torch" [flashlight] you can get along if you know the location of every path, road, building, fence, and so on. For 3 weeks our own American flashlights did not arrive and since none (of course) are purchasable here we did without . . .

Over the loud speaker (all buildings over the entire field are wired for public address) about 4:30 p.m. every day comes a voice announcing the correct time, then the duration of the blackout hours which are daily a few minutes earlier in the forenoon, and a few minutes later in the afternoon. At the proper times in the p.m., the heavy blackout curtains are drawn tightly. I was on the street of a nearby town of about 50,000 at blackout time. Within 10 minutes every source of light disappeared, every curtain was pulled, people left the streets and the few cars vanished. It seemed to me as though a fairly busy city suddenly turned into a ghost city where one heard things but saw very little. The town died in the few minutes I stood there and watched . . .

The English people . . . have a grimy, dirty look about them, and their skins, which never get any ultraviolet, are an ungodly soot-stained pallid white. . . . They are a hard-bitten lot and look as stubborn even from a distance as they really are. They even walk in a sort of dogged, plodding, determined way . . .

Performing war work in a machine shop, February 1943. *MNHS*

AM I PROUD!..

Dick Williams

I'm fighting famine . . .
by canning food at home

U. S. DEPARTMENT OF AGRICULTURE

I can give you an example though you've read of similar things many times. It seems so typical. I was the third person, and the only doctor, at the scene of a crash a few weeks ago. A censor would be interested to know that it was a non-combat, non-tactical flight and ship. I won't say more except that its military significance was nil. I was going down the road and I heard a plane. I looked up and though I'm no flier I had enough sense to realize that something was wrong. I watched the plane lose its altitude in an awful hurry and spread itself over about 100 yards of muddy ground. So I had the jeep driver go across the open field to the plane or what was left of it. The first two there had pulled the British pilot out on the ground. He was lying face down,

bloody, clothing torn, with his right leg from mid-shin down twisted in that gruesome, grotesque fashion that always means a smashing, shattering fracture. I assumed a corpse, since the body was motionless and broken. I looked at the face and through the blood I saw an open and viable eye, apparently scrutinizing sprigs of grass. So I said, "How do you feel?" The RAF raised its head—a plain, blondish English face, early twenties and so on. He studied me just the right-sized moment, then said, with Ronald Coleman coaching, "A bit dizzy."

So I said "Where do you hurt?" And the RAF said "A bit in the right foot—broken, you know." I looked him over, waiting for the ambulance. It came shortly, summoned from the same place the British had theirs. All American, four-speeds forwards, four-wheeled drive, it rumbled right through the mud to the spot. In it was another doctor from our squadron with bandages, etc. We splinted the leg where our patient lay; he volunteered only one offering: "Deuced shame—going on leave tomorrow—rawther, was going on leave tomorrow." We met a British antique serving as an ambulance just as we got back to the road. A Britisher leaned out and said, "We came as fawst as we could, you know, but you Ameddicans always seem to get there first."

We took the pilot back to the hospital, gave him the best care we know how probably because he had us so impressed with his matter-of-fact manner. . . . My conversation with him, as above, is verbatim—it occurred at the most 90 seconds after he was hurt . . .

All around here at road intersections, in the approaches to the littlest villages, at bridges, are the remnants of the sand-bags and earthwork barricades which were put up after the fall of France. They are pitiful in a way but mighty gallant.

So you see I wind up like all the rest I've heard talk. I don't like the English, I don't like their country and I don't think I ever will, but they've got guts for which we give them our greatest respect . . .

I am missing you very much; I was looking at your picture this afternoon, got on the broody side. I hope you enjoy letters like this—I am talking to you, darling, my favorite and ever-sympathetic audience. When in the hell is that little one going to arrive?

All my love, dearest,
Dick

SUNDAY, JANUARY 23, 1944
2:00 p.m. England
Dear darling wife:
. . . One of the biggest sources of quarrelling in a petty way or even to the point of fisticuffs between American and British soldiers is over the pay checks. As you no doubt know all our men receive fabulous amounts of money as compared to the British. Our sergeant's pay is greater than that of many British officers. Our lowest paid men, the privates, receive $60 per month plus all the food, clothing and housing that they need. That amount of money is greater than the average English war worker makes for long hard hours and he must also buy out of that money his food, his clothing, and pay his rent. Some of them don't have that much to start with after they have paid the heavy taxes. A great many of the young American airmen have $300 a month to spend (and they spend it all right!). We were warned before we arrived here that nothing so infuriates the British as the sight of our stuffed wallets. I have heard Americans price articles and be answered that the cost is "two and six," for instance, meaning 2 shillings and six-pence or about 50¢. The Americans, very blandly and innocently, ask if the shopkeeper means "two shillings and six pence" or "two pounds and 6 shillings" which is roughly

$9.20—it making little or no difference to them. Such things leave the British flabbergasted. But Americans, used to being stuck, go ahead and pay and pay—such as $14 to get inside a club in London (cover charge) and $15/quart for whisky—or they price eggs from a farmer willing to sell his eggs for "a shilling" (20¢). Says the American corporal, "Is that for one egg or for a dozen eggs?" Since the Englishman meant it for the whole dozen he is completely whipped by an American enlisted man who is calmly prepared to pay that price for a single lone egg . . .

Speculation as to when I'll be home is impossible and I think that it should be avoided to avoid disappointment and making my "foreign service tour" seem more prolonged than it will be anyway. There are

National Archives

those who can imagine Germany folding up in one great crash; there are those who imagine the war lasting over here for 2 more years. I don't forecast on things like that—but after the armistice it still might be months, for the combat troops will no doubt (at least they should be) be pulled out first and given a rest before a mighty veteran American Army, Navy and Air Force turn their incomprehensible power, with a viciousness not seen in this theater, against those damnable Japs. I can say that everything, absolutely everything, is very encouraging over here though . . .

My constant love,
Dick

JANUARY 28, 1944
Friday - 3:00 p.m.
Same place
Dear Darling:
. . . Yesterday one of the few meek surgical technicians that we have calmly announced that he was the father of an eight-pound baby boy born about 2 weeks ago. None of us knew

that his wife was expecting a baby and most of us didn't even know that he had a wife. I believe that that is about six fathers we have now in our squadron who have never seen their babies. The T/3 [technician] said that he didn't think it was important enough to tell everybody about the anticipated event. Not so with me. Not so with me. Time is now very, very short; when you read this it should be on the day, a few days before or a few days after at the most. I will wait as patiently as I am able.

The public address system just announced that we will play war for awhile. We are going to have a practice air raid shortly. I have my fur-lined flying jacket, steel helmet and gas mask ready on the bed. In a few minutes we will go out and sit in the ugly bomb shelter—

(Intermission here—sat in bomb shelter for 15 minutes just now.)

The bomb shelter is made of arched slabs of concrete in the usual hemi-cylinder shape—heavy, tunnelled brick-work for entrance and dirt heaped up over the entire thing. It provides 100% protection for anything close—0% for a direct hit, of course . . .

Baby, you ask what I would like to have from home. Frankly, I can think of so many things that I don't know where to start. The most important thing is razor blades. I get two cheap ones per week but they aren't much good and I am tired of scratching my face until it's sore every day. So I wish that you would paste a red or blue Gillette razor blade in every letter you send until you have sent about 30.

Next, I wish you would send me a pound or two of salted pecans, cashews, almonds, etc. Remember that they must be sturdily packed; a tin or can is preferable. I also would like a large and fine pocket knife with a loop on it, a cap opener and a screw driver, etc. and would Dad sharpen it good before you send it?

Waiting, waiting, waiting!
Love, Dick

[The Watson baby arrived on February 9 and was named Catherine.]

24 FEBRUARY 1944
10:00 a.m.
England
Dear Darlings:

. . . Many from our squadron have been on TD or DS [temporary duty or detached service] to the bomber bases of the 8th AAF. They are back with lots of first-hand stories of aerial warfare. "The easy way to win the war" (i.e., with bombing) infuriates me. I am ready to stand in bare-headed, silent awe for the combat airmen . . .

***

I dreamed last night I was eating white bread and butter.

***

How long will it be before the baby looks at you and smiles—I mean smiles with recognition? Do you think she will be afraid of me?

***

A nurse spent some time at a bomber base, got to know three young boys in the place very well. One week after she left she went back to visit them. All three are gone forever. She is stunned.

***

Do they still vote for the Hit Parade? I have one vote for a song I used to hear occasionally, one which once puzzled me. It is the no longer meaningless "Mad Dogs and Englishmen go out in the Mid-day Sun."

***

Our baby is the biggest of any yet born "in" our squadron. One of the other fathers is an officer—all the rest of the new fathers are enlisted. Two of the recent fathers had a serious argument day before yesterday on who had the better baby. Neither father has even seen a picture of his baby yet.

***

Excerpt from the Stars and Stripes: "Life must be getting 'rough' on the home front. We have a report from Detroit that residents of that city's ultra-ultra swanky section find things so tough that they are now sharing the few chauffeurs that remain. Ain't dat just too bad."

***

My stove, the "Cheltham Queen," [the brand name] is smoking up her last peanut-sized piece of coal. This means bed-time for me. Having no alarm clock I go to bed when it gets cold, get up as soon as the orderly builds a fire.

***

A blanket in English dampness here weighs one pound more in an unheated room than it does in a heated room.

***

The "Cheltham Queen" will expire in five minutes. . . . In five more minutes this room will be 89 degrees below zero.

***

Do you see the trend? First, the war, England, the fliers, the baby, me. Then, the war, England, the baby, the weather. Next, the baby, the weather, the baby, the weather. I must go to bed at once while it is still warm enough to be conscious of something else besides the moronic iron-working craftsman who fashioned the equally moronic "Cheltham Queen."

Lovingly,
Dick

2 MARCH 1944
2:15 p.m.
England
Dearest Babies:

. . . I have just finished censoring the mail. Next to sanitation work it is the stinkingest job. I have to write my name on each letter, stamp it, and seal it. We have an intelligent bunch of men compared to most G.I.s and they do quite a bit of writing. It takes quite a bit of time—just opening, closing, sealing, stamping, etc., 75 to 100 letters every day much less reading them. Long ago I learned which men I must watch—I use the scan method on the others—just look down the page for proper nouns, dates, figures, and for words like "enemy," "airplane," "bombs," etc. The letters are not very interesting. A devout Catholic boy, an Italian from Brooklyn, writes home in definite ecstasy about finding a priest. . . . The best surgical tech we have writes a glowing letter to "Darling Bonny" in California—his fourth this week. He also writes a very plain letter to his wife—the first this week. A Mexican boy writes home to Colorado and begs his father to send him a particular kind of 44-reed harmonica. He says that he feels "so much like playing a mouth harp" he will die if he doesn't get to do it soon. A 19 yr. old clerk writes home to his 17 yr. old girlfriend all sorts of stuff wherein he makes great dramatization of how he risked his life here and how luck was with him there, how hard he works, and what a hero he is. Actually, he got busted 3 weeks ago (from corporal back to private) for sheer laziness. None of the episodes he describes ever happened. His greatest risk is not moving fast enough when crossing streets. A Bible-student sort of a guy with horn rimmed glasses, a supply sergeant, writes a ghastly soliloquy on world fellowship, and "I shall never forget the kindness with which you opened your home and your hearts that night" . . . funny to read the end of the letter—he plans a horrible binge with whiskey and women, et al. A driver persists in writing "my darling angle" for angel. He is so nearly illiterate that I marvel that he tackles a letter to his wife and two girlfriends every other night. His letters are painfully scrawled out and one page must take him an hour or two. A cook asks to be sent some "writting papir." A kid from [New] Jersey (the one they call "Jersey" because he once remarked, hearing a twittering noise, "Must be boids on account they choip") wants to know where "Dominic, Tony and Legs" are now. One writes as though he has inside information on the date and hour of the invasion and I cut that out because the people at home would make a fine rumor out of it. Etc., etc. . . .

Yesterday I saw a fresh lemon. I never gave a damn about lemons anyway—but it is nice to see one so that I can think that I didn't eat it because I didn't want it rather than because I didn't have it . . .

Love, Dick

England
MARCH 13, 1944
Darling babies:

. . . Someplace, Lord knows where, trucks rumble. Someplace else, and we all know where and why, is the perpetual throb and roar, that heavy, penetrating, comforting (I always add this) roar of bombers' engines. As long as that hum fades out to the east we are unworried.

***

And now, how is home? I suppose the reason that I feel so good tonight is because the food itself, the sense of luxury, reminds me of home. [He and three other doctors had just had an exceptionally fine meal.] I am thinking about little Cathy a lot. I am thinking about you a lot. I am thinking about a lot a lot—and it is all good. I am not especially bothered about the British or Lend-lease or the war. There is just the faintest suggestion that it perhaps might not be too good a thing if I were always warm and well-fed and comfortable in those physical ways being away from you. For one thing they remind me of home right off the bat and I start dreaming about being home, what I'd do, how Cathy is, and I start coasting down the road to a lonesomeness that is harder to cope with. When there is no coal, and my hands and feet are numb, when it is so cold that I can't sleep, I am too damn mad and irritated to be depressed. When the food is canned and watery and cold I don't get too homesick because I'm too annoyed with . . . the whole stinking mess. But when I haven't these relentless thorns to keep me hood-winked about what I really want and where I really want to be and what I want to do, I am helplessly defenseless. When I am comfortable, home and all it means comes over me flood-like—playing with Cathy, teasing and loving you, reading and the radio, fireplaces, lights and a car, and always you and Cathy, you and Cathy.

Love,

Dick

PS. . . . Last week, when it was so very cold, and when there was no coal, our men got so desperate in their barracks that they became determined to have a fire somehow (incidentally, burning the furniture is not a joke—we have to watch them). They got shovels and axes, went out to the place where the coal is dumped (even the dust had been swept up by then) and chopped up buckets of ice. Then they took the buckets to the messhall and put them by the ranges until the ice melted, poured off the water, let the coal in the bottom dry, and came back and built a fire. They had enough for a couple of hours.

MARCH 23, 1944

England

. . . Sometimes we argue, we fathers here. One bunch says it's worse to have to leave a year-old baby than to have never seen it at all. We remote control men claim that it's far worse never to have seen our children at all. We have a sergeant who has one child of two years and a baby of two months which, of course, he's never seen. He says it's worse to be away never having seen the baby at all. He says the second one was bad enough, and that he doesn't know what he would do if the one he hasn't seen were his first. So that broke up that argument . . .

Much love, Dick

MARCH 31, 1944

England

Dear babies:

. . . I don't suppose that I could ever describe how much I hate this climate. I've been cold in Minnesota just like everyone who lives there has been. But it's different—there you get cold going to school or on the way home or downtown shopping. At home you get cold but shortly you can go someplace where it is warm and stay there long enough to spend another hour in the cold. Or downtown, for instance, you can stop in someplace and get warm. When I was on some of my DS and travelling in an open jeep (through the inevitable gray weather), the corporals and I used to get so thoroughly through-and-through chilled that we couldn't stand it. We'd stop some place, always in hopes of being able to find a fire, a sandwich and a hot drink. . . . It's quite a disappointment to open the door of a decent looking place (say, a tea-house) and see the people sitting in there with their hats, coats and gloves on. . . . It's the cold like you get about the fourth quarter of a football game, when you guessed the weather wrong and underdressed, except that you keep sitting there and the game is never over . . .

You and I have both seen pictures of soldiers minus arms, legs, or blind. We have read of pilots losing both legs—even seen movies which are never as rough as the real thing. Did you ever feel it really? I never could—really. In London I saw a young fellow of about 25 wheeled from the train to a big black car waiting at the curbing. People who were obviously his family were standing there. The young man, still in uniform, was smoking a pipe. And when it flashed across my mind that he had no legs, both off at the hip, God what a smack that has. Lots different, it is, from reading it. Have you ever heard of London being bombed? I have—saw the pictures too. Damned tingling feeling to stand in it though.

All around me are the men and machinery

of great scale warfare. I live amid the most staggering sights you have ever heard of. I am in the company of men who have been and are going to fight this war. This isn't playing—like training camps at home. This is the finished product. I can't tell you about what I see—I'm not permitted to . . .

As to the things at home: Again I say that it all seems ideal. . . . This place is disrupted and changed—all because of the war. This is the war—which you talk about, read about, hear about every single day. The war isn't a long way away for me like it is for you. The war is here, I live in it. My physical world, then, is all war. Everything we see connects with it, everything we do associates with it, everything we eat or don't have to eat is linked with it. You go to see a funny movie and that is not the war, except that it is the war you are getting away from and the war is the reason for showing it. Bob Hope is on the Service program and that is the war, too, because he is on the program to get the men away from war. And through all this there is one thing solid, one thing elevating, one thing hopeful and sustaining—and that one thing is my little baby Cathy, whom I have never seen, and all she represents to me, to her other closest relative and all her relatives, and her environment from her very crib and nursery right on up through town and country. . . . Tell Cathy I am in love with her mother.

Dick

MAY 3, 1944
Dear Babies:
. . . As you can probably tell from the tone of this letter, I am a little out of the box. My usual reaction of jaded morale, my response to things which are depressing, is to get somewhat ornery. It's sort of fighting back, I guess. Last week I had to go pronounce death on a British soldier. He had been run over by a truck. He was a dispatch rider and flew off his motorcycle. He was young and I didn't enjoy

looking through his letters at pictures, I suppose, of his wife and several children. 3 days ago, in my sphere, we had an officer decapitated in a runway accident. 2 days ago a truck ran over the head of a private (age 21) here and crushed his skull.

But today's news is shocking. For months, one of the nurses in my flight has been trying to get married to an officer she knew in the States. She had to produce papers, and so did he, and go through command channels for permission. Transfers and detached services for each of them upset their plans at the last minute a half a dozen times. . . . Day before yesterday I saw her and talked to her and she was very "low." She had planned to get married that afternoon at 6 p.m. and the bridegroom had been transferred and she didn't think that he could get an extra day. . . . The rest of the details you can get from the newspaper article which is accurate. Heightening the tragedy, if that is possible, is that she was married—about 6 hours. . . . [The enclosed clipping is headlined "American Army Honeymoon Party Crash in Jeep: Nurse Bride Killed, Husband Injured"]

I don't like to write morbidities home—but these are the things I live next to . . .

Much love, Dick.

MAY 11TH, 1944
England
Dear Babies, large and little:
Forgive me, darling, it [the salutation] is endearment—even if it is my weird brand . . .

This is written from my dispensary. I have had my evening coffee and brown bread toast and written you a V-mail letter. The stove is popping away—one of the technicians is boiling his underwear with GI soap in a bucket on the stove. Behind me are two tables covered with bed spreads. . . . The tables are covered with bottles of drugs, instruments of various sorts . . . rubber gloves, sterilizers, syringes, flashlights, pills, powders, liquids, tape, etc.,

etc. . . . plus my supreme accomplishment: 4 units of Army blood plasma. This is the finest set-up I've seen. It is a box, neatly packaged, ready to go. I could grab one of these plasma units, run out the door and transfuse a patient lying in the field in 5 minutes. The unit contains saline, plasma, tubing, tape, needles—everything set to go. It must cost horribly—but what the hell! I could save men with it if they needed it. I suppose each unit costs $25 or so because each has the full set of tubing and all in the hermetically sealed tins. But, as to "the hell with it," what if it was your husband who needed it—don't you suppose an extra $50 for the tax-payers would be meaningless? Or $5,000 for that matter? It is a source of satisfaction to me that our Army values human life so much. No other army does—not even the English . . .

Haven't heard from Dad for a long time. Is he all right?

Much love, Dick

16 MAY 1944
England
Dearest LaVonne and Cathy:
It is mid-afternoon and the weather is supposedly "freak" for this time of year. However, it seems just like the same old stuff to me. There is no sun—the sky immediately overhead is just about black, and it's dark gray until well toward the horizon. . . . How it can get down to just above freezing and stay there without ever going below I do not know . . .

Cannon [a roommate and fellow flight surgeon] and I haven't had a fire for about 5 days and going to bed, sleeping, getting up, and eating and toileting and working and what not always at 46 degrees is not my idea of coziness exactly. From my winter which seems to have extended well into a spring of discontent, I have had only one great urge. I want to sit by a fire, close by, and do nothing at all except let me eat all the horribly extravagant, delicious, fancy foods that I can. You notice I say that I

Crowd on Washington Avenue, Minneapolis, watching victory caravan, 1942. *MNHS*

want to sit by the fire. That deserves explanation. The idea that one could be comfortably warm anyplace in a house or a room except by the radiator or the heat register or the fireplace is one that vanished during my long and intimate association with the "Cheltham Queen." Yesterday I thought about how odd it would seem at home to be by the telephone and be warm or to be over by the radio and be warm there too. I somehow have a picture of myself being home and merely standing by the fireplace and looking at the rest of the room and at the rest of the house. I think of physical warmth as being in direct proportion to the linear measure from me to the symbol of heat.

When I get home I am going to heat the house up to a stifling 68 or 70, take off my shirt and undershirt, and go back and forth, sweating, from the living room and too many

cigarettes and lots of current magazines to the ice box which will contain many hundreds of things which haven't a goddam vitamin in them but taste good. . . .

Furthermore, should I ever become dissatisfied when I am back in America, I will merely turn off the fire and wait til the house gets, say, 46, and try to get warm by a cigarette lighter. After a few days of gray potatoes and stale coffee, dirty fingernails and smelly armpits (well, anyway it's nice to think that England is the cause of everything), I should be able to have a re-appreciation of where we live and how . . .

Much love, Dick

14 JUNE 1944
Dear Darlings:

. . . You know that I have often said that our amusements are simple here. There is a newly discovered past-time among us now. It has afforded the officers so much entertainment that it is odd to think it wasn't thought of before. It's simply owning a puppy. I suppose the idea behind it is easily understandable. These crazy young pilots go around in complete earnestness, carrying their "mascots" with them. They carry the dogs to the planes, to messhall, club, and quarters, sit up at night taking care of them, and fuss about the health of the pets like they were children. They even take them to town. There is "Darky"—a fine pup, glistening black with 4 white feet and a white face. The [name] "Darky" is because a kind of radio on large planes is called a "darky receiver." There is a 2 mos. old cocker whose owner gets drunk at night after "Flaps" has been fed. Another officer takes his tawny English bulldog to briefings with him. Another carries a 3 mos. old Yorkshire (weight less than one pound) under his jacket. Another has a young airdale which sleeps inside his sleeping bag with him. One fellow spends half his spare time searching the woods for a 6-weeks old mongrel. The lead up of all this is to the newest arrival on the field . . .

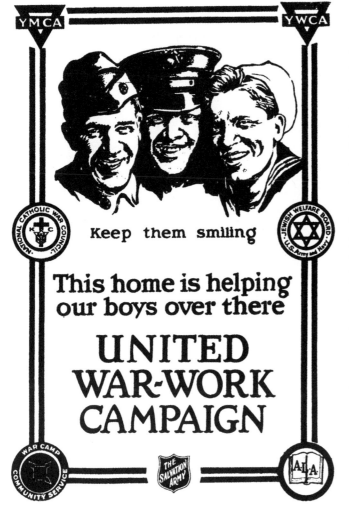

Watson en route by boxcar from his last post in northern France to Marseilles to board the ship for home, end of 1945. *Richard Watson*

He is six weeks old and has very large feet. His tail hasn't been cut but it looks like it should be. He is a cross between an English sheep dog and something unknown. . . . He is fat, curious and slightly aggressive in spite of a sad face. . . . His spots are brown instead of black; outside of that it's big T [Watson's dog, Toby, at home] all over again . . .

So this is my nostalgic story for today. It's not too nostalgic though—the pup is good for my morale and I notice that I sit and play with him and laugh most of the time. There are not many things here which remind me of home. It takes only a sheep-like puppy to remind me, not only of Toby, but of everything else . . .

***

No one clearly states what we may say and what we may not say about current ETO [European Theater of Operations] events. . . . So we will just play it safe. I have seen and talked to innumerable men who just came back and I've heard many, many stories. Some of my acquaintances of other fields won't be coming back—such news is received without noticeable reaction by any of us. It is easy to see how one gets beyond feeling or reacting. First-hand stories concern local encounters and they don't appear in the papers which give mainly the overall picture and only gentle doses of individual experiences. They give the stories of individuals when the individual was heroic or triumphant—but the real smack of war is when you hear about the catastrophes of individual men with all the details.

Though it is 10 p.m. it is approximately as light as mid-afternoon—lighter than noon of a dark cloudy day. I think that I shall pull the black-out curtains, pretend that it is midnight and go to bed . . .

Goodnight, daughter Cathy and wife LaVonne. I love you both all the time.

Dick

3 JULY 1944
Dear Babies:

Well, what horrible story should I write about today? What great misery has been mine now? We have the usual choices (food, weather, laundry, censorship, quarters, etc.) but these are all rather chronic. Tonight, while eating, a small incident occurred which I shall relate in greater detail than it warrants.

I was munching my gruel at the hospital (since I am O.D. [officer of the day] today) when a kid named Pendola came in with a plate of food. I said, "Take it away—I've already got some of the rotten stuff." . . . Said Pvt. Pendola, "There is something wrong with the food." I had two potatoes and I had eaten one half of one and I had just put the entire other half in my mouth (thinking I should get it over with as soon as possible). I continued to chew in my best phlegmatic (reverse Lend-Lease) fashion and said, "So?" and Pendola said, "There is worms on these potatoes." I carefully scrutinized the Pendola potatoes and saw that they did, indeed, crawl with a thin, maggot-like fauna. They had that maggot-like oozing and squirming. Even ETO maggots, I observed, are underweight. Meanwhile, I continued to chew in my best phlegmatic fashion. Next I examined my remaining potato—it, too, writhed. I continued to chew in my best phlegmatic fashion. About this time I had a thought—my short, stiff hair became stiffer but not shorter. Gawd, that's potato you are chewing on now! But,

I thought, any maggots there now are just a little more protein and there wasn't much I could do except swallow the mixture.

That is all there is to the story. I agreed with Pendola that there were worms in and on the potatoes . . .

5 JULY 1944
Dear Babies:

. . . A wave of foolishness has swept over me—I'm still feeling elevated. As I was censoring some mail the other night I came across two sentences in a letter by one of our G.I. illiterati, scribbled miserably, which struck me awfully funny—why I don't know. I shall copy the two sentences exactly as I found them: O I could wright a book about what we usted do Moor than a year has past since I last seen you.

How it came about that this reminded me of something out of some archaic English poet's book I don't know. But it did—seemed to make just about as much sense too. So consider what we could do with those two sentences from 5th grade, Private Joe Bard. Let's change them just a bit—we get something like this:

O,
I could wright a booke
About what we usted do.
O,
Moor than a year has past
Since did I last seen you.
Anon., ETO, circa, etc.

[Nearly ten months, about two hundred letters, and a one-week home leave (when the baby was thirteen months old) passed before this letter:]

30 APRIL 1945
France
My Darling Wife:

Tonight I am sitting here in the same bombed out buildings that I have been in for the last 6 or 7 weeks. At my elbow is some popcorn and

I am eating it as I write. It is a luxury "from the States." . . . Nothing here—Cannon has gone (permanently) to Nuremberg; Rasche is going to someplace else in France after he travels to England tomorrow. He went in to Paris today. I am left alone here now with this old beaten-up sick quarters and I am not liking the ETO any better than I ever did. Our (2nd) squadron is keeping the chateau that Col. Crouch had and I shall have a room in it. How much longer I will be here I do not know—the States? the States and then China? China without the States? Burma? India? the Pacific? the Army of Occupation? All I know is that eventually I shall come back to my beloved wife and daughter and that we shall live a happy life thereafter. These are boring days—the war is finished but the shooting seems to go on and on. Let me tell you this: that when the shooting stops, this miserable Europe only passes into a different phase of chaos. Food, government, transportation, housing, business, etc. are in horrible states. My theme is still the same only more deep-rooted: Europe is not worth American blood nor American money.

Every now and then I get that old feeling I knew so well in England. It sweeps over me all of a sudden—sort of a rush of realization that dams up and lets go all at once. I may be riding in a jeep through some back-road village where the gutter is the garbage can, or I may be urging the French civil police to arrest a mademoiselle who is grief to our Army, or I may be just sitting and staring out at signs I cannot read and at people I cannot understand—at people who think of me as a member of a race of rich fools. The thought I have is always the same—it condenses to this: just what in the real hell am I doing over here? There is only one place where I belong: with you.

Radio flash just this minute: Hitler is dead—the Germans have announced that to the Germans; he is probably in hiding. Radio flash followed by "Don't Fence Me In."

The celebrations at home over the "end of the war" have left us cold. Should the war end today, tomorrow would be exactly the same for all but about 10% of the people overseas. All the news, the good news, is received here with but casual comment, usually none. There is no news worth talking about except that which deals with: When do we go home?

It is time to go to bed. I am free of colds—my original blouse is again snug; I am washing my own socks; tomorrow is Wednesday; five to one we have beans and Spam at least one meal tomorrow; etc.

Write me often, baby. I am missing you and the littler baby so much . . . Dick

[Watson went home near the end of 1945, traveling by boxcar from northern France to Marseilles to board a troop transport for the States. He was discharged in April of 1946.]

Personal papers of Dr. and Mrs. Richard E. Watson, Minneapolis

Aboard Watson's ship, heading for home.
Richard Watson

NEWSPAPER CLIPPINGS

ST. PAUL STORES HAVE SPECIAL BLACKOUT PAINT—Don't blackout your windows with ordinary paint or enamel.

There's a special kind of blackout window paint and St. Paul paint stores have it on order. It's a powder that is mixed with water and after the blackouts are history it can be scrubbed off window glass. It is made for interior use only.

And black sateen is the new note in interior decoration. The material is used for blackout draperies and there is plenty of it on hand in St. Paul.

Experts here point out, however, that a simple method of blacking out a home is the turning off of all lights for the duration of the tests.

St. Paul Pioneer Press, December 17, 1941

The nationwide rubber campaign, which brought forth 219,000 tons of rubber in the first two weeks, closes at midnight Friday. By that time officials hope to pass the 300,000 tons mark.

The tin can campaign, stemming from the fact the Japanese have overrun the British Malay state and the Netherlands East Indies, started today in 36 cities, representing 47 per cent of the urban population. In September, residents of smaller urban areas will be asked to begin collecting tin cans.

Officials asked housewives to clean tin cans thoroughly, remove tops and bottoms, and paper labels and flatten the can to make collection easier.

(An estimated 990,000 tons of steel and 10,000 tons of tin could be salvaged from the hoped for goal of 1,000,000 tons of tin cans annually.)

Minneapolis Star Journal, July 6, 1942

Little things you notice: banks sending their statements stuck together with Scotch tape—no more rubber bands . . . a laundry that encloses a card with the words of the Star Spangled Banner with its bill . . . the nifty folding card. First Aid index, put out by the Minnesota Savings and Loan, telling quickly what to do with everything from snake bite to fractures.

Minneapolis Star Journal, July 8, 1942

IN THIS CORNER WITH CEDRIC ADAMS—PLENTY OF THANKS should go to Northwest girls for their splendid co-operation in the Servicemen's Ball at the Marigold last Saturday night. By bus, by trolley, by car, by hoof they came in droves. Total attendance mounted to 2,300. Only 333 servicemen could make it, but here's the reason: The very last minute a flock of soldiers were suddenly shipped from Fort Snelling up to Camp Ripley for holiday maneuvers. Uncle Sam is No. 1 gent with those guys, so they went. Out of the affair, Uncle Sam is $90 richer in tax money and the Servicemen's center on Eighth and Hennepin now has a check for $673.36, which will be ample for the purchase of the recording machine and records with which the boys will make transcriptions to send back home. Best follow-up on the party, though, is this: Private Bob Peterson reported to the center Friday and asked for a tall girl. He got her, Miss Margaret Weiss, took her to the dance. At the end of exactly six dances they were engaged and—they're going to be married THIS WEEK.

Minneapolis Star Journal, July 7, 1942

Flyover at St. Paul's Cathedral, London, in commemoration of the Battle of Britain, 1946.
National Archives

SEVEN CAVES RAID SHELTER—Sir:—I saw by the papers where many people ask where to go in case of air raids. Many suggestions were made like: Cellars, parks, big buildings, but I have the best place to offer. Come to St. Peter, Minn., to the Seven Caves, I can take care of many thousand persons. The caves are from 75 to 150 feet below the hills where you would be safe. The caves in winter are cosy and warm and a good place in case of cyclone and air raid by bombs. You are all welcome.—C. W. Meyers, St. Peter, Minn.

St. Paul Pioneer Press, December 23, 1941

6 GERMANS JAILED HERE AS ALIENS— Reporting on progress of the "enemy alien" roundup in the Twin cities territory, Clinton W. Stein, special agent in charge of the Federal Bureau of Investigation here, announced Wednesday that six now are in custody. All are Germans, he said, but beyond that no further identification was made. Four were picked up Tuesday and two more Wednesday, he stated.

St. Paul Pioneer Press, December 11, 1941

EVEN MAYONNAISE PLANT MAKES MUNITIONS NOW—A St. Paul manufacturer of general metal products now is making gun shells for the defense program.

A Minneapolis concern switched from making mayonnaise dressing to soldering name plates on gun mounts.

Formerly manufacturing auto air cleaners, a St. Paul plant is now making shell box liners.

Such are samples of the change-overs being accomplished by Northwest industry to fit the government's defense production drive.

St. Paul Pioneer Press, December 15, 1941

WE'LL HAVE A HEAVY LOAD CHRISTMAS, TOO!—LAST YEAR, WHEN AMERICA WAS AT PEACE, 12 times as many long distance calls were made to many points on Christmas Eve and on Christmas as on an average business day—many calls were delayed and some did not get through at all.

THIS YEAR WITH THE NATION AT WAR, the situation will be much worse unless a great many people refrain from making long distance calls at Christmas time.

TO KEEP TELEPHONE LINES OPEN for military operations and other defense activities, it will help if everyone who possibly can will make their long distance calls at other times than Christmas Eve and Christmas Day.

[Ad from the Tri-State Telephone and Telegraph Co.]

St. Paul Pioneer Press, December 22, 1941

ORCHESTRA TO CONTINUE CONCERTS—Expressing the view that during the emergency Duluth needs its symphony orchestra more than ever, directors of the Duluth symphony orchestra association yesterday voted to continue the concerts next season and approved a budget for operation of the organization during its 10th anniversary season.

The current season will come to a close April 17 with the internationally famous two-piano team of Fray and Braggiotti, as soloists.

Duluth News-Tribune, April 2, 1942

***

[Part of a facetious army memo, author unknown, distributed to some Minnesota servicemen:]

Subject: Indoctrination, for return to U.S.
To: All Units
The following points will be emphasized in the subject indoctrination course:

A typical American breakfast consists of such strange foods as cantaloupes, fresh eggs, milk, ham, etc. These are highly palatable and though strange in appearance, are extremely tasty. Butter, made from cream, is often served. If you wish some butter, you turn to the person nearest you and say quietly, "Please pass the butter." You do not say, "Throw me the goddam grease."

In the event the Helmet is retained by the individual, he will refrain from using it as a chair, wash bowl, foottub or bathtub. All these devices are furnished in the average American home. It is not considered good practice to squat Indian fashion [on one's heels] in a corner in the event all chairs are occupied. The host will usually provide suitable seats.

American dinners, in most cases, consist of several items, each served in a separate dish. The common practice of mixing various items, such as corn-beef and pudding, or lima beans and peaches to make it more palatable, will be refrained from. In time the "separate dish" system will become very enjoyable.

It is not proper to go around hitting every one of draft age in civilian clothes. He might have been released from the service for medical reasons; ask for his credentials, and if he can't show them, then and only then, go ahead and slug him.

Upon retiring, one will often find a pair of pajamas laid out on the bed. (Pajamas, it should be explained, are two piece garments which are donned after all clothing has been removed.) The soldier, confronted by these garments, should assume an air of familiarity, and act as though he were used to them. A casual remark, such as "My, what a delicate shade of blue," will usually suffice. Under no circumstances say, "How in hell do you expect me to sleep in a getup like this."

Personal papers of John Wickre, Cumberland, Wisconsin

EPILOGUE

With these recollections of World War II, we end this informal history of Minnesota. After the 1940s the style and substance of letters and diaries are much like today's. They don't offer the punch earlier ones do. Then, too, few letters and diaries after the 1920s have made their way to historical collections. Many people unfortunately—and wrongly— believe that any pioneer letter is a gem and any contemporary one is worthless. Future historians will need today's documents. Historical societies do not need another copy of a newspaper announcing John Kennedy's assassination or the moon walk. They probably do not want a single land certificate or stray letter. They do want collections of documents that give a vivid idea of a person's life. Yours? See your state or local historical society.

THANKS

Thanks again to those who made the 1981 book possible: Charles W. Bailey, Paul Verret, Dick Reid, Mike Carroll, Brian Cravens, Dorothy Meyer, Ingrid Sundstrom, Linda James, and many more. And for this 2023 version: Thanks to Josh Leventhal, Ann Regan, Em Poupart, Shannon Pennefeather, Daniel Leary, Judy Gilats, James Cihlar, and Riley Davis.

INDEX

Bring Warm Clothes was designed and set in type
by Judy Gilats in St. Paul, Minnesota. The text is set
in Escrow and the display typeface is Citrus Gothic.